# FAMILY LAW
# IN
# SCOTLAND

*For Robyn*

# Family Law in Scotland

### Seventh Edition

**Joe Thomson**
Formerly Regius Professor of Law at the University of Glasgow
and Commissioner at the Scottish Law Commission

Bloomsbury Professional

**Bloomsbury Professional Limited, Maxwelton House, 41–43 Boltro Road, Haywards Heath, West Sussex, RH16 1BJ**

© Bloomsbury Professional Limited 2014

Bloomsbury Professional, an imprint of Bloomsbury Publishing Plc

Reprinted 2020

A CIP Catalogue record for this book is available from the British Library.

ISBN: 978 1 78043 759 0

Typeset by Phoenix Photosetting, Chatham, Kent
Printed by CPI Group (UK) Ltd, Croydon CR0 4YY

# Preface

It is only three years since the last edition of this book. However, the fundamental changes to Scots family law introduced by the Marriage and Civil Partnership (Scotland) Act 2014 and the Children and Young People (Scotland) Act 2014 have necessitated a new edition. I have also taken the opportunity to consider the important judicial developments during this period.

I am deeply indebted to Alan Brown who was my research assistant. His work has been exemplary. As always my wife, Annie, has given me unstinting support throughout the gestation of this new edition.

One of the great pleasures of my career has been to appreciate how much I have learned from my students. None more so than Mrs Robyn Allardice-Bourne. Having had the privilege and pleasure of celebrating Robyn's birthday with her earlier this year, I think it is appropriate to dedicate this edition to her.

Joe Thomson
Campbeltown
1 September 2014

# Contents

**Chapter 4    The legal consequences of marriage and civil partnership, Part II: moveable property**

**Chapter 5    The legal consequences of marriage and civil partnership, Part III: the matrimonial and family home**

**Chapter 6    Divorce and dissolution**

**Chapter 7    Financial provision on divorce and dissolution**

**Chapter 8    Cohabitants**

## Chapter 9 Parents and children

## Chapter 10 Children's legal capacity and rights

## Chapter 11 Parental responsibilities and rights

## Chapter 12 Actions in relation to parental responsibilities and rights

## Chapter 13 Adoption

**Chapter 14    Children: responsibilities and powers of local authorities**

**Chapter 15    Children in need: emergency procedures and compulsory supervision orders**

# Table of Statutes

*References are to introduction and paragraph number.*

# Table of Orders, Rules and Regulations

# Table of Conventions, etc

# Table of cases

## D

## H

# M

**N**

# Introduction

In this short introduction it is proposed to explain the selection of subjects chosen for extended treatment and to discuss the policies underlying some of the most important features of contemporary family law.

Since the end of the eighteenth century the nuclear family has been the essential family unit in Scotland.[1] This comprised a man and a woman, who have a sexual relationship, and their children. Before their relationship gave rise to mutual legal rights and obligations, as a general rule the couple had to marry. More importantly, it was only when a couple married that the law regulated their income and capital when their relationship broke down, in the form of financial provision on divorce. Similarly, a spouse had important legal rights in respect of succession to a proportion of the deceased spouse's estate.[2]

It was a fundamental principle of the law that to be eligible to marry the parties had to be of the opposite sex viz only men could marry women and only women could marry men. With the increasing acceptance of gay and lesbian relationships in the latter part of the twentieth century, the Civil Partnership Act 2004 enabled parties of the same sex to register a civil partnership which gave them similar legal rights and obligations as spouses. In 2014, just ten years later, the Scottish Parliament accepted that it was wrong to continue to prevent persons from marrying on grounds of their sexual orientation. And so under the Marriage and Civil Partnership (Scotland) Act 2014, marriage is now open to same sex as well as opposite sex couples.[3] Thus in contemporary Scots Law marriage means 'marriage between persons of different sexes and marriage between persons of the same sex'.[4] References to the word 'marriage' (and related expressions) in any enactment, passed or to be passed, or in any document, is to be interpreted to include marriages between persons of the same sex as well as persons of the opposite sex.[5] In so far as being married is relevant for the operation of any rule of law,[6] the rule of law applies equally to opposite sex and same sex marriages[7].

Over the last years of the twentieth century, the law began to recognise that a large number of couples were living in opposite sex relationships outside marriage and that non-married opposite sex cohabitants faced similar problems to married couples, especially when their relationships broke down. Although there was no attempt to create a legal status of opposite sex cohabitant, the legislature began to provide them with certain rights in relation to particular matters, for example the occupation of the home in which they are, or had been, living.[8] These rights have been extended by the Family Law (Scotland) Act 2006 to include the right to financial provision when the couple separate or the relationship ends on the death of one of the parties and the deceased died without a will, ie intestate. These statutory provisions apply to same sex as well as opposite sex cohabitants.

Thus Scots law has responded to the different forms of lifestyle which are prevalent in Scotland in the twenty-first century by providing three legal regimes, *viz* marriage, civil partnership and cohabitation. This study of Scots family law attempts to examine these regimes.

Although marriage and civil partnership are central institutions in Scots family law, it should be noted that they are of very little legal significance for the spouses or civil partners *during* the marriage or civil partnership. Until the later years of the nineteenth century, a woman lost many important rights on marriage, for example in relation to her property. Since then, the law has endeavoured to achieve legal equality between the spouses by enacting that for various purposes, for example contract, delict and property, the spouses should be treated as though they were unmarried.[9] Similarly, for many legal purposes, civil partners are treated as though they have not registered their partnership. But while legal equality may have been achieved, the application of rules which ignore the fact that the persons concerned are married or have registered a civil partnership, leads, particularly in relation to property matters, to results which are both artificial and unjust. Consequently, legislation has introduced special rules for spouses, civil partners and to a lesser extent cohabitants which take into account the fact that they are living together.[10]

Of course, marriage and civil partnership do give rise to rights and obligations for the spouses and civil partners. Spouses and civil partners, but not cohabitants, owe a duty to aliment (ie maintain) each other during the marriage or civil partnership.[11] Moreover, when parents are married at the date of a child's conception or subsequently, the father will automatically have parental responsibilities and rights in relation to the child;[12] if the couple never marry, only the child's mother will have parental responsibilities and rights unless the man has been registered as the child's father, or until he obtains them as a consequence of a court order or agreement with the mother. But the most important legal consequence of marriage and civil partnership is that a court can award financial provision for the spouses or civil partners if their relationship ends in divorce or dissolution.[13]

Judicial divorce has been possible in Scots law since the Reformation in 1560, but divorce was not a prevalent feature of Scottish society until the twentieth century. The reasons for this are complex. While the grounds for divorce were restricted to the defender's adultery or desertion until the Divorce (Scotland) Act 1938, religious disapproval of divorce must also have acted as a considerable restraint. As a result of the increasing secularisation of Scottish society in the twentieth century, the social upheavals of two world wars and the emphasis on personal fulfilment in sexual relationships, divorce has become an accepted part of contemporary Scottish society. The law has responded to the demand for easier divorce with the introduction of a system based, theoretically at least, on the non-fault principle of irretrievable breakdown of marriage.[14] It is estimated that in Scotland at least one in three marriages now ends in divorce. As a divorced person will often enter a second marriage, it is not too cynical to suggest that we now live in a society where serial polygamy is common. There is no reason why the dissolution of civil partnership should prove to be less common.

Given this high incidence of breakdown, it is crucial that the law provides a system of financial provision which will enable the income and capital of the spouses or civil partners to be redistributed in a fair manner on divorce or dissolution. Until 1964, divorce was treated as judicial death: financial provision took the form of treating the defender as though dead and awarding the pursuer the legal rights to which a spouse would have been entitled from the defender's estate. That system was replaced[15] by one which gave the judge who was hearing the claim discretion to make financial provision which appeared just in the circumstances. Any advantages of flexibility which this system may have had were outweighed by the uncertainty that ensued. A much more sophisticated system was introduced in 1985; this provides a set of principles to be used in determining the financial provision that should be awarded in the circumstances of a particular marriage or civil partnership.[16] This gives greater certainty on the outcome of possible litigation and so enables spouses and civil partners – and their legal advisers – to negotiate a settlement without recourse to the courts.

The law on divorce and dissolution can be criticised on the ground of its complexity which inhibits the parties from being able to end their marriage or civil partnership with the minimum of legal intervention. On the other hand, the reform of the law on financial provision has, because of the increase in certainty as to the outcome of litigation, enabled the parties or their legal advisers to reach a settlement more frequently than in the past. It is generally accepted that modern family law should encourage spouses and civil partners to settle the property and other issues which arise when their relationship breaks down without recourse to litigation, thereby saving scarce legal aid resources. At present, Scots law only does this to a limited extent. The opportunity was not taken in the Family Law (Scotland) Act 2006 to introduce an even more simplified form of divorce and dissolution under which the parties simply give notice of an intention to do so: and more support could then be given to family mediation services to help spouses and civil partners reach agreement on such issues as property, financial provision and looking after their children.

Children have always had rights in Scots law. Most of these rights were, and are, exigible against their parents. The difficulty, of course, is that children will not have the capacity to exercise these rights because they are too young. However the United Kingdom is a signatory to the UN Convention on the Rights of the Child (UNCRC). Under the Children and Young People (Scotland) Act 2014, Scottish Ministers and public authorities must take steps to better or further effect the UNCRC requirements[17]. Reports of what steps have been taken must be produced every three years. In doing so, the Scottish Ministers must take into account any relevant views of children: they must also promote public awareness and understanding of the rights of children.[18] Moreover, every child and young person in

Scotland is to have a 'named person' to promote, support or safeguard the child or young person's well being. The named person is to be an employee of a 'service provider', for example a school teacher employed by a local authority. The named person cannot be the parent of the child.[19] In this way, it is anticipated that children's rights will be better respected and enforced.

Scots law has always recognised that parents owe duties towards their children, albeit that the parents never married. For centuries, however, the extent of a child's rights which were exigible from his or her parents – and remoter relatives – depended upon whether or not the child was legitimate. A child was legitimate if he or she was conceived or born during the parents' marriage. During the twentieth century piecemeal reforms alleviated the legal position of the illegitimate child. As a result of the Law Reform (Parent and Child) (Scotland) Act 1986,[20] the legal position of an illegitimate child was, for all but a few minor purposes, equated with that of a legitimate child. The status of illegitimacy was finally abolished by the Family Law (Scotland) Act 2006, s 21. Nevertheless it remains the case that when a child is a member of a one-parent family, he or she will more often suffer social disadvantages stemming from impoverished economic circumstances than a child who is brought up by two adults.

While parents owe responsibilities and obligations towards their children, for example the duty of aliment, they also enjoy important rights in respect of the care and upbringing of their child. The nature and extent of these parental responsibilities and rights has been one of the most controversial aspects of modern family law – in particular the question of when these rights cease and children can assert their liberty to make their own decisions on such important matters as contraception or medical treatment. Here the views of the child are at the centre of the decision-making process and should be adequately represented.

Given the prevalence of the breakdown of adult relationships, an important issue for modern family law is to attempt to ensure that the children of the family are well looked after when the parents or carers separate. Scots law has adopted the welfare principle as the criterion for the determination of such issues.[21] In practice, however, the courts are reluctant to disturb the arrangements which have *de facto* been operative prior to the breakdown, thus preserving the *status quo ante*: this is generally thought to be in the best interests of the child. Thus the law merely underpins the self-regulation by the parents or carers themselves of how the children of the family should be looked after when their relationship breaks down. Since in the vast majority of cases the mother will *de facto* be looking after any children when the breakdown occurs, the preservation of the *status quo* which is currently endorsed by the courts when applying the welfare principle reinforces the traditional view that the care of a child is primarily the responsibility of the mother. However, in theory at least, the law stresses that children need both parents and that parental responsibilities continue even where the child no longer lives with the parent concerned.

In a modern society, the state has a crucial role in supporting children who are at risk when their families have become dysfunctional. State agencies have certain powers and duties to help in this situation.[22] Scots law also has a system of children's hearings which can provide compulsory supervision orders for children in need.[23] The danger of any welfare-based system is, of course, that a parent's prima facie right to bring up a child and the child's prima facie right to be brought up in his or her family environment may be given insufficient weight when it is thought that the removal of the child from the family is desirable for the child's welfare. A delicate balance has therefore to be found and procedural safeguards must exist so that the rights of parents and children towards each other are given proper consideration. At the same time, the procedures must be compatible with the European Convention on Human Rights, most of which has been incorporated into domestic Scots law.[24]

One of the most remarkable features of contemporary Scots family law is that much of the law is of recent origin. As well as the introduction of civil partnerships[25] and same sex marriage[26], the last thirty years have, for example, seen the full-scale reform of financial provision on divorce,[27] illegitimacy,[28] parental responsibilities and rights[29] and financial provision for cohabitants on separation and death.[30] These reforms are the result of the work of the Scottish Law Commission which has played an important role in providing Scotland with a system of family law that is capable of meeting the needs of contemporary Scottish society.

1   Before that time the extended family in the form of clans was important, at least in the Highlands of Scotland.
2   On the spouses' rights to succession, see **Ch 3**.
3   Civil partnerships continue and, ironically perhaps, only same sex couples can register a partnership.
4   Marriage (Scotland) Act 1977, s 26(2).
5   Marriage and Civil Partnership (Scotland) Act 2014, ss 4(1), (5), (11), (12) and (13). This does not apply if the enactment or document otherwise provides.
6   For example the rules on marriage by cohabitation with habit and repute discussed at paras 1.14ff above.
7   MCP (S) A 2014, s 4(6).
8   See **Ch 9**.
9   On contract and delict, see **Ch 3**; on property, see **Chs 4** and **5**.
10  See, for example, the Family Law (Scotland) Act 1985, s 25: discussed in **Ch 4** and the Family Law (Scotland) Act 2006, s 26: discussed in **Ch 9**.
11  On aliment, see **Ch 3**.
12  Children (Scotland) Act 1995, s 3(1)(b): discussed in **Ch 10**.
13  On financial division on divorce and dissolution, see **Ch 7**.
14  Divorce and dissolution are discussed in **Ch 6**.
15  Succession (Scotland) Act 1964, Part V; later replaced by the Divorce (Scotland) Act 1976, s 5.
16  Family Law (Scotland) Act 1985, ss 8–17; discussed in **Ch 7**.
17  Children and Young People (Scotland) Act 2014, ss 1 and 2.
18  Ibid s 1(2) and (3).
19  Children and Young People (Scotland) Act 2014, Part 4.
20  The Law Reform (Parent and Child) (Scotland) Act 1986 is discussed in detail in **Chs 9** and **10**.
21  See **Ch 12**.
22  See **Ch 14**.
23  See **Ch 15**.
24  Convention for the Protection of Human Rights and Fundamental Freedoms (Rome, 4 November 1950; 213 UNTS 221; TS 71 (1953); Cmd 8969). Most, but not all, of the 1950 Convention has been incorporated into United Kingdom law, as Schedule 1 to the Human Rights Act 1998.
25  Civil Partnership Act 2004.
26  Marriage and Civil Partnership (Scotland) Act 2014.
27  See the Family Law (Scotland) Act 1985: discussed in **Ch 7**.
28  See the Law Reform (Parent and Child) (Scotland) Act 1986: discussed in **Ch 9**.
29  See the Children (Scotland) Act 1995, Pt I: discussed in **Ch 11**.
30  Family Law (Scotland) Act 2006, ss 28 and 29: discussed in **Ch 8**.

# Chapter 1

# Getting married and registering a civil partnership

## PART I: GETTING MARRIED

## Introduction

**1.1** Article 12 of the European Convention on Human Rights[1] provides:

> 'Men and women of marriageable age have the right to marry and to found a family, according to the national laws governing the exercise of this right.'

Scots law now goes further and recognises the right of men to marry men and women to marry women[2]. In this part we shall discuss how persons can marry under Scots law.

---

1  Convention for the Protection of Human Rights and Fundamental Freedoms (Rome, 4 November 1950; 213 UNTS 221; TS 71 (1953); Cmd 8969). Most, but not all, of the 1950 Convention has been incorporated into United Kingdom law as Schedule 1 to the Human Rights Act 1998.
2  Marriage Scotland) Act 1977, s 26 See generally Kenneth McK Norrie, 'Now the dust has settled; The Marriage and Civil Partnership (Scotland) Act' 2014 JR 135.

---

## Engagements

**1.2** It is customary for a couple to become engaged for a period before they marry. At common law an engagement was a contract and wrongful failure to implement the promise to marry gave rise to an action in damages. These damages included not only compensation for pecuniary loss arising from the breach, for example the cost of preparations for the wedding, but also for solatium to compensate the innocent party's injured feelings and wounded pride.[1] The Scottish Law Commission took the view that actions for breach of promise had become anachronistic in the late twentieth century and recommended abolition.[2]

By s 1(1) of the Law Reform (Husband and Wife) (Scotland) Act 1984, it is declared that:

'No promise of marriage or agreement between two persons to marry one another shall have effect under the law of Scotland to create any rights or obligations; and no action for breach of any such promise or agreement may be brought in any court in Scotland, whatever the law applicable to the promise or agreement.'[3]

The extent of this provision is wide. First, an engagement is no longer a legally enforceable contract; therefore any contractual remedies for breach of promise are no longer competent in Scottish courts.[4] Second, by stipulating that a promise or agreement to marry does not create any rights or obligations in Scots law, it would appear that the section excludes any delictual liability which might arise from a breach of promise. For example if a man, A, deliberately lied when he promised to marry a man, B, B would appear to have no right to sue A in delict on the ground of A's fraudulent misrepresentation.[5] Thus unlike the parallel English legislation[6] which only prevents agreements to marry operating as contracts, the Law Reform (Husband and Wife) (Scotland) Act 1984 prohibits delictual, as well as contractual, remedies.

The 1984 Act does not address itself to any of the property issues which can arise between engaged couples. Where the marriage does not take place, any property dispute, for example over the ownership of a house which was bought with a view to marriage, will be governed by the general principles of the law of property.[7] The law of unjustified enrichment may also be relevant. In *Shilliday v Smith*,[8] a woman provided her fiancé with funds so that he could improve the house in which they intended to live after they were married. When the marriage did not take place she obtained recompense for the expenditure since it was clear that she had not intended the money to be a gift and that the payment was conditional on the marriage taking place.

Where the couple do marry, any property acquired during the engagement for use as a family home, or to be used in the home, will be regarded as matrimonial property for the purpose of financial provision on divorce.[9]

There are no special property rules in relation to gifts between engaged couples. If the gift is intended to be outright, for example a birthday present, it need not be returned if the engagement is broken off. Where a gift is made expressly or impliedly[10] conditional on the marriage taking place, it must be returned if the condition fails: and the donor may use the *condictio causa data causa non secuta*[11] to recover the property.

Unlike the position in England,[12] there are no specific provisions in respect of gifts of engagement rings. In one sheriff court case it was held that the gift of an engagement ring is made unconditionally[13] but in another,[14] it was thought that the ring was returnable if the marriage did not take place – unless the donor had unjustifiably broken off the engagement. A third possibility is that the ring is given on the implied condition that it should be returned if the marriage does not take place for any reason. Given that engagements now give rise to no legal rights or obligations between the parties, it is thought that it would be consistent with the policy of the Law Reform (Husband and Wife) (Scotland) Act 1984 if engagement rings were presumed to be outright gifts; but that this presumption should be able to be rebutted on proof that the gift was intended to be subject to the condition that it should be returned if the marriage did not take place.

Where a couple receive engagement presents from third parties, it is thought that these are returnable if the marriage does not take place.[15]

It is expressly enacted in s 128 of the Civil Partnership Act 2004 that:

'No promise or agreement to enter into a civil partnership creates any rights or obligations under the law of Scotland; and no action for breach of such a promise or agreement may be brought in any court in Scotland, whatever the law applicable to the promise or agreement'.

---

1   *Hogg v Gow* 27 May 1812 FC.
2   Report of the Scottish Law Commission on Outdated Rules in the Law of Husband and Wife (1983) (Scot Law Com No 76).
3   By the Law Reform (Husband and Wife) (Scotland) Act 1984, s 1(2), the provision is expressly made retrospective.
4   This is so, whatever the proper law of the promise or agreement.
5   Similarly, there would be no right to sue in negligence if the promise was made carelessly: for example, if without taking reasonable care to discover whether he had the capacity to marry the promisee, a man gives a promise to marry which he cannot fulfil.

6    Law Reform (Miscellaneous Provisions) Act 1970, s 1(1).
7    In *Grieve v Morrison* 1993 SLT 852, an engaged couple bought a house, title to which was taken in joint names. Part of the price was the free proceeds from the sale of the woman's previous house. When the marriage did not take place, the woman failed to recover the proceeds because she had not established that the transfer of the proceeds to purchase the new house was made in consideration that the marriage would take place. Instead, the court ordered a division and sale under which both parties obtained half the free proceeds from the sale of the new house. On actions for division and sale, see **Ch 5**.
8    1998 SC 725.
9    Family Law (Scotland) Act 1985, s 10(4): discussed in **Ch 7**. Similarly, moveable property obtained in prospect of the marriage is subject to the presumption of equal shares in household goods: Family Law (Scotland) Act 1985, s 25: discussed in **Ch 4**.
10   For example, the gift of family jewellery.
11   Stair *The Institutions of the Law of Scotland* (6th edn, 1981) I 7.7. The *condictio* provides that, where payment or performance has been given and the counterpart consideration has failed, the money paid or the value of the performance should be restored under principles of unjustified enrichment. Before the *condictio* is applicable, it must be clear that the transfer of the property was subject to a mutually agreed understanding that it was made in consideration that the marriage would take place: *Grieve v Morrison* 1993 SLT 852. See also *Shilliday v Smith* 1998 SC 725. The obligation to make restiutiont arises when the marriage will no longer take place ie when the condition has failed, and not when the property was originally transferred. Therefore the five years prescriptive period only begins to run from the date of the failure of the condition:*Thomson v Mooney* [2013] CSIH 115.
12   See the Law Reform (Miscellaneous Provisions) Act 1970, s 3(2), where there is a rebuttable presumption that the gift of the ring is made unconditionally.
13   *Gold v Hume* (1950) 66 Sh Ct Rep 85.
14   *Savage v M'Allister* (1952) 68 Sh Ct Rep 11.
15   Stair I 7.7.

---

## The Formalities of Marriage

**1.3** A marriage will not be valid unless the parties have capacity to marry and the marriage conforms to the formalities required by the law of the place where the marriage is celebrated. In this section, the formal requirements of a valid marriage celebrated in Scotland are discussed. Scots law recognises two possible methods of marrying, ie regular or formal marriages and irregular or informal marriages.

## Regular marriages: formal marriages

**1.4** The law on the formalities of regular marriages is to be found in the Marriage (Scotland) Act 1977[1].

There are two types of regular marriage in Scotland: a civil marriage and a religious or belief marriage. However, before either can take place, the parties must follow certain civil preliminaries.[2]

---

1  As amended, particularly by the Marriage and Civil Partnership (Scotland) Act 2014.
2  Accordingly, the proclamation of banns has no legal significance in Scots law.

---

*Civil preliminaries*

**Marriage notices**

**1.5** Each of the parties to a marriage which is intended to be solemnised in Scotland, whether it is to be a civil, religious or belief ceremony, must submit a notice of intention to marry – a marriage notice – to the district registrar for the registration district in which the marriage is to be solemnised.[1] There is no need for either party to be resident in that registration district nor, indeed, in Scotland; but as one of the parties must appear to finalise arrangements for a civil ceremony or, alternatively, collect the marriage schedule for a religious or belief ceremony, in practice one of the parties must be present in Scotland before the date of the ceremony.

The marriage notice is accompanied by the prescribed fee and the birth certificate of the party submitting it. If either party has been married before and the marriage has been dissolved, a copy of the decree of divorce or declarator of nullity must be included; similarly, if either party is a person who had been married before and that marriage ended on the death of the previous spouse, the death certificate of the former spouse must be submitted.[2] If one of the parties is domiciled abroad,[3] he or she must 'if practicable' submit a certificate issued by a competent authority in the state in which the party is domiciled that he or she 'is not known to be subject to any legal incapacity (in terms of the law of that state) which would prevent his marrying':[4] this is known as a certificate of capacity.[5] There is no need to submit a certificate if no certificate has been issued only by reason of the fact that the parties to the intended marriage are of the same sex[6].

On receipt of the marriage notice, the registrar enters the following prescribed particulars in a marriage notice book: the party's name, address, marital status, date of birth and the proposed date of the marriage.[7] The names – but not the addresses – of the parties and the proposed date of the marriage are then displayed in a 'conspicuous' place at the registration office.

Any person claiming to have reason to submit an objection to an intended marriage can inspect any entry relating to the marriage in the marriage notice book. The objection to the marriage must be submitted in writing to the district registrar.[8] Where the objection is concerned with a trivial matter, for example an inaccuracy as to the age of the parties, the district registrar can, after notifying the parties, make the correction.[9] However, if the objection goes to the capacity of either party to marry,[10] for example if it is alleged that one of them is already a party to a subsisting marriage, then the district registrar must notify the Registrar General and the completion or issue of the marriage schedule is suspended until the matter has been investigated by the Registrar General.[11] If after investigation the Registrar General is satisfied that there is no legal impediment, he will inform the district registrar and the marriage can go ahead: but if there is a legal impediment, the Registrar General must direct the district registrar to take all reasonable steps to ensure that the marriage does not take place.[12]

It will be obvious that there must be sufficient time for objections to be made and any subsequent investigations to be carried out. As a general rule, there is a minimum waiting period of 28 days from the receipt of the marriage notice and a civil ceremony[13] or the issue of a marriage schedule for a religious or belief ceremony.[14] However, the Registrar General has a dispensing power to allow a marriage to be celebrated within a shorter period if the circumstances justify doing so. This power is used sparingly.[15]

---

1    Marriage (Scotland) Act 1977, s 3(1).
2    M(S)A 1977, s 3(1)(a) and (b). An extract of an entry in the Register of Divorces is sufficient evidence of the decree of divorce or declarator of nullity: see the Registration of Births, Deaths and Marriages (Scotland) Act 1965, s 28A(5).
3    And has not been resident in the UK for more than two years.
4    M(S)A 1977, s 3(5).

5   Where the *lex domicilii* does not recognise the party's divorce, but the divorce would be recognised in Scotland, a marriage can go ahead without a certificate of capacity: M(S)A 1977, s 3(5)(ii)(b). See also the Family Law Act 1986, s 50.
6   M(S)A 1977, s 3 (5)(ii) (c).
7   M(S)A 1977, s 4: the particulars are prescribed in the Marriage (Prescription of Forms) (Scotland) Regulations 1977, SI 1977/1671, reg 4.
8   M(S)A 1977, s 5(1).
9   M(S)A 1977, s 5(2)(a).
10  M(S)A 1977, s 5(4).
11  M(S)A 1977, s 5(2)(b).
12  M(S)A 1977, s 5(3).
13  M(S)A 1977, s 6(4)(a).
14  M(S)A 1977, s 19(1).
15  Nevertheless there was a case known to the author where a marriage had been arranged for two years but the parties failed to submit their marriage notices: after some frantic telephone calls, the Registrar General was prepared to issue the marriage schedule on the morning of the wedding!

**Marriage schedule**

**1.6** After the usual waiting period has expired and the district registrar is satisfied that the parties have capacity to marry, he makes up the marriage schedule. The schedule contains the details of the parties and serves as an initial record of the marriage for registration purposes. Where there is to be a religious or belief ceremony, in addition the marriage schedule acts as a licence authorising the celebrant to proceed. If more than three months have elapsed since the receipt of a marriage notice, the Registrar General has discretion to direct the district registrar not to complete the marriage schedule unless a new marriage notice is submitted.[1] A marriage schedule for a religious or belief ceremony will not be issued to the parties earlier than seven days before the ceremony.[2]

1   Marriage (Scotland) Act 1977, s 6(3).
2   M(S)A 1977, s 6(4)(b).

*Civil marriage*

**Opposite sex and same sex marriages**

**1.7** If there is to be a civil ceremony, the district registrar retains the marriage schedule until the date of the marriage. The ceremony is conducted by the registrar[1] and takes place in her office. There is no restriction on the time when the ceremony must take place but in practice it will be during the registrar's normal office hours. In addition the registrar may conduct a civil ceremony in an 'appropriate place'. It is for the district registrar to determine in each case whether the proposed place is appropriate for a civil wedding, for example, the bride's home or a local hotel.[2] It is expressly enacted that religious premises cannot be an appropriate place for a civil ceremony[3].

Both parties must be present with two witnesses professing to be over 16.[4] The marriage schedule is completed and the district registrar explains to the parties the nature of marriage in Scots law. The parties declare there are no legal impediments and are then asked if they take each other as spouses. The registrar declares them to be married and the marriage schedule is signed by both parties, the witnesses and the registrar. The marriage is then registered. A registrar cannot refuse to marry a couple on the ground that they are of the same sex, ie there is no conscientious exemption for registrars.

---

1    M(S)A 1977, ss 8(1)(b) and (1B)(b).
2    M(S)A 1977, s 18(1).
3    M(S)A 1977, s 18((1A).
4    M(S)A 1977, s 19(2).

---

*Religious or belief marriage*

**1.8**  If there is to be a religious or belief ceremony, the district registrar issues the marriage schedule *to the parties*. This is because the schedule acts as a licence to the celebrant to solemnise the marriage. A religious or belief ceremony can be carried out at any time, for example, in the evening if the couple come from a farming community, and any place, for example, in a hotel. The date and place chosen must be specified in the marriage schedule.[1]

**Opposite sex marriage**

The authorised celebrant is a person who is:[2]

　　(1)　　A minister or deacon of the Church of Scotland; or

(2)　A minister, clergyman, pastor, priest or other celebrant of a religious or belief body prescribed in regulations made by Scottish Ministers. A religious or belief body is an organised group of people: (a) which meets regularly for religious worship; or (b) the principal object (or one of the principal objects) of which is to uphold or promote philosophical beliefs and which meets regularly for that purpose[3]. Religious bodies will include the major Christian churches and denominations and non-Christian religions such as Islam and Hinduism. Belief bodies will include non-religious organisations such as Humanists. However Scottish Ministers can only prescribe a body if that body requests them to do so and the Ministers are satisfied that the body meets the qualifying requirements[4]. The qualifying requirements will be made in regulations but will be designed to ensure inter alia that marriages are not conducted as a profit making business and that the celebrants are aware of the risk of sham and forced marriages.

(3)　A person nominated to solemnise opposite sex marriages by a religious or belief body which is not prescribed under (2) above. The nominee is registered as a marriage celebrant by the Registrar General under s 9(1) of the Marriage (Scotland) Act 1977. The Registrar General can reject the nomination if the nominating body does not meet the qualifying requirements. The nominee is authorised for three years in the first instance.

(4)　A member of a religious or belief body temporarily authorised by the Registrar General under s 12 of the Marriage (Scotland) Act 1977 to solemnise opposite sex marriages. The religious or belief body must meet the qualifying requirements. These would include celebrants who are registered under s 9(1) but whose area of operation does not extend to the place where the marriage is to be celebrated, ministers from outside Scotland who have been asked to solemnise a marriage in Scotland, or ministers who are in Scotland on pulpit exchange. The authorisation must be in writing and is limited either to the marriage specified in the authorisation or for a specified period.

The celebrant must follow the form of ceremony approved by the Church of Scotland or the religious or belief body. The ceremony must be in an appropriate form which includes and is not inconsistent with: (a) a declaration of the parties, in the presence of each other, the celebrant and two witnesses, that they accept each other as husband and wife or spouses; and (b) a declaration thereafter by the celebrant that they are husband and wife or spouses[5].

**Same sex marriages**

The authorised celebrant is a person who is[6]:–

(1)     A minister, clergyman, pastor, priest or other celebrant of a religious or belief body prescribed by regulations made by Scottish Ministers, or who, not being of the foregoing, is recognised by a religious or belief body so prescribed as entitled to solemnise marriage between persons of the same sex on its behalf. Again Scottish Ministers can only prescribe a body if that body requests them to do so and the Ministers are satisfied that the body meets the qualifying requirements. At present the Church of Scotland does not intend to seek to become a prescribed body.

(2)     A person nominated to solemnise same sex marriages by a religious or belief body which is not prescribed under (1) above. The nominee is registered by the Registrar General under s 9(1A) of the Marriage (Scotland) Act 1977. The Registrar General can reject the nomination if the nominating body does not meet the qualifying requirements. So for example the Church of Scotland could nominate a particular minister who was prepared to conduct same sex marriages.

(3)     A member of a religious or belief body temporarily authorised by the Registrar General under s 12 of the Marriage (Scotland) Act 1977 to solemnise same sex marriages. The religious or belief body must meet the qualifying requirements. An authorisation for a specified period can only be made if the person is a member of a religious or belief body which has been prescribed under (1) above or has nominated celebrants under (2) above[7].

Section 8(1D) of the Marriage (Scotland) Act 1977 provides for the avoidance of doubt that no religious or belief body is obliged to seek to become a prescribed body or to nominate any member to be registered as empowered to solemnise same sex marriages. So a religious or belief body may request to be authorised to solemnise opposite sex marriages while not seeking authority to solemnise same sex marriages. Similarly no person is obliged to apply for temporary authorisation to solemnise such marriages. Moreover, where a person is an approved celebrant to conduct same sex marriages he or she is not obliged to do so. Accordingly, even where a religious or belief body has been prescribed to solemnise same sex marriages, any member of that body can still refuse to participate by relying on this conscientious exemption and need not secede from the body[8].

The ceremony must be in an appropriate form which includes and is in no way inconsistent with: (a) a declaration by the parties, in the presence of each other, the celebrant and two witnesses, that they accept each other in marriage; and (b) a declaration thereafter by the celebrant that the parties are then married.

In all marriages, the approved celebrant must not proceed unless:

(1)    the parties produce a marriage schedule issued in accordance with the Marriage (Scotland) Act 1977;

(2)    *both* parties are present; and

(3)    there are two witnesses professing to be over 16.[9]

After the ceremony the marriage schedule is signed by both parties, the witnesses and the celebrant. The schedule must be returned to the district registration office for registration within three days of the ceremony.[10] This was traditionally the task of the best man who paid the registration fee as part of his wedding gift!

---

1    Marriage (Scotland) Act 1977, s 6(5).
2    M(S)A 1977, s 8(1).
3.    M (S) A 1977, s 26.
4    M(S)A 1977, s 8(1A).
5    M(S)A 1977, s 9(3).
6    M(S)A 1977, s 8(1B).
7    M(S)A 1977, s 12(1C).
8    The Equality Act 2010 cannot be used to challenge the individual's decision not to conduct same sex marriages.
9    M(S)A 1977, s 13(1).
10   M(S)A 1977, s 15(2).

---

*Effect of irregularities*

**1.9** By virtue of section 23A, a marriage solemnised under the Marriage (Scotland) Act 1977 will not be invalidated by non-compliance with these formalities provided both parties were present at the ceremony and the marriage was duly registered.[1] There must be some form of ceremony but otherwise the marriage will not be invalidated by formal defects.

The scope of s 23A of the 1977 Act was considered in *Saleh v Saleh*.[2] The pursuer sought a declarator of nullity. The parties had originally intended to be married by a Church of Scotland minister in Grangemouth. Marriage notices were lodged but the registrar was unable to issue a marriage schedule as there was doubt as to the defender's freedom to marry. Faced with this difficulty, the couple decided to be married in a mosque in Edinburgh. No marriage notices were lodged with the appropriate district registrar nor was any marriage schedule made up, far less issued. Nevertheless the ceremony took place and the matour issued a certificate recording the ceremony; but because of the absence of a completed marriage schedule, the marriage could not be, and was not, registered. In granting the declarator, the Lord Ordinary (Clyde) held that this was not a case where s 23A of the 1977 Act was applicable because, although the parties were present at the ceremony, there was no registration. Lord Clyde thought that s 23A could save a marriage when, for example, the schedule had been issued prior to the time limits, or if the person who conducted the ceremony was not an approved celebrant, or a marriage schedule was not produced at the ceremony, always provided that the parties were present and the schedule had been issued, signed and registered.

In *Sohrab v Khan*[3] the Lord Ordinary (McEwan) held that s 23A of the 1977 Act could not save a marriage where a marriage schedule had not been issued at the time of the ceremony: it was irrelevant that a marriage schedule was issued and registered at a later date. In other words, there must be a marriage schedule which can be produced at the solemnisation of the marriage.

Even if the marriage can be saved by the Marriage (Scotland) Act 1977, s 23A, the parties and the celebrant may be liable to criminal sanctions for breach of the 1977 Act, for example if a person falsifies or forges a marriage schedule.[4]

1   However, if the registrar refuses to register the schedule because he believes that there
    has been non-compliance with the formalities, s 23A is not triggered and the marriage
    is not valid.
2   1987 SLT 633.
3   2002 SLT 1255.
4   See the M(S)A 1977, s 24 for a full list of offences.

## *Conclusion*

**1.10** The purpose of legal preliminaries to the solemnisation of marriage is to ensure that the parties to a marriage have legal capacity to marry. As a result of the Marriage (Scotland) Act 1977, all persons who wish to enter into a regular marriage in Scotland must follow the same preliminary procedure whether or not they intend to have a civil or a religious or belief ceremony. This makes for simplicity and uniformity. Moreover, it is submitted that the current rules give sufficient time for objections to be made and appropriate investigations to take place. The procedure itself is admirably simple without the complexities of residence requirements for the parties.

# Irregular marriages

## *Introduction*

**1.11** Before the Reformation in 1560, Scots law recognised the validity of irregular marriages.[1] These involved no ecclesiastical formalities whatsoever. There were three kinds:

(1)    a declaration by the parties that they took each other as husband and wife: marriage *per verba de praesenti*. The consent of the parties was sufficient to constitute the marriage and there was no need for the presence of an episcopally ordained priest or witnesses;

(2)    a promise to marry at some future date followed by sexual intercourse on the faith of that promise: marriage *per verba de futuro subsequente copula*. The sexual intercourse on the faith of the promise was deemed to be agreement to marry. Not

surprisingly, perhaps, there was no need for the presence of an episcopally ordained priest or witnesses;

(3)     marriage constituted by the tacit agreement of the parties to marry presumed from a period of cohabitation with habit and repute that they were husband and wife: marriage by cohabitation with habit and repute.

After the Reformation these forms of irregular marriage continued to be recognised as constituting valid marriages in Scots law. The first two forms of irregular marriage were abolished by s 5 of the Marriage (Scotland) Act 1939 which came into force on 1 July 1940.[2] However, the third form, marriage by cohabitation with habit and repute, remained a valid method of constituting marriage in Scotland.

Because many of the older cases involved irregular marriages, it is proposed to outline the salient features of *de praesenti* and *de futuro* marriages and then to consider marriage by cohabitation with habit and repute in some detail.

---

1     For full discussion see E M Clive *The Law of Husband and Wife in Scotland* (4th edn, 1997, W Greens/Sweet & Maxwell), Ch 5.
2     The section was not retrospective.

---

*Marriage by declaration de praesenti*

**1.12** The essence of this form of marriage was that the parties seriously and genuinely exchanged present consent to marriage. The couple were married as soon as consents were exchanged. Consummation was not required: *consensus non concubitus facit matrimonium*. Because there was no need for witnesses, there could be formidable problems of proof, particularly where one of the alleged spouses had died and the issue arose in a claim by the other for rights of succession.[1]

The exchange of consents had to take place in Scotland.[2] This explains the popularity of elopements from England to marry at Gretna Green. Eventually, a residence requirement of at least 21 days was introduced by the Marriage (Scotland) Act 1856. The *de praesenti* marriage has not been a competent form of contracting a marriage since 1 July 1940.[3]

---

1  See, for example, *Dunn v Dunn's Trustees* 1930 SC 131.
2  *Macdonald v Macdonald* (1863) 1 M 854.
3  See the Marriage (Scotland) Act 1939, s 5.

---

*Marriage by promise subsequente copula*

**1.13** In this form of irregular marriage, if a promise was made of marriage at some date in the future and sexual intercourse took place on the faith of the promise, the couple were taken to be married at the date of the intercourse. The theory was that while mutual consent was essential to marriage, where a woman permitted sexual intercourse in reliance on a man's promise to marry her, it was to be presumed that there and then the parties had exchanged consents to present marriage and, if this presumption was not rebutted, a marriage was constituted by promise *subsequente copula*.[1] Both the promise and the sexual intercourse had to take place in Scotland.

In time, this form of marriage was treated with scepticism. As Lord Sands explained in *N v C*:[2]

> 'According to the theory of the law, when two persons who are engaged to be married indulge in sexual intercourse, presumably they there and then exchange matrimonial consent and become married persons. But, according to the view which prevails in those sections of the community in which antenuptial fornication is most apt to occur, they do nothing of the kind. They yield to desire and indulge in immoral intercourse, robbed doubtless of some of its danger by the prospect of future marriage ... Parents, employers and clergymen in rural Scotland have often had occasion to deal sorrowfully with a girl whose betrothed had got her in the family way. I much doubt if it has ever happened that the girl advanced the plea in excuse that she was a married woman ... Marriage by promise cum subsequente copula is a plant nourished by the law which has never taken root in the understanding or the conscience of the common people.'

It is therefore not surprising that this has not been a competent form of contracting a marriage since 1 July 1940.[3]

---

1    See *N v C* 1933 SC 492.
2    1933 SC 492 at 501.
3    Marriage (Scotland) Act 1939, s 5.

---

*Marriage by cohabitation with habit and repute*

**1.14** The Marriage (Scotland) Act 1939 did not abolish the third form of irregular marriage, marriage by cohabitation with habit and repute. The theoretical basis of the doctrine has been the subject of controversy.[1] It is not simply a matter of evidence. Although there is a presumption from long cohabitation as husband and wife that a couple have been married,[2] this is rebuttable by evidence that the alleged ceremony did not take place.

However, marriage by cohabitation with habit and repute is not merely a rule of evidence that the parties are prima facie to be presumed to have married by declaration *de praesenti* or promise *cum subsequente copula*, for if that were so, marriage by cohabitation with habit and repute would have been impliedly abolished by the Marriage (Scotland) Act 1939. Instead, the basis of the doctrine is that the parties' tacit consent to marry, inferred from, and combined with, cohabitation with habit and repute constitutes marriage: a legitimate enunciation by the parties to themselves and others of their matrimonial consent which has never expressly been put into words.[3] Because of their cohabitation with habit and repute that they are married, the law presumes that the parties have tacitly agreed to be married, with the result that they are married unless evidence is led that they never intended to take each other as husband and wife.

---

1    See, for example, Ashton-Cross 'Cohabitation with Habit and Repute' 1961 JR 21.
2    Or before 1 July 1940, that the couple had married by *de praesenti* consents or promise *cum subsequente copula*.
3    *Campbell v Campbell* (1866) 4 M 867 at 924–925.

---

**The requirements**

**1.15**

(1)    There must be cohabitation, ie the couple must live together: merely to have sexual intercourse is not enough.[1]

(2)     The cohabitation must be as husband and wife: not as man and mistress or man and housekeeper. However, cohabitation which began on an indeterminate footing can ripen into a marriage if the couple later cohabit as husband and wife.[2] Where a couple live together with the intention that they will marry at a future date, since they are not cohabiting as husband and wife, they cannot become married as a result of the doctrine of marriage by cohabitation with habit and repute.[3] *A fortiori* the doctrine does not apply when a couple live together without any intention of ever marrying.[4]

(3)     The cohabitation must take place in Scotland.[5]

(4)     The cohabitation must be sufficiently long for the court to infer that the parties tacitly agreed to marry. At one time it was thought that this must be at least a year,[6] but in *Shaw v Henderson*[7] it was emphasised that there was no hard and fast rule: all that is required is that the evidence of cohabitation is sufficient for an inference of tacit agreement to be drawn. Eleven months cohabitation was enough in that case. It is ultimately a question of fact.[8]

(5)     The parties must be reputed to be husband and wife and this reputation must be 'uniform and undivided'. But it is not fatal if some persons know that the couple are not married provided they are generally thought by friends and society in general to be husband and wife.[9] But if a substantial number of relatives and friends do know that the couple are not married[10] or are merely contemplating marriage, the doctrine will not apply.[11]

(6)     The parties must have legal capacity to marry.[12] If for example, one of the parties is already married to a third party, the doctrine cannot apply; but once the impediment is removed by the death or divorce of the existing spouse then, as the party will now have capacity to marry, the doctrine is applicable.[13] However, the parties can only rely upon the cohabitation with habit and repute which occurs after the impediment has been removed.[14] Thus if A who is married to B begins to cohabit with C in 1980 and B dies in 2000, the period of relevant cohabitation only begins with B's death in 2000: the period of cohabitation – albeit with

habit and repute – between 1980 and 2000 is irrelevant except as background material.[15] Where a relationship begins illicitly, it may, of course, be difficult to establish the necessary repute that the couple are living as husband and wife. But the doctrine will still be applicable once the parties are aware that the impediment has been removed.[16] No weight is now given to the old idea that a relationship which begins illicitly should prima facie be presumed to continue illicitly. As Lord Caplan observed in *Gow v Lord Advocate*:[17]

> 'if the parties clearly showed an inclination to adopt the married state before they became free to marry, this could reflect on their attitude to the relationship if cohabitation continues when freedom to marry arises'.

Whether a man and a woman have cohabited as husband and wife with the necessary repute to draw the inference of tacit consent is essentially a question of fact.[18]

---

1   *Quaere* whether a couple can cohabit for this purpose if they do not have sexual intercourse.

2   See, for example, *Nicol v Bell* 1954 SLT 314 (woman began as man's housekeeper, became his mistress, but on the birth of his child was treated as his wife: they were married as a result of 20 years' cohabitation as his wife); *Vosilius v Vosilius* 2000 SCLR 679.

3   See, for example, *Low v Gorman* 1970 SLT 356; *Mackenzie v Scott* 1980 SLT (Notes) 9.

4   See, for example, *Gow v Lord Advocate* 1993 SLT 275 at 276, per Lord Caplan: 'The case must be viewed against the background of modern social conditions where it is not at all uncommon for a man and woman to live together openly in an intimate relationship while retaining a distinct disinclination to enter the marriage state'.

5   *Dysart Peerage Case* (1881) 6 App Cas 489; *Walker v Roberts* 1998 SLT 1133.

6   See, for example, *Campbell v Campbell* (1866) 4 M 867; *Wallace v Fife Coal Co Ltd* 1909 SC 682.

7   1982 SLT 211.

8   *Kamperman v MacIver* 1994 SLT 763 (a period of six-and-a-half months not necessarily insufficient).

9   *Shaw v Henderson* 1982 SLT 211; *Vosilius v Vosilius* 2000 SCLR 679. Nor is it fatal that the woman continued to use her maiden name: *Donnelly v Donnelly's Executor* 1992 SLT 13.

10  *Low v Gorman* 1970 SLT 356; *Walker v Roberts* 1998 SLT 1133.

11  *Mackenzie v Scott* 1980 SLT (Notes) 9.
12  A couple who were parties to a regular marriage and then divorced have capacity to marry again as a result of the doctrine of cohabitation with habit and repute: *Mullen v Mullen* 1991 SLT 205.
13  *S v S* 2006 SLT 471. But if the parties are not free to marry when they first begin cohabiting, once they gain capacity to marry there must be a change in the nature of their relationship and how it is regarded by the rest of the world.
14  *Low v Gorman* 1970 SLT 356; *Vosilius v Vosilius* 2000 SCLR 679. In *Kamperman v MacIver* 1994 SLT 763, the Second Division held that pre-removal cohabitation is not wholly irrelevant as it is part of the background material which could colour the nature of the cohabitation after the impediment is removed.
15  *Kamperman v MacIver* 1994 SLT 763.
16  *Campbell v Campbell* (1866) 4 M 867. The case proceeded on the assumption that the parties knew of the death of the first husband. Thus it would appear that the presumption of tacit consent would be rebutted if the parties continued to believe that the impediment existed.
17  1993 SLT 275 at 276.
18  *Kamperman v MacIver* 1994 SLT 763.

**Procedure**

**1.16** A party to the alleged marriage by cohabitation with habit and repute will raise an action in the Court of Session for declarator of marriage. But it should be emphasised that the couple are married by virtue of the doctrine: there is no need for a declarator to establish the marriage. A declarator has been granted where the couple were married by cohabitation with habit and repute albeit that they had separated before the husband's death.[1] By the nature of the doctrine it will be difficult to establish exactly when the couple were married. While the matter is not free from difficulty, there is force in Clive's view that the date should be when there was sufficient relevant cohabitation with habit and repute for the inference of tacit consent to be drawn.[2] When a declarator has been granted, the Principal Clerk of Session will intimate the relevant details to the Registrar General to enable the marriage to be registered.[3]

1  *Morris v Morris* 1987 GWD 39-1437.
2  See E M Clive *The Law of Husband and Wife in Scotland* (4th edn, 1997, W. Greens/ Sweet & Maxwell) at pp 57 ff.
3  Marriage (Scotland) Act 1977, s 21.

**The 'abolition' of marriage by cohabitation with habit and repute**

**1.17** There was no doubt that marriage by cohabitation with habit and repute was anomalous. The doctrine only applied when a couple who had legal capacity to marry *pretended* to be married. It was one of the few situations where Scots law recognised rights arising from bad faith. Where it was useful, however, was the case where a couple believed that they were regularly married but the marriage was void because of a temporary impediment: once the impediment was removed, they could become married by cohabitation with habit and repute. On the other hand, many couples were under the impression that they were validly married by virtue of marriage with cohabitation and repute when the doctrine was inapplicable to them either because they lacked capacity to marry or, more commonly, because they had made no pretence of being married and therefore lacked the requisite repute that they were husband and wife. In these circumstances both the Scottish Law Commission[1] and the Scottish Executive took the view that the doctrine should be abolished.

Section 3(1) of the Family Law (Scotland) Act 2006 provides that 'The rule of law by which marriage may be constituted by cohabitation with habit and repute shall cease to have effect.' Nevertheless, a couple may still become married by cohabitation with habit and repute: (i) if the cohabitation began and ended before the commencement of the Act[2] ie when they have already become married by cohabitation with habit and repute; and (ii) if the cohabitation began before but continues after that date.[3] In other words, a couple can still become married by cohabitation with habit and repute even though post Act cohabitation as well as pre-Act cohabitation has to be used to infer that they have done so. It will be evident that the rule has only been abolished in respect of couples whose cohabitation with habit and repute *begins* after the commencement of the 2006 Act. Knowledge of the law on marriage by cohabitation with habit and repute will still therefore be needed for many years.

Indeed there is one exceptional situation when a couple can still be married by cohabitation with habit and repute even though the cohabitation began after the commencement of the Act. This is when A and B go through a ceremony of marriage abroad. They believe that they are validly married but in fact the marriage is invalid under the law of the place where the wedding took place. A is, or becomes, domiciled in Scotland and they live here with the repute that they are married. If B dies domiciled in Scotland, a declarator that they were married by cohabitation and repute can be obtained if A became aware that the purported marriage was invalid after B had died.[4] It does not matter that the cohabitation with habit and repute began after the commencement of the 2006 Act. But the exception applies only when the invalid marriage took place abroad: if A and B went through a ceremony of marriage in Scotland which, unknown to them, was void they cannot become married by post commencement cohabitation with habit and repute. And B must have died before A discovered that their marriage is invalid: if B was still alive when A made the discovery, the exception does not apply and A and B would have to go through a new regular marriage.[5] This is very strange because if the discovery was not made until B had died, A can get a declarator that they had become married by cohabitation with habit and repute long before B had passed away!

In so far as the law of marriage by cohabitation with habit and repute remains relevant it applies to same sex as well as opposite sex marriages[6].

---

1    Report on Family Law (Scot Law Com No 135) rec 42.
2    4 May 2006.
3    Family Law (Scotland) Act 2006, s 3(2).
4    FL(S)A 2006, s 3(3) and (4).
5    This could be difficult if, for example, B then lacked capacity to marry because of mental impairment.
6    Marriage and Civil Partnership (Scotland) Act 2014, s 4(6).

---

## PART II: REGISTERING A CIVIL PARTNERSHIP

**1.18** In this part, we shall consider how a couple can register their same sex relationship as a civil partnership. Each of the intended civil partners must submit to the district registrar a notice of their intention to enter a civil partnership:[1] this is known as a notice of proposed civil partnership. Particulars from the notice are entered into the civil partnership book.[2] The names of the parties and the date on which the registration is to take place are then publicised.[3] The registration can only take place 28 days after these details have been publicised.[4] This gives persons the opportunity to raise an objection as to why the registration should not go ahead and the registrar the chance to make appropriate investigations. Once satisfied that there are no legal impediments, after the 28-day period has expired the registrar can complete a civil partnership schedule.

The civil partnership is formed by registration. The district registrar asks the intended civil partners to confirm that the particulars set out in the civil partnership schedule are correct.[5] Each of the partners then signs the civil partnership schedule in the presence of each other, two witnesses (both of whom have attained the age of 16) and the authorised registrar.[6] The schedule is then signed by the witnesses and the registrar in the presence of the civil partners and each other.[7] The registrar will then enter the details of the schedule into the civil partnership register.[8]

Part 2 of the Marriage and Civil Partnership (Scotland) Act 2014 introduces religious and belief registration of civil partnerships. The rules for the authorisation of non-registrar civil partnership celebrants are the same as those for the authorisation of religious or belief celebrants of same sex marriages[9].

Several points should be noted. Unlike a marriage, where the couple are married by mutual consent and the active involvement of a registrar or religious celebrant, a civil partnership is created by the partners registering as civil partners. It is the registration *per se* that creates a civil partnership: the parties do not register their partnership whereas a married couple do register their marriage. The registrar or religious or belief celebrant does not declare the parties to be civil partners: her function is simply to register them as civil partners. In contrast to marriage where the witnesses need only profess to be 16, witnesses to a civil partnership registration have to be 16 or older.

A civil registration can take place in a registration office or any appropriate place that the registration authority agrees can be the place of registration. However, civil registration cannot take place in religious premises ie premises which are used solely for religious purposes or have been used for such and have not subsequently been used solely or mainly for other purposes[10]. Thus for example, a civil registration of a civil partnership cannot be carried out in a university or college chapel but could be done in a restaurant or bar that had been a former church. It does not matter that the religious body endorses same sex marriage. A religious or belief civil partnership may be registered only on the date and at the place specified in the civil partnership schedule: the specified place can be religious premises.[11] The civil partnership schedule cannot be issued to one or both parties earlier than seven days before the date of the intended registration.[12]

By section 95A, once the civil partnership schedule has been registered under the Civil Partnership Act 2004, the civil partnership cannot be held to be invalid on the ground of failure to comply with the formalities of registration.[13] So for example, a civil partnership which has been registered would not be invalid if it was later discovered that one of the witnesses was not 16 or over.

A civil partnership can only be created by registration. Therefore there is not, and never has been, any possibility of a civil partnership arising by cohabitation with habit and repute of civil partnership.

---

1    Civil Partnership Act 2004, s 88.
2    CPA 2004, s 89. Each of the intended civil partners must submit their birth certificate and if previously married or civil partnered, a decree of divorce or dissolution or, where the former spouse or civil partner has died, the death certificate of the former spouse or civil partner.
3    CPA 2004, s 90.
4    CPA 2004, s 90(2)(b). There are provisions for early registration: CPA 2004, s 91.
5    CPA 2004, s 95(1).
6    CPA 2004, s 85(1).
7    CPA 2004, s 85(4). But the parties are civil partners by virtue of s 86(1) even though this does not take place: s 85(3).
8    CPA 2004, s 95(1).
9    Civil Partnership Act 2004, ss 94 A-94E. See para **1.8** above.
10   CPA 2004, s 93(1).
11   CPA 2004, s 93A.
12   CPA 2004, ss 94(2) and (3).
13   The parties and the registrar may, however, be guilty of an offence: CPA 2004, s 100.

**Conversion of civil partnership into same sex marriage**

**1.19**  The Marriage and Civil Partnership (Scotland) Act 2014 provides two methods under which the parties can convert their civil partnership into a same sex marriage. First there is to be an administrative process which will be contained in regulations made by the Scottish Ministers[1]. Secondly, the civil partners may simply marry in accordance with the rules for same sex marriages under the Marriage (Scotland) Act 1977[2]. The civil partnership must be a qualifying civil partnership. This is a civil partnership which was registered in Scotland and has not been dissolved, annulled or ended by death.[3] Scottish Ministers have the power to modify the definition to include civil partnerships registered abroad[4]. While it is a cardinal rule that a person who is married or in a civil partnership lacks the capacity to marry or register a civil partnership, this impediment to marry does not apply where the couple are parties to a qualifying partnership[5]. Once the civil partnership has been converted into a same sex marriage, the civil partnership is brought to an end[6] and the couple are treated as having been married for all purposes from the date of registration of the civil partnership[7]. For the avoidance of doubt any decree of aliment under s 3 of the Family Law (Scotland) Act 1985 continues after the civil partnership has been dissolved by marriage and any orders relating to the occupation of the family home under s 103(3) or (4) of the Civil Partnership Act 2004 are to be treated as having been made under the Matrimonial Homes (Family Protection) (Scotland) Act 1981[8].

There are no provisions enabling a couple to a same sex marriage to convert it into a civil partnership.

---

1    Marriage and Civil Partnership (Scotland) Act 2014, s 10.
2    MCP(S)A 2014, s 11(1)(a).
3    Marriage (Scotland) Act 1977, s 5(6).
4    MCP(S)A 2014, s 9(1).
5    M(S)A 1977, s 5(4)(b).
6    CPA 2004 s 1.
7    MCP(S)A 2014, s 11(2)(a) and (b).
8    MCP(S)A 2014, s 11(7) and (8) On aliment, see para **3.8** ff below. On occupation of the matrimonial and family home, see para **5.8**ff below.

Chapter 2

# Legal impediments to marriage and civil partnership

## INTRODUCTION

**2.1** As we saw in the last chapter,[1] as a result of section 23A of the Marriage (Scotland) Act 1977 and section 95A of the Civil Partnership Act 2004, non-compliance with the formalities for regular marriages or registered civil partnerships will not normally affect the validity of the marriage or the civil partnership. But in addition, both a marriage and a civil partnership may be defective if the parties lack legal capacity to marry or are not eligible to enter into a civil partnership or if there is not true consent. An opposite sex marriage, but not a same sex marriage or civil partnership, is also legally defective if it cannot be consummated as a result of the incurable impotency of one or both of the parties. In this chapter we shall examine the impediments to marriage and civil partnership that exist in Scots law.

---

1    See paras **1.9** and **1.18**.

---

## VOID MARRIAGES AND CIVIL PARTNERSHIPS

**2.2** As a general rule, where such impediments as described above exist a marriage will be void in Scots law. There is one exception to this principle, namely where an opposite sex marriage has not been consummated as a result of the incurable impotency of one or both of the parties. In this case, the marriage is voidable. A civil partnership is void if the parties were not eligible to register a civil partnership or either of them did not consent to the formation of the civil partnership.[1]

Where a marriage or civil partnership is void, prima facie, it has no legal effect whatsoever. There is no need for the parties to obtain a declarator of nullity. However, any person who has a legitimate interest may seek a declarator of nullity on the ground that a marriage or civil partnership was void. In certain circumstances, a void marriage may have legal consequences. For example, a child conceived during a void marriage is presumed to be the child of the mother's 'husband',[2] and the husband will have parental responsibilities and rights over the child if he and the mother entered into the 'marriage' believing in good faith at that time that the marriage was valid.[3] Moreover, if a declarator of nullity is obtained by one of the parties, the court has the same powers to award financial provision for the parties as it does in actions of divorce or the dissolution of a civil partnership.[4]

1    Civil Partnership Act 2004, s 123.
2    See the Law Reform (Parent and Child) (Scotland) Act 1986, s 5(1), (2); discussed in **Ch 9.**
3    Children (Scotland) Act 1995, s 3(1), (2); discussed in **Ch 11.**
4    Family Law (Scotland) Act 1985, s 17(1). Financial provision on divorce and dissolution is discussed in detail in **Ch 7.**

## VOIDABLE MARRIAGES

**2.3**  In the case of a voidable marriage, the marriage subsists unless and until a declarator of nullity of marriage is obtained. Only a party to the marriage can seek declarator and, unlike the case of a void marriage, declarator cannot be obtained if one of the parties is dead. However, the effect of the decree is to declare that the marriage has never existed, ie it has retroactive effect. Nevertheless, the court can award the parties financial provision in the same way as in an action of divorce.[1] Nor does the retroactive effect of the decree affect the status of any children of the marriage.[2] Given that the sole ground of a voidable marriage is the incurable impotency of one or both of the parties, the number of children is likely to be small, but with modern reproductive techniques, the existence of children of a voidable marriage is not impossible.

1    FL(S)A 1985, s 17(1).
2    Law Reform (Miscellaneous Provisions) Act 1949, s 4.

## CAPACITY TO MARRY AND ELIGIBILITY TO ENTER A CIVIL PARTNERSHIP

**2.4** We shall now consider the grounds on which a marriage or civil partnership is void in Scots law as a result of the parties' lack of legal capacity to marry or ineligibility to register a civil partnership.

### Nonage

**2.5** By s 1(1) of the Marriage (Scotland) Act 1977, no person domiciled[1] in Scotland may marry before he or she attains the age of 16. Thus for example, a 15-year-old girl who is domiciled in Scotland has no legal capacity to contract a marriage in Scotland or any other country in the world even if the law of the foreign country allows its domiciliaries to marry below the age of 16. Where a Scottish domiciliary is over the age of 16, he or she has legal capacity to marry a foreign domiciliary who is under the age of 16, provided the ceremony takes place abroad and the foreign party has capacity under his or her *lex domicilii* and the law of the country where the ceremony takes place (the *lex loci celebrationis*).[2] By s 1(2) of the Marriage (Scotland) Act 1977, a marriage solemnised between persons either of whom is under the age of 16 is void. Consequently, even if one or both of the parties have capacity to marry under the age of 16 under their *lex domicilii*, the marriage is void if the ceremony takes place in Scotland.

Two people are not eligible to register in Scotland as civil partners of each other if either has not attained the age of 16.[3]

---

1    Domicile is a complex legal concept: its essence is a person having his or her permanent home in Scotland or having a Scottish domicile of dependence as a result of his or her parent being domiciled in Scotland.
2    Family Law (Scotland) Act 2006, s 36.
3    Civil Partnership Act 2004, s 86(1)(c).

---

### Forbidden degrees of relationship

*Marriage*

**2.6** By s 2(1) of the Marriage (Scotland) Act 1977[1], a marriage between persons who are related to each other in a forbidden degree is void if solemnised: (a) in Scotland; or (b) at a time when either party is domiciled in Scotland. A person is related to another in a forbidden degree if related to that person in a degree specified in Schedule 1 to the 1977 Act.[2]. The list is exclusive in the sense that where the relationship is not mentioned in the Schedule, the parties may validly marry[3] unless it would be contrary to their *lex domicilii* or the *lex loci celebrationis* for them to do so. The list is as follows:

## 1 – Relationships by consanguinity

| | |
|---|---|
| Parent | Aunt or uncle |
| Child | Niece or nephew |
| Grandparent | Great-grandparent |
| Grandchild | Great-grandchild |
| Sibling | |

## 2 – Relationships by affinity

| | |
|---|---|
| Child of former spouse | Former spouse of grandparent |
| Child of former civil partner | Former civil partner of grandparent |
| Former spouse of parent | Grandchild of former spouse |
| Former civil partner of parent | Grandchild of former civil partner |

## 3 – Relationships by adoption

| | |
|---|---|
| Adoptive parent or former adoptive parent | Adopted child or former adopted child |

The prohibited relationships arise from: (1) blood ties (consanguinity); (2) marriage or civil partnerships (affinity); and (3) adoption.

---

1   As amended by the Marriage and Civil Partnership (Scotland) Act 2014, s 1.

2   M(S)A 1977, s 2(1ZA). For the purpose of paragraph 2 of the Schedule – relationships by affinity – 'spouse' means in the case of opposite sex marriages a husband in relation to his wife and a wife in relation to her husband and in the case of same sex marriages, one of the parties to the marriage in relation to the other: M(S)A 1977, s 2 (1C)).

3   Marriage (Scotland) Act 1977, s 2(3). Similar principles apply to marriages by cohabitation with habit and repute: see E M Clive *The Law of Husband and Wife in Scotland* (4th edn, 1997, W Greens/Sweet & Maxwell), p 76.

## *(1) Consanguinity*

**2.7** Prima facie we are concerned with persons who are genetically related. However, where a woman gives birth to a child as a result of a fertilised ovum donated by another woman, she is to be treated as the child's mother and not the woman who donated the egg.[1] Therefore the child cannot marry the woman who gave birth to him or her even though she is not genetically related to the child; but the child could marry the donor who is genetically related as she is not the mother for any legal purpose. Similarly, where a spouse agrees to the artificial insemination of his or her spouse using a donor's sperm (AID) or a civil partner agrees to her partner having a child by AID, the spouse or the civil partner is treated as the parent of the child for all legal purposes and not the donor.[2] And so, for example, even although she is not genetically related, an AID child cannot marry her mother's former spouse nor can she register a civil partnership with her mother's former civil partner; but she could marry the donor, who is genetically related to her, as he is not her father for any legal purpose.[3] Such children will also be deemed to be genetically related to the other members of the family, for example grandparents or siblings.

For the purpose of consanguinity, half-blood is treated as full blood[4] and illegitimacy is irrelevant.[5] For example, a man cannot marry his half-sister, ie his mother's daughter by a man who was not his father or his father's daughter by a woman who was not his mother. Similarly, a woman cannot marry her illegitimate son or her legitimate son's illegitimate son. It should be noted that first cousins are free to marry.

1   Human Fertilisation and Embryology Act 1990, ss 27(1) and 29 and the Human Fertilisation and Embryology Act 2008, ss 33(1) and 48.
2   HFEA 1990, ss 28(2), (4) and 29: HFEA 2008, ss 35(1), 42(1) and 48; Marriage (Scotland) Act 1977, s 2(7A).
3   Similar prohibitions apply when a man is the child's father or a woman is the child's second female parent under HFEA 2008, ss 36 and 43. For further discussion of these provisions see **Ch 9.**

4   Marriage (Scotland) Act 1977, s 2(2)(a).
5   Law Reform (Parent and Child) (Scotland) Act 1986, Schedule 1, para 17.

*(2) Affinity*

**2.8** A degree of affinity is created by marriage or civil partnership and not merely by the fact that sexual intercourse or other forms of sexual relations have taken place between the persons concerned. And so, for example, a man cannot prima facie marry his father's former wife but he can marry his father's cohabitant even if she has lived with his father for many years and borne him children. Stepbrothers and stepsisters are free to marry.

In certain circumstances a marriage between persons related by affinity is not prohibited. Persons who are related within the degrees of affinity may marry provided that both parties have attained the age of 21 at the time of the marriage and the younger party has not at any time before attaining the age of 18 lived in the same household as the other party and been treated by the other party as a child of the family.[1] For example, a man may marry his father's former wife provided both are over the age of 21 and, if he is the younger party, he has not lived in the same household as his stepmother and been treated by her as a child of the family before he had reached the age of 18. If he has been so treated, the parties cannot marry. In other words, provided the parties related within the specified degrees of affinity have never assumed, in effect, the roles of parent and child, they are free to marry if both are over the age of 21.

For these purposes, if one of the parties (the relevant person) has had sex realignment surgery and whose 'changed' gender has become the acquired gender under the Gender Recognition Act 2004,[2] then any reference to former wife or former husband of the relevant person includes (respectively) any former husband or former wife of the relevant person. For example, H and W are married. W has a son, S, from a previous marriage. H acquires a female gender. W divorces H. H cannot avoid the impediment to marrying S by arguing that at the time of the purported marriage, he is not the former husband of S's mother, W.

1    Marriage (Scotland) Act 1977, s 2(1A). Either party can petition the Court of Session
     for declarator that the conditions are satisfied which enable them to marry: see M(S)A
     1977, s 2(5).
2    Discussed below at para **2.12**.

## *(3) Adoption*

**2.9** The Marriage (Scotland) Act 1977 only prohibits marriage between
adoptive parents and their adopted children.[1] Thus, if H and W adopt A,
A cannot marry W, his adoptive mother, or H his adopted father; but if H
and W then adopt B, A can marry B unless they are genetically siblings.[2]

1    Adoption and Children (Scotland) Act 2007, s 41(2). Where a couple who have
     commissioned a surrogate child obtain parental rights by virtue of a parental order
     under the Human Fertilisation and Embryology Act 2008, ss 54, they are treated as
     being adopted for the purpose of the law on prohibited degrees of marriage: HFEA
     2008, s 55.
2    Adoption and parental rights orders do not affect the prohibitions on the grounds of
     consanguinity; so an adopted child cannot marry his genetic mother or father etc:
     AC(S) Act 2007, s 41(1).

## *Conclusion*

**2.10** There are two major policy reasons for having prohibited degrees.
The first, in relation to consanguinity, is biological. Marriage to a close
relative greatly increases the risk of conceiving a physically or mentally
disabled child. Yet marriage between first cousins is permitted even though
there is an enhanced risk of conceiving a physically or mentally disabled
child particularly if the woman is in her mid-thirties or older. Secondly, it
is argued that to allow marriage between persons who are closely related
will give rise both to feelings of disgust in society generally and possible
disruption within the family concerned. This can be the only justification
for prohibitions in respect of affinity and adoption. However, if this were
thought to be an important policy objective, why does the law, for example,
permit adopted siblings to marry even if for many years they believed
they were siblings by blood? Moreover, restrictions on marriage between
persons who are related only by affinity have been held to be a breach of

Article 8 (right to respect for private and family life) and Article 12 (the right to marry) of the European Convention of Human Rights.[1] This has led to the removal of restrictions on parents-in law marrying their former children-in-law.[2]

---

1    *B and L v UK* (2004) 42 HERR 195.
2    Family Law (Scotland) Act 2006, s 1.

---

## Civil partnership

**2.11**  By section 86(1)(b) of the Civil Partnership Act 2004[1], two people are not eligible to register in Scotland as civil partners of each other if they are related in a forbidden degree. The forbidden degrees are the same as for marriage[2] but, of course, are solely concerned with persons of the same sex. Thus for example, a man cannot register a civil partnership with his father or brother or son (consanguinity). Nor can he register a civil partnership with his mother's former husband (his step father) or his father's former civil partner or the son of his former wife (his step son) or his former civil partner's son (affinity).[3] However, in the case of affinity the prohibition is disapplied if: (a) both persons have reached the age of 21; and (b) the younger has not at any time before he was 18 lived in the same household as the elder and been treated by the elder as a child of his family.[4] An adopted son cannot enter into a civil partnership with his adoptive father and an adoptive mother cannot enter into a civil partnership with her adopted daughter[5].

---

1    As amended by the Marriage and Civil Partnership Act 2014, s 24(3).
2    Civil Partnership Act 2004, Schedule 10. A reference to mother includes a woman who is a parent of the child by virtue of the Human and Embryology Act 2008 ss 42 and 43: CPA 2004, s 86(5A).
3    When the relevant party's gender has become the acquired gender under the Gender Recognition Act 2004, former husband includes former wife (and vice versa): CPA 2004, s 86(4) and (5).
4    Civil Partnership Act 2004, s 86(3). The prohibition on persons entering into civil partnerships with their former children in law or the children of their former civil partners (and vice versa) has been abolished: Family Law (Scotland) Act 2006, s 33 and Schedule 1, para 2.
5    Adoption and Children (Scotland) Act 2007, s 41 (2).

---

## The sex of the parties

*Marriage*

**2.12** For centuries marriage in Scots law was regarded as a union between a man and a woman.[1] A marriage was therefore void if the parties purporting to marry were of the same sex. Section 5 (4) (e) of the Marriage (Scotland) Act 1977 expressly stipulated that there was an impediment to a marriage if 'both parties were of the same sex'. The Marriage and Civil Partnership (Scotland) Act 2014 has swept this restriction away and opened marriage to same sex couples. Section 5 (4) (e) of the 1977 Act is repealed[2] and marriage now means 'marriage between persons of different sexes and marriage between persons of the same sex'[3].

While only persons of the same sex can continue to register a civil partnership and there remain differences in the formalities between opposite sex and same sex marriages, it is still necessary to consider how a person's sex is to be determined for the purposes of family law. In *Bellinger v Bellinger,*[4] the House of Lords held that biological criteria only should continue to be used:[5] these are genital, gonadal and chromosomal.[6] In a case of genuine intersex, a choice must be made on the basis of the preponderance of biological criteria;[7] if later developments, including psychological factors, suggest that the original assignment of the child's sex was wrong, then it can be changed. But when all the criteria are congruent at birth, a child's sex is established: it cannot be changed[8] and that will be the child's sex for the purpose of family law.

This raised acute problems for transgender persons whose psychological sex is the opposite of their biological sex. Even after gender realignment surgery, their sex did not change for the purpose of the law of marriage. The House of Lords in *Bellinger* accepted that this constituted a breach of Article 8 and Article 12[9] of the European Convention of Human Rights as they could not marry in their realigned gender.

This led to the Gender Recognition Act 2004. A person of either gender who is aged 18 or over can apply for a gender recognition certificate on the basis that he or she is living in the other gender (the acquired gender).[10] The application is determined by the Gender Recognition Panel.[11] If the Panel was satisfied that the applicant (a) has or has had gender dysphoria;

(b) has lived in the acquired gender, and (c) intends to live in the acquired gender until death,[12] then the Panel had to issue a full gender recognition certificate[13] unless the applicant was married or had registered a civil parnership when an interim gender recognition was issued. If the applicant with an interim gender recognition certificate subsequently divorced or had the civil partnership dissolved on the ground that an interim gender recognition  certificate had been issued,[14] the Gender Recognition Panel could then grant a full gender recognition certificate. When a full gender recognition certificate was issued the legal effect is that the person's gender becomes for all purposes the acquired gender. Only then could the previously married or civilly partnered transgendered individual re-establish a legal relationship with their former spouse by registering a civil partnership or with their former civil partner by marrying.

With the introduction of same sex marriage, the Gender Recognition Act 2004 has been amended[15]. The rules apply to protected Scottish marriages and protected Scottish partnerships. These are marriages solemnised in Scotland and civil partnerships registered in Scotland[16]. Where the applicant for a gender recognition certificate is a party to a protected marriage and the application contains a declaration that the applicant wishes the marriage to continue and  a statutory declaration by the applicant's spouse that that spouse wishes the marriage to continue, then the General Recognition Panel will issue a full gender  recognition certificate and the marriage will continue. If the applicant's spouse does not consent, the Panel will issue an interim gender recognition certificate. The applicant can then apply to a sheriff for a full gender recognition certificate which if the application was made within 6 months of the issue of the interim recognition certificate, the sheriff must grant.[17] While the marriage continues, the interests of the non-consenting spouse are protected as that spouse-and indeed the applicant-retains the right to obtain a divorce on the ground which arose when the interim gender recognition certificate was issued as that ground does not lapse when the full gender certificate was granted[18].

When a party to a protected civil partnership seeks a gender recognition certificate, the civil partnership cannot continue as a civil partnership can only exist between partners of the same sex. After a full gender recognition certificate has been issued, the applicant and the former civil partner are free to marry.

1   Stair *The Institutions of the Law of Scotland* (6th edn, 1981), I 4.1–I 4.6.
2   Marriage and Civil Partnership (Scotland) Act 2014, s 2 (a).
3   Marriage Scotland) Act 1977, s 26 (2) as inserted by MCP(S)A 2014, s 4(14).
4   [2004] AC 467.
5   This was the approach taken by Ormrod J in *Corbett v Corbett* [1971] P 83.
6   In the cells of biological males, Y as well as X chromosomes are present; no Y chromosomes are present in the cells of a biological female.
7   This appears to be the approach that was taken by the Lord Ordinary (Hunter) in the mysterious case of Forbes-Sempill (unreported). This case proceeded on the basis that the person concerned was a true hermaphrodite. See A I L Campbell 'Successful sex in succession: sex in dispute – the Forbes Sempill case and possible implications' 1998 JR 257 and 325.
8   *X, Petitioner* 1957 SLT (Sh Ct) 61.
9   The European Court of Human Rights had finally reached the same conclusion in *Goodwin v UK* and *I v UK* (2002) 35 EHHR 18.
10  Gender Recognition Act 2004, s 1(1)(a).
11  GRA 2004, s 1(3).
12  GRA 2004, ss 2 and 3.
13  GRA 2004, s 4(1).
14  On divorce on this ground see para **6.11**.
15  By the Marriage and Civil Partnership Act 2014, Sch 2.
16  GRA 2004, s 25.
17  GRA 2004 s 4E.
18  Divorce (Scotland) Act 1976, s 1 (3B).

## Civil partnership

**2.13** In Scotland two people are not eligible to register as civil partners of each other if they are not of the same sex.[1] If they are of opposite sex the purported civil partnership is void. Sex will be determined by biological criteria. An acquired gender can be obtained under the Gender Recognition Act 2004 so that a person whose acquired gender is male can register a civil partnership with another man and a person whose acquired gender is female can register a civil partnership with another woman. Where a person has obtained a full gender recognition certificate as a consequence of divorce, there is an expedited procedure under which he and his former husband or she and her former wife can register a civil partnership.[2]

1   Civil Partnership Act 2004, s 86(1)(a).

2    CPA 2004, s 96. Each must issue a s 88 notice of intention to register a civil partnership within 30 days of the issue of the full gender recognition certificate whereupon the civil partnership can be registered on any of the 30 days following receipt of the s 88 notices. There does not appear to be an expedited procedure for marrying a former civil partner when a civil partnership is dissolved because an interim gender recognition certificate has been issued to one of the partners.

## Prior subsisting marriage or civil partnership

**2.14**  A person who is already a party to a valid marriage or civil partnership lacks legal capacity to enter into a subsequent marriage or civil partnership while the first marriage or civil partnership continues to subsist.[1] There is no legal impediment if the first marriage or civil partnership is void; if, however, a marriage is only voidable, it will operate as a bar to a second marriage or civil partnership unless and until a declarator of nullity of marriage has been obtained.[2]

Even though the parties entered into marriage or a civil partnership with the belief held in good faith that any prior marriage or civil partnership had ended as a result of the death of the spouse or civil partner or divorce or dissolution, the marriage or civil partnership will still be void if *in fact* the prior marriage or civil partnership was subsisting at the time of the ceremony or registration. However, if a decree or declarator of nullity were obtained, financial provision for the spouses or the civil partners would be available.[3] Moreover, once the prior marriage was dissolved and the impediment to marriage thereby removed, the parties could have become married as a result of subsequent cohabitation with habit and repute.[4]

Where one of the parties is aware of this impediment, the innocent party may obtain damages for fraud. This can be illustrated by *Burke v Burke.*[5] In this case H was living with W1. He went through a ceremony of marriage with the pursuer, W2. He told her that he was divorced from W1. He also informed W2 that he was working night shifts but he spent his evenings with W1. When W2 discovered that no divorce had taken place, she sought declarator of nullity and aliment for her child who had been conceived during the 'marriage'. The court held that W2 did not have to prove the validity of the first marriage: she could rely on the doctrine *omnia praesumuntur rite et solemniter acta esse.*[6] The onus lay on the defender to establish, which in the circumstances he could not, that the first marriage was void. Accordingly, she obtained declarator and aliment for the child. In addition, the court held that the pursuer was entitled to damages in delict as a result of the defender's fraud and awarded her £2,500.[7]

A marriage or civil partnership will be void even though the parties believed, in good faith, that a prior marriage or civil partnership had been dissolved as a result of the death of the spouse or civil partner. This can raise difficulties for a person whose spouse or civil partner has disappeared and who wishes to enter a second marriage or civil partnership. At common law, there was a very strong presumption of life and a person who had disappeared was presumed to live to a ripe old age.[8] This presumption could be rebutted by evidence establishing beyond reasonable doubt that a spouse was dead but even so, a subsequent marriage was void if the spouse was in fact still alive.

This unsatisfactory position was resolved as a result of the Presumption of Death (Scotland) Act 1977. Under this statute, any person with sufficient interest may petition the Court of Session or the sheriff court for a declarator of death. The court may grant decree if satisfied on a balance of probabilities that either:

(1)   the missing person is dead – including the date and time of death; or

(2)   the missing person has not been known to be alive for a period of at least seven years: in this case, the court will declare the missing person to have died at the end of the day occurring seven years after the date on which he was last known to be alive.[9]

The Presumption of Death (Scotland) Act 1977 therefore covers two situations. In the first, a person has disappeared in circumstances which point to his death at a particular time, for example if a person was travelling in an aeroplane which disappeared. Here there is no need to wait seven years before bringing the action. In the second, a person has simply gone missing and there are no circumstances to suggest that he is dead. Here no action can be raised until seven years have elapsed during which there is no evidence that the missing person is alive.

A declarator of death is effective 'for all purposes including dissolution of a marriage or of a civil partnership to which the missing person is a party'.[10] Once a marriage or civil partnership has been dissolved as a result of a decree, 'the dissolution of the marriage or civil partnership shall not be invalidated by the circumstance that the missing person was in fact alive at the date specified in the decree'.[11] Thus if, for example, a person has obtained a declarator of death of a missing spouse, that person will have capacity to enter a subsequent marriage or civil partnership and this later marriage or civil partnership is not affected even if the missing spouse was in fact alive at the date of the later ceremony.

Although there are provisions for the variation or recall of the declarator if the missing person is found to be alive within five years of the date of the decree, no variation or recall 'shall operate so as to revive a marriage of the missing person dissolved by virtue of a decree in an action of declarator'.[12] It should be noted that any person, for example a beneficiary under the missing person's will, may apply for declarator. If it is granted, it will have the effect of dissolving the missing person's marriage or civil partnership, even though the missing person's spouse or civil partner continues to entertain the belief that the missing person is still alive and does not wish the marriage to be dissolved.

It is a criminal offence to purport to enter into a marriage knowing that either or both parties are already married to, or in a civil partnership with, another person[13] and it is a criminal offence to purport to register a civil partnership knowing that either or both parties are already in a civil partnership with, or married to, another person[14]. However, by s 13 of the Presumption of Death (Scotland) Act 1977 it is a defence to these offences for the accused to prove that at no time within a period of seven years immediately preceding the date of a subsequent 'marriage' had he or she any reason to believe that a prior spouse or civil partner was alive.[15]

---

1   Marriage (Scotland) Act 1977, s 5(4)(b); Civil Partnership Act 2004, s 86(1)(d).
2   Even though a declarator of nullity of marriage renders the marriage retrospectively null, it will probably not operate to validate a second marriage which was entered into before declarator was obtained.
3   See para **2.2**.
4   See para **1.15**.
5   1983 SLT 331.

6   The Latin means that 'all things are presumed to have been solemnly done and with the usual ceremony'. This is a rebuttable presumption of compliance with the appropriate formalities.

7   It has been held that a woman in this position is not entitled to compensation from the Criminal Injuries Compensation Board as she has not been the victim of a crime of violence when she had sex with a man whom she believed was her husband – her remedy was to sue him for fraud: *Gray v Criminal Injuries Compensation Board* 1999 SC 137.

8   Stair IV 45.17. See, for example, *Muhammad v Robertson or Kettle or Muhammad* 1972 SLT (Notes) 69.

9   Presumption of Death (Scotland) Act 1977.

10  PD(S)A 1977, s 3(1).

11  PD(S)A 1977, s 3(3).

12  PD(S)A 1977, s 4(5). It does not appear that this section has been amended to prevent a civil partnership which has been dissolved from reviving if the missing person turns out to be alive.

13  Marriage (Scotland) Act 1977, s 24A(1). The common law offence of bigamy has been abolished: Marriage and Civil Partnership (Scotland) Act 2014, s 28(3).

14  Civil Partnership Act 2004, s 100(1).

15  It is possible to call the Lord Advocate as a defender in an action of declarator of death, but as a general rule the missing person should be called as defender: *Horak v Lord Advocate* 1984 SLT 201.

# DEFECTIVE CONSENT

## Marriage

**2.15** Marriage is a contract and like any other contract requires consent. At common law a marriage was null if the parties did not truly consent to take each other as husband and wife. The law has now been put on a statutory basis and is to be found in s 20A of the Marriage (Scotland) Act 1977. The provisions only apply to marriages which are solemnised in Scotland.

## Mental incapacity

**2.16** By s 20A(3) of the 1977 Act, a marriage is void if at the time of the ceremony a party to the marriage was incapable of understanding the nature of marriage or of consenting to the marriage. This could arise from mental illness or mental impairment. However, the fact that a person is suffering from a mental illness, for example depression, does not necessarily prevent the giving of valid consent, provided the necessary capacity is present at the time. Marriage is a simple contract and persons of limited intelligence can validly consent to marriage. It has been held[1] that there is a very heavy burden on any person denying the validity of a marriage to establish that one or both parties were incapable of understanding the nature of marriage as a result of mental impairment or mental illness at the time of the ceremony. But if this burden can be discharged, the marriage will be void. A person may be of sound mind but physically or mentally weak, ie facile: as a result, such persons may easily be persuaded to act against their interests. For example, an unscrupulous nurse might persuade a rich old lady who is ill in hospital to marry him. In the absence of duress,[2] such a marriage is valid! Scots law has firmly rejected the contention that a marriage can be voidable on the grounds of facility and circumvention or undue influence.[3]

A party may lack capacity to consent as a result of drunkenness or abuse of drugs at the time of the ceremony. The effect of alcohol or drugs must be extreme before capacity is lost. In *Johnston v Brown*,[4] the pursuer, Mary Brown, obtained declarator of nullity of marriage on the ground that at the time of the ceremony, and for three days thereafter, she was so inebriated that she lacked capacity to consent to the marriage. Accordingly, the marriage was void.

---

1    *Long v Long* 1950 SLT (Notes) 32.
2    See para **2.18** ff.
3    *Scott v Kelly* 1992 SLT 915.
4    (1823) 25 495.

---

## Error

**2.17** By s 20A(2) of the 1977 Act a marriage is void if, at the time of the ceremony, a party who was capable of consenting to the marriage purported to give consent but did so under error. For this purpose, error is restricted to error as to the nature of the ceremony or the identity of the other party.[1]

An error as to the nature of the ceremony would arise if A goes through a ceremony of marriage with B, believing it to be merely a betrothal, An error as to identity is only operative in cases of impersonation. Thus when Jacob married Leah, believing he was marrying Rachel, the marriage would have been void in Scots law as a result of error.[2] In *M'Leod v Adams*[3] no error as to identity arose. The defender had deserted from the army. Using a false name to avoid detection by the authorities, he told a young and gullible widow that he was a sergeant in the Black Watch. The couple married by exchanging *de praesenti* consents whereupon the defender promptly deserted his wife taking her savings with him. Lord Sands held that there was no operative error as the widow clearly intended to marry the man before her and accordingly there was no error as to the identity of the parties to the marriage.[4] It is thought that the same result would be obtained under s 20A of the 1977 Act.

At common law it was settled that an error as to the qualities of a party to the marriage does not operate to vitiate consent. 'Errors in qualities or circumstances vitiate not: as if one supposing he had married a maid, or chaste woman, had married a whore.'[5] In the contract of marriage parties take each other 'for better or worse' and the Scottish courts refused to imply resolutive conditions into the contract which would be inconsistent with this fundamental principle.[6]

Moreover, in *Lang v Lang*,[7] the Inner House of the Court of Session held that it was irrelevant that an error as to qualities was induced by the fraudulent misrepresentation or concealment of facts by the spouse concerned. The pursuer in this case sought a declarator of nullity on the ground that he had been induced to marry the defender as a result of her representation that she was pregnant by him when, in fact, she was carrying another man's child. The court maintained that neither concealment of pregnancy *per alium*, nor a fraudulent misrepresentation of the true source of a disclosed pregnancy, was a ground of nullity in Scots law as these merely gave rise to errors as to qualities of the spouse and were therefore not sufficiently essential to vitiate consent. Again it is submitted that the same result would be obtained under s 20A of the 1977 Act.

The limited scope of operative error in relation to marriage can be the cause of considerable injustice. Although a person in the position of the pursuer in *Lang v Lang*[8] could seek divorce, he may well have to wait two years before he has a relevant ground.[9] The fraudulent misrepresentation cannot constitute grounds for divorce as behaviour for this purpose is restricted to the defender's conduct *'since the date of the marriage'*.[10]

1    Marriage (Scotland) Act 1977, s 20A(5).
2    *Genesis* 29: 21–30.
3    1920 1 SLT 229.
4    Declarator of nullity was however granted on the grounds that the marriage was a sham: see para **2.20** ff.
5    Stair I 9.9.
6    There is one exception: the marriage is voidable if one or both of the parties are unable to consummate the marriage as a result of incurable impotency. See para **2.22** ff.
7    1921 SC 44, overruling *Stein v Stein* 1914 SC 903.
8    1921 SC 44.
9    That is two years' non-cohabitation: Divorce (Scotland) Act 1976, s 1(2)(e). See **Ch 6**.
10   Divorce (Scotland) Act 1976, s 1(2)(b): see **Ch 6**.

## Duress

**2.18** Section 20A(2) of the Marriage (Scotland) Act 1977 provides that a marriage is void if at the time of the marriage ceremony a party to a marriage who was capable of consenting to the marriage purported to give consent but did so only by reason of duress. However, duress is not defined.

At common law a marriage was void if the will of one of the parties was overcome as a result of force or fear. The test was subjective.[1] In other words, the question was 'was this particular person overcome by force or fear?' not 'would a person of reasonable fortitude have been terrified?' The Scottish cases were concerned with arranged marriages. It was accepted that where a child marries out of deference to the parents' wishes, the marriage was not void. But unremitting pressure intentionally sustained by the parents,[2] or the threat of being cut off from financial support and being sent to a foreign country,[3] went beyond the limits of proper parental influence and could constitute duress.[4] It is submitted that duress for the purpose of s 20A of the 1977 Act should be construed in the same way.

As a matter of principle, duress may emanate from a third party, for example state authorities or the bride's irate father with his shotgun! In the leading English case of *Buckland v Buckland*,[5] the Court of Appeal held that before it is relevant the fear must have been unjustifiably imposed. Thus for example, if a man is forced to marry a girl whom he has made pregnant because of the threat that paternity proceedings would be brought against him unless he did so, he could not rely on the fear as it was justly imposed. Clive has argued[6] that this distinction is hard to justify as the consent is no more free where the fear is justly imposed. This may well be a case where reasoning from legal principle must give way to considerations of public policy.

The concept of duress in Scots law is narrow. And even if a marriage is void as a result of duress, there will have been a ceremony and the victim may have been compelled to leave her family and live with her 'spouse'. Put another way, while a marriage can be null because of duress, the law does nothing to prevent the 'marriage' being performed in the first place. In order to alleviate public concern about forced marriages, the Forced Marriage etc (Protection and Jurisdiction) (Scotland) Act 2011 enables a court to make a forced marriage protection order.[7] The purpose of the order is to protect a person from being forced into a marriage or from any attempt to force the person into a marriage. The order will require persons, for example the victim's family, to stop using violent, threatening or intimidating conduct to force the protected person to marry.[8] An application for an order can be made by the protected person or a local authority or a person specified by Scottish ministers, for example, a representative from a women's refuge.[9] An application can be made after the marriage, for example to prevent the protected person from being compelled to leave the country.[10] Breach of a protection order is a criminal offence.

---

1   *Mahmood v Mahmood* 1993 SLT 589; *Mahmud v Mahmud* 1994 SLT 599; *Sohrab v Khan* 2002 SLT 1255.
2   *Mahmud v Mahmud* 1994 SLT 599. It was irrelevant that the pursuer in this case was a young man rather than a girl. In *Sohrab v Khan* 2002 SLT 1255, part of the pressure was the threat by the pursuer's mother that she would kill herself unless her daughter (the pursuer) entered into an arranged marriage.
3   *Mahmood v Mahmood* 1993 SLT 589. The disapproval of the parents' or the child's community is not per se enough.
4   While it may be easier to infer duress when, as in *Mahmud*, the 'marriage' was never consummated and the parties never lived together, in *Mahmood* declarator was granted even though the marriage was consummated.
5   [1967] 2 All ER 300; [1968] P 296.
6   E M Clive *The Law of Husband and Wife in Scotland* (4th edn, 1997, W Greens/Sweet & Maxwell), p 86.

7    Forced Marriage etc (Protection and Jurisdiction) (Scotland) Act 2011, s 1(1)(a).
8    FM(PJ)(S)A 2011, s 2.
9    FM(PJ)(S)A 2011, s 3.
10   FM(PJ)(S)A 2011, s 1(1)(b).

## Civil Partnerships

**2.19**  By s 123(1) of the Civil Partnership Act 2004, a civil partnership is void if the parties are ineligible to register in Scotland as civil partners.[1] A person who is incapable of understanding the nature of civil partnership, or validly consenting to its formation, is not eligible to register.[2] A civil partnership is also void if at the time of registration one of the parties who was capable of consenting to the formation of the civil partnership purported to consent but did so by reason only of duress or error.[3] Error is restricted to error as to the nature of civil partnership or the identity of the other party.[4] The issues which arise have been discussed in the context of marriage. Scottish Ministers have the power to apply the provisions of the Forced Marriage etc (Protection and Jurisdiction) Act 2011 to civil partnerships.[5]

1    Civil Partnership Act 2004, s 123(1)(a).
2    CPA 2004, s 86(1)(e).
3    CPA 2004, s 123(1)(b) and (c).
4    CPA 2004, s 123(2).
5    Forced Marriage etc (Protection and Jurisdiction) Act 2011, s 10.

## Sham marriages

**2.20**  At common law it was recognised that a marriage was null if it could be established that one or both parties had, for religious or other reasons, intended not to become married at the time of the ceremony,[1] ie that at the time of the ceremony one or both of them had tacitly withheld consent to the marriage. Put another way they were saying 'yes' when they meant 'no'. This was known as the sham marriage doctrine. It became controversial because parties could go through a ceremony of marriage in order to obtain certain rights deriving from the status of matrimony, for example in relation to immigration, then later obtain a decree of declarator of nullity on the basis that their marriage was a sham.

Section 20A(4) of the Marriage (Scotland) Act 1977 provides:

'If a party to a marriage purported to give consent to marriage other than by reason only of duress or error, the marriage shall not be void by reason only of that party's having tacitly withheld consent to the marriage at the time when it was solemnised'.

Accordingly it would appear that the sham marriage doctrine has been abolished. However, it has been held that a marriage is void as a sham not only when the parties tacitly withhold consent but also when they positively intend not to be married.[2] On a strict construction, s 20A would not cover this latter situation and such marriages would still be null by virtue of the common law. Since the mischief of the provision is clear, it is thought that the courts would not favour a construction that would keep alive any remnant of the sham marriage doctrine.

There is not, and has never been, a sham civil partnership doctrine. This is why there is no equivalent of s 20A(4) of the Marriage (Scotland) Act 1977 in the Civil Partnership Act 2004.

1   See, for example, *Orlandi v Castelli* 1961 SC 113; *Mahmud v Mahmud* 1977 SLT (Notes) 17; *Akram v Akram* 1979 SLT (Notes) 87; *H v H* 2005 SLT 1025. A marriage could be void as a sham where only one party withheld consent: *McLeod v Adams* 1920 1 SLT 229.
2   See, for example, *H v H* 2005 SLT 1025.

## Validation of marriages void for absence of consent

**2.21** There is some authority for the principle that a marriage which is void as a result of absence of consent will be validated if the parties choose to overlook the impediment and continue to live as husband and wife.[1] However, it is thought that the better view is that a couple became married as a result of the doctrine of marriage by cohabitation with habit and repute, in the same way as if their original marriage was void because of a temporary impediment to their marriage. As we have seen,[2] marriage by cohabitation with habit and repute has now been prospectively 'abolished'.

1   E M Clive *The Law of Husband and Wife in Scotland* (4th edn, 1997, W. Greens/Sweet & Maxwell), pp 92 ff.
2   See para **1.17**.

## VOIDABLE MARRIAGES: INCURABLE IMPOTENCY

**2.22** The parties' consent is the essential element of marriage in Scots law: *consensus non concubitus facit matrimonium*. However, an opposite sex marriage[1] is voidable if, and only if, one or both of the parties is at the time of the ceremony permanently and incurably impotent. As Lord President (Clyde) explained in *L v L*,[2] *potentia copulandi* is a resolutive condition of the contract of marriage: if it is not fulfilled the marriage is a nullity. But before the marriage will be treated as null, a party to the marriage must obtain a declarator of nullity of marriage whereupon the marriage is retrospectively void from the date of decree.[3] It has been recommended that incurable impotency should cease to be a ground on which a marriage is voidable.[4]

---

1   Section 5 (1) of the Marriage and Civil Partnership (Scotland) Act 2014 provides that ' For the avoidance of doubt,the rule of law which provides for a marriage to be voidable by reason of impotence has effect only in relation to a marriage between persons of different sexes'. Nor does the law affect civil partnerships.
2   *L v L* 1931 SC 477 at 481.
3   See para **2.2**.
4   Report on Family Law (Scot Law Com No 135) rec 49. There are only about eight declarators of nullity a year and it is doubtful whether they are all concerned with incurable impotency. The numbers concerned are therefore very small. It is true that specific matrimonial relief on the ground of incurable impotency is anomalous: there is no specific relief, for example, if a spouse marries when suffering from sterility or an incurable or infectious disease, for example AIDS. It is argued by the Scottish Law Commission that divorce on the ground of irretrievable breakdown should be a sufficient remedy in cases of incurable impotency. This recommendation was not accepted by the Scottish Executive and the Family Law (Scotland) Act 2006 did not reform this area of the law apart from extending the jurisdiction to grant declarator to the sheriff court: FL(S)A 2006, s 4. The sheriff can grant declarator when the marriage is void as well as when it is voidable.

---

### The meaning of incurable impotency

**2.23** 'Impotency' means incapacity to have sexual intercourse. The Scottish courts have taken the view that sexual intercourse involves full and complete sexual intercourse: *vera copula perfecta* accomplished *modo naturalis*. Partial penetration by the husband of the wife is not enough.[1]

However, once full penetration has been achieved, the marriage has been consummated. It is irrelevant that the husband has used a contraceptive sheath.[2] Moreover, impotency is incapacity for sexual intercourse not the capacity to procreate. Consequently, sterility does not amount to impotency. If a spouse is capable of sexual intercourse but refuses to consummate the marriage, that is not a ground of nullity in Scots law though it could give rise to grounds for divorce.[3]

The impotency may be the result of physical or psychological causes. It may exist only in relation to the other spouse: *quoad hanc* (vis-à-vis the wife) or *quoad hunc* (vis-à-vis the husband). Indeed, both spouses may be impotent in relation to each other: *quoad hanc et quoad hunc*. The impotency must exist at the date of the marriage and must be permanent and incurable at the date of the action for declarator of nullity. The courts have taken a realistic approach on the question of incurability and have held that the issue is whether the impotency is incurable in the context of the particular marriage. Thus for example, in *M v W or M*,[4] the husband suffered from a nervous or psychological inability to consummate the marriage. He was advised by his doctor that the impotency was curable if he had hormone treatment and had the full support and help of his wife. After the hormone treatment was administered, his wife refused to have sexual intercourse with him. The Inner House held that the husband's impotency was incurable *quoad hanc* as the cure involved both the hormone treatment and the wife's help which had not been forthcoming.[5] While this decision illustrates the court's sympathy towards the pursuer, it must be restricted to its own special facts: a potent spouse cannot argue that he is impotent *quoad hanc* merely because his wife refuses to have sexual intercourse with him since this would, in effect, be recognising wilful refusal to consummate as a ground of nullity.

If the impotency is curable, where the action is brought by the potent spouse, decree is not granted until the impotent spouse has had an opportunity to undergo the necessary treatment: if the defender refuses treatment, decree will then be granted.[6] If the impotent spouse is the pursuer, the action will fail if reasonable steps could be taken to effect a cure. Where the treatment carries a risk to life or intolerable pain, the impotent spouse is not expected to undergo such an ordeal and the impotency will be regarded as incurable.[7]

The potent spouse can obviously bring an action. But in *F v F*,[8] the Inner House held that because impotency was an involuntary condition, the impotent spouse can also seek a declarator of nullity on the ground of his or her own incurable impotency.

---

1    *J v J* 1978 SLT 128.
2    *Baxter v Baxter* [1947] 2 All ER 886, [1948] AC 274, HL, an English case which it is thought would be followed in Scotland.
3    On the behaviour ground: Divorce (Scotland) Act 1976, s 1(2)(b). See **Ch 6.**
4    1966 SLT 152.
5    But the Lord President (Clyde) thought that the question was whether the husband was impotent throughout the marriage rather than whether it was curable at the date of the action: *M v W or M* 1966 SLT 152 at 154.
6    *WY v AY* 1946 SC 27.
7    Such risks are unlikely to arise in the context of modern medicine.
8    *F v F* 1945 SC 202.

---

### Personal bar

**2.24** A spouse may be personally barred from obtaining declarator of nullity on the ground of incurable impotency. Personal bar will arise if, with knowledge of the impotency and the availability of a legal remedy, the pursuer has either approbated the marriage or taken advantage of, or derived benefits from, the matrimonial relationship with the result that it would be unfair or inequitable to permit the pursuer to treat the marriage as null.[1]

Two points should be noticed. First, personal bar will arise only if the pursuer knows of the facts and the availability of a legal remedy. But knowledge of the law will prima facie be assumed and the onus should therefore be on the pursuer to show that he or she did not have knowledge of a legal remedy. Secondly, it is the pursuer's *conduct* which constitutes approbation or the taking of advantages etc which renders it unfair or inequitable to grant decree. The following are illustrations of the principle.

---

1    *CB v AB* (1885) 12 R (HL) 36 at 38, per Lord Selborne.

---

*(1) Delay*

**2.25** Delay per se is not enough[1] but if it would result in serious prejudice to the defender, it could be.[2]

1 See, for example, *Allardyce v Allardyce* 1954 SC 419.
2 *AB v CB* 1961 SC 347.

*(2) Knowledge of impotency*

**2.26** Where the pursuer entered into the marriage with knowledge of the defender's impotency this will result in personal bar. By marrying in these circumstances, the pursuer has adopted or homologated the defender's failure to perform a condition whose failure would otherwise have entitled the pursuer to have the marriage resolved.[1] Conversely, an impotent spouse who has allowed the potent spouse to enter the marriage with knowledge of the impotency is personally barred from seeking declarator on the ground of his or her own impotency.

1 *L v L* 1931 SC 477 at 481, per Lord President Clyde.

*(3) Children*

**2.27** Personal bar will arise where the pursuer has homologated or adopted the voidable marriage by agreeing to adopt a child or have a child by artificial insemination.[1]

1 *AB v CB* 1961 SC 347. *Quaere* if the child was conceived by *fecundatio ab extra* during an unsuccessful attempt to consummate the marriage.

# Chapter 3

# The legal consequences of marriage and civil partnership

## PART I: GENERAL

### Introduction

**3.1** In this and the following two chapters, it is proposed to discuss the major legal consequences for the parties of marriage and civil partnership. This chapter is concerned with a diverse but not exhaustive range of subjects and certain important matters, for example bankruptcy, evidence, immigration and taxation, are not discussed. In Chapters 4 and 5 the implications of marriage and civil partnership on the law of property are treated in some detail.

The twentieth century saw a drastic decline in the legal consequences of marriage.[1] In the interests of equality between the spouses, many changes in the law have taken the form of regarding the spouses as though they were unmarried. But, particularly in relation to property, as long as our society continues to perceive that the primary responsibility for child rearing should be the mother's, formal legal equality will often result in a wife's economic dependence on her husband as in fact she does not have the same opportunities to acquire property during the marriage. On the other hand, under the system of financial provision on divorce, a wife can be compensated for economic disadvantages sustained by her as a result of the marriage. Moreover, when a marriage is terminated by death, Scots law protects the surviving spouse (who will usually be a widow) by providing her with rights to a proportion of the deceased's estate which cannot be defeated by the deceased. It is perhaps not too cynical to observe that during the marriage the legal consequences of being married are, with some important exceptions, such as aliment[2] and the right to occupy the matrimonial home,[3] relatively insignificant compared with being married when the marriage is terminated by divorce or death.

Unless there is a child of the family, the economic disadvantages of being a same sex spouse or a civil partner are less acute. But the legal position of same sex spouses or civil partners vis a vis each other is the same as that of opposite sex spouses.

1    See generally, E M Clive *The Law of Husband and Wife in Scotland* (4th edn, 1997, W Greens/Sweet & Maxwell), Part II.
2    Discussed at paras **3.8** ff.
3    See **Ch 5**.

## Personal effects

*Domicile*

**3.2**  At common law spouses had a duty to adhere to each other: if a spouse refused to adhere without reasonable cause, that spouse was in desertion. Now that desertion is no longer a ground of divorce or dissolution,[2] it is thought that the obligation of adherence no longer subsists. The right of a husband to choose where the spouses should live was abolished in 1984.[3] Because she had to live with her husband, the rule developed that a wife's domicile depended on that of her husband. Accordingly, while the marriage subsisted, a wife could not have a domicile which was different from her husband's. The wife's domicile of dependency was abolished by s 1 of the Domicile and Matrimonial Proceedings Act 1973 and a wife can now acquire an independent domicile.[4] Of course, none of these rules applied to same sex spouses or civil partners.

1    E M Clive *The Law of Husband and Wife in Scotland* (4th edn, 1997, W Greens/Sweet & Maxwell), Ch 11.
2    Discussed below at para **6.7**.
3    Law Reform (Husband and Wife) (Scotland) Act 1984, s 4.
4    See the Domicile and Matrimonial Proceedings Act 1973, s 1(2): a wife who had a domicile by dependence retains that domicile unless and until it is changed by acquisition or revival of another domicile on or after the 1973 Act came into force.

*Sexual relations*

**3.3** If a spouse in an opposite sex marriage is unable to consummate the marriage as a result of incurable impotency, the marriage is voidable.[1] If a spouse or civil partner wilfully refuses to have sexual relations, this could give rise to an action of divorce or dissolution on the ground of unreasonable behaviour.[2] If a spouse voluntarily has sexual intercourse with a third party during the subsistence of the marriage, this can give rise to an action of divorce on the ground of adultery.[3] While adultery is a ground of divorce of a same sex marriage[4] it is not a ground for dissolution of a civil partnership.

At one time, it was thought that a husband could not be guilty of raping his wife if he had sexual intercourse with her without her consent: this was based on the view that, on marriage, a wife is prima facie deemed to have surrendered her person to her husband. Where there was evidence, for example if the couple were *de facto* separated, from which it could be inferred that the wife was no longer prepared to surrender her body to her husband, then he could be prosecuted for rape and not merely indecent assault.[5] In 1989, the High Court of Justiciary held that these rules were anachronistic and that a husband could be guilty of raping his wife even though the couple were living together.[6] In the course of his judgment the Lord Justice-General (Emslie) said:[7]

> 'Nowadays it cannot seriously be maintained that by marriage a wife submits herself irrevocably to sexual intercourse in all circumstances. It cannot be affirmed nowadays, whatever the position may have been in earlier centuries, that it is an incident of modern marriage that a wife consents to intercourse obtained only by force. There is no doubt that a wife does not consent to assault upon her person and there is no plausible justification for saying today that she nevertheless is to be taken to consent to intercourse by assault.'

Of course, even though a husband can be charged with the rape of his wife, there remain formidable problems of proof.[8]

On marriage or the registration of a civil partnership, a spouse or civil partner lacks capacity to enter into another marriage or register another civil partnership unless the existing marriage or civil partnership is terminated by divorce or dissolution or death.[9]

1    Discussed at paras **2.22** ff.
2    Discussed below at para **6.6**.
3    Divorce (Scotland) Act 1976, s 1(2)(a), discussed at paras **6.3** ff
4    Divorce (Scotland) Act 1976, s 1(3A).
5    *HM Advocate v Duffy* 1983 SLT 7; *HM Advocate v Paxton* 1985 SLT 96.
6    *S v HM Advocate* 1989 SLT 469.
7    1989 SLT 469 at 473.
8    In *S v HM Advocate* 1989 SLT 469, for example, the jury found the charge of rape not proven.
9    The incapacity to marry while being a party to a valid subsisting marriage is not a breach of Article 12 (right to marry) of the European Convention on Human Rights. Indeed, it has been held that there is no violation of the Article if a state prohibits a divorced person from remarrying: *Johnston v Ireland* (1986) 9 EHRR 203.

*Name*

**3.4**  There is no legal requirement for a wife to take her husband's surname on marriage. It is, however, still common for a wife to use her husband's surname but this is mere usage. In formal legal documents a married woman will sign using her maiden name and her husband's surname, for example, Mrs Elizabeth Smith (maiden name) or Brown (husband's name).[1] There is no similar usage in relation to same sex spouses or civil partners.

1    For the form of names used in court proceedings, see E M Clive *The Law of Husband and Wife in Scotland* (4th edn, 1997, W Greens/Sweet & Maxwell), pp 149 ff.

## Obligations

*Contract*

**3.5**  At common law a wife had no contractual capacity. In time the courts recognised exceptions to the general rule and in a series of statutes culminating in the Married Women's Property (Scotland) Act 1920, a married woman was deemed to 'be capable of entering into contracts and incurring obligations ... as if she were not married'.[1] There was, of course, no similar disability in the context of same sex marriage or civil partnership. Nevertheless s 24(1)(b) of the Family Law (Scotland) Act 1985 provides that, subject to the provisions of any enactment, marriage or civil partnership does not of itself affect the legal capacity of the parties to the marriage or the partners in a civil partnership. Thus marriage or registration of a civil partnership per se has no effect on the contractual capacity of the spouses or civil partners.

At common law a wife was presumed to have been placed by her husband in charge of his domestic affairs and consequently she could pledge his credit for household expenses, for example food and clothing. This was known as the wife's *praepositura*. The *praepositura* was thought to have become anachronistic and was abolished in 1984.[2]

It is however perfectly possible that one spouse or civil partner may expressly appoint the other spouse or civil partner to act as his or her agent in a particular transaction. Moreover, one spouse or civil partner may *impliedly* authorise the other spouse or civil partner to act as his or her agent by acquiescing in a series of transactions. For example if a husband has paid the accounts incurred by his wife at a dress shop, he will remain liable to pay future accounts unless he has informed the shopkeeper that he will no longer be prepared to pay her accounts in the future: merely to tell his wife no longer to pledge his credit is not sufficient to avoid liability.[3]

When a spouse, A, enters into an obligation with a third party which benefits the other spouse, B, for example the grant to a bank of a standard security over A's property to be used to guarantee B's debts, there is no *presumption* in Scots law that A acted under the undue influence of B. Where A has *in fact* acted under B's undue influence, or under error as a consequence of B's misrepresentation,[4] the third party may be unable to enforce the obligation unless it can be shown that the third party acted in good faith towards A throughout the transaction.[5] For example this could involve the third party being under a duty to advise A of the nature of the transaction and suggest that A seeks independent legal advice.[6] In the absence of the third party fulfilling these duties, A can have the obligation with the third party reduced. This duty of good faith does not arise if A also received a benefit from the third party such as an increased borrowing facility at a bank.[7] It is thought that the law is the same when one civil partner enters into a gratuitous obligation with a third party for the benefit of the other civil partner.

1    Married Women's Property (Scotland) Act 1920, s 1. For a full account of these developments, see E M Clive *The Law of Husband and Wife in Scotland* (4th edn, 1997, W Greens/Sweet & Maxwell), pp 211 ff.
2    Law Reform (Husband and Wife) (Scotland) Act 1984, s 7.
3    The husband's liability to pay his wife's debts incurred before marriage has been abolished: see the Law Reform (Husband and Wife) (Scotland) Act 1984, s 6.
4    *Clydesdale Bank v Black* 2002 SLT 764, approving *Braithwaite v Bank of Scotland* 1999 SLT 25 and *Wright v Cotias Investments Inc* 2001 SLT 353.
5    *Smith v Bank of Scotland* 1997 SC (HL) 111.
6    When the wife has a solicitor who appears to represent her interests, the third party can assume that she was properly advised even though the solicitor was also acting for the husband: *Forsyth v Royal Bank of Scotland* 2000 SLT 1295; *Ahmed v Clydesdale Bank* 2001 SLT 423. The detailed duties under the analogous doctrine in English law laid down in *Royal Bank of Scotland v Etridge (No 2)* [2001] 4 All ER 449 do not apply in Scots law: *Clydesdale Bank v Black* 2002 SLT 764; *Thomson v Royal Bank of Scotland* 2002 GWD 18-591.
7    *Royal Bank of Scotland v Wilson* 2003 SLT 25.

*Delict*[1]

**3.6** At common law, spouses could not sue each other in delict. The anachronistic nature of this rule can be illustrated by the case where as a result of a husband's negligent driving, the wife was injured but could not sue her husband. This was indefensible particularly as the loss would ultimately fall on her husband's insurance company. This position was modified by s 2(1) of the Law Reform (Husband and Wife) Act 1962, which provided that each of the spouses had 'the like rights' to bring proceedings against the other in respect of a delict 'as if they were not married'. If the action was brought during the subsistence of the marriage, the court had a discretion to dismiss the proceedings if it appeared that no substantial benefit would accrue to either party if the action continued.[2] The court's discretion was unlikely to be invoked as the action had to proceed if a benefit accrued to the *pursuer* even though the couple as a family unit did not benefit. The opportunity was taken in the Family Law (Scotland) Act 2006[3] to repeal the 1962 Act. The original common law rules do not, of course, revive.[4] The common law rules never applied to same sex spouses or civil partners.

Under the Damages (Scotland) Act 2011, where a spouse or civil partner has died from personal injuries caused by a delict of a third party, the surviving spouse or civil partner[5] has a right to damages for loss of support, including a reasonable sum for loss of the deceased's personal services,[6] funeral expenses and compensation for grief, distress and the loss of the deceased's society.[7] As a general rule, it is presumed that loss of support amounts to 75% of the deceased's income[8]. A surviving *divorced* spouse or former civil partner can only obtain damages for loss of support and funeral expenses.[9] While it is not necessary that the deceased was under a legal obligation to aliment the claimant, the divorced spouse or civil partner can only obtain compensation for the actual loss of support he or she was receiving from the deceased[10]. Where a housewife was killed, her husband and child obtained damages for the loss of her services as a housekeeper.[11]

The Damages (Scotland) Act 2011 is concerned with the situation where the delict results in death. Where a person is injured it was held at common law that the defender did not owe a duty of care to the victim's spouse or relatives if they suffered loss as a result of the delict. Accordingly, the family could not sue for damages.[12] Moreover, the victim could not sue for losses sustained by a relative, for example a spouse, who had given up his or her job to nurse him.[13] As a result of s 8 of the Administration of Justice Act 1982,[14] where a person has sustained personal injuries, the injured person can now recover damages which amount to reasonable remuneration for necessary services rendered to him or her by a relative.[15] For these purposes, a relative includes a spouse, a divorced spouse, a civil partner or former civil partner.[16] The pursuer, ie the injured person, will then account to the relative for any damages recovered under this provision.[17]

When the victim is not earning, at common law he or she had no right to sue for loss of earnings. This was particularly unfair to wives who had given up their employment to look after the home or children. Section 9 of the Administration of Justice Act 1982 now provides that an injured person who has been providing *unpaid* personal services to a relative can sue for damages if, as a result of the injuries, he or she is unable to continue to do so. Again a relative includes a spouse, divorced spouse, civil partner or former civil partner.[18] The personal services must be services which:

(1)    were or might have been expected to have been rendered by the injured person before the injury;

(2)     were of a kind which when rendered by a person other than a relative would ordinarily be obtainable on payment; and

(3)     the injured person but for the injuries in question might have been expected to render gratuitously to a relative.

These would include a spouse or civil partner's unpaid housekeeping and DIY services for the benefit of the other spouse or civil partner and their family.[19] Because the personal services must have been rendered gratuitously before s 9 applies, the 1982 Act recognises the fact that work at home is still prima facie unpaid but that its economic value to the community is such that justice demands that the injured person receive compensation even though he or she has not suffered patrimonial loss.[20]

---

1     See generally Joe Thomson *Delictual Liability* (5th edn, 2014, Bloomsbury Professional) Ch 13.
2     Law Reform (Husband and Wife) Act 1962, s 2(2).
3     Family Law (Scotland) Act 2006, s 45 and Schedule 2.
4     Interpretation Act 1978, s 16.
5     Damages (Scotland) Act 2011, ss 3 and 14(1).
6     D(S)A 2011, s 6. See, for example, *Ingham v John G Russell Transport Ltd* 1991 SCLR 596.
7     D(S)A 2011 ss 4 (1) (a), (3)(5) and 14). Compensation was not reduced where a wife married her husband knowing that he was suffering a fatal disease allegedly caused by the negligence of the defender: *Phillips v Grampian Health Board* 1989 SLT 538.
8     D(S)A 2011, s 7(1)(a).
9     D(S)A 2011, ss 4(1)(b),(3),(5) and 14.
10    D(S)A 2011, s 7(1)(b).
11    *Brown v Ferguson* 1990 SLT 274. See also *McManus' Executrix v Babcock Energy Ltd* 1999 SC 569.
12    *Robertson v Turnbull* 1982 SLT 96.
13    *Edgar v Lord Advocate* 1965 SC 67.
14    Administration of Justice Act 1982, s 8.
15    Damages can also be awarded as reasonable remuneration for necessary services to be rendered by a relative after the date of the action: Administration of Justice Act 1982, s 8(3). This reverses the decision in *Forsyth's Curator Bonis v Govan Shipbuilders* 1988 SLT 321.
16    Administration of Justice Act 1982, s 13(1)(a) and (aa).
17    Administration of Justice Act 1982, s 8(2). Damages will not be paid if the relative has expressly agreed that no payment should be made for these services: s 8(1) and (3). For an example of the operation of the provisions, see *Denheen v British Railways Board* 1986 SLT 249. There is no equivalent to s 8(2) in respect of recovery of damages for future services under s 8(3).

18  See above note 15.
19  See, for example, *Ingham v John G Russell Transport Ltd* 1991 SCLR 596.
20  Of course, if the victim was being paid for his or her services, they could recover damages for loss of wages in the usual way.

## Income support

**3.7** For the purpose of obtaining income support it is necessary to aggregate the needs and resources of any couple who are living together. Spouses or civil partners who are members of the same household are a couple for this purpose.[1]

The relationship between the system of state support and the private law obligation of aliment is discussed in the next section.

1  Social Security Contributions and Benefits Act 1992, s 137(1).

## Aliment

*The nature and extent of the obligation*

**3.8**  A spouse has a duty to aliment, ie *maintain* the other spouse and vice versa.[1] Similarly a partner in a civil partnership is under an obligation to aliment the other partner and vice versa.[2]

A spouse or civil partner's duty of aliment is 'to provide such support as is reasonable in the circumstances', having regard to the matters which a court is required or entitled to consider in determining the amount of aliment awarded.[3] The effect of this provision is that a spouse or civil partner will always have a prima facie right to aliment from the other, but the extent of the defender's duty to aliment will depend on the same factors as govern quantification of an award.

The factors which must be considered are set out in the Family Law (Scotland) Act 1985, s 4(1). They are:

'(a)  the needs and resources of the parties;[4]

(b)  the earning capacities of the parties;[5]

(c)  generally, all the circumstances of the case.'

---

1    Family Law (Scotland) Act 1985, s 1(1)(a) and (b). Obligations of aliment exist between parents and children: these are discussed in **Ch 9**.
2    Family Law (Scotland) Act 1985, s 1(1)(bb).
3    FL(S)A 1985, s 1(2).
4    'Needs' means present and foreseeable needs; 'resources' means present and foreseeable resources: FL(S)A 1985, s 27.
5    The court is concerned with earning *capacity*, not merely a party's likely future earnings: consequently a claimant cannot elect to be unemployed.

---

**Family Law (Scotland) Act 1985, s 4(3)(a)**

**3.9** In relation to s 4(1)(c), s 4(3)(a) provides that the court '*may*, if it thinks fit, take account of any support, financial or otherwise, given by the defender to any person whom he maintains as a dependant in his household, whether or not the defender owes an obligation of aliment to that person'. The effect of this provision can be illustrated by the following example: H leaves W, who is unemployed, and sets up home with his cohabitant, C. H supports C financially. In an action for aliment brought by W against H, the court *may* take into account the fact that H is supporting C. If it does, there will be fewer resources available for W and consequently a smaller amount of aliment will be awarded. Section 4(3)(a) of the 1985 Act reverses the previous rule under which financial or other support *in fact* made by a defender to a third party was *not* taken into account unless he was under a legal obligation to aliment that person, for example his child.[1]

It is submitted that the courts should be prepared to exercise their discretion under s 4(3)(a), particularly where the defender is a low wage earner. If H in the example above was earning very little, then if the fact that he was supporting C was taken into account, W would probably receive no aliment at all. This is a sensible result in the circumstances for it allows W to have full recourse to income support and other benefits. If it were not taken into account, the amount of aliment awarded would be small: even if H paid it regularly, W would be no better off financially since the aliment would merely reduce the amount payable in income support.

Where either spouse or civil partner is being financially or otherwise supported by a third party, this will be a relevant factor under s 4(1)(c) as it is clearly one of the circumstances of the case. For example, in an action for aliment by a wife against her husband, the court was entitled to take into account the fact that the husband's cohabitant was contributing to their joint outlays; but the joint incomes of the husband and cohabitant could not simply be aggregated as that would subject the cohabitant to an obligation of aliment to the wife, which the cohabitant did not owe.[2]

---

1  *Henry v Henry* 1972 SLT (Notes) 26. Moreover, a pursuer's entitlement to income support was ignored, with the result that defenders could be ordered to pay awards of aliment which they could not afford while continuing to support the third party: *McAuley v McAuley* 1968 SLT (Sh Ct) 81; *McCarrol v McCarrol* 1966 SLT (Sh Ct) 45.
2  *Munro v Munro* 1986 SLT 72; *Firth v Firth* 1990 GWD 5-266. Cf *Pryde v Pryde* 1991 SLT (Sh Ct) 26.

---

**Family Law (Scotland) Act 1985, s 4(3)(b)**

**3.10**  In relation to s 4(1)(c), s 4(3)(b) provides that the court 'shall not take account of any conduct of a party unless it would be manifestly inequitable to leave it out of account'. The effect of this provision is that a spouse or civil partner has a prima facie right to aliment from the other, even though the pursuer has committed adultery,[1] has behaved in an intolerable way, or refuses to live with the defender. Moreover, in assessing the amount of aliment such conduct is to be ignored by the court unless it would be 'manifestly inequitable to leave it out of account'.[2] It is submitted that it should only be in very extreme circumstances that the pursuer's conduct should be taken into account to reduce the amount of aliment which would otherwise be awarded.[3] When a relationship is breaking down, there is usually fault on both sides: certainly, it is most unjust to penalise a spouse or civil partner financially for conduct, for example sexual misconduct such as adultery, which is a symptom not a cause of matrimonial breakdown.

Nor does this raise injustice to the defender. The purpose of aliment is to oblige spouses and civil partners to maintain each other *during the marriage or civil partnership*: the obligation to aliment ends on divorce or dissolution of the civil partnership. Consequently, if a defender feels aggrieved at being obliged to aliment a pursuer who has committed adultery or other matrimonial misconduct, the remedy is to sue for divorce or dissoluton.[4] On divorce or dissolution, the obligation to aliment ceases and, instead, financial provision can be ordered which will hopefully result in a financial clean break between the parties.[5] It is thought this approach is consonant with current public policy which is to encourage marriages or civil partnerships which have irretrievably broken down, as evidenced inter alia by sexual or other misconduct, to be decently buried.

---

1    This issue is discussed in the context of divorce in **Ch 6**.
2    Family Law (Scotland) Act 1985, s 4(3)(b).
3    One example might be where the pursuer's conduct had reduced the defender's resources: for example by injuring the defender so that his earning capacity was impaired. Another is illustrated by the facts of *Kyte v Kyte* [1987] 3 WLR 1114 where the wife had actively encouraged her husband's attempts at suicide! In *Walker v Walker* 1991 SLT 649, Lord Clyde stated that where the defender had lied as to his income and assets, this *was* conduct which it would be manifestly inequitable to leave out of account.
4    See **Ch 6.**
5    See **Ch 7**.

---

*Defences*

**3.11** Section 2(8) of the Family Law (Scotland) Act 1985 gives a general defence to a claim for aliment[1] if the defender makes an offer to receive the pursuer into the defender's household and to fulfil the obligation of aliment *provided* it is reasonable to expect the pursuer to accept the offer. In considering whether it is reasonable for the pursuer to accept the defender's offer, s 2(9) enjoins the court to look at all the relevant circumstances including conduct and any decree, for example an interdict against violence,[2] which has been obtained.

So, for example, if W has been the victim of H's domestic violence, she will obtain aliment even though she is unwilling to live with him and despite the fact that H makes her an offer to return to his household; as a result of H's conduct, the offer is not one which it would be reasonable to expect W, the victim of his violence, to accept. Even if she had committed adultery, it is thought that H would not have a defence if he had been violent towards her; because of the violence, it is still not reasonable to expect W to return. Moreover, her adultery will not lead to any reduction in the amount of aliment awarded as it is thought that adultery per se is not conduct which it would be manifestly inequitable to leave out of account.[3]

Where a couple have agreed to separate, s 2(9) of the Family Law (Scotland) Act 1985 provides that the mere fact that they have agreed to live apart does not of itself establish that it is unreasonable to expect the pursuer to accept the defender's offer. For example, if civil partners agree to part and one of them later seeks aliment, if the other makes him an offer to return to his household, this may constitute a s 2(8) defence because it is not unreasonable to expect the pursuer to accept such an offer merely because he and the defender have earlier agreed to part. Of course, other circumstances, for example the defender's excessive drinking or violence while they lived together, may make it unreasonable to expect the pursuer to accept the defender's offer.

---

1   Except where the claim is brought by or on behalf of a child under the age of 16: see **Ch 10.**
2   Discussed in **Ch 5.**
3   Family Law (Scotland) Act 1985, s 4(3)(b), discussed at para **3.10.**

---

*Aliment where the parties are living together*

**3.12** At common law a spouse who was being inadequately maintained had to leave the matrimonial home before an action for aliment could be brought.[1] Section 2(6) of the Family Law (Scotland) Act 1985 provides that an action for aliment is competent notwithstanding that the pursuer is living in the same household as the defender. Thus for example, a same sex spouse can sue the other spouse for an adequate housekeeping allowance. But it is a defence to an action in these circumstances if the defender can show that he or she is fulfilling the obligation to aliment the pursuer and intends to continue doing so.[2] These provisions also apply to civil partners.

---

1   *M'Donald v M'Donald* (1875) 2 R 705.
2   Family Law (Scotland) Act 1985, s 2(7).

---

*The nature of an award*

**3.13** On granting a decree of aliment, s 3(1) of the Family Law (Scotland) Act 1985 provides that the court may, if it thinks fit:

(1)    order the making of a periodical payment, whether for a definite or an indefinite period or until the happening of a specified event: but the court cannot substitute a lump sum for a periodical payment;[1]

(2)    order the making of alimentary payments of an occasional or special nature, for example hospital expenses: these will usually be small amounts;

(3)    backdate awards to the date of bringing the action or, on special cause shown, even earlier;

(4)    award less than the amount claimed even if the claim is undisputed.[2]

The prohibition of lump sum payments and the continued insistence that an award takes the form of a periodical payment reflect the fact that aliment is an obligation which arises from, and continues throughout, a marriage or civil partnership. In contrast, on divorce or dissolution of a civil partnership it is envisaged that financial provision will generally take the form of capital payments, ie lump sum payments, to encourage a financial clean break between the parties.[3]

On an application by either party, a decree of aliment can be varied or recalled if there has been a material change of circumstances since the date of decree.[4] If the value of the original award has been undermined by inflation, the decree may be varied upwards; conversely, if the defender has been made redundant since the date of the original award the decree can be varied downwards or indeed recalled. The mere fact that at the time of the original award the court proceeded upon a particular hypothesis which turned out to be incorrect is not a material change of circumstances.[5] In an action for variation, the court has the same powers, for example to backdate awards, as in an original application for aliment.[6]

A decree of aliment comes to an end if the parties divorce or a civil partnership is dissolved. Where the couple are a qualifying civil partnership, a decree of aliment does not come to an end if the civil partnership is converted into marriage[7].

---

1    FL(S)A 1985, s 3(2). A defender cannot be ordered to provide security for an alimentary payment: *MacDonald v MacDonald* 1995 SLT 72.

2    This overrules *Terry v Murray* 1947 SC 10 where it was held that the court was bound to grant decree for the amount claimed in an undefended action for aliment.

3    See **Ch 7**.

4    Family Law (Scotland) Act 1985, s 5(1); *Walker v Walker* 1991 SLT 649. There is, however, no need for a change of circumstances before a decree of interim aliment can be varied: *Bisset v Bisset* 1993 SCLR 284. An agreement to aliment a spouse can also be varied on a change of circumstances: FL(S)A 1985, s 7(2). It cannot be varied after the parties have divorced: *Drummond v Drummond* 1995 SCLR 428, 1996 SLT 386. The court has the power to backdate the variation: FL(S)A 1985, ss 7(2ZA)–(2ZC).

5    *Walker v Walker* 1995 SLT 375.

6    FL(S)A 1985, s 5(2) impliedly incorporating s 3: see *Hannah v Hannah* 1988 SLT 82. However, there is authority that in a variation the court cannot backdate beyond the date of the decree sought to be varied: *Walker v Walker* 1991 SLT 649, *sed quaere*.

7    Marriage and Civil Partnership (Scotland) Act 2014, s 11(7). On qualifying civil partnerships and their conversion to marriage, see para **1.19** above.

*Procedural matters*

**3.14** A spouse or civil partner may bring a claim for aliment *simpliciter* in the Court of Session or the sheriff court.[1] In practice a claim for aliment is often brought along with other proceedings, for example separation. In addition, in an action for aliment or in an action for divorce or dissolution, separation, declarator of marriage or declarator of nullity of marriage or civil partnership, the court can order interim aliment until the final disposal of the action.[2]

When decree of divorce or dissolution has been granted, but a claim for financial provision is still pending, an award of interim aliment remains competent.[3] Because an action for interim aliment is not technically an action of aliment within the meaning of the Family Law (Scotland) Act 1985,[4] it has been held that the court does not have the power to vary or recall a decree of interim aliment with *retrospective* effect.[5] The factors in s 4 of the 1985 Act have also been held to be relevant to a claim for interim aliment.[6]

As interim aliment is awarded to a party to the proceedings, it does not matter that the proceedings finally establish that, for example, because the marriage or civil partnership was void, the parties did not owe an obligation to aliment each other because they were never spouses or civil partners. A pursuer in an action of declarator of nullity can apply for interim aliment, although denying the existence of the marriage or civil partnership.[7]

1   FL(S)A 1985, s 2(1).
2   FL(S)A 1985, s 6(1).
3   *Neill v Neill* 1987 SLT (Sh Ct) 143.
4   FL(S)A 1985, s 2(2) and (3).
5   *McColl v McColl* 1993 SLT 617. This can cause difficulties if the award of aliment is backdated to cover the period when the defender was obliged to pay an award of interim aliment. Because the decree of interim aliment cannot be recalled with retrospective effect, the defender would have to pay both the backdated award of aliment *plus* any arrears of interim aliment.
6   *McGeachie v McGeachie* 1989 SCLR 99: for the s 4 factors, see para **3.8** ff. An appeal from an award of interim aliment is possible with leave of the sheriff: *MacInnes v MacInnes* 1990 GWD 13-690; *Richardson v Richardson* 1991 SLT (Sh Ct) 7.
7   Family Law (Scotland) Act 1985, s 17(2).

*The relationship between aliment and income support*

**3.15**  It will be clear that the guidelines in the Family Law (Scotland) Act 1985, s 4 are sufficiently wide to allow a court considerable discretion in assessing the amount of aliment. Apart from the prima facie exclusion of misconduct and the fact that the defender's financial or other support to a third party may be taken into account, there are few guidelines on how the court should exercise its discretion. Wealthy couples should be able to negotiate an appropriate figure with the advice of their lawyers. But where the couple is in the lower income bracket, there may not be enough money to aliment the family adequately when the relationship breaks down, particularly if the wage earner has become involved with another family. Consider the following example.

**Example**

H, a small wage earner, leaves W who is unemployed in order to live with another woman, M. H supports M financially and does not provide aliment for W. What can W do?

(1)   At common law W could pledge her husband's credit for necessaries – if she could obtain food and clothing on credit.

This right was distinct from her *praepositura* and has not been abolished.[1] The third party who supplied W with the necessary support can recover from H, provided H was liable to aliment W. H's liability to the third party is based on principles of recompense.

(2)     W could bring an action for aliment against H. However, if the court exercised its discretion and took into account the fact that he was supporting M, W would receive little, if any, aliment.[2] If this factor were ignored, it could cause hardship to M who is unable to obtain income support because of the cohabitation rule.[3]

(3)     In practice W would apply for income support. There is no longer an obligation on a spouse to seek a decree of aliment before applying for income support. In financial terms, W is no worse off: indeed, she could be better off than if an award of aliment had been obtained from H.[4] At the very least, she receives regular income and there is no problem of enforcement of a decree of aliment against H.

By s 78 of the Social Security Administration Act 1992, because they are 'couples' for the purposes of the legislation, spouses and civil partners are liable relatives. This means that when income support is paid to or on behalf of a person who is not being alimented by a liable relative, the Secretary of State can take proceedings against the liable relative to make a contribution towards the amount of support paid.[5] A sheriff having regard to all the circumstances, including the defender's resources, can order the defender to pay such sum, weekly or otherwise, as may be appropriate.[6] Thus, in the above example, the Secretary of State could take proceedings against H (the liable relative) who has failed to aliment W (the dependent) for a contribution towards the amount of income support W has received.[7] If W has a decree of aliment against H, the Secretary of State can enforce the decree.[8]

But, in practice, the Secretary of State will only take proceedings against a liable relative, if the relative's resources are in excess of the following: the income support, including any premiums and housing costs which the relative could claim, plus a quarter of the relative's net earnings.[9] If H is on a low wage, it is unlikely that he would have income in excess of the formula and the Secretary of State would therefore not approach him for a contribution. Approximately only 11 per cent of the money paid out in income support is recovered from liable relatives.

It should be noted that for the purposes of the Social Security Administration Act 1992, neither a man nor a woman is a liable relative in respect of a former spouse or civil partner. However, parents are liable relatives in respect of their children.[10]

---

1    On the *praepositura*, see para **3.5**. It is thought that the right has not been affected by the repeal of the Married Women's Property (Scotland) Act 1920, s 3(2). It is not thought that a civil partner has such a right.
2    Family Law (Scotland) Act 1985, s 4(3)(a), discussed at para **3.9**. If W's entitlement to income support was ignored as a resource, W would obtain *some* aliment; but this would simply reduce her income support and leave her no better off financially.
3    Parties living together as husband and wife or as civil partners are a couple for these purposes.
4    See para **3.9**.
5    Social Security Administration Act 1992, s 106.
6    The sheriff's discretion is very wide: the sheriff can, for example, order the liable relative to pay only a small fraction of the income support paid out: *Secretary of State for Social Services v McMillan* 1987 SLT 52.
7    The court can order payments to be made to W rather than the Secretary of State; in other words, the Secretary of State, in effect, raises an action of aliment on behalf of W: Social Security Administration Act 1992, s 106(4)(b) and (c).
8    SSAA 1992, s 108.
9    The formula was first published in the *Report of the Committee on One-Parent Families* (the Finer Report) (Cmnd 5629) (1974) para 4.188. It has subsequently been modified: it is not clear whether the formula will continue to be applied.
10   The aliment of children is discussed in Ch 9. If A and B have a child C, A is a liable relative in respect of B if B is looking after C; it does not matter if A and B are divorced or were never married: SSAA 1992, s 107.

---

## Succession

*Introduction*

**3.16** As submitted at the outset, in modern family law it is important for a person to have been married or have registered a civil partnership. This is particularly true in relation to succession where Scots law gives a surviving spouse or civil partner certain rights to succeed to a proportion of the deceased spouse or civil partner's estate which cannot be defeated by testamentary deed. In this section it is proposed to give an outline of these rights: as they are closely related to similar rights enjoyed by the deceased's children it is convenient also to discuss these at this stage.

## *Legal rights*

**3.17** Since the Succession (Scotland) Act 1964, a surviving spouse is entitled to legal rights out of the deceased spouse's free moveable estate; a surviving civil partner has legal rights out of the deceased civil partner's free moveable estate: these we will call the relict's legal rights.[1] Children[2] are entitled to *legitim* out of their deceased parent's moveable estate.

The relict's right is to one-third of the deceased's free moveable estate if the deceased is survived by children or to one-half of the deceased's free moveable estate if there are no surviving children. *Legitim* is the right to one-third of the deceased parent's free moveable estate if survived by a spouse or civil partner or to one-half of the deceased's free moveable estate if there is no surviving spouse or civil partner. Moveable estate consists of money, shares, pictures, cars etc, but excludes land ie heritable property, of which the most important is likely to be the matrimonial or family home.

For example, if H dies survived by W and children, W is entitled to a third of his free moveable estate as her legal rights, the children are entitled to a third of his free moveable estate as *legitim* and the deceased can only effectively test ie make testamentary provisions on the remaining third. But if the estate includes heritable property, for example the matrimonial home, H is free to dispose of the property as he wishes by testamentary deed, as legal rights are not exigible out of heritage. So H could, by will, leave his house to his girlfriend, or the dogs' and cats' home.

Legal rights may be discharged in the lifetime of the spouses or civil partners or parents. Similarly legal rights may be renounced after a spouse's, civil partner's or parent's death. This can be done either expressly or impliedly by acceptance of testamentary provisions which were intended by the deceased to be in satisfaction of legal rights.[3] If, however, the surviving spouse, civil partner or children elect to take legal rights, they will forfeit any testamentary provisions in testamentary deeds executed after 1964, unless forfeiture is expressly excluded.[4]

1    Civil Partnership Act 2004, s 131.
2    Scots law makes no distinction between legitimate and illegitimate children in this context: Law Reform (Parent and Child) (Scotland) Act 1986, Schedule 1, para 7(2), discussed in **Ch 8.**
3    By the Succession (Scotland) Act 1964, s 13, acceptance of a provision in a post-1964 testamentary disposition is, in the absence of express provision to the contrary, deemed to be an implied renunciation of legal rights in so far as they would conflict with the settlement.
4    Succession (Scotland) Act 1964, s 13; for deeds executed pre-1964, see *Ballantyne's Trustees v Ballantyne* 1993 SLT 1237.

*Prior rights*

**3.18**   Where a spouse or civil partner dies intestate,[1] ie without a will, the surviving *spouse* or *civil partner* enjoys substantial prior rights out of the intestate estate.

By s 8 of the Succession (Scotland) Act 1964, the surviving spouse or civil partner is entitled to the dwelling house (which was owned by the intestate) in which he or she was ordinarily resident at the date of the death of the intestate.[2] If the house is worth more than £300K, the surviving spouse or civil partner is entitled to a sum of £300K instead.[3] In addition, the surviving spouse or civil partner is entitled to the furniture and plenishings (which were owned by the deceased) of a dwelling house[4] in which he or she was ordinarily resident at the date of the death of the intestate. However, if the value of the furniture or plenishings exceeds £24K, the surviving spouse or civil partner is entitled to such parts of them as he or she may choose, to a value not exceeding £24K.

By s 9 of the Succession (Scotland) Act 1964 the surviving spouse or civil partner is entitled to financial provision out of the intestate's estate. If the intestate is survived by issue,[5] however remote, the surviving spouse or civil partner is entitled to £42K; in other cases, the surviving spouse or civil partner is entitled to £75K.[6] Where the net intestate estate is less than £42K or £75K, as the case may be, the surviving spouse or civil partner is entitled to the whole of the intestate estate. Where it is more, the surviving spouse or civil partner's financial provision is borne by the heritable and moveable parts of the estate in proportion to the respective amounts of those parts.[7]

After satisfaction of these prior rights, the surviving spouse or civil partner is entitled to claim legal rights from the remaining free moveable estate.[8] Only then is the remaining intestate estate distributed to the deceased's heirs.[9]

It will be obvious that the prior rights of a surviving spouse or civil partner will exhaust the value of most estates. Consequently, the surviving spouse or civil partner may well be better off if the deceased dies intestate rather than leave a testamentary deed bequeathing all the estate to the surviving spouse or civil partner. For in this latter case, any surviving children will be entitled to claim *legitim*; but on an intestacy, children can only succeed to the intestate estate after satisfaction of the surviving spouse or civil partner's prior rights.

---

1    For these purposes intestacy includes partial intestacy.
2    If more than one house qualifies, the surviving spouse has six months to elect which house is to be subject to prior rights.
3    S(S)A 1964, s 8(1). The current amounts were set by the Prior Rights of Surviving Spouses (Scotland) Order 2005, SI 2005/252.
4    It does not matter if the dwelling house did not form part of the deceased's intestate estate.
5    There is no distinction between legitimate and illegitimate issue: see S(S)A 1964, s 36(1).
6    The current sums were set by SI 2005/252.
7    S(S)A 1964, s 9(3).
8    Discussed at para **3.17**.
9    These will in the first place be the deceased's children and their issue. No distinction is made between legitimate and illegitimate issue: see the Succession (Scotland) Act 1964, s 36(1). For a full list of heirs see S(S)A 1964, s 2; on representation see S(S)A 1964, s 5.

---

*Conclusion*

**3.19** As a result of the system of prior rights, a surviving spouse or civil partner is generously treated on an intestacy. Where the deceased has left a will, the system of legal rights affords some degree of protection for the deceased's surviving spouse or civil partner and family. But there is nothing to stop the deceased from defeating claims to legal rights by converting all the property into heritage and disposing of it by testamentary deed to whomsoever he or she chooses.[1] The same result can be achieved if the deceased has transferred his or her moveable property to a third party during his or her lifetime. The inter vivos transfer must be genuine: a simulate or sham transaction will not suffice.

It should be noted that neither marriage nor the registration of a civil partnership has the effect of revoking prior testamentary writings. It is a question of construction whether a legacy to the deceased's 'wife' or 'husband' or 'partner' means the deceased's spouse or civil partner at the time the will was executed or the person who was the deceased's spouse or civil partner at the date of death.

In the present writer's view, there is force in the argument that at present the deceased's family may be over protected. While protection for a spouse or civil partner is perhaps justified, it is difficult to see why *adult* children should be entitled to *legitim*, when they may have had no interest in their parent's welfare before his or her death.

---

1    In these circumstances, the surviving spouse has an equitable claim for continuing aliment from the deceased spouse's estate: see E M Clive *The Law of Husband and Wife in Scotland* (4th edn, 1997, W Greens/Sweet & Maxwell), pp 604 ff. It does not appear that a surviving civil partner would have such a claim.

Chapter 4

# The legal consequences of marriage and civil partnership

## PART II: MOVEABLE PROPERTY

### Introduction

**4.1** Until the Married Women's Property (Scotland) Act 1881,[1] as a general rule all moveable property – money, shares, furniture etc – owned by a wife or subsequently acquired by her during marriage, for example by legacy, passed to her husband as a result of his *jus mariti*. The husband could do anything he wished with the property. There were limited exceptions to this rule such as alimentary provisions in favour of the wife under a marriage contract and the wife's *paraphernalia*, ie her dresses and jewellery including their receptacles. The 1881 Act abolished the *jus mariti*.[2] Where a wife owned heritable property, for example land or a house, it remained hers, but the property was administered by her husband as a result of his *jus administrationis*.[3] The *jus administrationis* was abolished by the Married Women's Property (Scotland) Act 1920.[4]

As a result of the Married Women's Property (Scotland) Acts of 1881 and 1920, Scots law accepted that marriage should have no effect on the property rights of spouses during marriage and that for this purpose they should be treated as strangers. Accordingly, in relation to the property of spouses, Scots law has a system of separate property. The common law rules did not apply to civil partners. Nevertheless, s 24 of the Family Law (Scotland) Act 1985 states:

'… marriage or civil partnership shall not of itself affect—

(a) the respective rights of the parties to the marriage or as the case may be the partners in the civil partnership in relation to their property'.

Scots law therefore proceeds on the basis that prima facie the ordinary rules of property law apply to spouses and civil partners as though they were unmarried or had not registered their partnership. The separate property system achieves legal equality between the spouses and civil partners in respect of their property. In practice this can lead to injustice as in our society women are still expected to bear the major burden of child rearing; consequently, wives in particular frequently do not have the same opportunities as their husbands to acquire property during the marriage.[5]

Moreover, the separate property system ignores the fact that when spouses or civil partners acquire property, they do not regard themselves as strangers. Often they will pool their resources to purchase a matrimonial or family home and other domestic property. In addition property is often bought not for the use and enjoyment of the purchasing spouse or civil partner but for the use and enjoyment of the family, for example furniture. In relation to such property, the application of the ordinary rules of the law of property is difficult and likely to lead to unrealistic results. It has now been recognised in Scotland that the property rules relating to spouses and civil partners cannot ignore the 'family' element in their property transactions. Consequently, special property rules have been introduced which are specifically applicable to spouses and civil partners and do not treat them as strangers.

Thus, while the basic property regime is still that of separate property, there are now some special property rules that recognise that the parties are married or have registered a civil partnership. These rules are designed to take into account the 'family' element in the parties' property dealings. To some extent, these rules have alleviated the injustices which in practice arise from a strict application of the separate property system.

The law as it relates to moveable property is examined in this chapter; the law in relation to the matrimonial and family home is considered in Chapter 5.

---

1   For the history of the law, see E M Clive *The Law of Husband and Wife in Scotland* (4th edn, 1997, W Greens/Sweet & Maxwell), pp 219 ff.

2   Married Women's Property (Scotland) Act 1881, s 1(1).

3   Until 1881, income arising from her lands, for example rents, belonged to the husband by virtue of his *jus mariti* as the rents were, of course, moveable property.

4   Married Women's Property (Scotland) Act 1920, s 1.

5   A spouse or civil partner can now obtain compensation for any economic disadvantages suffered as a result of marriage or civil partnership in the form of financial provision on divorce or dissolution: see Ch 7.

## Wedding presents

**4.2** The ownership of a wedding present depends on the intention of the donor. Did the donor intend the gift to be owned in common by the spouses or only by one of the spouses? There is no difficulty if there is direct evidence of the donor's intention. But problems can arise if such evidence is not available.

In *McDonald v McDonald*,[1] the sheriff took the view that 'the practical rule which is normally applied is to regard as the owner of the present the spouse from whose friends or relatives the gift was received'.[2] Moreover, because a gift was intended to be *used* by the spouses, for example an electric toaster or bathroom scales, it does not follow that the donor intended that the present should be *owned* in common by them.[3] Sometimes the donor's intention can be inferred from the nature of the gift: for example, a necklace can be presumed to be a gift to the wife and a set of guns can be presumed to be a gift to the husband. Similar issues arise when persons receive gifts on registering their civil partnership.

---

1    1953 SLT (Sh Ct) 36.
2    1953 SLT (Sh Ct) 36 at 36.
3    *Traill v Traill* 1925 SLT (Sh Ct) 54.

---

## Gifts between spouses and civil partners

**4.3** The ordinary law of donation applies in relation to the transfer of corporeal moveable property between spouses and civil partners. Accordingly, the presumption *against* donation is prima facie applicable.[1] But as gifts between spouses and civil partners are not uncommon, the presumption is not difficult to rebut.[2] For example, H transfers a dress to W. The onus is on W to show that H intended to make a gift of the dress to her. The presumption is easily rebutted if W brings evidence that the transfer took place on her birthday or on their wedding anniversary or at Christmas! In addition to rebutting the presumption against donation, before the ownership of the property passes to the donee it must be established that the property was delivered to him or her. This can give rise to difficulties where the property is already in the matrimonial or family home before the gift is made.

The common law rule that gifts between spouses were revocable during the donor's lifetime has been abolished.[3]

---

1   *Jamieson v M'Leod* (1880) 7 R 1131; *Smith v Smith's Trustees* (1884) 12 R 186; *Beveridge v Beveridge* 1925 SLT 234 at 236.
2   There is no presumption against donation in transfers of property between parent and child: Stair *The Institutions of the Law of Scotland* (6th edn, 1981) I 8.2.
3   Married Women's Property (Scotland) Act 1920, s 5. The gift may be struck down as a gratuitous alienation if the donor becomes bankrupt.

---

## Corporeal moveables bought by the spouses

**4.4** It is a cardinal principle of a system of separate property that the spouse or civil partner who buys or otherwise acquires corporeal moveable property prima facie owns it; so if H buys a motor car, he is the owner. Where both spouses or civil partners contribute to the purchase price, they own the property in common in proportion to their contributions to the price. But in the absence of evidence of joint contribution to the price, the common law does not assume common ownership merely because the property is used by both spouses or civil partners or the family.[1]

Apart from the problems of proving which of the spouses or civil partners paid for the property, perhaps many years after the date of its purchase, the separate property system could give rise to injustices in the following situations.

(1)   Where W gives up her job for several years to look after the children of the family she will lose the opportunity to earn and acquire property. The common law gave her no proprietary interest in the property acquired by H during that period.

(2)   Where both same sex spouses, A and B, are working and they agree that, for example, A's earnings should be used to run the household while B uses her earnings to purchase antiques or lay down vintage claret, the common law gave A no proprietary interest in the property purchased by B.

The injustices of the application of the system of separate property in practice are obvious and the position has been alleviated to some extent by legislation.

---

1   *Harper v Adair* 1945 JC 21 at 28, per the Lord Justice-General (Normand); *Preston v Preston* 1950 SC 253 at 261, per Lord Keith.

---

*Household goods*

**4.5**  Section 25(1) of the Family Law (Scotland) Act 1985 provides that:

> 'If any question arises (whether during or after a marriage or civil partnership) as to the respective rights of ownership of the parties to a marriage or the partners in a civil partnership in any household goods obtained in prospect of or during the marriage or civil partnership other than by gift or succession from a third party, it shall be presumed, unless the contrary is proved, that each has a right to an equal share in the goods in question'.

In other words, there is a presumption that the household goods are *owned* in common by the spouses or civil partners.[1]

Household goods are defined[2] as 'any goods (including decorative or ornamental goods) kept or used at any time during the marriage or civil partnership in any family home for the joint domestic purposes of the parties to the marriage or the partners'. However: (a) money or securities; (b) any motor car, caravan or other road vehicle;[3] and (c) any domestic animal, are expressly excluded.[4]

Consider the following examples:

(1)   If A buys antique paintings before the registration of his civil partnership with B, the presumption of common ownership does not apply as the property was acquired before the civil partnership. But if before registration, A buys a Chinese carpet with the intention that it is to be used in the family home after registration, the presumption of equal shares will apply as the goods were bought in prospect of civil partnership.

(2)   If W inherits a grandfather clock during the marriage the presumption of common ownership will not apply as property acquired by gift or succession from a third party is excluded.

(3)   If H wins £10,000 on the lottery during the marriage and invests £5,000 in a bank account and uses the remainder to buy antiques

which are kept in the family home, the presumption of equal shares does not apply to the money deposited with the bank as money and securities are expressly excluded, but it will apply to the antiques as these are household goods.

(4)    If A buys a motor car during the marriage which is used by B, A's same sex spouse, for work and leisure purposes, the presumption of common ownership does not apply as road vehicles are expressly excluded.

It must be stressed that the Family Law (Scotland) Act 1985, s 25 gives rise only to a *presumption* of equal shares in household goods: it is therefore open to the purchasing spouse or civil partner, if he or she alleges that the goods were not intended to be owned in common, to bring evidence to rebut the presumption and establish that they were to be owned outright by the purchasing spouse or civil partner. However, s 25(2) provides that the presumption of equal shares will not be rebutted merely by the fact that while the parties were married or in civil partnership *and living together* the goods in question were purchased from a third party by either party alone or by both in unequal shares. Consider the following examples:

(1)    During the marriage and while the spouses were living together, H buys a silver teapot from a dealer. Prima facie the teapot is household goods and the presumption of equal shares applies. The mere fact that H bought the teapot from a third party using his own money is not in itself sufficient to rebut the presumption. Consequently the teapot is owned in common by H and W.

(2)    During the marriage and while the spouses were living together, H buys a silver teapot from a dealer. Prima facie the teapot is household goods and the presumption of equal shares applies. H had collected silver before he was married but not with the prospect of marriage. This fact, combined with the fact that he bought the teapot from a third party using his own money, could be sufficient to rebut the presumption and establish that the teapot was intended for his collection and to be owned outright by H, along with the rest of the silver.[5]

(3)    During the marriage but when the spouses were not living together, H buys a silver teapot from a dealer. Prima facie the

teapot is household goods and the presumption of equal shares applies. But as the teapot was bought when the couple were not living together, s 25(2) does not apply and the fact that H bought the teapot from a third party using his own money may in itself be sufficient to rebut the presumption of common ownership and consequently establish that the teapot is owned outright by H.

There may be difficulties in the interrelationship between the Family Law (Scotland) Act 1985, s 25 and the law of gifts between spouses and civil partners.[6] If A purchases a painting during the civil partnership, prima facie s 25 applies as the painting is household goods and therefore there is a presumption of common ownership with A's civil partner, B. If A transfers the painting to B on his birthday, B may be able to rebut the presumption *against* donation and establish that A intended the painting to be an outright gift to him. It is submitted that if B can do so, he would thereby rebut the presumption of equal shares in household goods in s 25.

The examples given are perhaps esoteric and the theoretical difficulties in s 25 of the Family Law (Scotland) Act 1985 must not be thought to undermine its evident utility. In the vast majority of cases the presumption will not be capable of being rebutted and consequently spouses and civil partners will be taken to have equal shares in the normal contents of the family home, ie consumer durables such as furniture, carpets, televisions, fridges, cookers and kitchen utensils.

Moreover, the definition of household goods[7] demands that not only must the goods be kept or used in the family home, but also that they must be kept or used 'for joint domestic purposes'. Thus corporeal moveables used exclusively for a spouse or civil partner's business (for example, a computer) or hobby (for example, golf clubs) will be excluded. But difficulties arise where property is bought both as a collector's item and for use by the spouses or civil partners as in the example of the silver teapot: such property could be defined as household goods so giving rise to the problems outlined above.

More difficult to justify, perhaps, is the exclusion of motor cars, caravans or other vehicles, as these are often bought as a result of a couple pooling their resources: the application of the separate property system may give a result which is entirely fortuitous. The exclusion of family pets is, on the other hand, perhaps more understandable.

It should also be noted that as common owners, either spouse or civil partner, can apply for an action of division and sale of the property.[8]

---

1   *Kinloch v Barclay's Bank* 1995 GWD 24-1316.
2   Family Law (Scotland) Act 1985, s 25(3).
3   For example, a bicycle.
4   Family Law (Scotland) Act 1985, s 25(3)(a), (b) and (c).
5   If the teapot was kept in a display cabinet and never used, arguably it is not household goods as it has not been kept or used for joint domestic purposes.
6   See para **4.3**.
7   Family Law (Scotland) Act 1985, s 25(3).
8   Actions for division and sale are discussed in the context of heritage: see para **5.11** ff.

---

*Furniture and plenishings in the matrimonial or family home*

**4.6** The Matrimonial Homes (Family Protection) (Scotland) Act 1981 contains provisions which enable a spouse to continue living in a matrimonial home although the marriage or relationship is breaking down.[1] It was appreciated by Parliament that these rights would be of limited value if the spouse who owned the furniture and plenishings of the home could sell them leaving the house empty. Accordingly, a spouse who has a right to occupy the matrimonial home[2] can apply under s 3(2) of the 1981 Act for an order granting the applicant the possession or use in the matrimonial home of any of its furniture and plenishings owned by the other.[3] Section 103(2) of the Civil Partnership Act 2004 provides a similar remedy for a civil partner in relation to the possession and use of furniture and plenishings in a family home.[4] 'Furniture and plenishings' mean any article situated in the matrimonial home or family home which is owned or hired by either spouse or civil partner[5] and 'is reasonably necessary to enable the home to be used as a family residence'.[6] In the writer's opinion, an order is not available when the spouses or civil partners own the property in common. Here as common owner of the property, a spouse or civil partner can apply for an interdict to stop the other spouse or civil partner preventing the applicant from using or possessing the property.[7]

The court[8] must first make an order declaring that the applicant has occupancy rights in respect of the matrimonial or family home.[9] The court can then make such an order as appears just and reasonable having regard to all the circumstances of the case, including inter alia:

(1)     the conduct of the spouses or civil partners;

(2)     the needs and financial resources of the spouses or civil partners;

(3)     the needs of any children of the family; and

(4)     the extent, if any, to which the matrimonial or the family home, or any item of furniture and plenishings is used in connection with a trade, business or profession of either spouse or civil partner.[10]

An interim order can be made provided the non-applicant has been afforded an opportunity of being heard or represented before the court.[11] But the court cannot make an order if the effect of the order would be to exclude the non-applicant spouse from the matrimonial or family home: for example an order for the sole and exclusive possession or use of the fitted carpets throughout the home.

Where the furniture or plenishings are being paid up under a hire-purchase or a conditional sale agreement, an order does not prejudice the rights of the hirer or creditor to recover the property for non-performance of any obligations under the agreements.[12] But the spouse or civil partner in whose favour the order is made is entitled to make any payments under the agreements in lieu of the debtor.[13] Similarly, he or she can carry out any essential repairs to the furniture and plenishings.[14] On the application of either spouse or civil partner the court can apportion any such expenditure between the parties.[15]

The effect of an order is therefore to override the property rights of a spouse or civil partner in relation to the furniture and plenishings of the matrimonial or family home to the extent that the applicant is entitled to the use and possession of the relevant property for the duration of the order. It must be stressed that such an order regulates only the possession and use of the property. The ownership of the property is still determined by reference to s 25 of the Family Law (Scotland) Act 1985[16] and the common law rules. Moreover, the definition of furniture and plenishings in the 1981 and 2004 Acts is narrower than that of household goods for the purposes of s 25 since it is only furniture and plenishings which are *reasonably necessary* to enable the home to be used as a family residence which can be the subject of a s 3(2) or s 103(2) order.[17] The following examples illustrate the interrelationship between the two provisions.

(1)    H buys a bed during the marriage. The presumption of equal shares applies and is not rebutted. H and W therefore own the bed in common. Although a bed is an article reasonably necessary to enable the home to be used as a family residence, W cannot apply for a s 3(2) order for the use and possession of the bed because s 3(2) applies only where the furniture and plenishings are owned solely by one of the spouses. At common law, W as common owner would be entitled to an interdict preventing H from disposing of the bed.[18]

(2)    During the civil partnership A inherits a dining room suite from his grandmother. The presumption of equal shares does not apply[19] and the suite is owned outright by A. But if they are the only table and chairs in the house, A's civil partner, B, can apply for a s 103(2) order for their use and possession as they are articles reasonably necessary to enable the house to be used as a family residence.

(3)    A inherits an oil painting during the marriage. The presumption of equal shares does not apply. A therefore owns the painting outright. But as the painting is not reasonably necessary to enable the home to be used as a family residence, B, A's same sex spouse, will be unable to obtain a s 3(2) order for the use and possession of the painting.

Again it should be emphasised that these theoretical difficulties should not be allowed to detract from the evident utility of these provisions. It is further recognition that the incidents of ownership of property may have to be overridden in the interests of the family for whose benefit the property was acquired. In particular, it should be noted that the needs of the children of the family will be an important factor in determining whether or not an order should be made.[20]

---

1    The Matrimonial Homes (Family Protection) (Scotland) Act 1981 is discussed in detail in **Ch 5**.

2   See Ch 5. For the definition of 'matrimonial home', see MH(FP)(S)A 1981, s 22.
3   MH(FP)(S)A 1981, s 3(2).
4   For the definition of 'family home', see the Civil Partnership Act 2004, s 135.
5   Or is being acquired by either spouse or civil partner under a hire-purchase agreement or conditional sale agreement.
6   MH(FP)(S)A 1981, s 22; CPA 2004, s 135: vehicles, caravans or houseboats are expressly excluded.
7   MH(FP)(S)A 1981, s 3(2) was, of course, enacted before the Family Law (Scotland) Act 1985, s 25, discussed above. Since the presumption of common ownership will usually apply, the scope of s 3(2) of the MH(FP)(S)A1981 and s 103(2) of the CPA 2004 are greatly reduced. Ironically, it can be argued that the remedies under ss 3(2) and 103(2) are more sophisticated than that of a common owner at common law. However, it is possible that the provisions may be capable of being interpreted as including household goods owned in common by the defender and the applicant: *sed quaere.*
8   The Court of Session or the sheriff court: MH(FP)(S)A 1981, s 22; CPA 2004, s 135.
9   MH(FP)(S)A 1981, s 3(1); CPA 2004, s 103(1): *Welsh v Welsh* 1987 SLT (Sh Ct) 30.
10  MH(FP)(S)A 1981, s 3(3); CPA 2004, s 103(3).
11  MH(FP)(S)A 1981, s 3(4); CPA 2004, s 103(4): *Welsh v Welsh* 1987 SLT (Sh Ct) 30.
12  MH(FP)(S)A 1981, s 3(2); CPA 2004, s 103(2).
13  MH(FP)(S)A 1981, ss 2(5)(a) and 3(2); CPA 2004, ss 102(a) and 103(2).
14  MH(FP)(S)A 1981, ss 2(5)(a) and 3(2); CPA 2004, ss 102(a) and 103(2).
15  MH(FP)(S)A 1981, s 2(5)(b); CPA 2004, s 102(5)(b).
16  Discussed at para **4.5** ff.
17  MH(FP)(S)A 1981, s 22; CPA 2004, s 135.
18  Since the bed is common property and H and W each own a one-half pro indiviso share of its value, an action for division and sale is competent to enable H to realise his share. This is discussed in the context of heritage in **Ch 5.** Theoretically, H could attempt to sell his one-half pro indiviso share of the bed, if anyone would like to buy half a bed!
19  Household goods inherited from third parties are expressly excluded by the Family Law (Scotland) Act 1985, s 25(1).
20  MH(FP)(S)A 1981, s 3(3); CPA 2004, s 103(3).

## Money and securities

**4.7** Money and securities are expressly excluded from the presumption of equal shares in household goods.[1] The ownership of money or securities will therefore be determined by the ordinary property rules, ie in accordance with the separate property system. For example, if H deposits £5,000 in a bank account in his name, the money in the account prima facie belongs to him. It is open to W to claim that she transferred the money to H to invest on her behalf and consequently the investment belongs to her. She will have the benefit of the presumption against donation[2] and she is not restricted in the type of evidence she can bring to substantiate her claim.[3]

Problems have arisen in relation to joint bank accounts. When an account is opened in the joint names of spouses or civil partners, depending on the terms of the agreement with the bank, this may oblige the bank to honour cheques drawn by either spouse or civil partner. In the case of a deposit account, the bank may be obliged to pay money over to either of the spouses or civil partners when called upon to do so. But the fact that the account is in joint names does not determine the ownership of the money in it.

Where one spouse or civil partner has been the sole contributor of the funds in the account, in the absence of evidence of donation, it will be presumed that the account was opened for administrative convenience only and the money in the account belongs to the contributing spouse or civil partner. Where *both* spouses or civil partners contributed to the fund, it will be readily inferred that they intended the account to be used as a common purse and that the money in the account is owned in common.[4]

Where a spouse or civil partner draws on a joint account to buy property, prima facie the property belongs to the purchaser outright – even though the account was opened for administrative purposes only.[5] However, where a spouse or civil partner purchases household goods, the presumption of equal shares will apply by virtue of s 25 of the Family Law (Scotland) Act 1985.[6]

Similar principles will apply to money investments.

---

1    Family Law (Scotland) Act 1985, s 25(3)(a).
2    Discussed at para **4.3**.
3    *Smith v Smith* 1933 SC 701.
4    That is, the court will infer donation to the extent necessary to give each spouse a half share of the money in the account.
5    Unless there is evidence that the property was bought as a joint investment.
6    Discussed at para **4.5** ff.

## Savings from housekeeping

**4.8** One of the harshest consequences of the system of separate property was where a husband provided his wife with a housekeeping allowance and the wife, being thrifty, was able to save some of the money. Because the husband had intended the money to be used to run the home, donation could not be inferred. Consequently, the husband was the owner of the savings made by the wife.[1] The Married Women's Property Act 1964 attempted to alleviate the position. It provided that savings made by a wife from a housekeeping allowance made to her by her husband should be presumed to be owned jointly by the spouses in the absence of an agreement to the contrary. The 1964 Act was defective in that it was not applicable to savings made by a husband from a housekeeping allowance paid to him by his wife: in these circumstances, any savings would still be owned by the wife.

This discriminatory element has been removed and the provision amended to include civil partners. Section 26 of the Family Law (Scotland) Act 1985 provides:

'If any question arises (whether during or after a marriage or civil partnership) as to the right of either party to a marriage or as the case may be of a partner in a civil partnership to money derived from any allowance made by either party or partner for their joint household expenses or for similar purposes, or to any property acquired out of such money, the money or property shall, in the absence of any agreement between them to the contrary, be treated as belonging to each party or partner in equal shares'.

It will be clear that s 26 of the 1985 Act applies to allowances made by one spouse to the other spouse and civil partner to civil partner. The allowances must be for 'their joint household expenses or for similar purposes'. It is not thought that money given to a spouse or civil partner for payment of mortgage instalments would be included within the definition.[2]

Money or property 'derived from the allowance' has been given a wide meaning. In *Pyatt v Pyatt*[3] Lord Fraser held that the prize money won by a wife on Littlewoods Football Pools was 'derived from' the allowance when the wife had taken the stake money from her housekeeping. The winnings had resulted both from the allowance which had provided the stake money and the wife's luck. Since the stake money had been essential, the prize money had been derived from the allowance and consequently the husband was entitled to half the winnings.

The application of s 26 of the Family Law (Scotland) Act 1985 can lead to some odd results. Consider the following example. W gives H a housekeeping allowance. H uses some of the allowance to bet on a horse. H wins £1,000. He puts £500 in a building society account and buys a second hand caravan with the rest of the money. Following *Pyatt v Pyatt*[4] W is entitled to half the £500 in the building society account, ie £250 and is an owner in common of the caravan.[5] W is not entitled to choose the full £500 in the account in lieu of her half share of the caravan.[6]

---

1    *Smith v Smith* 1933 SC 701; *Preston v Preston* 1950 SC 253. This did not apply to savings from aliment paid by a husband when the couple were separated.
2    *Tymoszczuk v Tymoszczuk* (1964) 108 Sol Jo 676 (interpreting the similar phrase in the Married Women's Property Act 1964); but cf *Re John's Assignment Trusts, Niven v Niven* [1970] 2 All ER 210 (Note), [1970] 1 WLR 955.
3    1966 SLT (Notes) 73.
4    1966 SLT (Notes) 73.
5    Family Law (Scotland) Act 1985, s 25 is inapplicable since caravans are expressly excluded from the definition of household goods: FL(S)A 1985, s 25(3)(b).
6    Moreover, if H used the £1,000 together with £1,000 of his own savings in order to buy a pony, W would own a quarter of the pony! Domestic animals are also excluded from the definition of household goods: FL(S)A 1985, s 25(3)(c).

---

## Policies of assurance

**4.9** Where A takes out an insurance policy for the benefit of B, B has no rights in the policy until it is delivered to B or the rights under the policy have been intimated to B. There is an exception to this principle where a spouse or civil partner takes out a life policy on his or her life for the benefit of the other spouse or civil partner (or children): in these circumstances, the policy is deemed to be held by the insured in trust for the beneficiaries who take an immediate right without the necessity of delivery or intimation of the policy to them.[1]

---

1    Married Women's Policies of Assurance (Scotland) Act 1880, s 2; Civil Partnership Act 2004, s 132.

---

Chapter 5

# The legal consequences of marriage and civil partnership

## PART III: THE MATRIMONIAL AND FAMILY HOME

### Introduction

**5.1** The most important heritable property which spouses or civil partners are likely to possess is their matrimonial or family home. A married couple or civil partners are likely to live in accommodation which is owned by one or both of them. In Scots law, the person who has title is the owner of the heritable property. When property is sold, the title must be registered in the Land Register of Scotland. Until registration, the buyer does not have a real right in the property, ie he is not the owner with a title which is good against the world; as against the seller, however, the buyer will have a personal right to sue for breach of contract if the seller disposes of the property to a third party before registration.

Many couples are unable to purchase a house outright and have to borrow the necessary sum from a bank (the heritable creditor). Until the loan is repaid, the bank will usually have a heritable security (often referred to as a mortgage) over the house; this enables the heritable creditor to sell the house if the loan (and interest thereon) is not repaid. The only form of heritable security is now the standard security, which is itself registered in the Land Register of Scotland.

Some couples cannot afford to buy their home. Instead, they will simply rent accommodation. Since 1974, a lease of residential property cannot be granted for more than 20 years.[1] Most residential leases are not for long periods and are terminable by notice, stipulated in the lease. As a result of legislation,[2] tenants enjoy a considerable measure of security of tenure in both the public and private housing sectors. The person who has security of tenure is the tenant. Joint tenancies are possible but it is more usual for the tenancy to be in the name of one of the spouses, usually the husband in opposite sex marriages, or one of the civil partners.

It will be obvious that where, for example, property is owned by one of the spouses or one of the civil partners, the other spouse or civil partner may experience difficulties in relation to the continued occupation of the matrimonial home if their relationship begins to break down. As a result of the Matrimonial Homes (Family Protection) (Scotland) Act 1981, the rights of a spouse to occupy the *matrimonial* home have been greatly improved: under the Civil Partnership Act 2004[3] a civil partner has similar rights in respect of the *family* home. These rights will be discussed in this chapter. Before doing so, consideration must be given to the operation of the system of separate property on the question of the ownership of the matrimonial or family home.

---

1    Land Tenure Reform (Scotland) Act 1974, s 8.
2    See in particular the Rent (Scotland) Act 1984, the Housing (Scotland) Act 1987, and the Housing (Scotland) Act 1988. Discussion of these statutes is outwith the scope of the present book.
3    Sections 101–112.

---

## The ownership of the matrimonial or family home

*Title in the name of one of the spouses or civil partners*

**5.2**  When a person purchases heritable property, title to which is taken in that person's name, it is a cardinal principle of the Scots law of property that that person is the owner of the property. For example, if H buys a house, title to which is taken in H's name, he is the owner of the house. This is an inevitable consequence of a system of separate property. The fact that the house is to be used as the matrimonial home is irrelevant to the question of its ownership.

When a house is purchased solely from the funds of one of the spouses or civil partners then the application of the separate property principle is justified. But in practice it is more likely that a house will be purchased through the means of a loan and a standard security. A couple will often agree to pool their resources in order to acquire their house. For example, a wife may make a direct financial contribution to the down-payment or the mortgage instalments. Alternatively, the spouses may agree that while the husband's earnings are used to pay the instalments, the wife's earnings will be used for household expenses: in these circumstances, the wife will have made an indirect contribution to the acquisition of the matrimonial home. Yet if the title has been taken in the husband's name, he will be the sole owner of the house even though it could not have been purchased without the wife's direct or indirect financial assistance. The injustice of the application of the separate property principle in these circumstances is readily apparent.

In England, a wife who has made a direct or indirect financial contribution towards the acquisition of the matrimonial home may obtain an interest in the property because in these circumstances a court can infer that the couple intended that the husband was holding the property on a constructive trust for the benefit of the wife. The extent of the wife's interest in the house is proportional to the size of her contribution. Such a solution is doubtful in Scots law.[1]

If H obtained the funds from W by telling her that he would put the title in joint names, W could sue H in delict if he did not do so.[2] If W transferred the money in the erroneous belief that title would be taken in joint names, then even in the absence of fraud on H's part, W would have a claim for recompense under principles of unjust enrichment.[3]

Where a spouse or civil partner has made a direct or indirect contribution to the acquisition of a house, title to which has been taken in the name of the other spouse or civil partner, it is possible to regulate the ownership of the *value* of the property by agreement. While this agreement need not be in writing,[4] it is thought that such an agreement will not be readily inferred. Even if such an agreement existed it would only be binding between the spouses or civil partners and would not prevent the spouse or civil partner who has the title from selling the property to a third party who is entitled to rely on the title as it appears in the Land Register of Scotland.[5]

---

1    At one time it was thought that the scope of a constructive trust was limited because, as a result of the Blank Bonds and Trusts Act 1696, proof of the existence of the trust was restricted to the writ or oath of the alleged trustee. For example, if W transferred funds to H which H used to purchase a house, title to which was taken in H's name,

W could not argue that H held the property on trust for W unless she could prove by H's writ or oath that he held the house on trust for her. The 1696 Act was repealed by the Requirements of Writing (Scotland) Act 1995, s 11 and Schedule 5. Consequently, in the example W may be able to argue that since there is a fiduciary relationship between her and H, H was holding the property on a constructive trust for her benefit. This would enable her to obtain an accounting from H if he had sold the house to a bona fide third party. As yet, there is no indication that the Scottish courts are going to develop the law along such lines: see Norrie 1995 JR 209.

2   *Marshall v Lyall and Marshall* (1859) 21 D 514.
3   Similarly an action for recompense would lie if W made improvements to the property in the belief that the house was hers: *Newton v Newton* 1925 SC 715. It is important to note that it is the law of obligations which provides W with a remedy, not the law of property. This was recognised by Lord Hope in the English case of *Stack v Dowden* [2007] UKHL 17. As these issues will in practice be of more importance for cohabitants, they are explored in greater depth at para **8.4**.
4   Requirements of Writing (Scotland) Act 1995, s 1(1) and (2); *Denvir v Denvir* 1969 SLT 301.
5   For further discussion of these property issues, see Joe Thomson *Scots Private Law* (2006) Chs 2–4.

## Title in the name of both of the spouses or civil partners

**5.3** Spouses and civil partners are increasingly taking title to their homes in joint names. While this will alleviate many of the problems discussed in the previous section, to take title in both names raises its own difficulties.

Where title to a house is taken in joint names, the property is regarded as common property. This means that while the property is possessed undivided, each of the spouses or civil partners has his or her own separate title to half of the property, ie each owns a one-half pro indiviso share of the value of the property.[1] During his or her lifetime, each co-owner is entitled to dispose of their share to a third party without the knowledge or consent of the other co-owning spouse or civil partner.[2] Similarly, each co-owner is free to dispose of his or her one half pro indiviso share by will.

Complications have arisen from the conveyancing practice of taking the title in the names of husband and wife *and the survivor*. This is known as a special destination. For example, if the property is taken in the names of husband and wife and the survivor, on the death of the husband, his share of the property will automatically pass to his wife, the survivor. The wife will take the deceased husband's pro indiviso share burdened with her husband's debts up to the value of the property.[3]

There are other difficulties. While the spouses remain free to dispose of their share during their lifetime,[4] a special destination may prevent a spouse disposing of his or her share by will. Where both spouses have contributed to the purchase of the property, the courts will readily infer from a special destination to the survivor that there is a contractual relationship between the parties and neither can revoke the arrangement by testamentary deed.[5] Where only one of the parties has purchased a house, this principle does not apply to the spouse who bought the property and he or she remains free to dispose of his or her pro indiviso share by will – but not, of course, the other spouse's share. Since the latter has in effect received his or her share as a gift, the court will readily imply that the donee took the gift under the condition that the donor should obtain that share if the donor is the survivor and consequently the donee cannot dispose of his or her share by will. But even in these circumstances, the donee is free to dispose of his or her share during his or her lifetime.[6] The same difficulties arise if title is taken in the name of both civil partners and the survivor.

A particular difficulty arose if the couple divorced or had their civil partnership dissolved. For example, title to a family home is taken in the names of A and B and the survivor. A and B are civil partners. When their civil partnership is dissolved, they agree that B should have the former family home. If A conveys his one half pro indiviso share to B, B becomes the sole owner of the house. But the survivorship destination to A of B's original pro indiviso share has not been evacuated. If B dies a one half pro indiviso share of the property will automatically be transferred to A.[7] If both A and B contributed to the purchase of the house, there will be an implied agreement that B could not dispose of his original one half pro indiviso share by will: so A will obtain a half share even if B had willed the house to his new civil partner, C. To avoid this result, at the time of the dissolution of their civil partnership *both* A and B must convey their one half pro indiviso shares to B thus evacuating the special destination of B's share. Alternatively, A and B could expressly agree to renounce all rights of succession to each other's property thereby evacuating the special destinations.[8]

The law was complex and held pitfalls for the unwary or badly advised. However, it has now been enacted that a special destination should automatically be revoked on divorce[9] or on dissolution of a civil partnership.[10] This is done by having a statutory fiction that if the special destination has not been evacuated, the person who would succeed under it is deemed not to have survived the deceased.[11] Accordingly, where title to heritable property is taken by A with a special destination to B or by A and B with a special destination to the survivor, then if A and B divorce or have their civil partnership dissolved, if B subsequently dies without having evacuated the destination, A is deemed to have failed to survive B for the purpose of inheriting under the special destination. Therefore A does not acquire the property or B's pro indiviso share from B's estate.[12]

---

1    If the title is in joint names, it is presumed that prima facie each owner has a one-half pro indiviso share. If the proportions are not to be so then the parties should have an agreement stipulating what the actual proportions are.

2    But see *McLeod v Cedar Holdings Ltd* 1989 SLT 620 where H took out a further heritable security over property owned by H and W. H had forged W's signature. The Inner House granted W reduction in respect of her pro indiviso share.

3    *Fleming's Trustee v Fleming* 2000 SC 206.

4    *Steele v Caldwell* 1979 SLT 228.

5    *Perrett's Trustees v Perrett* 1909 SC 522.

6    *Hay's Trustee v Hay's Trustees* 1951 SC 329.

7    *Gardner's Executor v Raeburn* 1996 SLT 745.

8    *Redfern's Executors v Redfern* 1996 SLT 900.

9    Family Law (Scotland) Act 2006, s 19.

10   Civil Partnership Act 2004, s 124A.

11   FL(S)A 2006, s 19(1) and (2) (spouses): CPA 2004, ss 124A(1) and (2) (civil partners).

12   As a result of this rule, the title to property may become inaccurate. For example, A acquires property in his own name with a destination over to his civil partner, B. The civil partnership is dissolved. A dies. As a result of the new rule B is deemed not to have survived A and the property remains in A's estate. But as far as title is concerned, it remains subject to the special destination and it will not be evident from the Land Register that there has been a dissolution. B may therefore appear to be the owner of the property because of the special destination. In ignorance of the law or in bad faith, B may transfer the property to a third party who will attempt to acquire title through the special destination to B. Section 124A(3) of CPA 2004 (s 19(3) of the FL(S)A 2006 in the case of divorce) provides that when the third party has acquired in good faith and for value in such circumstances, his title is not challengeable on the ground that the special destination was revoked by the dissolution and the property remains in A's estate. A's estate can recover the proceeds of B's sale to the third party under the law of unjustified enrichment.

---

## The occupation of the matrimonial or family home

**5.4** In the last section, we discussed the question of the ownership of the matrimonial or family home. In this section we shall consider the different but related question of the occupation of the matrimonial or family home. There are two situations:

(1)     where one spouse or civil partner has the title to the property or is the tenant, and the other spouse or civil partner has no real right in the property; and

(2)     where both spouses or civil partners have a title to the property, ie they are common owners of the property.

*Where one spouse or civil partner has title or is the tenant*

**5.5** At common law the owner or the tenant had the right of exclusive possession of his or her property. Thus for example, if H owned the matrimonial home, he could tell W to leave: if W refused, H could obtain an interdict preventing her access to the house. While H remained under a duty to aliment W, this did not oblige him to continue to allow W to occupy the matrimonial home.[1] The common law rule that a spouse who owned or was the tenant of a matrimonial home was entitled to order the non-owning spouse to leave has been radically altered as a result of the Matrimonial Homes (Family Protection) (Scotland) Act 1981.[2] A similar legal regime was introduced for civil partners by the Civil Partnership Act 2004.[3]

---

1     *MacLure v MacLure* 1911 SC 200; *Millar v Milla*r 1940 SC 56.
2     See generally, E M Clive *The Law of Husband and Wife in Scotland* (4th edn, 1997, W Greens/Sweet & Maxwell), Ch 15.
3     Sections 101–112.

---

### The nature of the statutory rights

**5.6** By s 1(1) of the 1981 Act and s 101(1) of the 2004 Act, where one spouse or civil partner, 'the entitled spouse' or 'entitled partner', is the owner or tenant of the matrimonial or family home[1] and the other spouse, 'the non-entitled spouse' or 'non-entitled partner' is not the owner or tenant,[2] then the non-entitled spouse or civil partner has the following statutory rights:

(1)    if in occupation, to continue to occupy the matrimonial or family home;

(2)    if not in occupation, to enter into and occupy the matrimonial or family home.[3]

These statutory rights of a non-entitled spouse or civil partner to occupy the matrimonial or family home expressly include the right to do so 'together with any child of the family'.[4]

The effect of this provision is to give the non-entitled spouse or non-entitled partner a positive right to occupy the matrimonial or family home together with any child of the family. 'Matrimonial home' and 'family home' have wide meanings. They include any house, caravan, houseboat or other structure which has been provided as, or become, a *family* residence.[5] Although the term 'family residence' is used, it is clear that it is not limited to a family where there are children. It is enough that a house has been acquired with the intention that it should be used as a family home; the couple do not need to have lived there.[6]

Conversely, if the house was acquired without the intention that it should be used as a family residence, nevertheless it can become a matrimonial or family home. For example, if A bought a flat before he met and married B, his same sex spouse, it will become a matrimonial home if B lives there after their marriage.[7] If there are two or more family residences, for example a town house and a country cottage, the non-entitled spouse or civil partner will have a statutory right to occupy both (or more) houses. On the other hand, a matrimonial or family home does not include a residence provided for one spouse or civil partner to live in separately from the other spouse or civil partner even if children of the family also reside there.[8]

A child of the family includes any child or grandchild of either spouse or civil partner or any person brought up or treated by either spouse or civil partner as if he or she was a child of that spouse or civil partner. The age of the child is irrelevant.[9] For example, a severely disabled adult son or daughter of either spouse or civil partner will be a child of the family for the purposes of the 1981 and 2004 Acts.

The statutory rights arise as soon as the parties marry or register their civil partnership and the entitled spouse or civil partner acquires a family residence. The rights continue throughout the marriage or civil partnership even if the couple separate. But if they do not cohabit for a continuous period of two years during which the non-entitled spouse or civil partner does not occupy the matrimonial or family home, then the statutory rights come to an end.[10] Having lost the statutory rights in this way, the non-entitled spouse or civil partner cannot apply for a declarator that they exist even though the couple may have become reconciled and resumed cohabitation.[11] The statutory rights also cease when the marriage or civil partnership ends in death, divorce or dissolution.[12] Most importantly, the rights of the non-entitled spouse or civil partner are not defeated if, during the marriage or civil partnership, the matrimonial or family home is sold or otherwise disposed of to a third party.[13]

---

1   Or is permitted by a third party to occupy the home: Matrimonial Homes (Family Protection) (Scotland) Act 1981, s 1(1); Civil Partnership Act 2004, s 101(1). This only arises if the third party has waived his or her right to occupy the home in favour of the entitled spouse: MH(FP)(S)A 1981, s 1(2); CPA 2004, s 101(3); *Murphy v Murphy* 1992 SCLR 62.
2   Or is not permitted by a third party to occupy the home: MH(FP)(S)A 1981, s 1(1); CPA 2004, s 101(1).
3   MH(FP)(S)A 1981, s 1(1); CPA 2004, s 101(1).
4   MH(FP)(S)A 1981, s 1(1A); CPA 2004, s 101(2).
5   MH(FP)(S)A 1981, s 22; CPA 2004, s 135: any garden or outbuildings, for example a garage, are included.
6   *O'Neill v O'Neill* 1987 SLT (Sh Ct) 26.
7   But it will not be matrimonial or partnership property for the purpose of fair division under the Family Law (Scotland) Act 1985, s 9(1)(a): discussed in **Ch 7**.
8   MH(FP)(S)A 1981, s 22: CPA 2004. This includes a house provided by a spouse or civil partner for himself or herself; or a house provided by a spouse or civil partner for the other spouse or civil partner; or a house provided for one spouse or civil partner by a third party.
9   MH(FP)(S)A 1981, s 22; CPA 2004, s 101(7).
10  MH(FP)(S)A 1981, s 1(7); CPA 2004, s 101(6A).
11  MH(FP)(S)A 1981, s 1(8); CPA 2004, s 101(6B).
12  Where on divorce or dissolution, the court makes an incidental order entitling the applicant spouse or civil partner to continue to occupy the matrimonial or family home after the divorce or dissolution, certain of the rights in s 2 of the MH(FP)(S)A 1981 and s 102 of the CPA 2004, which enable a non-entitled spouse or civil partner to take steps in relation to the upkeep of the home and its contents, will continue:

FL(S)A 1985, s 14(5) and (5A). Nevertheless it is common and accepted practice to incorporate craves for relief under the 1981 Act or 2004 Act in divorce or dissolution proceedings: *Nelson v Nelson* 1988 SLT (Sh Ct) 26.

13    Discussed in detail at para **5.10**.

### Upkeep and maintenance of the matrimonial home

**5.7** For the purpose of securing the statutory rights of occupation, a non-entitled spouse or civil partner has the right, without the consent of the entitled spouse or civil partner, inter alia to pay any rent, mortgage instalments etc instead of the entitled spouse or civil partner; to carry out essential repairs; to carry out non-essential repairs approved by a court as appropriate for the reasonable enjoyment of the occupancy rights; and to take any other steps necessary to ensure the occupancy of the matrimonial or family home.[1] The court has the power to apportion such expenditure between the spouses or civil partners.[2]

1    Matrimonial Homes (Family Protection) (Scotland) Act 1981, s 2(1); Civil Partnership Act 2004, s 102(1). The court is the Court of Session or the sheriff court.
2    MH(FP)(S)A 1981, s 2(4); CPA 2004, s 102(4).

### Regulatory orders

**5.8** By s 3 of the Matrimonial Homes (Family Protection) (Scotland) Act 1981 and s 103 of the Civil Partnership Act 2004 the court has the power to regulate the spouse or civil partner's occupancy of the matrimonial or family home. An order may be sought by either the entitled or non-entitled spouse or civil partner. The court can make orders declaring or enforcing the applicant's rights of occupation, restricting the non-applicant's occupancy rights and regulating the occupancy rights of both parties. While the court is obliged to declare that the applicant has occupancy rights when it is satisfied that the property constitutes a matrimonial or family home,[1] the exercise of its other powers under ss 3 and 103 is discretionary. By ss 3(3) and 103(3) the court is obliged to make such orders as appears to the court to be just and reasonable having regard to all the circumstances of the case including:

(a) the conduct of the spouses and civil partners in relation to each other and otherwise;

(b) the respective needs and financial resources of the spouses or civil partners;

(c) the needs of any child of the family;

(d) the extent (if any) to which the matrimonial or family home is used in connection with a trade, business or profession of either spouse or civil partner; and

(e) whether the entitled spouse or civil partner offers or has offered to make available to the non-entitled spouse or civil partner any suitable alternative accommodation.

Interim orders are possible if considered necessary or expedient[2] and compensation is available for loss or impairment of occupancy rights.[3] However, a court cannot make an order under ss 3(3) or 103(3) if its effect would be to exclude the entitled spouse or civil partner from the matrimonial or family home. While the power to grant declarator of a non-entitled spouse or civil partner's statutory rights is important, in practice little use has been made of the court's powers to make regulatory orders under ss 3(3) or 104(3).[4]

---

1   Matrimonial Homes (Family Protection) (Scotland) Act 1981, s 3(3); Civil Partnership Act 2004, s 103(3). Indeed, it would appear that declarator is essential before other relief can be given under s 3 or s 103: *Welsh v Welsh* 1987 SLT (Sh Ct) 30.

2   MH(FP)(S)A 1981, s 3(4); CPA 2004, s 103(4): the non-applicant spouse or civil partner must have been afforded an opportunity of being heard or represented in court.

3   MH(FP)(S)A 1981, s 3(7); CPA 2004, s 103(8).

4   Where a s 104(3) order is in force when a qualifying civil partnership ends because the civil partnership has been converted into a same sex marriage, the order continues as if made under MH(FP)(S)A 1981, s 3(3): Marriage and Civil Partnership (Scotland) Act 2014, s 11(8). On qualifying civil partnerships, see para **1.19** above.

**Exclusion orders**

**5.9** By s 4 of the 1981 Act and s 104 of the 2004 Act the court has the power to exclude either of the spouses or civil partners from the matrimonial or family home. The order may be sought by either the entitled or non-entitled spouse.[1] By s 4(2) of the 1981 Act the court:

> '*shall* make an exclusion order if it appears to the court that the making of an order is *necessary* for the protection of the applicant or any child of the family from any *conduct* or threatened or reasonably apprehended conduct of the non-applicant spouse which is or would be injurious to the physical or mental health of the applicant or child'.[2]

In spite of the mandatory wording of s 4(2), by s 4(3)(a) the court shall not make an exclusion order if it would be unjustified or unreasonable having regard to all the circumstances of the case, including the factors specified in s 3(3).[3] The wording of s 104(2) of the 2004 Act is a little different. It provides that:

> '... the court *is* to make an exclusion order if it appears to it that to do so is *necessary* for the protection of the applicant or any child of the family from any *conduct*, or any threatened or reasonably apprehended conduct, of the non-applicant partner which is or would be injurious to the physical or mental health of the applicant or child'.[4]

Once again, even if the necessity criterion is satisfied, the court is not to make an exclusion order if it appears to the court that to do so would be unjustified or unreasonable to do so having regard to all the circumstances, including the matters specified in s 103(3). Interim exclusion orders are available[5] but the necessity criterion must still be satisfied.[6]

The construction of s 4 of the 1981 Act initially caused the Scottish courts much difficulty. At first there was a reluctance to grant an interim exclusion order when the court was proceeding on affidavit evidence. In *Bell v Bell*[7] and *Smith v Smith*,[8] the Inner House of the Court of Session held that the necessity criterion in s 4(2) was a 'high and severe' test. The judges indicated that it would be unlikely to be satisfied unless the applicant was living in the matrimonial home at the time of the application. This caused considerable apprehension until the Lord Justice-Clerk (Wheatley) attempted to remove such fears in *Colagiacomo v Colagiacomo*:[9]

> 'If there is any misconception that following *Bell v Bell* an interim exclusion order will only be granted if the parties are both occupying the matrimonial home, the sooner that misconception is removed the better. The fact that only one of the parties is occupying the matrimonial home is a factor to be taken into account but is not per se to be regarded as a conclusive one'.[10]

Although exclusion orders were granted in later cases where the applicant had left the matrimonial home,[11] s 4(1) of the 1981 Act was amended expressly to provide that an application for an exclusion order can be made, 'whether or not that spouse [the applicant] is in occupation at the time of the application'.[12]

In *Bell v Bell*[13] and *Smith v Smith*[14] the judges also indicated that an exclusion order should not be made if a matrimonial interdict prohibiting the molestation of the applicant would be sufficient protection.[15] This could lead to a 'Catch 22' situation: a wife could not be granted an interim exclusion order unless she had applied for a non-molestation interdict, but if she obtained such an interdict, an exclusion order would not be granted without evidence that the husband had been in breach of the interdict.[16]

However, in *Brown v Brown*,[17] Lord Dunpark held that a matrimonial interdict was not a pre-requisite for an exclusion order, although in considering whether it would be unjustified or unreasonable to make the order, the sheriff or Lord Ordinary must consider inter alia whether a matrimonial interdict would suffice.[18] Moreover, when granting a s 4 order, the judge should state the reasons why an interdict did not afford sufficient protection.[19] On the facts of *Brown* an interdict was not enough since the husband was violent only when he was drunk and this conduct would not be affected by the existence of an interdict.[20] In *Roberton v Roberton*[21] the Inner House held that a sheriff was entitled to grant an interim exclusion order because it was almost impossible to frame an effective interdict given the husband's unreasonably intrusive and jealous nature: the exclusion order was therefore necessary to protect the wife from injury to her health.

Lastly, there are dicta in *Bell v Bell*[22] to support the contention that an interim exclusion order should only be made if the court is satisfied that the applicant would be in danger of 'serious injury or irreparable damage' if the order is not granted. In *McCafferty v McCafferty*[23] the Inner House of the Court of Session held that these dicta were an unnecessary gloss on the necessity test which stipulates that it is sufficient that the non-applicant's conduct or threatened or reasonably apprehended conduct 'is or would be injurious to the physical or mental health of the applicant or child'.

While these developments were concerned with exclusion orders under the 1981 Act, it is submitted that exclusion orders under the 2004 Act will be approached in the same way.

It has never been doubted that the criterion for an exclusion order is not easy to satisfy. The applicant must satisfy the court that the order is *necessary* for the protection of the applicant or any child of the family because the non-applicant's conduct (or threatened or reasonably apprehended conduct) is, or would be, injurious to the physical or mental health of the applicant or child.[24] The fact that, on a balance of convenience test, it is desirable that the applicant and the child of the family should have exclusive occupation of the matrimonial home will not suffice.[25] Although s 4(2) of the 1981 Act and s 104(2) of the 2004 Act expressly include harm to the applicant's or child's mental as well as physical health,[26] this must be occasioned by the non-applicant's *conduct* and not merely be the result of the breakdown of the marriage or civil partnership.[27]

It should also be remembered that, even if the necessity test is satisfied, the court can refuse an exclusion order if in all the circumstances of the case, including the factors listed in s 3(3) of the 1981 Act and s 103(3) of the 2004 Act, it would be unjustified or unreasonable to do so.[28] But as Lord Dunpark observed in *Brown v Brown*,[29] the Inner House of the Court of Session:

> 'had difficulty in envisaging circumstances in which an order which is necessary for the protection of the spouse may be "unjustified or unreasonable" ...'.

Nevertheless, the court has suspended the operation of an exclusion order for three months in order to enable the defender to find alternative accommodation. This is difficult to accept given that the exclusion order was *ex hypothesi* 'necessary'.[30] In *McCafferty v McCafferty*,[31] Lord Dunpark said that in an application for an exclusion order the court should ask four questions:

'(1)   What is the nature and quality of the alleged conduct?

(2)   Is the court satisfied that the conduct is likely to be repeated if cohabitation continues?

(3)   Has the conduct been or, if repeated, would it be injurious to the physical or mental health of the applicant or to any child of the family?

(4)   If so, is the order sought necessary for the future protection of the physical or mental health of the applicant or child?'[32]

The necessity for an exclusion order will only be established if the court is satisfied that a matrimonial interdict will not afford sufficient protection but a matrimonial interdict is not a pre-requisite for an exclusion order.

It will be clear that the success of an application for an exclusion order will greatly depend on the readiness of the judge at first instance, the Lord Ordinary or the sheriff, to find the necessity test satisfied. This is important, for an appellate court will not interfere with a judge's discretion unless 'no reasonable Lord Ordinary [or sheriff] could have reached the decision, and that he was completely wrong'.[33]

Whatever the difficulties inherent in the legislation and experienced in practice, it cannot be doubted that the protections afforded by ss 4 and 104 are an important step in the protection of the victims of domestic violence.[34]

The necessity criterion can be criticised as too narrow but it will clearly cover at least the most blatant forms of domestic abuse. But there is much weight in the contention that where a relationship is breaking down the needs of any children of the family should be paramount and that the courts should have the power to exclude a spouse or civil partner from the matrimonial or family home when giving paramount consideration to the welfare of the children of the failing relationship, on the balance of convenience it is desirable that the person looking after the children should have exclusive occupation of the home. To some extent, this has been remedied by the introduction of exclusion orders under s 76 of the Children (Scotland) Act 1995.[34]

---

1    See, for example, *Brown v Brown* 1985 SLT 376; *Millar v Millar* 1991 SCLR 649 where the applicant was the entitled spouse. A local authority has title to sue for an exclusion order under s 76 of the Children (Scotland) Act 1995, discussed at para **14.6** ff.

2    Italics added.

3    See para **5.8**. Exclusion orders are also not available if the matrimonial or family home is part of an agricultural tenancy or has been let as an incident of employment: Matrimonial Homes (Family Protection) (Scotland) Act 1981, s 4(3)(b); Civil Partnership Act 2004, s 104(3)(b).

4    Italics added.

5    MH(FP)(S)A 1981, s 4(6); CPA 2004, s 104(6). The non-applicant spouse or civil partner must be afforded an opportunity of being heard or represented before the court. It has been held that affidavit evidence is of little value to the defender and a proof should take place at an early stage unless the circumstances are exceptional: *Armitage v Armitage* 1993 SCLR 173.

6    *Bell v Bell* 1983 SLT 224; *Smith v Smith* 1983 SLT 275; *Ward v Ward* 1983 SLT 472; *Roberton v Roberton* 1999 SLT 38.

7    1983 SLT 224.

8    1983 SLT 275.

9    *Colagiacomo v Calagiacomo* 1983 SLT 559.

10   1983 SLT 559 at 562.

11   See, for example *Ward v Ward* 1983 SLT 472; *Brown v Brown* 1985 SLT 376.

12   Law Reform (Miscellaneous Provisions) (Scotland) Act 1985, s 13(5). In *Millar v Millar* 1991 SCLR 649 a spouse obtained an exclusion order although she had left the home ten months before: the delay was not the fault of the pursuer.

13   *Bell v Bell* 1983 SLT 224.

14   *Smith v Smith* 1983 SLT 275.

15   Matrimonial interdicts are granted under the Matrimonial Homes (Family Protection) (Scotland) Act 1981, s 14. The equivalent for civil partners are relevant interdicts which are granted under the Civil Partnership Act 2004, s 113.

16   As happened in *Smith v Smith* 1983 SLT 275.

17   *Brown v Brown* 1985 SLT 376.

18   MH(FP)(S)A 1981, s 4(3); CPA 2004, s 104(3).

19   *McCafferty v McCafferty* 1986 SLT 650.

20   See also, for example, *Oliver v Oliver* 1988 GWD 26-1110.

21   *Roberton v Roberton* 1999 SLT 38.

22   *Bell v Bell* 1983 SLT 224 at 231, per Lord Robertson and at 232, per Lord Grieve.

23   *McCafferty v McCafferty* 1986 SLT 650 at 652 per Lord Justice-Clerk (Ross); at 654 per Lord Robertson and at 655 per Lord Dunpark.

24   In *Barbour v Barbour* 1990 GWD 3-135, for example, it did not appear that an exclusion order was necessary to protect anyone. Cf *Raeburn v Raeburn* 1990 GWD 8-424.

25 *Smith v Smith* 1983 SLT 275. In *Hampsey v Hampsey* 1988 GWD 24-1035, the Sheriff Principal (Caplan) held that a sheriff has 'no power to grant an exclusion order simply because the best interests of the child required it'. See also *Millar v Millar* 1991 SCLR 649.

26 *McCafferty v McCafferty* 1986 SLT 650. In *Roberton v Roberton* 1999 SLT 38, the court held that the wife's deteriorating health was caused by the husband's obsessive, jealous behaviour and was not merely the result of the tension which often arises when a marriage is breaking down.

27 *Matheson v Matheson* 1986 SLT (Sh Ct) 2.

28 It is ironic that the needs of the children is one of the factors listed in the MH(FP)(S)A 1981, s 3(3) and CPA 2004, s 103(3), and is, therefore, only relevant when considering whether it would be unjustified or unreasonable to make an exclusion order!

29 *Brown v Brown* 1985 SLT 376 at 378. See also *Millar v Millar* 1991 SCLR 649 at 651, per the Sheriff Principal (Maguire).

30 *Mather v Mather* 1987 SLT 565.

31 *McCafferty v McCafferty* 1986 SLT 650.

32 1986 SLT 650 at 656.

33 *McCafferty v McCafferty* 1986 SLT 650 at 655, per Lord Robertson. In *Brown v Brown* 1985 SLT 376, Lord Dunpark held that an appellate court could only interfere if the judge at first instance did not apply the proper test or the decision was wholly unwarranted on the facts. In *Coster v Coster* 1992 SCLR 210, an appeal from a sheriff refusing an exclusion order was allowed on the basis that the sheriff had given too much weight to whether the pursuer had alternative accommodation available rather than the averments of serious assault by the defender. See also *Roberton v Roberton* 1999 SLT 38.

34 Where a s 104(4) order is in force when a qualifying civil partnership ends because the civil partnership has been converted into a same sex marriage, the order continues as if made under MH(FP)(S)A 1981, s 3(4): Marriage and Civil Partnership (Scotland) Act 2014, s 11(8). On qualifying civil partnerships, see para **1.19** above.

35 Discussed at para **14.6** ff.

## Statutory rights and third parties

**5.10** A non-entitled spouse or non-entitled civil partner's statutory right of occupation is not prejudiced as the result of the entitled spouse or civil partner's dealings with the property.[1] Dealings include the sale or lease of the matrimonial or family home or the grant of a heritable security over it. For example, while an entitled spouse may still sell the matrimonial home, the purchaser will take the property subject to the non-entitled spouse's statutory rights of occupation. Moreover, by s 6(1)(b) of the 1981 Act and s 106(1)(b) of the 2004 Act, the purchaser is not entitled to occupy the matrimonial or family home or any part of it while the non-entitled spouse or civil partner continues to enjoy statutory rights of occupation in relation to the property.

Although this provision is laudable in so far as it protects the non-entitled spouse or non-entitled partner's statutory rights vis-à-vis third parties, it clearly causes conveyancing difficulties as the statutory rights are not registered in the Land Register of Scotland. Thus a third party could buy a house in good faith and in reliance upon the Register only to find that he cannot occupy the property because it is a matrimonial or family home in which the seller's non-entitled spouse or non-entitled partner has statutory rights of occupation.

The 1981 Act and the 2004 Act provide various solutions to this problem. A non-entitled spouse or civil partner can renounce in writing the statutory rights in relation to a particular matrimonial or family home provided that at the time it was made, the non-entitled spouse or civil partner swore or affirmed before a notary public that the renunciation was made freely and without coercion of any kind.[2] Where such a renunciation is made, the property is no longer subject to statutory rights of occupancy.[3]

Similarly, occupancy rights are not effective against a third party if the non-entitled spouse or non-entitled civil partner has consented to the dealing.[4] When a non-entitled spouse or civil partner refuses to consent to the dealing, the court has power to dispense with the consent on the ground that it is being unreasonably withheld.[5] A non-entitled spouse or civil partner will be taken to have withheld consent unreasonably if:

(1)   the entitled spouse or civil partner had been led to believe that the consent would be forthcoming and there has been no change of circumstances which would prejudice the non-entitled spouse or civil partner; or

(2)   having taken all reasonable steps, the entitled spouse or civil partner has been unable to obtain an answer to a request for consent.[6]

In all other cases, the onus rests on the entitled spouse or civil partner to show that the non-entitled spouse or civil partner has unreasonably withheld consent to the dealing. Before the court could consider the issue, the proposed dealing had to have reached a stage of negotiations where price and other conditions of the sale had been agreed.[7] This effectively prevented the entitled spouse or civil partner from selling the house on the open market without first obtaining the non-entitled spouse or civil partner's consent. It is now possible for the court to dispense with consent even though negotiations have not reached that stage provided that the house is sold within the period specified in the order at no less than the price stipulated by the court in the order.[8] In determining whether the consent is being unreasonably withheld the court will consider all the circumstances of the case, including the factors listed in s 3(3) of the 1981 Act and s 103(3) of the 2004 Act.[9] In *O'Neill v O'Neill*[10] where the non-entitled spouse had no intention of living in the house but was merely withholding consent as a bargaining lever in relation to a financial settlement on divorce, the court indicated that her consent was being withheld unreasonably. If the court dispenses with the non-entitled spouse's consent to the dealing,[11] the third party is not affected by the statutory rights.

There are also exceptions when the entitled spouse or civil partner entered into a binding obligation in respect of the dealing before the marriage or registration of the civil partnership.[12] If the entitled spouse or civil partner has permanently ceased to be entitled to occupy the matrimonial home, for example by selling it to a third party, the non-entitled spouse or civil partner's statutory rights cease to be exercisable against the third party if the non-entitled spouse or civil partner has, at any time thereafter, not occupied the property for a continuous period of two years.[13] For example, H is the entitled spouse. He sells the matrimonial home to X in 2012. W, the non-entitled spouse, leaves the matrimonial home in January 2014. Provided W does not occupy the matrimonial home for any period during the next two years, her statutory rights of occupation will not be enforceable against X after January 2016.

In practice the most important exceptions are to be found in s 6(3)(e) of the 1981 Act and s 106(3)(e) of the 2004 Act.[14] These provide respectively that the non-entitled spouse or civil partner's statutory rights are not enforceable against a third party where:

> 'the dealing comprises a transfer [for value] to a third party who has acted in good faith, if there is produced to the third party by the transferor—

(i) a written declaration signed by the transferor ... declaring that the subjects of the transfer are not or were not at the time of the dealing, a matrimonial [family] home in relation to which a spouse [civil partner] of the transferor has or had occupancy rights; or

(ii) a renunciation of occupancy rights or consent to the dealing which bears to have been properly made or given by the non-entitled spouse [civil partner] ...'.[15]

Provided the third party is in good faith, then if there is such a written declaration, a transferee *for value*, for example a buyer, will take the property free from the occupancy rights of the transferor's non-entitled spouse or civil partner. If the written declaration is false, the non-entitled spouse or civil partner will have recourse against the entitled spouse or civil partner for compensation for loss of occupancy rights as a result of their fraud.[16] The provision is so worded that it enables a transferor who is not married or in a civil partnership to declare that the property is not a matrimonial or family home. But it also enables a transferor who is married or in a civil partnership and whose spouse or civil partner does have statutory rights to make a written declaration when the property which is subject to the dealing is not *in fact* a matrimonial or family home. A similar written declaration is used to prevent the rights of a heritable creditor[17] being prejudiced by a non-entitled spouse or civil partner's statutory rights of occupation.[18]

To summarise. A is an entitled spouse or civil partner, B is A's non-entitled spouse or civil partner with statutory rights of occupation in respect of the matrimonial or family home owned by A. A transfers the property to C who acts in good faith and gives value. If A has made a written declaration that the house is not subject to statutory rights of occupation, then C will take it free of B's statutory rights. If C is in bad faith, ie knows about B, or does not give value, then B's statutory rights will prevail over C even if C obtained a written declaration from A. But if C later transfers the property to D who is in good faith and gives value, it has been enacted that D will take the property free of B's statutory rights.[19] If D then transfers the property to E, E takes free of B's statutory rights, even if E is not in good faith or has not given value.[20]

Where a dealing has occurred and the third party has taken the property subject to the non-entitled spouse or civil partner's statutory rights, the third party can apply to a court for an order dispensing with the consent of the non-entitled spouse or civil partner to the dealing, if the consent was being unreasonably withheld.[21] If successful, the third party will then take the property free from the non-entitled spouse or civil partner's statutory rights.

Since the Matrimonial Homes (Family Protection) (Scotland) Act 1981 came into effect, in spite of initial conveyancing difficulties, these provisions have been the cause of little, if any, litigation. In particular, where a third party has relied on a s 6(3)(e) declaration, there has been no reported case in which a non-entitled spouse has claimed that occupation rights are nevertheless enforceable against the third party because of an absence of good faith. There is no reason to believe that the position will not be the same under s 106(3)(c) of the Civil Partnership Act 2004.

---

1 Matrimonial Homes (Family Protection) (Scotland) Act 1981, s 6(1)(a); Civil Partnership Act 2004, s 106(1)(a). This protection does not apply where the entitled spouse occupies the home by permission of a third party or shares the occupation of the home with a third party: MH(FP)(S)A 1981, s 6(2)(a) and (b); CPA 2004, s 106(2) (a) and (b).

2 MH(FP)(S)A Act 1981, s 1(5) and (6): CPA 2004, s 101(5) and (6). It is not necessary that the non-entitled spouse or civil partner comes to Scotland to swear or affirm provided it is done before a person authorised to administer oaths or receive affirmations under the law of the country where the non-entitled spouse swears or affirms.

3 MH(FP)(S)A 1981, s 6(3)(a)(ii); CPA 2004, s 106(3)(a)(ii).

4 MH(FP)(S)A 1981, s 6(3)(a)(i); CPA 2004, s 104(3)(a)(i).

5 MH(FP)(S)A 1981, s 7(1); CPA 2004, s 107(1). The other grounds for dispensation are that the non-entitled spouse or civil partner is unable to consent because of physical or mental disability; or cannot be found after reasonable steps have been taken to trace the spouse; or is under the age of 16. This could only arise in the case of a marriage or registration of a civil partnership celebrated abroad.

6 MH(FP)(S)A 1981, s 7(2); CPA 2004, s 107(2).

7 *Fyfe v Fyfe* 1987 SLT (Sh Ct) 38.

8 MH(FP)(S)A 1981, s 7(1A) and (1B); CPA 2004, s 107(1A) and (1B). There are similar provisions where the proposed dealing is the grant of a heritable security: 1981 Act, s 7(1C) and (1D); 2004 Act, s 107(1C) and (1D). If the application for dispensation is refused and the non-entitled spouse or civil partner continues to live in the house, he or she can be ordered to make payments to the entitled spouse or civil partner: MH(FP)(S)A 1981, s 7(3A); CPA 2004, s 107(3A).

9 MH(FP)(S)A 1981, s 7(3); CPA 2004, s 107(3).

10  *O'Neill v O'Neill* 1987 SLT (Sh Ct) 26. The house was only a matrimonial home because the husband had hoped that his wife would live there: see para **5.6**.
11  The court will proceed as expeditiously as possible, but there must be evidence to justify dispensing with consent: see *Longmuir v Longmuir* 1985 SLT (Sh Ct) 33.
12  MH(FP)(S)A 1981, s 6(3)(c); CPA 2004, s 106(3)(c).
13  MH(FP)(S)A 1981, s 6(3)(f); CPA 2004, s 106(3)(f). Continuity is not broken even if during that period the non-entitled spouse or civil partner had taken court proceedings to assert his or her statutory rights. But the time during which the proceedings were taken does not count towards the two years; MH(FP)(S)A 1981, s 9A, s 15; CPA 2004, s 111A. These provisions in effect reverse *Stevenson v Roy* 2002 SLT 446.
14  MH(FP)(S)A 1981, s 6(3)(e); CPA 2004, s 106(6)(e).
15  The time of the dealing in the case of a sale of the property is the date of delivery of the deed transferring title to the property: MH(FP)(S)A 1981, s 6(3)(c); CPA 2004, s 106(4).
16  MH(FP)(S)A 1981, s 3(7); CPA 2004, s 103(8).
17  For example, a bank.
18  MH(FP)(S)A 1981, s 8(1) and (2); CPA 2004, ss 108(1) and (2).
19  MH(FP)(S)A 1981, s 6(1A); CPA 2004, s 106(1A).
20  MH(FP)(S)A 1981, s 7; CPA 2004, s 107.
21  MH(FP)(S)A 1981, s 7; CPA 2004, s 107.

*Where both spouses and civil partners have legal title or are joint tenants*

**5.11** The statutory rights of occupation of the matrimonial or family home are only available to a non-entitled spouse or civil partner, ie a spouse or civil partner who has no real right of ownership in the property. Where a spouse or civil partner has a real right of ownership in the matrimonial or family home, at common law he or she is entitled to occupy it. Both the Matrimonial Homes (Family Protection) (Scotland) Act 1981 and the Civil Partnership Act 2004 contain important provisions which strengthen the position of spouses and civil partners who are common owners of their family residence. These provisions will be discussed in this section.

Although it was contrary to principle that a co-owner or co-tenant could be ejected by the other from the common property, there was a suggestion in *Price v Watson*[1] that this was possible. Section 4(7) of the MH(FP)(S)A 1981 has clarified the position: it provides that where both spouses are entitled, or permitted by a third party, to occupy a matrimonial home, it shall be incompetent for one spouse to bring an action of ejection from the matrimonial home against the other spouse. While at common law either co-owner could carry out necessary repairs and pay essential outgoings, there was no power to carry out non-essential repairs. The 1981 Act and the 2004 Act give co-owners who are spouses or civil partners the power to do so and allows a court to apportion the expenditure between them.[2]

Where the spouses or civil partners are common owners of the matrimonial or family home, each spouse or civil partner is free to sell his or her own half pro indiviso share of the property without the agreement of the other. This could lead to problems where the purchaser insisted on occupying the property. Section 9(1) of the 1981 Act and s 109(1) of the 2004 Act provide that the right to occupy the matrimonial or family home enjoyed by a co-owning spouse or civil partner is not to be prejudiced by reason only of any dealing of the other spouse or civil partner in respect of the property and that a third party shall not by reason only of such a dealing be entitled to occupy the matrimonial or family home or any part of it. The effect of these provisions is that, while a co-owning spouse or civil partner is still entitled to sell his or her one half pro indiviso share, the purchaser of the pro indiviso share is unable to occupy the matrimonial or family home while the other co-owning spouse or civil partner continues to reside there.

It was an axiomatic principle of the common law that where property was held in common, either of the co-owners was entitled to obtain a decree of division and sale to realise his or her share of the value of the property. The court had no discretion to refuse the decree. In *Dickson v Dickson*,[3] for example, the Lord Ordinary (Kincraig) held that a husband was entitled to a decree of division and sale in respect of property he owned in common with his wife; it was irrelevant that she would not agree to the sale because she wished to use the house as a home for herself and the children of the family. Thus by applying for a decree of division and sale, a spouse could frustrate the underlying purpose of owning a matrimonial home, ie to provide a home for the co-owning spouse and their family.

Section 19 of the 1981 Act and s 110 of the 2004 Act provide a partial solution to this problem. Where a matrimonial or family home is owned in common by a married couple or civil partners, if one of the spouses or civil partners brings an action for the division and sale of the property, the court has a discretion, after having regard to all the circumstances of the case, to refuse or postpone the granting of the decree, or only to grant the decree subject to conditions. The court is expressly directed to consider the factors listed in s 3(3) of the 1981 Act and s 103(3) in the 2004 Act and whether the spouse or civil partner bringing the action has offered to make suitable alternative accommodation available to the other spouse or civil partner.[4]

It is not clear where the onus lies in respect to s 19 and s 110 applications. In *Hall v Hall*,[5] the Sheriff Principal (Caplan), arguing by analogy with dispensation of consent under s 7 of the 1981 Act,[6] held that the onus lay on the spouse seeking the sale to show that the sale is reasonable. On the other hand, in *Berry v Berry*,[7] Lord Sutherland held that as a co-owner has a prima facie right to an action of division and sale, the onus lay on the defender to show why it was unreasonable for the sale to go ahead. In practice, however, the court will not allow a sale to go ahead when the continued occupation of the matrimonial home is clearly in the interests of the defender and the family.

The needs of children are important.[8] In *Crow v Crow*,[9] Lord Wylie held that s 19 of the 1981 Act had made very material inroads into the rights of pro indiviso proprietors who were married. In particular, he stressed that the needs of the family were crucial. Accordingly, he had no hesitation in postponing the grant of a decree of division and sale beyond a date when the marriage would be terminated by divorce.[10] So for example, if H applies for an action of division and sale, the court could delay granting decree until any children of the marriage reach the age of 18, even though the couple may divorce before the youngest child has reached that age.

It is important to note that s 19 of the 1981 Act and s 110 of the 2004 Act are only applicable when the co-owners are spouses or civil partners. If after divorce or dissolution, an ex-spouse or civil partner applies for an action of division and sale, he or she must be granted decree.[11] Moreover, if, during the marriage or civil partnership, a spouse or civil partner sells his or her one half pro indiviso share to a third party, the third party is entitled to a decree of division and sale as s 19 and s 110 only apply when both co-owners of the matrimonial or family home are married to or in a civil partnership with each other.[12]

Where both spouses and civil partners are common owners of the matrimonial or family home, ie entitled spouses, the court has the same powers under s 3 of the 1981 Act and s 103 of the 2004 Act to make regulatory orders in respect of its occupation as it has when there is an entitled and non-entitled spouse or civil partner.[13] Similarly, the court may make an exclusion order under s 4 of the 1981 Act and s 104 of the 2004 Act where both spouses or civil partners are entitled in exactly the same way as in the case of an entitled and non-entitled spouse or civil partner.[14] The availability of exclusion orders as an important step towards the protection of victims of domestic violence cannot be over-estimated.

1    1951 SC 359.
2    Matrimonial Homes (Family Protection) (Scotland) Act 1981, s 2(4) and (6); Civil Partnership Act 2004, s 102(4) and (6).
3    1982 SLT 128.
4    MH(FP)(S)A 1981, s 19(a) and (b); CPA 2004, s 110(a) and (b). The offer must be of specific alternative accommodation; a general offer to help a co-owning spouse find somewhere to live is not enough. See *Hall v Hall* 1987 SLT (Sh Ct) 15.
5    1987 SLT (Sh Ct) 15. See also *Milne v Milne* 1994 SLT (Sh Ct) 57, where the approach in *Hall* was followed.
6    Discussed at para **5.10**.
7    1988 SCLR 296. The sale was ordered in this case. The most appropriate method of sale is by private treaty in open market: *Berry v Berry (No 2)* 1989 SLT 292. Where a spouse refused to pay a capital sum payment as financial provision on divorce, he was forced to sell his pro indiviso share of the former matrimonial home to his co-owning former spouse: *Scrimgeour v Scrimgeour* 1988 SLT 590. This was an exceptional case.
8    See, for example, *Milne v Milne* 1994 SLT (Sh Ct) 57 (W and children lived in home for 18 years: not fair and reasonable that they should have to move). Significantly, in *Berry v Berry* 1998 SCLR 296, the couple had no children; but a home was not required for the children in *Hall v Hall* 1987 SLT (Sh Ct) 15, yet the sale was refused. In *Rae v Rae* 1991 SLT 454, *Berry* was distinguished on the ground that in *Rae* the home was required for the wife and child of the marriage.
9    1986 SLT 270.
10   Indeed a divorce action was pending in this case.
11   *Burrows v Burrows* 1996 SC 378. H agreed to refrain from bringing an action of division and sale for five years after the couple divorced; although H could not raise the action during that period, he had an absolute right to division and sale after the five years had expired.
12   However, this 'dodge' may be caught by Matrimonial Homes (Family Protection) (Scotland) Act 1981, s 9(1)(a) which provides that the co-owning spouse's rights 'in that home' are not to be prejudiced by any dealing of the other spouse: Civil Partnership Act 2004, s 109(1)(a) is to the same effect. Curiously, s 9(2) appears to apply ss 6(3) and 7 of the 1981 Act to the situation where both spouses are entitled. But these provisions would appear to be concerned with the statutory rights of

occupation of non-entitled spouses: it could hardly have been Parliament's intention that, for example, a spouse could be compelled to sell his or her pro indiviso share on the grounds of withholding consent unreasonably. *Sed quaere*. Again the CPA 2004, s 109(2) raises a similar question.

13   See para **5.8** ff.

14   See para **5.9** ff.

*Tenancies*

**5.12** By s 13(1) of the 1981 Act and s 112(1) of the 2004 Act, a non-entitled spouse or civil partner can apply to a court for an order transferring the tenancy of the matrimonial or family home from the entitled to the non-entitled spouse or civil partner subject to the non-entitled spouse or partner paying just and reasonable compensation to the entitled spouse or civil partner.

Notice must be given to the landlord who has to be given an opportunity to be heard in the proceedings. In deciding whether the tenancy should be transferred, the court is directed to consider the factors in s 3(3) of the 1981 Act and s 103(3) of the 2004 Act[1] and whether the non-entitled spouse or civil partner is suitable to become a tenant and to perform the obligations in the lease. There are exceptions where the matrimonial home is, for example, part of an agricultural holding or a croft.[2] An order granting an application under s 13(1) of the 1981 Act or s 112(1) of the 2004 Act can be made on granting a decree of divorce or dissolution or declarator of nullity of marriage or civil partnership.[3]

Where both spouses or civil partners are joint or common tenants there is a similar right to apply to a court for an order vesting the tenancy in the applicant's name solely, provided that the applicant pays just and reasonable compensation to the other spouse or civil partner.[4] Where an entitled spouse or civil partner is the tenant of a matrimonial or family home, the non-entitled spouse or civil partner retains possession of the tenancy and therefore the protection of the Rent (Scotland) Act 1984 if the entitled spouse or civil partner leaves home.[5]

1   See para **5.8**. Thus in *McGowan v McGowan* 1986 SLT 112, Lord Kincraig ordered the transfer of a tenancy in H's name to his wife. H had been violent during the

marriage and had had an adulterous affair. W was living with the son of the marriage in overcrowded conditions with her married daughter. Lord Kincraig thought it would be a 'travesty of justice' if H was allowed to retain occupation of the matrimonial home.

2   For a full list, see the Matrimonial Homes (Family Protection) (Scotland) Act 1981, s 13(7) and (8); Civil Partnership Act 2004, s 112(8).
3   MH(FP)(S)A 1981, s 13(2); CPA 2004, s 112(2).
4   MH(FP)(S)A 1981, s 13(9); CPA 2004, s 112(10).
5   MH(FP)(S)A 1981, s 2(8), reversing the decision in *Temple v Mitchell* 1956 SC 267; CPA 2004, s 102(8).

## Matrimonial and relevant interdicts

**5.13** A spouse or civil partner's right to occupy the matrimonial or family home can, of course, be undermined as a result of the other spouse or civil partner's violent behaviour. Since this is so, it is thought to be convenient to discuss the law relating to matrimonial and relevant interdicts in this section.

In the leading case of *Tattersall v Tattersall*, the Lord President (Emslie) opined[1] that 'interdict in the law of Scotland is designed only to prevent the apprehended commission of a wrong'. Interdict is granted at common law to protect property rights. Thus in *MacLure v MacLure*,[2] for example, a husband who owned a hotel which was also used as the matrimonial home obtained an interdict against his wife who had no real right in the property from entering the hotel. Interdict is also granted to protect the integrity of the person and therefore one spouse can obtain interdict against molestation by the other.[3]

It is a fundamental principle of Scots law that an interdict must be granted in sufficiently precise terms to leave the defender in no doubt as to what he or she can or cannot do and that the conduct prohibited should be no wider than is necessary to curb the defender's illegal actions. Thus in *Murdoch v Murdoch*[4] an interim interdict preventing a husband from telephoning his wife or calling at her house was incompetent by reason of being too wide.

The major drawback of an interdict at common law was the question of enforcement. Where there was an alleged breach of interdict, a petition and complaint had to be brought with the concurrence of the Lord Advocate or procurator fiscal, to establish to the courts that a breach of the interdict had taken place.[5] The action was civil and the police had no power to arrest a person merely because he or she was in breach of interdict, though they could, of course, intervene if a crime or offence, for example an assault, had occurred.

The Matrimonial Homes (Family Protection) (Scotland) Act 1981 introduced a system of matrimonial interdicts to which the court must, in certain circumstances, attach a power of arrest. Where a power of arrest is attached to an interdict, a police constable may arrest the defender without warrant if the constable has reasonable cause to suspect that the defender is in breach of an interdict. The Civil Partnership Act 2004 introduced a similar system of relevant interdicts for civil partners.

Section 14(1) of the 1981 Act and s 113(1) of the 2004 Act provide that it shall not be incompetent for a court to entertain an application by a spouse or civil partner for a matrimonial or relevant interdict by reason only that the spouses or civil partners are living together. This clarifies the doubt which had existed at common law about the competency of such an application.[6]

By s 14(2) of the 1981 Act and s 113(2) of the 2004 Act a matrimonial or relevant interdict means an interdict, including an interim interdict, which:[7]

   '(a)   restrains or prohibits any conduct of one spouse or civil partner towards the other spouse or civil partner or a child of the family; or

   (b)   prohibits a spouse or civil partner from entering or remaining in—

      (i)   a matrimonial or family home,

      (ii)  any other residence occupied by the applicant spouse or civil partner,

      (iii) any place of work of the applicant spouse or civil partner,

      (iv) any school attended by a child in the permanent or temporary care of the applicant spouse or civil partner ...'

There is little difficulty in relation to s 14(2)(a) or s 113(2)(a) interdicts, ie non-molestation interdicts. It appears that the criteria in *Murdoch v*

*Murdoch*[8] are still followed and that the interdict must specify the conduct prohibited which should be no wider than necessary to prevent the illegal act, ie the molestation of the other spouse or a child of the family.

In relation to s 14(2)(b)(i) and s 113(2)(b)(i), it will be clear that the effect of such an interdict is to exclude the defender from the matrimonial or family home. Where the applicant is a non-entitled spouse or civil partner or both applicant and defender are entitled, resort must be made to s 4 or s 104 for an exclusion order and the interdict can be granted as ancillary to that order. Even where the applicant is an entitled spouse or civil partner and the defender non-entitled, the interdict can only be granted as ancillary to a s 4 or s 104 exclusion order unless the defender has not been given leave to exercise his or her statutory rights.[9] As a result, before a s 14(2)(b)(i) or s 113(2)(b)(i) interdict is granted, in the vast majority of cases the applicant must have obtained an exclusion order which will only be granted if it is necessary to do so.[10]

Where a matrimonial or family interdict is made which is ancillary to an exclusion order the court *must* attach a power of arrest to such an interdict if this is requested by the applicant.[11] In relation to any other matrimonial or family interdict, for example a non-molestation interdict under s 14(2)(a) or s 113(2)(a), the court must attach a power of arrest if it is satisfied that it is necessary to do so to prevent the interdict being breached. When a power of arrest is attached to a matrimonial or family interdict, a police constable may arrest the non-applicant spouse without a warrant if the constable has reasonable cause for suspecting that the defender is in breach of the interdict.

Where the court considers that an interdict may not be sufficient to stop the molestation, it is competent to make a non-harassment order under the Protection from Harassment Act 1997, s 58.[12]

---

1    *Tattersall v Tattersall* 1983 SLT 506 at 509.
2    1911 SC 200.
3    This was certainly the case if the spouses were living apart; it was uncertain whether interdict was available when they were cohabiting: but see now Matrimonial Homes (Family Protection) (Scotland) Act 1981, s 14 and Civil Partnership Act 2004, s 113.
4    1973 SLT (Notes) 13.
5    *Gribben v Gribben* 1976 SLT 266.

6   See note 3 above.
7   MH(FP)(S)A 1981, s 14(2); CPA 2004, s 113(2).
8   1973 SLT (Notes) 13.
9   MH(FP)(S)A 1981, s 14(3), (4) and (5); CPA 2004, s 113(3), (4) and (5). Before these provisions were enacted an entitled spouse could obtain such an interdict against a non-entitled spouse on the balance of convenience as the interdict was treated as simply protecting the entitled spouse's real right of ownership in the property: the entitled spouse did not have firstly to obtain an exclusion order. See *Tattersall v Tattersall* 1983 SLT 506.
10   On exclusion orders, see para **5.9** above.
11   Protection from Abuse (Scotland) Act 2001, s 1(1A).
12   *McCann v McGurran* 2002 SLT 592. Interim non-harassment orders are not competent. See also *McGuire v Kidston* 2002 SLT (Sh Ct) 66.

## Mortgage Rights (Scotland) Act 2001

**5.14**   A creditor in a standard security has a statutory right to enforce the security on default of the debtor. This can include inter alia the sale of the property. When the debtor's land is residential property, the Mortgage Rights (Scotland) Act 2001 provides that inter alia the following persons can apply to have the exercise of the creditor's rights suspended for a reasonable period:[1]

(1)   the debtor, where the property is his or her sole or main residence;[2]

(2)   the non-entitled spouse or civil partner of the debtor, if the property is a matrimonial or family home and the sole or main residence of the non-entitled spouse or civil partner;[3]

Where a house has been acquired by means of a loan which is secured by a standard security over the property in favour of the lender, the effect of the 2001 Act is to ensure that the debtor and his family are given some protection from eviction in the event of the debtor's default in the re-payment of the loan.

1   Mortgage Rights (Scotland) Act 2001, s 2. In theory, the suspension could be indefinite as no maximum period is stipulated.
2   MR(S)A 2001, s 1(2)(a).
3   MR(S)A 2001, s 1(2)(b).

# Chapter 6

# Divorce and dissolution

## INTRODUCTION

**6.1** Divorce on the ground of adultery has been recognised at common law since the Reformation and divorce for desertion was introduced by statute in 1573.[1] Until the Divorce (Scotland) Act 1938, these remained the only two grounds of divorce. The 1938 Act introduced further grounds: cruelty, incurable insanity, sodomy and bestiality.[2] With the exception of incurable insanity, the grounds of divorce were fault-based and divorce was perceived as a punishment for the defender's matrimonial offence.

Divorce for incurable insanity was manifestly a non-fault ground and to this can be traced the idea that divorce should be regarded as a remedy to enable a spouse to escape from a dead marriage. This view of divorce gradually became more prevalent. For example, as the result of judicial and statutory developments,[3] any requirement of moral fault on the part of a defender was whittled away from the concept of cruelty so that the pursuer could obtain a divorce whenever the defender's conduct was detrimental to the pursuer's health.

By the 1960s the movement for the reform of divorce law on the basis of a 'non-fault' ground of irretrievable breakdown of marriage had built up considerable momentum.[4] The Law Commission took the view that a system based on the matrimonial offence did not achieve the objectives of a good divorce law which were:

'(1)  to buttress, rather than to undermine, the stability of marriage; and

(2)  where, regrettably, a marriage has irretrievably broken down, to enable the empty legal shell to be destroyed with the maximum fairness, and the minimum bitterness, distress and humiliation.'[5]

However, the Law Commission considered that it was impracticable to make irretrievable breakdown of marriage the sole ground of divorce. How was breakdown to be established without some form of inquisitorial procedure alien to an adversarial system of adjudication? Would not this involve a new system of courts or tribunals manned by social workers rather than lawyers? Was not the equation of matrimony with a commercial partnership too revolutionary a concept for contemporary British society? The Scottish Law Commission recommended merely the addition of new separation grounds to the existing grounds of divorce but considered that the legal effect of the grounds was that they established that a marriage had in fact broken down.[6]

In England, a compromise was reached between the concept of non-fault divorce based on irretrievable breakdown and the existing matrimonial offences in the Divorce Reform Act 1969, later consolidated in the Matrimonial Causes Act 1973. Although irretrievable breakdown was to be the sole ground of divorce, it could only be established by proof of at least one of five guideline facts, which included modified versions of the previous matrimonial offences and two new facts based on separation.[7]

The Divorce (Scotland) Act 1976 follows a similar compromise. In its Report on the Reform of the Ground of Divorce[8] the Scottish Law Commission recommended important changes to the ground of divorce which were implemented in the Family Law (Scotland) Act 2006. An additional ground of divorce, that an interim gender recognition certificate has been issued to either party, was added by the Gender Recognition Act 2004.

The grounds for the dissolution of a civil partnership mirror those of divorce, with one important exception: adultery is not a ground for the dissolution of a civil partnership.

---

1   Act of 1573 (c 55).
2   The Divorce (Scotland) Act 1938 also enabled a marriage to be dissolved on the ground of the presumed death of one of the spouses.
3   Most importantly, the Divorce (Scotland) Act 1964, s 5.
4   See, for example, *Putting Asunder: A Divorce Law for Contemporary Society* (1996) Society for Propagation of Christian Knowledge.
5   Reform of the Grounds of Divorce: The Field of Choice (Cmnd 3123), para 15.
6   Divorce: The Grounds Considered (Cmnd 3256) (1967).
7   Matrimonial Causes Act 1973, s 1.
8   Scot Law Com No 116.

## IRRETRIEVABLE BREAKDOWN OF MARRIAGE OR CIVIL PARTNERSHIP

**6.2** If a system of divorce or dissolution is based on the sole ground of irretrievable breakdown of marriage or civil partnership as opposed to the concept of matrimonial offence, two consequences should follow. First, a pursuer should be entitled to a divorce or dissolution whenever the marriage or civil partnership has in fact broken down irretrievably. It is irrelevant that the defender's conduct was morally blameless. Moreover, and more importantly, it is irrelevant that the pursuer's conduct could be perceived to have contributed to the failure of the relationship. If, for example, a pursuer has committed adultery, this should not be held against him or her; the adultery is merely a symptom of the breakdown. Secondly, even though the defender's conduct amounts to what formerly constituted a matrimonial offence, for example adultery, the pursuer should not be entitled to a divorce unless the marriage has in fact broken down. There should therefore be built into the system provisions for establishing whether or not reconciliation is possible and to encourage reconciliation where this possibility exists.

As a result of the fact that the current law is a compromise between the concept of irretrievable breakdown and misconduct, the full implications of a non-fault theory of divorce or dissolution have been ignored. Section 1(1)(a) of the Divorce (Scotland) Act 1976 and s 117(2)(a) of the Civil Partnership Act 2004 provide that irretrievable breakdown of marriage or civil partnership is a ground of divorce or dissolution. However, irretrievable breakdown is only relevant if, and only if, it is established in accordance with later provisions in the legislation. Section 1(2) of the D(S)A 1976 and s 117(3) of the CPA 2004 provide that irretrievable breakdown will be taken to be established on proof of:

(a)  the defender's adultery (this does not apply to dissolution of a civil partnership);

(b)  the defender's behaviour;

(c)  the non-cohabitation of the parties for one year and their consents; or

(d)  the non-cohabitation of the parties for two years.

Thus a pursuer will be unable to obtain a divorce or dissolution unless he or she can prove one of the facts or guidelines in s 1(2) or s 117(3) even though the marriage or civil partnership has in fact irretrievably broken down. Conversely, a pursuer will be entitled to a divorce or dissolution if one of the facts or guidelines is established, even though the marriage or civil partnership has not in fact irretrievably broken down. In other words, proof of a s 1(2) or s 117(3) fact or guideline is both a necessary and sufficient condition of establishing irretrievable breakdown within the meaning of the Divorce (Scotland) Act 1976 and the Civil Partnership Act 2004. Irretrievable breakdown in the context of the Scots law of divorce and dissolution is simply an artificial legal construct enabling a party who can prove one or more of the facts and guidelines in s 1(2) or s 117(3) to obtain a divorce or dissolution.[1] The concept of fault has therefore not been eroded from the law.

Moreover, because the 1976 and the 2004 Acts are not concerned with whether a marriage or civil partnership has *in fact* broken down irretrievably, it is significant that they contain no provisions for compulsory attempts at reconciliation nor is there any obligation on solicitors to discuss with clients the possibility of reconciliation.[2] If, however, it appears to the court that there is a reasonable prospect of reconciliation, the court can continue the action for an attempt to be made,[3] but in practice it is unlikely that reconciliation is possible once the action has begun. In these circumstances, it is hypocritical to regard irretrievable breakdown as the ground of divorce or dissolution: the provisions of s 1(2) of the D(S)A 1976 and s 117(3) of the CPA 2004 constitute grounds for divorce and dissolution in Scots law, not simply facts or guidelines to determine whether a marriage or civil partnership has in fact irretrievably broken down.

---

1   The phrase could as well be 'abracadabra': see W A Wilson 'Divorce for Abracadabra' 1976 SLT (News) 27.
2   Cf the Matrimonial Causes Act 1973, s 6. However, a Court of Session *Practice Note* of 11 March 1977 enjoins practitioners to encourage clients to seek marriage counselling if the clients might benefit. There are also provisions in the Court of Session and sheriff court rules under which parties can be advised to attempt mediation in respect of the residence of any children of the marriage.
3   Divorce (Scotland) Act 1976, s 2(1); Civil Partnership Act 2004, s 118.

---

# THE GROUNDS OF DIVORCE AND DISSOLUTION

## Adultery

**6.3** By s 1(2)(a) of the Divorce (Scotland) Act 1976, irretrievable breakdown of marriage is established if 'since the date of the marriage the defender has committed adultery'.

Adultery has been defined as voluntary sexual intercourse between a married person and a person of the opposite sex, not being the married partner. The sexual intercourse must be voluntary; thus a woman who is the victim of rape is not guilty of adultery.[1]

The physical requirements of adultery were discussed by Lord Wheatley in *MacLennan v MacLennan*.[2] The pursuer sought a divorce on the ground of his wife's adultery. She had gone to the United States and returned with a child which the pursuer could not have fathered. Her defence was that she had conceived the child as a result of artificial insemination from a donor (AID). Although Lord Wheatley regarded the wife's conception of a child by AID without her husband's consent as 'a grave and heinous breach of the contract of marriage', it did not amount to adultery. Adultery involved a mutual surrender of the sexual and reproductive organs and some degree of penetration of the woman's vagina was necessary: in Lord Wheatley's words adultery necessitated 'physical contact with an alien and unlawful sexual organ, and without that element there cannot be what the law regards as adultery'.[3] He therefore dismissed the argument that adultery could be committed by a woman 'when alone in the privacy of her bedroom, she injects into her ovum by means of a syringe the seed of a man she does not know and has never seen'.[4]

A defender's adultery is only relevant if it has occurred 'since the date of the marriage'. Thus, if a young man commits adultery with a married woman and subsequently marries, his spouse cannot rely upon his pre-marital adultery to found an action of divorce. A single isolated act of adultery will suffice.

Where the defender has been found guilty of rape or incest by a United Kingdom court evidence of his conviction can be used to establish adultery provided a third party identifies the defender as the person convicted.[5]

Moreover, a finding of adultery in earlier matrimonial proceedings is admissible in divorce proceedings to establish adultery, but, once again, a third party must identify the defender as the party in the earlier proceedings.[6]

Section 1(3A) of the D(S)A 1976 provides 'For the avoidance of doubt, in relation to marriage between persons of the same sex, adultery has the same meaning as it has in relation to marriage between persons of different sexes.' This means that a same sex spouse can be divorced on the ground of adultery if that spouse has sexual intercourse with a person of the opposite sex. If the spouse has a homosexual relationship with another person during the marriage, that does not amount to adultery but would constitute unreasonable behaviour. This is in contrast with civil partnerships where adultery is not a ground for dissolution but would constitute unreasonable behaviour.

In an action of divorce on the ground of adultery, the pursuer may be met by certain defences. It should be noted that as a result of s 14 of the Family Law (Scotland) Act 2006, collusion is no longer a bar to divorce on any of the grounds of divorce.

---

1   The fact that a person believes in good faith that he or she is not married does not prevent them from being guilty of adultery: *Sands v Sands* 1964 SLT 80.
2   1958 SC 105.
3   *MacLennan v MacLennan* 1958 SC 105 at 114.
4   1958 SC 105 at 114. AID without the husband's consent could give rise to a divorce based on the Divorce (Scotland) Act 1976, s 1(2)(b), as would other forms of sexual gratification not involving sexual intercourse.
5   Law Reform (Miscellaneous Provisions) (Scotland) Act 1968, s 10; *Andrews v Andrews* 1971 SLT (Notes) 44.
6   LR(MP)(S)A 1968, s 11.

---

*Lenocinium*

**6.4** The common law defence of *lenocinium* was preserved by s 1(3) of the Divorce (Scotland) Act 1976. The defence of *lenocinium* is difficult to define.[1] The essence of the defence is that the pursuer actively promoted the defender's adultery or was art and part in the offence. This would cover, for example, a husband who encouraged his wife to take up prostitution or a wife who suggested to her husband that they should join a 'spouse swapping' party. The defence can be illustrated by the leading case of *Gallacher v Gallacher*,[2] where a husband sent a letter to his wife entreating her to do something to enable him to divorce her. A few months later, the wife fell passionately in love with another man. In divorce proceedings based on adultery, the action failed on account of *lenocinium*. The court refused to accept the husband's contention that the adultery arose as a result of the wife's passion for her lover rather than his letter. As Lord Anderson said,[3]

'No woman invited by her husband to commit adultery would go into the street and offer herself to the first man she met. Affection for her lover must always be a cause, and it may be the main cause of her lapse from virtue'.

However, the husband's letter had been the reason why she had even contemplated adultery. Lord Ormidale took the view that:[4]

'Passion no doubt was a factor before she finally fell, but I have no doubt that but for the letter and invitation of her husband, she would have resisted and not responded to the advances [of her lover]'.

Thus the pursuer's conduct does not have to be *the* cause (*causa causans*) of the adultery; it is sufficient if it is a cause (*conditio sine qua non*).

Six years later, Gallacher again attempted to obtain a divorce.[5] This time he was successful. The wife had continued to live with her lover but the court held that her continuing adulterous relationship was no longer caused by the pursuer's letter. Lord Hunter maintained[6] that the husband's act of connivance six years before could not be regarded as a perpetual licence to the wife to commit adultery for the rest of her lifetime: on the facts, the defender no longer required his encouragement. Consequently, the defence of *lenocinium* failed as the wife could no longer show that her husband's letter was a cause of her continuing her adulterous affair.

It is important to stress that before *lenocinium* can be established, the pursuer must actively encourage the defender's adultery. In *Thomson v Thomson*,[7] the pursuer thought that his wife was having an affair. When she asked him for money to visit friends, he suspected she was going to meet her lover. Nevertheless he gave her the money she requested but had her followed by inquiry agents. They discovered her committing adultery in Gateshead. The wife's defence of *lenocinium* failed on the ground that since she believed she had succeeded in keeping the knowledge of her affair from her husband, he could not have been actively encouraging her to commit adultery when he gave her the money she requested – albeit that he suspected how she would in fact use it. Similarly, it is not *lenocinium* to hire inquiry agents to watch a spouse suspected of adultery.[8]

1   See *Gallacher v Gallacher* 1928 SC 586 at 591, per Lord Justice-Clerk (Alness).
2   1928 SC 586.
3   1928 SC 586 at 599.
4   1928 SC 586 at 595.
5   *Gallacher v Gallacher* 1934 SC 339.
6   1934 SC 339 at 346.
7   1908 SC 179.
8   For proposals that *lenocinium* should be replaced by a defence of actively promoting or encouraging adultery, see Report on Family Law (Scot Law Com No 135) Recommendation 67. This recommendation was not implemented by the Family Law (Scotland) Act 2006.

*Condonation*

**6.5** By s 1(3) of the Divorce (Scotland) Act 1976, the defender's adultery will not be a ground of divorce if it has been 'condoned by the pursuer's cohabitation with the defender in the knowledge or belief that the defender has committed the adultery'. Section 13(2) of the 1976 Act provides that for the purposes of the Act 'the parties to a marriage shall be held to cohabit with one another only when they are in fact living together as man and wife'.[1] Thus the parties must in fact live together as man and wife before the defence is operative; verbal forgiveness[1] or an isolated act of sexual intercourse will not suffice.

But s 1(3) must be read with s 2(2) of the 1976 Act. Section 2(2) provides that adultery will not be condoned unless the pursuer has continued or resumed cohabitation with the defender at any time after the end of a period of three months from the date on which cohabitation was continued or resumed.

Some examples will illustrate how this section operates: in all cases it is assumed that the pursuer knows or believes the defender has committed adultery.

(1)     If the pursuer continues to cohabit with the defender for less than three months, adultery is not condoned.

(2)     If the pursuer continues to cohabit with the defender for more than three months, adultery is condoned.

(3)     If the pursuer continues to cohabit with the defender for less than three months but then resumes cohabitation, the adultery will be condoned if cohabitation takes place at any time after a three-month period beginning from the date when he knew or believed the defender was committing adultery and continued to cohabit.

**Example**

(a)     P learns of D's adultery on 31 January. P continues to cohabit with D for a week. If P resumes cohabitation, for however short a period, after 30 April, the adultery will be condoned as the resumption of cohabitation took place outside the three-month period beginning on 31 January.

(b)     P learns of D's adultery on 31 January. P continues to cohabit with D for a week. If P resumes cohabitation on 1 April, the adultery will not be condoned if P leaves before 1 May. But if the cohabitation continues beyond or is resumed after 30 April, the adultery will be condoned as cohabitation has taken place outside the three-month period beginning on 31 January.

(4)     If P ceases cohabitation with D but resumes cohabitation for less than three months, the adultery will not be condoned.

(5)     If P ceases cohabitation with D but resumes cohabitation for more than three months, the adultery will be condoned.

(6)     If P ceases cohabitation with D but resumes cohabitation for less than three months, the adultery will be condoned if cohabitation takes place at any time after a three-month period from the date of the initial resumption.

**Example**

(a)     P learns of D's adultery. He ceases to cohabit for a year. P resumes cohabitation on 31 January. P continues to cohabit with D for a week. If P resumes cohabitation, for however short a period, after 30 April, the adultery will be condoned as cohabitation has taken place outwith the three-month period beginning on 31 January when cohabitation was first resumed.

(b) P learns of D's adultery. He ceases to cohabit for a year. P resumes cohabitation on 31 January. P continues to cohabit with D for a week. If P resumes cohabitation on 1 April, the adultery will not be condoned if he leaves before 1 May. But if cohabitation continues beyond or is resumed after 30 April, the adultery will be condoned as cohabitation has taken place outwith the three-month period beginning on 31 January.

It is thought that s 1(3) of the Divorce (Scotland) Act 1976 only operates as a defence in relation to the adultery on which the action is founded. Thus if the pursuer cohabited in the knowledge or belief that the defender committed adultery with A, it would not operate as a bar to an action based on the defender's adultery with B. Similarly, if the pursuer knew or believed that the defender had committed specific acts of adultery, s 1(3) would not operate in relation to other acts of adultery which subsequently came to the pursuer's knowledge.

As we have noted, adultery is not a ground for the dissolution of a civil partnership.

---

1    'Man and wife' must be read as referring to same sex as well as opposite sex spouses: Marriage and Civil Partnership (Scotland) Act 2014, s 4.
2    This was the position at common law: *Annan v Annan* 1948 SC 532.

---

## Behaviour

**6.6** By s 1(2)(b) of the Divorce (Scotland) Act 1976, and s 117(3)(a) of the Civil Partnership Act 2004, irretricvable breakdown of marriage or civil partnership is established if:

'since the date of the marriage [or registration of the civil partnership] the defender has at any time behaved (whether or not as a result of mental abnormality and whether such behaviour has been active or passive) in such a way that the pursuer cannot reasonably be expected to cohabit with the defender'.

The defender's conduct must have occurred after the date of the marriage or registration of the civil partnership; a spouse or civil partner's behaviour before the marriage or registration of the civil partnership is irrelevant. Thus for example, a husband cannot use s 1(2)(b) to obtain a divorce on the ground that he was induced to marry the defender as a result of her fraudulent misrepresentation that she was pregnant by him: the wife's behaviour, ie the lie, took place *before* the date of the marriage.[1] Similarly, a man who discovers that his civil partner had committed a heinous offence before the registration of their civil partnership, cannot rely on this offence to obtain a dissolution.[2]

Before s 1(2)(b) of the D(S)A 1976 or s 117(3) of the CPA 2004 is applicable, the defender must have behaved. What does behaviour mean in this context? A mere physical condition does not per se constitute behaviour. For example, if a defender is incontinent, that in itself does not amount to behaviour. But if an incontinent spouse refused to wear protective underwear, the refusal to do so would constitute behaviour. However, it is settled that symptoms of an illness can in certain circumstances amount to behaviour. If for example, a civil partner became violent as a result of an illness, the violence would clearly constitute behaviour. But it can be difficult to determine when the symptom of an illness is merely a physical condition and when it amounts to behaviour. Thus a husband's sleepiness and general lack of interest in his family caused by schizophrenia has been held to amount to behaviour[3] and bad personal hygiene as a result of disseminated sclerosis has not.[4]

A solution to this problem may be that the D(S)A 1976 and the CPA 2004 include behaviour 'whether such behaviour has been active or passive'. In *Thurlow v Thurlow*[5] it has been accepted in England that where as a result of a debilitating illness a spouse is unable to fulfil the obligations of marriage, this failure can constitute behaviour for the purposes of divorce. As the 1976 and 2004 Acts have expressly enacted that behaviour may be passive,[6] it is thought that the principle in *Thurlow* has been transplanted into Scots law. Thus for example, if an illness prevents a spouse from fulfilling the obligations of married life, this passive negative behaviour – as opposed to the illness – can amount to grounds for divorce.[7]

The fact that a defender's behaviour is caused by mental illness is irrelevant: s 1(2)(b) of the D(S)A 1976 and s 117(3)(a) of the CPA 2004 expressly state that conduct will constitute behaviour 'whether or not as a result of mental illness'.[8]

The pursuer must establish that the defender behaved 'in such a way that the pursuer cannot reasonably be expected to cohabit with the defender'. The test is a compromise between a subjective and objective test. The criterion is whether the particular pursuer can, at the time of the action,[9] reasonably be expected to cohabit with the defender. Thus a highly sensitive spouse or civil partner may not reasonably be expected to put up with conduct which a spouse or civil partner of ordinary fortitude could withstand.[10] But because of the phrase 'reasonably be expected', utterly trivial conduct (for example, snoring)[11] or socially useful conduct (membership of a lifeboat or mountain rescue team) will not constitute grounds for divorce or dissolution, however sensitive the pursuer may be. In *Taylor v Taylor*,[12] the court held that the defender could not bring evidence to try to establish that, because of her Christian religious beliefs, the pursuer had to forgive his conduct and therefore it was not unreasonable for her to continue living with him!

The range of behaviour which could satisfy s 1(2)(b) of the D(S)A 1976 and s 117(3)(a) of the CPA 2004 is as wide as human conduct. It includes both physical[13] and verbal assaults. Moreover, as Lord Davidson explained in *Hastie v Hastie*,[14]

'conduct on the part of a defender, by word or act, may be of such a nature that even if there is no risk of a repetition it is so destructive of a marriage relationship as to make it unreasonable to expect the pursuer to cohabit with the defender'.

In relation to sexual behaviour, this would include, for example, excessive demands for sexual relations, wilful and unjustified refusal of sexual relations,[15] and sexual relations with a third party. Thus while homosexual relations with a third party do not amount to adultery, they will constitute unreasonable behaviour.[16] Excessive drunkenness[17] or abuse of other drugs would also suffice.

The mere fact that the pursuer has continued to cohabit with the defender after the alleged behaviour took place does not per se prevent the pursuer relying upon it for the purposes of s 1(2)(b) of the D(S)A 1976 or s 117(3)(a) of the CPA 2004. A woman who has been the victim of violence may continue to live with her husband or civil partner after the assaults through fear or because she has simply nowhere else to go.[18] But where the alleged behaviour is objectively trivial, the longer the pursuer remains with the defender, the more difficult it will be to establish that the pursuer cannot reasonably be expected to cohabit with the defender as a result of that conduct. The pursuer's conduct after separation, for example forming a new relationship, may be used as evidence to establish that the pursuer cannot reasonably be expected to live with the defender.[19]

By s 3(1) of the D(S)A 1976 and s 121 of the CPA 2004 if a decree of separation[20] has previously been granted in respect of the same, or substantially the same facts, an extract of the decree may be regarded as sufficient proof of these facts in an action for divorce or dissolution on the ground, inter alia, of behaviour, but the court must still receive further evidence from the pursuer of what has occurred between the parties since the date of the decree.[21] Finally, where the behaviour relied upon led to a criminal conviction of the defender by a United Kingdom court, s 10 of the Law Reform (Miscellaneous Provisions) (Scotland) Act 1968 is applicable.[22]

There are no specific defences in relation to s 1(2)(b) of the D(S)A 1976 or s 117(3)(a) of the CPA 2004.

---

1   On fraudulent misrepresentation, see para **2.17** ff.
2   Cf *Hastings v Hastings* 1941 SLT 323.
3   *Fullarton v Fullarton* 1976 SLT 8. However, the effect of the behaviour on the pursuer was not serious enough for the divorce to be granted.
4   *Grant v Grant* 1974 SLT (Notes) 54.
5   [1975] 2 All ER 979, [1976] Fam 32.
6   There is no express reference to passive behaviour in the Matrimonial Causes Act 1973, s 1(2)(b).
7   If this thesis is accepted doubt must be cast on such pre-1976 cases as *H v H* 1968 SLT 40, where a wife's frigidity which was caused by neurotic depression was held not to constitute cruelty. However, the frigidity would now amount to passive behaviour and the fact that it was a symptom of an illness is irrelevant.
8   In so doing the Divorce (Scotland) Act 1976 follows the policy of the Divorce (Scotland) Act 1964, s 5; *Williams v Williams* [1963] 2 All ER 994, [1964] AC 698, HL.

9  In *Findlay v Findlay* 1991 SLT 457, H drank and stayed out late. W suspected H was seeing another woman. The couple separated. At the time of the proof, W was living with another man. Her association was not per se enough to conclude that she could no longer reasonably be expected to cohabit with H. Lord Prosser stressed that there had to be a causal link between H's behaviour and the conclusion that W could not reasonably be expected to live with H. On the facts, H's behaviour led to W's separation and new relationship: there was therefore a causal link. Accordingly, because she was now living with another man, she could not reasonably be expected to cohabit with H at the time of the divorce action. See also *Knox v Knox* 1993 SCLR 381.

10 See, for example, *Livingstone-Stallard v Livingstone-Stallard* [1974] 3 All ER 766, [1974] Fam 47; *O'Neill v O'Neill* [1975] 3 All ER 289, [1975] 1 WLR 1118, CA. In *Meikle v Meikle* 1987 GWD 26-1005, a wife who came from a town background and went to live on her husband's hill farm obtained a divorce on the grounds that her husband spent too much time at work and she was disillusioned with life in the country. However, the fact that a husband had to work long hours in order to support his family has been held not to be sufficient to amount to unreasonable behaviour: *Ross v Ross* 1997 SLT (Sh Ct) 51.

11 Assuming, of course, that snoring constitutes behaviour.

12 2001 SCLR 16.

13 The assault need not be directed at the pursuer: *AB v CB* 1959 SC 27.

14 1985 SLT 146 at 148: wife's false accusation that husband was engaging in an incestuous association. See also *MacLeod v MacLeod* 1990 GWD 14-767: husband's unfounded suspicions of wife's adultery. A husband's boast that he was having an affair has been held to constitute unreasonable behaviour even though the wife could not establish adultery: *Stewart v Stewart* 1987 SLT (Sh Ct) 48.

15 In *Mason v Mason* (1980) *Times,* 5 December, CA, a wife's limitation of sexual intercourse to once a week was held in England not to be such that her husband could no longer reasonably be expected to cohabit.

16 *White v White* 1966 SC 187.

17 *Campbell v Campbell* 1973 SLT (Notes) 82.

18 See, for example, *Britton v Britton* 1973 SLT (Notes) 12; *Bradley v Bradley* [1973] 3 All ER 750, [1973] 1 WLR 1291, CA.

19 *Findlay v Findlay* 1991 SLT 457; *Knox v Knox* 1993 SCLR 381.

20 See para **6.11**.

21 This will usually simply be that the parties have neither lived together nor had sexual relations since the date of the decree of separation.

22 Discussed in the context of adultery at para **6.3**.

## Non-cohabitation for one year

**6.7** By s 1(2)(d) of the Divorce (Scotland) Act 1976 and s 117(3)(c) of the Civil Partnership Act 2004 irretrievable breakdown of marriage or civil partnership is established if:

'there has been no cohabitation between the parties [or civil partners] at any time during a continuous period of one year after the date of the marriage [or registration of the civil partnership] and immediately preceding the bringing of the action and the defender consents to the granting of the decree [or decree of dissolution of the civil partnership]'.

First, there must be no cohabitation between the parties for the requisite period. Section 13(2) of the 1976 Act provides that 'the parties to a marriage shall be held to cohabit with one another only when they are in fact living together as man and wife'.[1] Interpreted literally, a couple who are not *in fact* living together as man and wife are not cohabiting for the purpose of s 1(2)(d). The reason why they are not in fact living together is irrelevant. Thus, for example, if a couple are not living together because the husband is in prison or in hospital or working abroad, they are not cohabiting within the meaning of the D(S)A 1976.

Conversely, a couple may not be cohabiting within the meaning of s 13(2) of the D(S)A 1976 even though they live in close physical proximity. They will only be treated as cohabiting if they are in fact living together *as man and wife*. The absence of sexual relations will be an important factor in determining whether they are living in that capacity – but absence of sexual relations per se will probably not be enough. But if sexual relations have ceased, or the spouses provide no services for each other, or if they have no joint social life, then it is possible to argue that they are not living together as husband and wife even though they occupy the same house.[2]

There is no equivalent of s 13(2) in the CPA 2004. It is submitted, however, that the concept of non-cohabitation for the purposes of s 117(3)(c) should be interpreted in a similar way.

The non-cohabitation must be for a continuous period of at least one year after the date of the marriage or registration of the civil partnership and immediately preceding the bringing of the action. By s 2(4) of the D(S)A 1976 and s 119(3) of the CPA 2004, resumption of cohabitation for a period or periods not exceeding six months in all does not break the continuity of the period of non-cohabitation but does not count towards it.

### Example 1

D leaves P on 1 January 2013. The couple resume cohabitation on 1 July 2013. They separate on 1 October 2013. The action can be brought after 1 April 2014. The three-month period of cohabitation between 1 July and 1 October 2013 is less than six months and therefore does not break the continuity of the one year's non-cohabitation but does not count towards it.

**Example 2**

D leaves P on 1 January 2013. The couple resume cohabitation on 1 November 2013. They separate on 30 June 2014. The period of cohabitation between 1 November 2013 and 30 June 2014 is greater than six months. The continuity of the non-cohabitation after the separation on 1 January 2013 is broken and it is therefore impossible to establish that they have not cohabited for a continuous period of a year from that date. A divorce or dissolution based on continuous non-cohabitation for a year immediately preceding the bringing of the action can only be brought on 1 July 2015.

Finally, the defender must positively consent to the granting of the decree. Consent can be withdrawn at any time before decree. Moreover in *Boyle v Boyle*[3] Lord Maxwell held[4] that 'it is perfectly open to a defender to withhold consent for any reason he thinks fit or for no reason'. Thus the defender's consent can be used as a bargaining counter between the parties in reaching agreement over ancillary matters like financial provision on divorce or dissolution.

The divorce or dissolution can proceed as a simplified application for divorce or dissolution.[5] The pursuer is able to use s 3 of the D(S)A 1976 or s 121 of the CPA 2004 if a decree of separation has previously been granted on the ground of non-cohabitation.[6]

---

1   'Man and wife' must be read as referring to same sex as well as opposite sex spouses: Marriage and Civil Partnership (Scotland) Act 2014, s 4.
2   See, for example, *Samurai v Al-Samurai* [2014] CSOH 95.
3   1977 SLT (Notes) 69. See also *Donnelly v Donnelly* 1991 SLT (Sh Ct) 9.
4   1977 SLT (Notes) 69 at 69.
5   Simplified divorce and dissolution procedure is discussed at para **6.12** ff.
6   Discussed in relation to behaviour at para **6.6**.

## Non-cohabitation for two years

**6.8** By s 1(2)(e) of the Divorce (Scotland) Act 1976 and s 117(3)(d) of the Civil Partnership Act 2004 irretrievable breakdown of marriage or civil partnership is established if 'there has been no cohabitation between the parties [the civil partners] at any time during a continuous period of two years after the date of the marriage [or the date of registration of the civil partnership] and immediately preceding the bringing of the action'.

In relation to the meaning of non-cohabitation and continuity of non-cohabitation, this ground raises precisely the same legal issues as those in s 1(2)(d) and s 117(3)(c).[1] The difference is, of course, that the period of non-cohabitation is two years and the consent of the defender is *not* necessary. Accordingly, a defender who has not been guilty of a matrimonial or partnership offence can be divorced against his or her will. The rationale of this ground is that since the parties have not cohabited for two years, the marriage or civil partnership has in fact broken down irretrievably and consequently should be legally brought to an end.

The divorce or dissolution can proceed as a simplified application for divorce or dissolution.[2] The pursuer is able to use s 3 of the D(S)A 1976 or s 121 of the CPA 2004 if a decree of separation has previously been granted on the ground of non-cohabitation.

---

1   Discussed at para **6.7**.
2   Simplified divorce procedure is discussed at para **6.12** ff.

---

## Postponement of decree where religious impediment to remarry exists

**6.9** The grant of a decree of divorce, but not of dissolution of a civil partnership, may be postponed if s 3A of the Divorce (Scotland) Act 1976 is applicable. In certain religions, for example Judaism, a woman who has been divorced under Scots law is not allowed to enter a religious marriage unless she has also been divorced under the law of her religion. This may involve her husband divorcing her by delivering to her a document of divorce. In Judaism this is known as a gett. If he refuses to do so, not only will the woman be unable to re-marry in accordance with her religion, but she may also be ostracised by her family. Section 3A gives the court power to postpone the grant of decree of divorce until a religious divorce has taken place. So if H is seeking a divorce from W, W can apply under s 3A to have the grant of the decree of divorce postponed until H divorces her under the law of their religion so that she will have no religious impediment to having a religious marriage in the future.

The power to postpone grant of decree arises '[n]otwithstanding that irretrievable breakdown of a marriage has been established in an action of divorce'. The pursuer is therefore being denied a remedy to which he would otherwise be legally entitled. This is done for religious reasons, namely because the applicant is prevented from entering into a religious marriage by virtue of a requirement of that religion and the other party can remove or contribute to the removal of the impediment which prevents the religious marriage. In addition, the court must be satisfied that it is just and reasonable to postpone the grant of the decree.[1] The court can recall the postponement when it has received a certificate from the relevant religious body that the other party has acted to remove the impediment.[2] Where W is seeking a divorce from H, postponement of the decree will not help W to obtain a religious divorce from H if H does not want to divorce her.

---

1   Divorce (Scotland) Act 1976, s 3A(1)(b)(ii).
2   It can also recall the postponement even though this has not occurred: D(S)A 1976, s 3A(4).

---

### Divorce or dissolution on the ground that either party has been issued with an interim gender recognition certificate

**6.10** As we have seen,[1] a post-operative transsexual can apply for a gender recognition certificate when the acquired gender will be recognised as the applicant's sex. Where the applicant is married or is a party to a civil partnership, only an interim gender recognition certificate could be issued until the applicant divorced or the civil partnership was dissolved. The grant of an interim recognition certificate to a spouse or civil partner is a ground of divorce[2] or dissolution.[3] *Either* party to the marriage or civil partnership can seek a divorce or dissolution on this ground. The divorce or dissolution can proceed as a simplified application for divorce or dissolution.[4]

With the introduction of same sex marriage, the Gender Recognition Act 2004 has been amended[5]. The rules apply to protected Scottish marriages and protected Scottish partnerships. These are marriages solemnised in Scotland and civil partnerships registered in Scotland[6]. Where the applicant for a gender recognition certificate is a party to a protected marriage and the application contains a declaration that the applicant wishes the marriage to continue and a statutory declaration by the applicant's spouse that that spouse wishes the marriage to continue, then the General Recognition Panel will issue a full gender recognition certificate and the marriage will continue. If the applicant's spouse does not consent, the Panel will issue an interim gender recognition certificate. The applicant can then apply to a sheriff for a full gender recognition certificate which if the application was made within 6 months of the issue of the interim recognition certificate, the sheriff must grant[7]. While the marriage continues even though a full gender recognition certificate has been granted by the sheriff, the interests of the non-consenting spouse are protected as s 1 (3B) of D(S)A 1976 provides that the right to obtain a divorce which arose when the interim gender recognition certificate was issued does not lapse when the full gender certificate was granted.

Section 3A of the Divorce (Scotland) Act 1976[8] does not apply to a divorce on this ground.

---

1   See para **2.12**.
2   Divorce (Scotland) Act 1976, s 1(1)(b).
3   Civil Partnership Act 2004, s 117(2)(b).
4   Simplified divorce or dissolution procedure is discussed at para **6.12**.
5   By the Marriage and Civil Partnership Act 2014, Sch 2.
6   GRA 2004, s 25.
7   GRA 2004, s 4E.
8   See para **6.9**.

---

## JUDICIAL SEPARATION

**6.11** The grounds for judicial separation are exactly the same as the grounds for divorce or dissolution and the same defences apply.[1] The marriage or civil partnership still subsists and the spouses and civil partners remain under their obligation to aliment each other[2] and their obligations of fidelity and tolerable behaviour continue. Thus for example, a divorce can be sought on the ground of adultery committed after the decree of separation. If a decree of separation is obtained the same facts can be used as a ground for a subsequent divorce or dissolution.[3]

---

1  Divorce (Scotland) Act 1976, s 4; Civil Partnership Act 2004, s 120.
2  Discussed at para **3.8** ff. A pursuer can seek a decree of separation without craving for aliment: *Gray v Gray* 1991 SCLR 422.
3  Divorce (Scotland) Act 1976, s 3; Civil Partnership Act 2004, s 121.

---

## PROCEDURAL MATTERS

### Proof and simplified procedure

**6.12** As a general principle, a divorce or dissolution cannot be granted unless the ground of action has been proved, whether or not the action has been defended.[1] There is no need for corroboration but there must be evidence emanating from a source other than a party to the marriage or the civil partnership.[2] But where an action is undefended, unless the court otherwise directs, proof is by way of affidavits instead of parole evidence.[3] A simplified procedure – in effect a do-it-yourself divorce or dissolution – is possible.[4] However, its scope is severely restricted. An application can proceed if, and only if:

(1)  the pursuer relies on the facts set out in ss 1(2)(d) or (e) of the Divorce (Scotland) Act 1976, or ss 117(3)(c) or (d) of the Civil Partnership Act 2004 or the divorce or dissolution is based on the issue of an interim gender recognition certificate;

(2)  in relation to a divorce based on s 1(2)(d) of the D(S)A 1976, or a dissolution based on s 117(3)(c) of the CPA 2004, the other spouse or civil partner consents;

(3)  there are no proceedings pending in any court which could have the effect of bringing the marriage or civil partnership to an end;

(4)  there are no children of the marriage or of the family under the age of 16;

(5)  neither party is seeking financial provision on divorce or dissolution; and

(6)    neither party is suffering from a mental disorder.

The simplified procedure is an exception to the rule that in divorce actions the evidence from a source other than one or both of the spouses is required.

---

1    Proof is on the balance of probabilities: Divorce (Scotland) Act 1976, s 1(6) and the Civil Partnership Act 2004, s 117(8).
2    Civil Evidence (Scotland) Act 1988, ss 1(1), 8(1) and (3). See, for example, *Taylor v Taylor* 2001 SCLR 16.
3    Evidence in Undefended Divorce Actions (Scotland) Order 1983, SI 1983/949.
4    Divorce Jurisdiction, Court Fees and Legal Aid (Scotland) Act 1983, s 2. Rules of Court of Session 1994, rr 49.72 to 49.80; Act of Sederunt (Ordinary Cause Rules) Amendment (Civil Partnership Act 2004) 2005, SSI 2005/638, rr 33A.66 to 33A.75.

---

## Conclusion

**6.13** This chapter has primarily been an attempt to outline the substantive Scots law of divorce and dissolution of a civil partnership. In theory, the right to a divorce or dissolution is restrictive but in practice little difficulty is experienced in obtaining the necessary grounds. The vast majority of divorces and dissolutions are undefended[1] and there have been few reported decisions on the legal difficulties which the grounds in the Divorce (Scotland) Act 1976 and the Civil Partnership Act 2004 raise. In short, it would appear that in relation to establishing a ground of divorce or dissolution, as opposed to ancillary matters such as financial provision and the residence of children, the role of the court is largely administrative. But there must still be cases where a marriage or civil partnership has in fact irretrievably broken down, yet divorce or dissolution is not possible because a s 1(2) of the D(S)A 1976 or s 117(3) of the CPA 2004 ground cannot be established.

It should be accepted that in twenty-first century society there is and will continue to be a high rate of matrimonial and partnership breakdown.[2] The primary concerns of a modern divorce or dissolution law should be to attempt to protect the children of the relationship as much as possible and to provide a fair system for the re-allocation of the family's income and capital. There is force in the view that if the spouses and partners are agreed on these matters, they should be able to divorce or have their civil partnership dissolved by consent provided the court approves of the settlement. If the couple are not agreed, then the court, on an application by one of the spouses or civil partners, should allow the couple a period of say six months in which, with the assistance of their legal advisers, a settlement could be reached. If this is not achieved during that period, the court, on the application of one of the parties, should then make orders relating to parental responsibilities and financial provision and grant decree without the necessity of any grounds for divorce.

In its Discussion Paper, *The Ground for Divorce*,[3] the Scottish Law Commission put forward a radical proposal that divorce should be obtained by the lapse of a period after notice had been given on the lines suggested in the preceding paragraph: delayed divorce on demand. However, in its final Report[4] this proposal was abandoned. Instead, the Commission recommended that desertion be abolished as a ground of divorce and the periods of non-cohabitation for the purposes of the Divorce (Scotland) Act 1976, s 1(2)(d) and (e) be reduced to one year and two years respectively.[5] These recommendations were enacted in the Family Law (Scotland) Act 2006. The momentum for more radical change appears to have dissipated.[6]

---

1    Approximately 90 per cent.
2    At present, approximately one in three marriages ends in divorce.
3    The Ground for Divorce (Scot Law Com Discussion Paper No 76).
4    Report on the Reform of the Ground for Divorce (Scot Law Com No 116).
5    Report on the Reform of the Ground for Divorce (Scot Law Com No 116), paras 1.1 and 1.2.
6    In England, reform of the law along the lines of delayed divorce on demand has failed: see the Family Law Act 1996. The pretext was lack of resources.

---

# Chapter 7

# Financial provision on divorce and dissolution

## INTRODUCTION

**7.1** A major function of contemporary family law is to provide a system of rules whereby a couple's capital and income can be redistributed in a just way when their marriage or civil partnership ends in divorce or dissolution. Before the enactment of the Family Law (Scotland) Act 1985, Scots law left this important matter largely to the discretion of the judges.[1] The Scottish Law Commission considered the options for reform in a very full and detailed report[2] which led to the system of financial provision on divorce in the Family Law (Scotland) Act 1985.[3] The 1985 Act has been amended by the Civil Partnership Act 2004[4] so that the same system of financial provision applies on the dissolution of a civil partnership as on divorce. Before considering this system in detail, several important issues must be discussed.

For many couples whose relationship breaks down there is little property or income to be redistributed. Nevertheless where couples do have considerable assets, they are surely entitled to a rational system of redistribution of their property and income when their marriage or civil partnership ends in divorce or dissolution. A major difficulty in determining the criteria for financial provision is that any system must endeavour to accommodate the different kinds of marriages and civil partnerships which end in divorce or dissolution. These include short, childless marriages or civil partnerships where both parties work; medium-range marriages or civil partnerships where there are dependent children; long marriages or civil partnerships where a spouse or civil partner has given up paid employment to look after the children of the family and has no prospect of a job in the future; and a civil partnership or marriage where one partner or spouse has provided all the income while the other ran the home.

The Scottish Law Commission concluded that, given the variety of marriages, there was no one principle which, if followed, would produce a satisfactory financial settlement in every case. For example, in a short, childless marriage or civil partnership it is simply not fair – even if it were practicable – that a spouse or civil partner should as a result of financial provision be placed in the same financial position he or she would have enjoyed if the marriage or civil partnership had not broken down. On the other hand, if a  spouse or civil partner has given up their career in order to look after the children of the family and has, in effect, been an unpaid housekeeper for many years, why should they lose the expectation that the other spouse or civil partner would maintain them in old age merely because the marriage or partnership has ended in divorce or dissolution? Again, even after a short marriage or civil partnership, the financial needs of a spouse or partner who is unable to earn because they are looking after dependent children may not be met merely by the equal division of the spouses' or civil partners' capital assets. Accordingly, the Scottish Law Commission took the view that it was necessary to provide a set of principles or objectives which were to be achieved by a system of financial provision on divorce but which at the same time would allow the courts to retain a considerable degree of discretion so that orders could be made which took account of the particular circumstances of the marriage or civil partnership in question.

Finally, it must be stressed at the outset that the provisions of the Family Law (Scotland) Act 1985 are concerned only with financial provision for *spouses and civil partners*. In Scots law children have an independent right to aliment from their parents or those who have accepted them as children of their family.[5] When for example a marriage breaks down, the children will often live with one of their parents and not with the other. In these circumstances the absent parent, ie the parent with whom the child does not live, is obliged to pay maintenance calculation for the child until the child is 16.[6] In addition, there is the possibility that the parents will have to pay aliment to the child. A child's claims for maintenance calculation and/or aliment are determined *before* a court considers financial provision for the spouses or civil partners. In this way, Scots law gives primacy to the financial needs of the children of a family when a marriage or civil partnership ends in divorce or dissolution.

---

1     See the Divorce (Scotland) Act 1976, s 5(2). For a short discussion of the pre-1985 law, see the second edition of this book (1991, Butterworths), pp 120 ff.

2   Report on Aliment and Financial Provision (Scot Law Com No 67).
3   The Family Law (Scotland) Act 1985 came into force on 1 September 1986. On the
     effect of the 1985 Act on the practice of solicitors, see *The Impact of the Family Law
     (Scotland) Act 1985 on Solicitors' Divorce Practice* (November 1990) Scottish Office
     Central Research Unit Papers.
4   Part 2 of Schedule 28 to the Act.
5   Family Law (Scotland) Act 1985, s 1(1)(c) and (d).
6   On maintenance calculation, see paras **10.11** ff.

## THE NATURE OF THE ORDERS

**7.2** By s 8(1) of the Family Law (Scotland) Act 1985, in an action for
divorce or dissolution,[1] the court[2] has the power to make one or more of the
following orders by way of financial provision for the applicant.

1   The regime on financial provision also applies in an action of declarator of nullity of
     marriage or a civil partnership: Family Law (Scotland) Act 1985, s 17.
2   That is the Court of Session or the sheriff court: FL(S)A 1985, s 27.

## (1) An order for the payment of a capital sum or the transfer of property

**7.3** The court has the power to make orders for the payment of a capital
sum and/or a transfer of property.[1] Such an order can be made either
at the date of divorce or dissolution or within a period specified by the
court.[2] The court can stipulate that the order is to come into effect at a
specified future date.[3] For example, if a married couple's only substantial
asset is the matrimonial home and this would have to be sold to raise the
finance necessary for the payment of a capital sum, the court may delay
the operation of such an order until a specified date, for instance when the
youngest child of the family has reached the age of 18 and the property is
no longer required as a home for the family.

The court can order that a capital sum be paid by instalments.[4] This is
important where a couple's assets are not in an easily realisable form. For
example, if a wife was granted a capital sum of £50K but the husband's
assets were tied up in a small business, the court could order that the £50K

be paid in five annual instalments of £10K. It will also be useful where a spouse has few capital assets but a high income. The advantages of a capital sum payable by instalments over periodical allowances is that the total capital sum awarded cannot be varied[5] and it will not therefore be perceived by the payer as an indefinite financial burden.

A property transfer order obliges one of the parties to transfer the ownership of his or her property to the other. For example, if H and W are common owners of the matrimonial home, the court could order H to transfer his one-half pro indiviso share of the house to W.[6] This is useful where the children of the parties are to reside with W after the divorce. A property transfer order and a capital sum payment can be made in the same action: but neither has a preference over the other.[7]

---

1    FL(S)A 1985, s 8(1)(a) and (aa). The court can also order a capital sum payment in respect of lump sums due under pension schemes: FL(S)A 1985, s 8(1)(ba). See para **7.8**.
2    FL(S)A 1985, s 12(1)(a) and (b).
3    FL(S)A 1985, s 12(2). See, for example, *Little v Little* 1990 SLT 230, approved by the Inner House 1990 SLT 785. In this case, the major asset – the defender's interest in a pension fund – was not in an easily realisable form thus justifying the court in delaying payment of one-half of the capital sum for six years.
4    FL(S)A 1985, s 12(3).
5    The date or method of payment of an order can be varied on a material change of circumstances: FL(S)A 1985, s 12(4).
6    H and W would both convey their one-half pro indiviso shares to W.
7    FL(S)A 1985, s 8(1)(a) and (aa). See *Mc Kinnon v McKinnon* 2008 GWD 12-226. Whether there should be a property transfer order or a capital sum payment 'will depend on the facts of each case': ibid at para 10.

---

## (2) Periodical allowances

**7.4** The court has power to make an order for the payment of a periodical allowance.[1] It is an axiomatic principle of the Family Law (Scotland) Act 1985 that before ordering a periodical allowance the court must be satisfied that the payment of a capital sum or a transfer of property order is inappropriate or insufficient in the circumstances.[2] Moreover, a periodical allowance can only be made if it is justified by one of the principles in ss 9(1)(c), (d) or (e).[3] Thus the whole thrust of the 1985 Act is that the 'normal' orders for financial provision should take the form of capital sum payments or transfer of property orders rather than periodical allowances. This is to encourage 'a clean break' with the consequence that the spouses or civil partners cease to be economically dependent on each other after the divorce or dissolution. It is for this reason that the court's power to order a capital sum to be paid by instalments is so important.

Only in exceptional circumstances should orders for periodical allowances be made. The order can be for a definite or indefinite period, or until a specified event happens.[4] If there has been a material change of circumstances, a periodical allowance can be varied or recalled and an order for a periodical allowance can be converted into the payment of a capital sum or property transfer order.[5] A periodical allowance ends with the death or remarriage of the payee,[6] but it continues if the payer dies though the executor can apply to the court to recall the order.[7]

---

1    Family Law (Scotland) Act 1985, s 8(1)(b). The court can also make a pension sharing order: s 8(1)(baa). Pension sharing orders are discussed at para **7.8** ff.

2    FL(S)A 1985, s 13(2). 'If a pursuer seeks an award of periodical allowance she must aver and prove that the conditions in section 13(2) are satisfied. If she does not do so, the principle of the '"clean break" embodied in the 1985 Act prevents the court from considering the question of periodical allowance at all': *Mackin v Mackin* 1991 SLT (Sh Ct) 22 at 24, per the Sheriff Principal (Ireland). Where the pursuer has obtained a substantial capital sum payment and/or property transfer order, it is most unlikely that the criteria in s 13(2) will be satisfied and no periodical allowance should be made: *McConnell v McConnell* 1995 GWD 3–145.

3    FL(S)A 1985, s 13(2). The principles are discussed in detail at paras **7.18–7.20**. See *Thirde v Thirde* 1987 SCLR 335. The pursuer's pleadings must refer to the principle(s) in FL(S)A 1985, s 9(1)(c)–(e) being relied upon.

4    FL(S)A 1985, s 13(3). See, for example, *Mitchell v Mitchell* 1993 SLT 419.

5    FL(S)A 1985, s 13(4). The making of a maintenance calculation in respect of a child living with the payee is a material change of circumstances: FL(S)A 1985, s 13(4A). Any variation or recall can be backdated to the date of the application or, on cause shown, to an earlier date: FL(S)A 1985, s 13(4)(b). On variation, the periodical allowance can be made for a definite or indefinite period or until a specified event happens: FL(S)A 1985, s 13(5), impliedly incorporating inter alia s 13(2). See, for example, *Kerray v Kerray* 1991 SLT 613.

6    FL(S)A 1985, s 13(7)(b).

7    FL(S)A 1985, s 13(7)(a) and (4).

## (3) Incidental orders

**7.5** In addition, the court has the power to make incidental orders. These are listed in s 14 of the Family Law (Scotland) Act 1985. They include an order for the sale of the couple's property,[1] the valuation of their property[2] and a declarator as to the ownership of any disputed property.[3] The court can also make an order regulating the occupation of the matrimonial or family home and the use of its furniture and plenishings,[4] including an order regulating liability as between the parties for outgoings in respect of the home and its contents.[5] Under these provisions the court can exclude one of the parties from the property. As long as an order subsists as to the occupation of the matrimonial or family home and its contents, the occupant retains[6] the powers of management conferred by the Matrimonial Homes (Family Protection) (Scotland) Act 1981 and the Civil Partnership Act 2004.[7] The provisions of the 1981 Act and the 2004 Act protecting a spouse or civil partner's occupancy rights against dealings with third parties do not apply.

Other incidental orders include an order that security should be given for any financial provision[8] and an order as to the date from which any interest on any amount awarded should run.[9] In *Geddes v Geddes,*[10] the Inner House of the Court of Session held that a court could order interest to run from a date *prior* to the date of decree provided it was justified by the principles in s 9 of the FL(S)A 1985 and reasonable to do so.[11] For example, H and W separate and W lives in the matrimonial home until the divorce five years later. H is prima facie entitled to a capital sum payment of half the net value of the house at the date of separation, the relevant date.[12] The court can order interest on the capital sum payment to run from the relevant date rather than the date of divorce, ie H will get the capital sum payment *plus* five years' interest on that sum. The interest represents consideration for W's exclusive use of the matrimonial home for five years.[13] The provision is also useful where payment of a capital sum is postponed until a future date because the payer's assets are not easily realisable at the date of divorce or dissolution. For example, a civil partner has pension interests and rights under a life insurance policy. These are not easily realisable. In these circumstances the court can make a capital sum order and defer payment for several years. But it can also order that interest on the capital sum is to be paid to the payee during this period thus compensating her for the deferment of the payment.[14]

Powers also exist for the payment or transfer of property to a trustee on behalf of a party to the marriage or civil partnership,[15] and for setting aside or varying any term in an antenuptial or postnuptial marriage settlement or any corresponding settlement in respect of a civil partnership.[16] The court can also dispense with the need for one of the parties to execute a deed and can order the sheriff clerk to do so instead: this power exists where the deed is concerned with moveable as well as heritable property.[17] Finally, the court can make any ancillary order which is expedient to give effect to the principles set out in s 9 of the FL(S)A 1985, or any order made under s 8(2) of the same Act.[18]

Armed with this plethora of powers, the court can make orders for financial provision which can be tailor-made for the particular couple concerned.

---

1 Family Law (Scotland) Act 1985, s 14(2)(a). See for example, *Porter v Porter* 1990 SCLR 752; *Reynolds v Reynolds* 1991 SCLR 175. Because of the exceptionally uncertain state of the current property market, the court may order the sale of the former matrimonial home giving the pursuer the free proceeds (or a proportion thereof) instead of making an order for a capital sum payment based on a valuation of the property: *Smith v Smith* [2009] CSOH 2. In *Thomson v Thomson* 2003 Fam LR 22 the sale of the former matrimonial home was delayed until a seven years-old child had completed his primary education at a local school. It has been held that this order cannot be sought post decree to enforce a capital sum order which has not been paid: *Amin v Amin* 2000 SLT (Sh Ct) 115. *Sed quaere* if the incidental order is an ancillary order rather than an order for financial provision. Sale was ordered *post* divorce in *Jacques v Jacques* 1995 SLT 963 at the Inner House stage.
2 FL(S)A 1985, s 14(2)(b).
3 FL(S)A 1985, s 14(2)(c).
4 FL(S)A 1985, s 14(2)(d); see *Little v Little* 1989 SCLR 613, approved by the Inner House 1990 SLT 785. By FL(S)A 1985, s 14(3), orders under s 14(2)(d) and (e) of the 1985 Act can be made only on or after divorce or dissolution; this is because before divorce or dissolution these matters are regulated by the Matrimonial Homes (Family Protection) (Scotland) Act 1981 and the Civil Partnership Act 2004.
5 FL(S)A 1985, s 14(2)(e).
6 FL(S)A 1985, s 14(5), (5A) and (5B).
7 That is MH(FP)(S)A 1981, s 2 and the CPA 2004, s 102.
8 FL(S)A 1985, s 14(2)(f). See for example, *Macdonald v Macdonald* 1995 SLT 72. It would appear that the order must be made to secure an order for financial provision, eg the payment of a capital sum: *Trotter v Trotter* 2001 SLT (Sh Ct) 42.

9    FL(S)A 1985, s 14(2)(j).
10   *Geddes v Geddes* 1993 SLT 494; cf *Kennedy v Kennedy* 2004 Fam LR 70.
11   On the s 9 principles, see paras **7.6** ff.
12   Discussed at para **7.7** ff.
13   See, for example, *Welsh v Welsh* 1994 SLT 828.
14   *Bannon v Bannon* 1993 SLT 999.
15   FL(S)A 1985, s 14(2)(g).
16   FL(S)A 1985, s 14(2)(h). A contract of copartnery is not a marriage settlement for the
     purposes of this section.
17   Section 14(2)(ja) (moveable property); s 5A of the Sheriff Courts (Scotland) Act 1907
     (heritage).
18   FL(S)A 1995, s 14(2)(k). See *McDonald v McDonald* 1993 SCLR 132; *Murley v
     Murley* 1995 SCLR 1138; *Lindsay v Lindsay* 2005 SLT (Sh Ct) 81. In *Murdoch v
     Murdoch* [2012] CSIH 2, 2012 Fam LR 2 the court held that it was competent for
     the pursuer to seek a principal order in her favour- in this case a property transfer
     order- and an incidental order-in this case a counter balancing payment- in favour
     of the defender ie the pursuer can seek an order against herself. This approach was
     'consistent with common sense': ibid at para 22. But before such an order is competent
     it must be necessary to do justice between the parties: *R v C* 2013 GWD 22-431.

## THE PRINCIPLES

**7.6** In an application for financial provision, s 8(2) of the Family Law
(Scotland) Act 1985 provides that the court shall make such order, if
any, as is justified by the principles set out in s 9 of the 1985 Act, and
is reasonable having regard to the resources of the parties.[1] Resources
include the couple's present and foreseeable resources.[2] Thus the court's
discretion is limited in that the order must be justified by the s 9 principles
but the discretion is still wide as, even if justified by the principles, the
order must still be reasonable in the light of the couple's resources.

This discretion can be used to reduce an award of financial provision which
is otherwise due in the light of both the payer's[3] and payee's[4] resources
at the date of the divorce or dissolution. For example, if W is prima
facie entitled to a capital sum payment of £100K but H's resources have
substantially declined since the couple separated, the court can reduce the
capital sum to be paid because it is not reasonable for H to pay such a
large amount in the light of his resources at the date of divorce.[5] However,
this discretion cannot be used *to increase* an award beyond that justified
by the s 9 principles.[6] A discussion of the s 9(1) principles follows.

1 Family Law (Scotland) Act 1985, s 8(2)(a) and (b). The onus rests on the party seeking financial provision to establish both these considerations: *Fraser v Fraser* 2002 Fam LR 53.

2 So, for example, a spouse's interest in a pension fund is a resource for these purposes: *Gribb v Gribb* 1995 SCLR 1007, 1996 SLT 719. But in determining what is reasonable, the court is not entitled to allow the issue of expenses, for example, the effect of the legal aid clawback, to determine that choice of orders: see *McKinnon v McKinnon* 2008 GWD 12-226.

3 *Buczynska v Buczynski* 1989 SLT 558 (capital sum reduced because payee (wife) had resources which did not constitute matrimonial property). On the other hand, in *Cunniff v Cunniff* 1999 SC 537 W received an outright transfer of the matrimonial home even though this would lead to the bankruptcy of H!

4 *Welsh v Welsh* 1994 SLT 828.

5 In *Wallis v Wallis* 1993 SLT 1348, there are dicta in the speeches of Lord Keith at 1351 and Lord Jauncey at 1352 to the effect that amending legislation might be necessary to achieve this result: however, it is thought that the FL(S)A 1985, s 8(2)(a) and (b) do not inhibit a court reducing an award in the way described above. While (a) and (b) are cumulative in the sense that an award must be justified by s 9 principles and reasonable in the light of the parties' resources, it does not follow that the court can make no order at all if the order which is prima facie justified by the s 9 principles is unreasonable in the light of the payer's resources: instead the court can *reduce* the award to a reasonable level. In these circumstances, it is still justified by s 9 principles. *Sed quaere.*

6 *Latter v Latter* 1990 SLT 805. FL(S)A 1985, s 8(2)(a) and (b) are cumulative in this sense; see discussion in preceding note. If otherwise, the s 9 principles would be otiose and the financial provision would simply be whatever the court in its discretion regarded as reasonable.

| **Principle 9(1)(a):** | The net value of the matrimonial or partnership property should be shared fairly between the parties to the marriage or civil partnership. |
| --- | --- |

**7.7** The first principle is s 9(1)(a) of the Family Law (Scotland) Act 1985. This provides that the net value of the matrimonial or partnership property should be shared fairly between the parties. The *net* value of the matrimonial or partnership property is the value of the property at the relevant date after deduction of any outstanding debts incurred by the parties: (a) during the marriage or partnership; or (b) before the marriage or registration of the partnership in so far as the pre-marital or pre-registration debts relate to matrimonial or partnership property. For example, if the couple's only property is a house bought during the marriage by means of a loan secured by a standard security over the property, the net value of the property at the relevant date will be the value of the house after deducting the outstanding loan.[1] Potential liability for any capital gains tax which might be incurred by a payer if property has to be realised in order to pay financial provision is not taken into account in determining the net value of the property. Instead it will be a relevant factor in deciding whether or not it is reasonable in the light of the payer's resources that he should pay the amount of financial provision to which the payee is otherwise entitled under the s 9 principles.[2]

The relevant date is the date on which the parties cease to cohabit as husband and wife or civil partners, or the date of service of the summons in the action of divorce or dissolution if they continue living together.[3] Thus if a couple cease to cohabit in June 2014, that will be the relevant date for this purpose even though the action for divorce or dissolution is not brought until several years later.[4] Because a couple are deemed not to cohabit unless they are in fact living together as man and wife,[5] the relevant date may occur before a couple finally separate if they were not in fact living together as man and wife, albeit residing in the same house.[6] This is important as it will follow that the net value of their matrimonial property may be much less than the value of their property at the date they finally separated.

---

1   Family Law (Scotland) Act 1985, s 10(2)(a) and (b). The value of a house should not be discounted if it is still subject to a clawback provision in favour of a local authority. But the fact that there may be a clawback if the house has to be sold is a relevant factor in determining whether it is reasonable to order the amount of financial provision otherwise due under the s 9 principles: *Sweeney v Sweeney* 2004 SLT 125; *Stuart v Stuart* 2001 SLT (Sh Ct) 20. Where property was encumbered before the marriage or civil partnership, and subsequently becomes matrimonial or partnership property, then the encumbrances at the relevant date must be proportioned as between pre marital or pre partnership debts and debts incurred during the marriage or partnership: this can be very complex. Only the latter are used to determine the net value of the matrimonial or partnership property: *Willson v Willson* [2008] CSOH 161.

2   *Sweeney v Sweeney* 2004 SLT 125; *Sweeney v Sweeney (No 2)* 2005 SLT 1141; *Coyle v Coyle* 2004 Fam LR 2. Expenses are not a relevant factor in determining what is reasonable:*McKinnon v McKinnon* 2008 GWD 12-226.

3   FL(S)A 1985, s 10(3).

4   This is subject to the FL(S)A 1985, s 10(7) which determines the relevant date after unsuccessful attempts at reconciliation. For discussion of s 10(7), see E M Clive *The Law of Husband and Wife in Scotland* (4th edn, 1997, W. Greens/Sweet & Maxwell), p 445.

5    FL(S)A 1985, s 27(2). The phrase 'man and wife' must be interpreted to include same
     sex spouses: Marriage and Civil Partnership (Scotland) Act 2014, s 4. This provision
     does not appear to have been amended to include civil partners but it is thought that
     similar principles apply.
6    *Buczynska v Buczynski* 1989 SLT 558, *Samurai v Al-Samurai* [2014] CSOH 95
     (Spouses ceased to cohabit as man and wife, when wife sent a solicitor's letter to
     her husband informing him she wanted a divorce albeit that they continued to live
     under the same roof but as separated persons). For full discussion of the meaning of
     cohabitation see para **6.7**. The statutory definition of cohabitation for the purpose of
     divorce is identical to that in FL(S)A 1985, s 27(2).

## (i) Matrimonial and partnership property

**7.8** Matrimonial and partnership property is defined[1] as *all* the property
belonging to the spouses, civil partners or either of them at the relevant
date that was acquired by the spouse(s) or civil partner(s):

(1)    before the marriage or registration for use by them as a family
       home or as furniture or plenishings for such a home, ie the family
       home and its contents; or

(2)    during the marriage or partnership *but before the relevant date.*

The following property is excluded:

(1)    property acquired before marriage or registration, with the
       important exception of property acquired for use as a family
       home and its contents;

(2)    property acquired by a spouse or civil partner *after* the relevant
       date; and

(3)    property acquired during the marriage or civil partnership from a
       third party by way of gift or succession.

We shall now consider the definition of matrimonial or partnership
property in some detail.

The only property acquired before the marriage or registration which can
constitute matrimonial or partnership property is the family home and its
furniture and plenishings. Any other kind of property, such as a business
which was acquired before marriage, is *not* matrimonial or partnership
property; moreover, any increase in value of such property does not

constitute matrimonial property even if the increase in value is attributable to the efforts of the spouses during the marriage.[2]

In *Mitchell v Mitchell*,[3] the Inner House of the Court of Session held that a house bought before the marriage would be treated as matrimonial property only if it was acquired by the purchaser *with the intention* that it was to be used as a family home for the purchaser and the other partner.

Consider the following examples:

(1)    A buys a house as a bachelor pad. If A marries B, the house is not matrimonial property even if A and B live there: A did not acquire the house with the intention that it should be a family home for A and B.[4]

(2)    A buys a house when he is cohabiting with B with the intention that it should be a family home for A and B. If A and B marry, the house is matrimonial property as it was bought before the marriage with the intention that it should be a family home for A and B. It does not matter that at the time it was acquired A did not intend to marry B; it is enough that it was intended as a family home for A and B.[5]

(3)    A buys a house when he is cohabiting with B with the intention that it should be a family home for A and B. A and B separate. A registers a civil partnership with C. The house is not partnership property as it was not acquired by A with the intention that it should be a family home for A and C.

(4)    H buys a house during his marriage to W1. The house is matrimonial property. H and W1 divorce. H remains in the house. H marries W2. The house is not matrimonial property vis-à-vis the second marriage because it was not acquired with the intention of being a family home for H and W2.[6]

(5)    H buys a house during his marriage to W. The house is matrimonial property. H and W divorce. H remains in the house. H and W remarry. The house is matrimonial property because, although acquired before the second marriage, it was bought with the intention of being used as a family home for H and W, albeit when they were parties to the first marriage.[7]

(6)     H buys a house during his marriage to W. The house is matrimonial property. H and W divorce. H sells the house and buys a new property. H and W remarry. The house is not matrimonial property. It was bought before the second marriage when H did not intend it to be used as a family home for H and W.[8]

In *Corbett* v *Corbett*[9] before she married, W was the tenant of a local authority house. She decided to buy the property. Her cohabitant did not wish to contribute to the purchase of the house. After the house was purchased, the couple married. It was held that the house was not matrimonial property. At the time of purchase the house was already a family home: consequently it had not been *bought* with the intention that it should be the couple's family home but simply as an investment. However the court accepted that a house could be bought both as an investment and with the intention that the purchaser would live in it with the person who subsequently becomes a spouse or civil partner ie that it should be a family home: in these circumstances, the house would be matrimonial or partnership property.

This area of the law remains very significant as more and more couples cohabit before they marry. It is particularly relevant in cases of dissolution of civil partnerships where the couple were cohabiting in a house belonging to one of the partners before the partnership was registered.

Where a spouse or civil partner owned a house before the marriage or registration, if he or she conveys a one half pro indiviso share of the property to the other spouse or civil partner during the marriage or civil partnership, only the transferee's one half pro indiviso share constitutes matrimonial or partnership property: the transferor's one half pro indiviso share is not matrimonial or partnership property and therefore is not subject to fair sharing under s 9(1)(a).[10]

All property acquired by spouses or civil partners during the marriage or partnership but before the relevant date is prima facie matrimonial or partnership property. This includes the house, furniture, motor cars, jewellery, savings and investments. It is irrelevant whether, as a matter of property law, the property is owned individually or in common. For example, although money, vehicles and pets are not household goods[11] and therefore are not presumed to be owned in common, they nevertheless constitute matrimonial or partnership property if acquired during the marriage or civil partnership. Matrimonial and partnership property includes a business owned by a spouse or civil partner.[12]

Any property acquired by way of gift *from a third party* or inheritance is excluded. Several points should be noted. First, gifts from one spouse or civil partner to the other constitute matrimonial or partnership property. For example, if A gives her civil partner, B, a necklace, or B gives A a watch, the necklace and watch are partnership property: the exception only applies if A or B receives a gift from a third party, for example their parents.

Secondly, where a gift from a third party or an inheritance increases in value during the marriage or civil partnership, the increase in value does *not* constitute matrimonial or partnership property and is excluded.[13] However, where a gift of money from a third party or an inheritance is used by a spouse or civil partner to buy property during the marriage or the partnership, the property acquired is matrimonial or partnership property. For example, W inherits £200K in shares. She sells shares worth £100K to purchase a house. The house is matrimonial property but the unsold shares are not because they remain part of her inheritance. As Lord McLean observed,[14]

> '... any property acquired by the parties during the marriage but before separation is matrimonial property even if it is purchased with funds which one of the parties has acquired by way of gift or succession. The funds themselves before their application in acquiring the property, would not, according to s 10(4), be matrimonial property'.

Property acquired after the relevant date but before the divorce or dissolution is not matrimonial or partnership property for the purpose of s 9(1)(a) – although it would be a part of a spouse or civil partner's resources for the application of other provisions in the Family Law (Scotland) Act 1985. Nevertheless, difficulties can arise. For example, a claim for damages awarded *after* the relevant date in respect of a delict suffered by a spouse before the relevant date is matrimonial or partnership property.[15] A redundancy payment paid before the relevant date is matrimonial or partnership property but *not* if paid after the relevant date.[16] A tax refund paid after the relevant date in respect of income earned before the relevant date is matrimonial or partnership property.[17]

Most importantly, matrimonial and partnership property includes the portion of any rights or interests of either spouse or civil partner:

(1)     under a life policy or similar arrangement; and

(2)     in any benefits under a pension which either party has or may have (including such benefits payable in respect of the death of either party), which is referable to the period of marriage or civil partnership before the relevant date.[18]

It is necessary to determine the cash equivalent transfer value (CETV) of the pension at the relevant date (unless this is less than 12 months before the date of receipt, when the date of receipt is used).[19] After this is received, the parties must apportion it to determine the part which is referable to the period of marriage before the relevant date.[20] Where a lump sum is payable under the pension scheme on the death of one of the parties, the court on ordering a capital sum payment under s 8(1) of the FL(S)A 1985 can direct the trustees or managers to pay the whole or part of the lump sum when it becomes due to the other party to the marriage or civil partnership. This is known as a 'pension lump sum order'.[21]

It is now possible for the spouses or civil partners to share a pension when it matures. This is done by the parties reaching agreement (a qualifying agreement)[22] or by obtaining a pension sharing order under s 8(1)(baa) of the FL(S)A 1985.[23] The basic state pension cannot be shared. Where there is to be pension sharing the court cannot make a pension lump sum order under s 12A of the 1985 Act.[24] The idea is that on divorce or dissolution the transferor spouse or civil partner's shareable rights in his or her pension arrangement are subject to a debit of the appropriate amount, and the transferee spouse or civil partner becomes entitled to a credit of that amount which is enforceable against the person responsible for running the pension scheme.[25] The pension credit can then be used to purchase rights in the pension arrangement in the transferee's own name. The pension will become payable when the transferee retires.

Most pension sharing is achieved by qualifying agreements. Before any agreement is signed, the transferor must have intimated to the managers of the pension scheme his or her intention to have his or her pension rights shared with the transferee.[26] The agreement must then be registered in the Books of Council and Session.[27] Qualifying agreements cannot be made after the parties have divorced or the partnership has been dissolved. Alternatively, the court can make a pension sharing order which will specify the percentage value or the amount to be deducted from the transferor's pension rights.[28] On divorce or dissolution, the parties send the decree, the qualifying agreement or pension order to the pension scheme managers; this should be done within two months of the extract decree. The pension sharing can then be effected.[29] Pension sharing is an attractive option for younger persons who have their own career and sufficient funds to withstand the financial difficulties which usually accompany the breakdown of a relationship. Older payees might prefer to have the family home or an immediate capital sum payment since they will have less time to build up an alternative source of income for their retirement.

1    Family Law (Scotland) Act 1985, s 10(4) and (4A). In *AB v CD* [2006] CSOH 200 where H set up a trust to manage his property in favour of a company which he controlled, the court nevertheless held that some of the property technically owned by the trust still constituted matrimonial property belonging to H; H had simply treated the trust as a 'piggy bank'.

2    *Wilson v Wilson* 1999 SLT 249. Such property will constitute a spouse or civil partner's resources for the application of other provisions of the FL(S)A 1985. If a spouse or civil partner uses pre-marital or pre-registration property to acquire property during the marriage or civil partnership, the new property is matrimonial or partnership property for the purposes of FL(S)A 1985, s 9(1)(a). The existence of business interests before the marriage or civil partnership which engendered the acquisition of matrimonial or partnership property is a ground for unequal division of that property: *Watt v Watt* 2009 SLT 931.

3    1995 SLT 426.

4    The house *would* be a matrimonial home for the purpose of the Matrimonial Homes (Family Protection) (Scotland) Act 1981: see para **5.6** ff.

5    *Mitchell v Mitchell* 1995 SLT 426 at 427, per the Lord Justice-Clerk (Ross).

6    *Ranaldi v Ranaldi* 1994 SLT (Sh Ct) 25.

7    These were the facts in *Mitchell v Mitchell* 1995 SLT 426.

8    Unless H bought the house with the intention to lure W to remarry him!

9    2009 WL 2392276.

10    *Willson v Willson* [2008] CSOH 161.

11    That is for the purposes of the FL(S)A 1985, s 25: discussed at para **4.5** ff.

12    *Crockett v Crockett* 1992 SCLR 591; *McConnell v McConnell* 1993 GWD 34–2185. Acute difficulties can arise in the valuation of such a business. Where the business is a partnership, the increase in the value of a spouse's capital account during the marriage

is matrimonial property but land in the spouse's name may be owned on behalf of the partnership and not constitute matrimonial property: *Marshall v Marshall* [2007] CSOH 16. In *K v K* 2013 GWD 26-530 H deliberately ran down a business after the relevant date which W subsequently rescued. The value of the business at the relevant date was not treated as matrimonial property on the basis that it was not fair that W should compensate H in respect of property which he had squandered and abandoned: *sed quare?* Surely special circumstances existed under FL(S)A 1985, s 10(6)(c) to deviate from equal sharing in W's favour. On s 10(6), see paras **7.11** ff below.

13   *Whittome v Whittome (No 1)* 1994 SLT 114 at 125, per Lord Osborne, disapproving the dictum of Lord Marnoch in *Latter v Latter* 1990 SLT 805. Lord Marnoch appeared to accept these strictures in *Wilson v Wilson* 1999 SLT 249.

14   *Davidson v Davidson* 1994 SLT 506 at 508. These provisions must not be construed too technically. If for example, W's parents wish to give H and W a house as a wedding present, the fact that they give W the money to pay for the house and the missives of sale are signed by W would not prevent the house being regarded as a gift from W's parents and therefore *not* matrimonial property: see for example, *Latter v Latter* 1990 SLT 805. In *Willson v Willson* [2008] CSOH 161, Lord Drummond Young held that funds owned by W before marriage or funds which are the realisation of property owned before marriage or acquired by gift or succession from a third party do not become matrimonial property merely because they are deposited in a joint bank account during the marriage. See also *B v B* [2012] CSOH 21, 2012 Fam LR 65, *Harris v Harris* 2013 GWD 16-337.

15   *Skarpaas v Skarpaas* 1993 SLT 343. Damages paid before the relevant date in respect of a delict before the marriage would also be matrimonial property. Damages paid after the relevant date in respect of a delict suffered before the marriage would not be matrimonial property: *Petrie v Petrie* 1988 SCLR 390. Damages for solatium and future loss of earnings are excluded. When the claim has not been settled at the relevant date, any tender offered around that time could be a suitable valuation of the claim: *Carrol v Carrol* 2003 Fam LR 108. See also *McGuire v McGuire's Curator Bonis* 1991 SLT (Sh Ct) 76 (criminal injuries compensation).

16   *Tyrrell v Tyrrell* 1990 SLT 406: the court refused to treat a redundancy payment as analogous to an interest under a life policy or pension.

17   *Macritchie v Macritchie* 1994 SLT (Sh Ct) 72.

18   FL(S)A 1985, s 10(5).

19   This information must be given by the pension scheme managers to the member on request within specified time limits. On valuation, see generally the Pensions on Divorce etc (Provision of Information) Regulations 2000, SI 2000/1048. The member's spouse or civil partner cannot apply for this information.

20   The formula is A × B/C where A is the CETV, B is the period of membership within the marriage and before the relevant date and C is the period of membership before the relevant date.

21   FL(S)A 1985, s 12A.

22   Welfare Reform and Pensions Act 1999, s 28(1)(f); Pensions on Divorce etc (Pension Sharing) (Scotland) Regulations 2000, SI 2000/1051, regs 3 and 5.

23   The order is defined in FL(S)A 1985, s 27.

24 FL(S)A 1985, s 8(4), (5) and (6) .
25 WRPA 1999, s 29.
26 Pensions on Divorce etc (Pension Sharing) (Scotland) Regulations 2000, SI 2000/1051.
27 WRPA 1999, s 28(3)(b).
28 FL(S)A 1985, s 27. The court can include in the order provisions about the apportionment between the parties of any charges in respect of the costs of pension sharing: s 8A.
29 Where a spouse or civil partner is entitled to compensation payable under the Pensions Act 2004, the court is disempowered from making a pension sharing order or a pension lump sum order out of such compensation: s 10(4A) and (5A). But once the compensation is paid, the proportion referable to the period of the marriage or civil partnership is matrimonial or partnership property and is subject to fair division and subject to all the orders under s 8 except those relating to pensions. If a pension lump sum order has already been made, references to the pension are to be taken as references to any compensation that has been paid out: ss 12A(7ZA), (7ZB) and (7ZC). Any agreements which contain provisions in relation to pensions remain liable to be set aside or varied by the court even if the Board of the Pension Protection Fund assumes responsibility for the pension scheme: ss 16 (2A), (2B) and (2C).

---

*(ii) Identifying matrimonial and partnership property*

**7.9** In applying principle 9(1)(a) of the Family Law (Scotland) Act 1985, the first task is to identify the matrimonial or partnership property which should be shared fairly between the parties. In *Little v Little*,[1] the Inner House of the Court of Session held that there was no need for the court to calculate a single value of the total matrimonial property at the relevant date; moreover, the court could leave out certain items, for example a couple's motor cars or personal possessions, if this would have no practical result on the claim for financial provision. In addition, it was accepted that the matrimonial home could be excluded if a property transfer order was desirable in the circumstances of the case.[2] It is submitted that the approach of the Inner House runs counter to the express language of s 10(4) and (4A) of the FL(S)A 1985 which refers to *all* the couple's property at the relevant date and therefore a court should still proceed to calculate the total net value of their property at that date.[3]

Let us consider a typical example:

H bought a house for £10K shortly before he married W. H bought the house intending that it should be used as their family home. H paid a down payment of £1K and raised the rest of the price by a loan secured by a standard security over the house. Title to the house was taken in H's name. When H left W after 16 years of marriage, the house was worth £140K with an outstanding loan of £2K. During the marriage H bought furniture, a car, and golf clubs: these were worth £16K, £9K and £1K respectively at the time that H left W. During the marriage W bought furs and jewellery: these were worth £4K and £6K respectively at the time that H left W. She also inherited a diamond ring worth £10K at the time that H left W. H had contributed to an occupational pension scheme which he joined four years before he married. The CETV of H's interest in the scheme when H left W was £120K. He has shares that he bought before the marriage which were worth £60K when H left W. W's savings made from her earnings during the marriage were worth £10K. After H left W, she won £5K on the lottery. The relevant date is the date when the parties ceased to cohabit, ie when H left W. At that date, the net value of the matrimonial property consists of the following:

(1) The matrimonial home. While the property was acquired by H *before* marriage, it was acquired for use as a family home for H and W and therefore qualifies. Its net value at the relevant date was: £140K – £2K (outstanding mortgage) = £138K.

(2) H's furniture, car and golf clubs, ie property acquired by him during the marriage and before the relevant date was worth: £16K + £9K + £1K = £26K.

(3) W's furs and jewellery, ie property acquired by her during the marriage and before the relevant date, but excluding the diamond ring which was acquired by way of succession from a third party, was worth: £4K + £6K = £10K.

(4) W's savings made during the marriage and before the relevant date are worth £10K. H's shares are excluded as he acquired them *before* marriage. W's lottery winnings are excluded because she acquired them *after* the relevant date.

(5) The proportion of H's interest in the occupational pension scheme which is referable to the period of marriage before the relevant date has to be calculated. H has been in the scheme for 20 years, 16 of which were during the marriage and before the

relevant date. At the relevant date CETV is £120K. Therefore the portion referable to the period of marriage is:

$$£120 \times \frac{16}{20} = £96K$$

Thus the total value of the matrimonial property at the relevant date is £280K.

By s 10(1) of the FL(S)A 1985, fair sharing of matrimonial and partnership property is prima facie equal sharing. In the example, H and W are each prima facie entitled to £140K. As W already owns property valued at £20K, ie £10K furs and jewellery and £10K savings, H must transfer £120K to her. In deciding whether this should be done, the court must consider whether it is reasonable to do so in the light of the couple's resources.[4] These will include the non-matrimonial property belonging to the spouses, ie H's shares worth £60K and W's diamond ring and lottery win which are worth £10K and £5K respectively, ie £15K. In these circumstances, it is thought that it would be reasonable to order H to make a payment to W of £120K – to be paid in instalments if his capital is not easily realisable.

It should be emphasised that it is the net value of matrimonial or partnership property which is subject to fair division. If for example H has assets worth £100K and W has no assets but has incurred credit card debts of £20K, the outstanding debt must be deducted from the value of H's assets. Thus the net value of the matrimonial property is £80K. It might be thought that to obtain an equal division of the property, H should transfer £40K to W. But W still has a debt of £20K and once it is paid she is left with only £20K while H has £40K. In these circumstances, in order to achieve an equal division, H must make a capital sum payment of £50K to W so that after the debt is paid both H and W are left with £30K from the property.[5] While this result is fair if W's debt was incurred for the benefit of the family, it is less so if W had done so for selfish or self indulgent reasons. However if that were the case, the court could deviate from a 50:50 division in H's favour on the ground that W dissipated the matrimonial property.[6]

---

1    1990 SLT 785.

2    The court maintained that the court's discretion to depart from equal sharing in special circumstances under the Family Law (Scotland) Act 1985, s 10(1) and (6)

was wide enough to exclude certain items from being treated as matrimonial property at all. However, it is thought that the discretion only operates *after* all the couple's matrimonial property at the relevant date has been valued: see para **7.11** ff. But cf *Jacques v Jacques* 1995 SLT 963; *R v R* 2000 Fam LR 43.
3    Nevertheless the Inner House continues to allow judges at first instance considerable latitude: 'The sheriff decided to take a broad and practical approach, without finding it necessary to do what is required by a strict reading of s 10(4) of the Act, which is to take into account all the property belonging to the parties or either of them at the relevant date which is comprised within the definition of matrimonial property ... The question whether it was necessary to value every item of property comprised in the matrimonial property and to calculate a single lump sum representing the net value of the entirety of it was a matter for the discretion of the sheriff': *Jacques v Jacques* 1995 SLT 963 at 965, per the Lord President (Hope). *Sed quaere.*
4    FL(S)A 1985, s 8(2)(b).
5    See for example *Russell v Russell* 2005 Fam LR 96.
6    See paras **7.14**.

*(iii)  The* Wallis v Wallis *problem*

**7.10**  It must always be remembered that the fund that is to be shared fairly is the net value of the matrimonial or partnership property *at the relevant date*. Consider the following situation: A and his civil partner, B, own the family home in common. At the relevant date the house is worth £100K, ie A and B have a one-half pro indiviso share worth £50K. After separation, B remains in the family home. At the time of the dissolution, the house is worth £120K. B wishes to live in the house. In these circumstances, it might be thought sensible that A transfers his one-half pro indiviso share to B in return for a counter-balancing capital sum payment of £60K, ie the value of A's pro indiviso share of the property *at the date of dissolution*.

However, in *Wallis v Wallis*[1] it was held that the maximum capital sum payment which could be awarded in this situation was half the value of the house *at the relevant date*, ie £50K in our example. Accordingly, if a property transfer order was made, B would receive an asset worth £60K in return for a capital sum payment of £50K, ie B would obtain a windfall of £10K. This result is clearly unfortunate.[2] It is to deal with the *Wallis* problem that s 10(3A) has been added to the Family Law (Scotland) Act 1985. This provides that *when a property transfer order is made*, the date when the property being transferred is to be valued is no longer to be the relevant date but the 'appropriate valuation date'. The appropriate valuation date is to be the date agreed by the parties or in the absence of such an agreement, the date on which the property transfer order is made: this will usually be the date of divorce or dissolution. So in the example, in the absence of an agreement between A and B, the house will be valued at the date of dissolution rather than the relevant date so that B must make a capital payment of £60k to A and no longer receives the *Wallis* windfall. Given that s 10(3A) is only triggered when the court intends to make a transfer of property order under s 8(aa), it is designed to make the smallest possible inroad into the fundamental principle that for the purpose of fair sharing under s 9(1)(a) the property is valued at the relevant date.

In the absence of a date agreed between the parties, the appropriate valuation date is to be the date when the property transfer order is made, ie the date of divorce or dissolution. But s 10(3A) also provides that in exceptional circumstances the appropriate valuation date can be determined by the court being a date as near as may be to the date when the transfer of property order is made. In *Willson v Willson*[3] W obtained a transfer of property order of H's one half pro indiviso share of the former matrimonial home. Because of delays on the part of H, if the value of the property had increased at the date of the order, Lord Drummond Young was prepared to treat the delay as exceptional circumstances and revert to an earlier date as the appropriate valuation date when the house had a lower value: it was unfair that H should benefit from the higher value as W had paid the mortgage and running costs of the house since the relevant date. However if, because of even further delays on H's part, the value of the house had fallen substantially at the date of the order, the date of the order would be the appropriate valuation date.

Nevertheless difficulties can be anticipated in determining the appropriate valuation date. Consider the following example:-.

At the relevant date, A and B, same sex spouses, are owners in common of a family home valued at £300K; A has investments valued at £250K and B has investments valued at £50K. The matrimonial property is therefore £600K and both are entitled to an equal share ie £300K. As B already has property worth £200K, ie B's one half pro indiviso share of the house (£150K) and B's investments (£50K), A has to make a capital sum payment to B of £100K. At the time of divorce, the value of the house is £500K. A's investments are worth £750K but B's have collapsed and are worthless. B seeks a property transfer order of A's one half pro indiviso share of the property. Under *Wallis*, A's share is valued at the relevant date ie £150K. Given that B is entitled to £100K from A, B need only transfer £50K to A in return for A's share of the house. Under s 10(3A), A's share will be valued at the appropriate date, the date of the transfer order ie £250K. B is still only entitled to £100K from A and now B must transfer £150K in respect of the transfer of A's one half pro indiviso share to B. Given that A's investments have prospered and that B's have failed, would these constitute exceptional circumstances when the court could depart from the rule that prima facie the appropriate valuation date is the date of divorce? For in our example, although B's *pro indiviso* share of the house has also risen since the relevant date, B has no other assets and cannot afford to purchase A's share if it is valued at the date of divorce as opposed to the relevant date.

---

1   1992 SLT 672 (IH); 1993 SLT 1348 (HL).
2   In *Dible v Dible* 1997 SLT 787 for example, at the relevant date the matrimonial property was valued at £164K: this included a house valued at £59K. W obtained a property transfer order of the house which at the time of divorce was worth £83K. The sheriff ordered H to make a capital sum payment of £12K so that she received approximately 60 per cent of the value of the matrimonial property at the relevant date. (The sheriff thought a 40:60 split was fair sharing in the circumstances.) On appeal, following *Wallis v Wallis* 1993 SLT 1348, it was held that the sheriff should have ignored the increase in value of the house when considering the appropriate balancing capital sum payment, ie the property transfer accounted for only £59K of what was due as opposed to £83K. Consequently, the capital sum payment was increased by £21K to £33K. Again, the injustice inherent in *Wallis* is readily apparent. Although criticised, the decision was binding on the courts: *Kennedy v Kennedy* 2004 Fam LR 70: *Christie v Christie* 2004 SLT (Sh Ct) 95. Courts became reluctant to make property transfer orders unless there was other matrimonial property and the transferee's 'windfall' could be treated as her share of that property. The injustice could also be alleviated by an award of interest on the transferor's capital sum being backdated to the relevant date. Where the house was owned in common, instead of a property transfer order, the court could order division and sale of the property, enabling both parties to benefit from any increase in its value since the relevant date: Family Law (Scotland) Act 1985, s 14(2)(a): *Lewis v Lewis* 1993 SCLR 33; *Jacques v Jacques* 1995 SLT 963; *McCaskill v McCaskill* 2004 Fam LR 123 (incidental orders for sale of property owned in common).
3   [2008] CSOH 161.

*(iv) Special circumstances*

**7.11** By s 10(1) of the Family Law (Scotland) Act 1985, fair sharing is prima facie equal sharing of the net value of all the matrimonial and partnership property. But s 10 (1) also provides that the court can depart from equal sharing if other proportions are justified by special circumstances. It is important to appreciate that the provision is general:[1] it is always open to argue that the facts of a particular case constitute special circumstances which justify the court deviating from the principle that fair sharing means equal sharing. Nevertheless, it is expressly enacted that special circumstances include those listed in s 10(6) of the 1985 Act. Whether to deviate, and the extent of the deviation, is a matter entirely at the discretion of the court and a judge is not obliged to deviate when there are facts which amount to special circumstances in s 10(6).[2] Moreover, it has been emphasised again and again that a 50:50 split will normally be fair.[3]

The special circumstances listed in s 10(6) of the 1985 Act are discussed below.

---

1   See for example, *Peacock v Peacock* 1994 SLT 40; *Cunniff v Cunniff* 1999 SC 537; *Trotter v Trotter* 2001 SLT (Sh Ct) 42. The fact that the value of the matrimonial or partnership property has changed between the relevant date and the date of divorce is not per se a special circumstance for deviation under s 10(1): *Wallis v Wallis* 1993 SLT 1348; *Welsh v Welsh* 1994 SLT 828. Prospective tax liabilities can amount to special circumstances: *W v W* [2013] CSOH 136, 2014 SCLR 63.
2   *Jacques v Jacques* 1997 SC (HL) 20.
3   See for example, *Adams v Adams (No 1)* 1997 SLT 144: this case is an exemplary decision on how the Family Law (Scotland) Act 1985 should be applied and merits careful study.

---

(a) The terms of any agreement between the parties on the ownership or division of any of the matrimonial or partnership property.[1]

**7.12** The most common example of such an agreement is a joint minute tendered to the court hearing the divorce or dissolution, but it could also be an agreement made before the marriage or registration on how the matrimonial or partnership property should be divided on divorce or dissolution.[2] Such agreements are of increasing importance and often deal with all the couple's property. On the other hand the agreement might relate to a particular piece of property. For example, while a gift made by one spouse or civil partner to another is matrimonial or partnership property, the couple might agree expressly or impliedly that gifts inter se should be excluded from fair sharing under s 9(1)(a) of the Family Law (Scotland) Act 1985.

---

1   Where the agreement is concerned with heritable property, it does not have to be in writing: *Little v Little* 1990 SLT 785.
2   See for example, *Jongejon v Jongejon* 1993 SLT 595. In *Kibble v Kibble* 2010 SLT (Sh Ct) 5 it was argued that the parties had entered into an ante nuptial contract that a house owned by the husband before marriage but which would have constituted matrimonial property because it had been bought with the intention of being the couple's family home was not to be treated as matrimonial property in the event they should divorce.

---

(b)   The source of the funds or assets used to acquire any of the matrimonial property where these funds or assets were not derived from the income or efforts of the parties during the marriage.

**7.13** Where a spouse or civil partner buys property during the marriage or civil partnership from funds which were not matrimonial or partnership property, for example the proceeds of the sale of a house prior to the marriage or registration, the court can use this provision to give the spouse or civil partner an increased share of the matrimonial or partnership property purchased from these funds.[1] Although property acquired from a third party as a result of gift or inheritance is excluded from the definition of matrimonial and partnership property, where a spouse or civil partner uses funds acquired in this way to purchase property during the marriage or civil partnership, for example a painting or a motor car, this will prima facie be matrimonial or partnership property which is subject to fair sharing. In these circumstances, the court has been prepared to deviate from the principle that equality is fairness in order to compensate the party who purchased the property as it was not bought from funds deriving from the income or efforts of the parties during the marriage.[2] Thus in *R v R*[3] a wife was awarded approximately a third, as opposed to a half, of the net value of the matrimonial property because 'to a very large extent it derive[d] from inherited or gifted assets which, had they not been sold, would have been outwith the scope of matrimonial property'.[4]

Conversely, if the property did derive from the income and efforts of the parties during the marriage or civil partnership, there is no ground for deviation under s 10(6)(b) of the Family Law (Scotland) Act 1985. This can lead to some harsh decisions. For example, if W worked to support an unemployed and drunken H, any property she acquired during the marriage, for example if she purchased her council flat, would be subject to equal division between them. There is no room for deviation under s 10(6)(b) as the property was acquired as a result of W's income and efforts during the marriage: s 10(6)(b) only applies when the funds did *not* come from this source.[5]

---

1   See for example, *Jesner v Jesner* 1992 SLT 999. *Cf Jacques v Jacques* 1997 SC (HL) 20.
2   See for example, *Davidson v Davidson* 1994 SLT 506; *Willsons v Willsons* [2008] CSOH 161; *Watt v Watt* 2009 SLT 931.
3   2000 Fam LR 43 at 47, per the Lord Ordinary (Eassie).
4   See also *Campbell v Cambell* [2008] CSOH 101 (matrimonial property split 75/25 in favour of the defender as it derived from a large proportion of the proceeds of the sale of a very successful pharmacy business owned by the defender before the marriage); *B v B* [2012] CSOH 21 (matrimonial property split 60/40 in H's favour since it derived substantially from property owned by H before the marriage.); *Harris v Harris* 2013 GWD 16-337 (matrimonial property split 55/45 in W's favour as she had paid significant sums to reduce the mortgage on the former matrimonial home from an inheritance from both her parents).
5   See for example, *Cunningham v Cunningham* 2001 Fam LR 12; *Pressley v Pressley* 2002 SCLR 804.

---

(c)  Any destruction, dissipation or alienation of property by either party.

**7.14** This provision enables the court to deviate from the principle that fair sharing is equal sharing when a spouse or civil partner has destroyed, dissipated or alienated matrimonial property before or after the relevant date. This provision is additional to the general protection in s 18 of the Family Law (Scotland) Act 1985 against transactions likely to defeat claims for inter alia financial provision on divorce or dissolution.[1]

---

1   Family Law (Scotland) Act 1985, s 18, is discussed at para **7.23** ff. This provision should perhaps have been applied in *K v K* 2013 GWD 26-530 discussed above para **7.8** note 12.

---

(d) The nature of the matrimonial property, the use made of it (including use for business purposes or as a matrimonial home) and the extent to which it is reasonable to expect it to be realised or divided or used as security.

**7.15** This is probably the most important of the special circumstances which may justify deviation from the principle that fair sharing is equal sharing. If A, a same sex spouse, uses the family home for business purposes, it might be unreasonable to order A to sell the property in order to realise its value to make a capital payment to B, the other same sex spouse. In those circumstances, the court could allow A to retain the property and order A to pay to B whatever capital sum A could afford to compensate B for the loss of B's prima facie entitlement to half the value of the house. This capital sum need not be equivalent to half the net value of the house, ie the court could decrease B's share, but it would normally still be substantial. A could be required to raise the capital by a second mortgage or the capital sum could be paid by instalments out of A's income. Similarly, while a spouse's business assets acquired during the marriage constitute matrimonial property, the court may award less than half their net value to the other spouse as clearly they may not be easily realisable.[1]

Where there are children of the family who need a home, the court could order that the family home be transferred outright to the spouse or civil partner who is looking after the children. If the children reside with W, her share of the rest of the matrimonial property would be reduced proportionately even if the reduction does not fully compensate H for the loss of half the value of all the matrimonial property.[2] In *Peacock v Peacock*[3] the couple had few assets except their house, title to which was in joint names. W looked after the children and H was unemployed and unable to contribute to the children's aliment. W had paid the mortgage instalments after H left. The Inner House of the Court of Session ordered H to transfer his one-half pro indiviso share of the house to W in return for W's assignation to him of her interest in a small life policy. The fact that there was little matrimonial property apart from the house which was required as a home for the children constituted special circumstances reducing H's share of the net value of the house to nil. On the other hand, if a couple have substantial resources so that there would be little difficulty in the party who looks after the children acquiring suitable alternative accommodation for the family, the court might well simply order the home to be sold and the proceeds divided equally between the spouses or civil partners, provided evidence was brought that it would not be contrary to the interests of the children to do so.[4]

It should be noticed that this provision is concerned with the use made of the property as a matrimonial home. In *Hales v Hales*[5] after the couple separated W continued to live in the former matrimonial home. Subsequently she began a new relationship and her partner moved into the house. He suffered a brain aneurism and the house was modified by Glasgow City Council at significant cost so as to be suitable for the partner's ongoing needs. In the action for divorce, W resisted the proposed sale of the house on the basis of special circumstances under s 10(6)(d) due to the substantial modifications that had been carried out and her inability to finance similar modifications on an alternative property. The court held that the defence was irrelevant as s 10(6)(d) referred to the matrimonial home and was therefore confined to the circumstances of the parties to the marriage and their children.

Where the matrimonial or partnership property is a spouse or civil partner's interest in a life policy or pension fund, the asset will often not be easily realisable. Unless the payer has other substantial capital,[6] it is not reasonable to expect that spouse or civil partner to make a capital sum payment of half the net value of the interest to which the payee is prima facie entitled. In these circumstances, the courts have ordered capital sum payments of less than half the value of the interest.[7] The advantage to the payee of doing so is that the capital sum payment, though less than the amount to which the payee is prima facie entitled, is paid at the date of the divorce or dissolution. Alternatively, the court may delay the payment of the capital sum until the policy or the pension matures.[8] The disadvantage to the payee of doing so is that while the payee will obtain half the value of the interest, payment of the capital sum is deferred. To compensate the payee for the deferment, the court could increase the share beyond 50 per cent[9] or order interest to be paid on the capital sum from the date of divorce or dissolution (or earlier) even though the capital sum does not have to be paid until a future date.[10] Of course, if a pension sharing order is made, there is no need to deviate from equal sharing of pension funds.[11]

If the matrimonial or partnership property is damages, there could be deviation on the grounds that they were intended to be used to support the party who was the victim of the personal injuries.[12]

---

1   *Morrison v Morrison* 1989 SCLR 574; *Crockett v Crockett* 1992 SCLR 591. Alternatively the capital sum could be ordered to be paid by instalments or payment delayed until a later date, with interest to run on the capital sum from the date of divorce (or earlier). In *Sweeney v Sweeney (No 2)* 2005 SLT 1141 the Inner House of the Court of Session accepted that there could be a deviation under s 10(6)(d) even though the assets, which were difficult to realise, had been invested by H in his business between the relevant date and the date of divorce. But in the event the court preferred to take account of this, not by awarding W less than 50 per cent, but by making the capital sum payable by instalments.

2   *Cooper v Cooper* 1989 SCLR 347 (wife obtained a property transfer of the matrimonial home even though it was the couple's major capital asset: however, the husband did not require accommodation as he was seriously ill). In *JR v AR* 2012 GWD 39-765, W received a larger share of the proceeds of the sale of the former matrimonial home so that she could purchase a suitable home for herself and their children. The sheriff accepted that an unequal share of the proceeds would be appropriate referring to 'a legitimate objective under the principles of the Act: namely that account should be taken of the parties' housing needs'. A pension sharing order was made in respect of W's pension to offset the imbalance and achieve equal division.

3   1994 SLT 40. A similar approach was taken in *Cunniff v Cunniff* 1999 SC 537, where H had to transfer his one-half pro indiviso share of the house to W even though he would then face bankruptcy!

4   *Adams v Adams (No 1)* 1997 SLT 144. The Lord Ordinary (Gill) refused to transfer the matrimonial home to W because she could not afford to run that house which was too big for her and the children; she could afford a smaller property.

5   2012 GWD 7-123.

6   *Brooks v Brooks* 1993 SLT 184.

7   *Muir v Muir* 1989 SCLR 445; *Carpenter v Carpenter* 1990 SCLR 206.

8   *Gulline v Gulline* 1992 SLT (Sh Ct) 71; *Bannon v Bannon* 1993 SLT 999; *Shand v Shand* 1994 SLT 387.

9   *Bannon v Bannon* 1993 SLT 999. Cf *Murphy v Murphy* 1996 SLT 91.

10  *Gulline v Gulline* 1992 SLT (Sh Ct) 71: on interest, see para **7.5**.

11  On pension sharing, see para **7.8**.

12  *Petrie v Petrie* 1988 SCLR 390.

(e) Actual or prospective liability for any expenses of valuation or transfer of property in connection with the divorce.

**7.16** In applying the principle in s 9(1)(a) of the Family Law (Scotland) Act 1985, prima facie the conduct of either party is not taken into account.[1] For example, if a marriage has irretrievably broken down as a result of a wife's adultery or a husband's behaviour, this is irrelevant and does not affect the principle that fair sharing of matrimonial property prima facie means equal sharing. Where a spouse or civil partner's conduct has adversely affected the financial resources of the couple, for example by dissipation of assets or unreasonably refusing to find employment, the conduct will be relevant.[2] Often, of course, such conduct may well have already been taken into account by virtue of s 10(6)(c) of the FL(S)A 1985, ie deviation from equality of sharing as a result of destruction, dissipation or alienation of property.[3] The reason why, as a general rule, misconduct is not relevant is that the principle in s 9(1)(a) is intended to recognise that a spouse or civil partner deserves a fair share of the matrimonial or partnership property as a result of his or her contribution to the marriage or civil partnership: responsibility for its breakdown should not undermine that entitlement unless the spouse or civil partner's conduct has adversely affected the assets which are to be divided.

---

1   Family Law (Scotland) Act 1985, s 11(7). See, for example, *Gracie v Gracie* 1997 SLT (Sh Ct) 15.
2   FL(S)A 1985, s 11(7)(a). In *Skarpaas v Skarpaas* 1991 SLT (Sh Ct) 15, H's alcoholism was regarded as such conduct.
3   Discussed at para **7.14**.

---

| **Principle 9(1)(b)** | Fair account should be taken of any economic advantage derived by either party from contributions by the other, and of any economic disadvantage suffered by either party in the interests of the other party or of the family. |
| --- | --- |

**7.17** This principle is intended to compensate a spouse or civil partner who, whether before or during the marriage or partnership, has either:

(1)     made a contribution to the economic advantage of the other, for example by putting money into the other party's business or working in the business as an unpaid employee;[1] or

(2)     has suffered an economic disadvantage in the interests of the other party or the family, for example by a wife giving up a well-paid job to bear and look after children[2].

Where a spouse or civil partner has suffered an economic disadvantage, there need not be a corresponding economic advantage to the other; it is sufficient if the economic disadvantage was sustained in the interests of the other party or the family.[3] Economic advantage includes gains in capital, income and earning capacity and economic disadvantage is to be construed accordingly.[4] Contributions include indirect and non-financial contributions, for example gardening or decorating the family home. A contribution made by a spouse or civil partner in keeping the home and caring for the family is expressly recognised.[5] However, where items of matrimonial or partnership property have simply increased in value between the relevant date and the date of divorce or dissolution, the courts have consistently refused to allow s 9(1)(b) to be used to give the applicant a share in the increase in value of the asset: this is because the increase is not a result of any economic contribution of the applicant during that period.[6]

It is important to note that principle 9(1)(b) applies to economic advantages made, economic disadvantages suffered and contributions made by a party *before* the marriage or registration took place.[7] Thus for example, if W had worked before a couple married in order to support H when he was undergoing training for a profession, that contribution could be taken into account under s 9(1)(b) of the Family Law (Scotland) Act 1985 even though it was made before the parties married.

Claims under this principle are particularly difficult to quantify. By s 11(2) of the FL(S)A 1985, the court must consider whether the economic advantages or disadvantages sustained by either spouse have been balanced by the economic advantages or disadvantages sustained by the other: it is only when there is an economic imbalance in the applicant's favour that an award can be made. As the Lord Ordinary (Lady Smith) observed in *Coyle v Coyle*[8]:

'It is important to recognise that Parliament did not, in the 1985 Act, provide that whenever a couple divorce after a marriage in which one has been the breadwinner and one has been the homemaker, the latter must receive extra compensatory financial provision on divorce'.

The onus rests on the applicant to show such an imbalance.[9] However, the need for this balancing exercise has sometimes been ignored by the courts.[10]

The court will also have to determine whether or not any resulting imbalance has been or will be corrected by a sharing of the value of the matrimonial or partnership property under principle 9(1)(a) or otherwise.[11] Since any awards under principle 9(1)(b) must take the form of capital sum payments or property transfer orders, in practice principles 9(1)(a) and (b) are considered together. Thus a claim under s 9(1)(b) has been met by making a property transfer order which gave the transferee not only her fair share of the matrimonial property but also the increase in value of the house between the relevant date and the date of divorce: this increase in value satisfied the s 9(1)(b) claim.[12] Again a claim by W under s 9(1)(b) was used to justify refusing to give H a share of the matrimonial property which had all been purchased by W.[13] In particular, having determined that a wife or civil partner should receive compensation under principle 9(1)(b) for her contributions to the family during the marriage or the partnership, the court may decide that the most appropriate form it should take is an outright transfer of the family home to her even though she would thereby receive more than half the value of the matrimonial or partnership property to which she was prima facie entitled under principle 9(1)(a).[14]

Section 9 (1)(b) has been used where there is no matrimonial or partnership property which is subject to fair sharing under s 9(1)(a). In *Ranaldi v Ranaldi*,[15] the couple's home was not matrimonial property and therefore W was not entitled to a share of its value under principle 9(1)(a). During the marriage, W had taken in boarders, paid off the loan over the property and enhanced its value. As a result of principle 9(1)(b), she was awarded a capital sum payment of half the increase in the value of the property during the marriage. A similar approach was taken in *Wilson v Wilson*[16] when a farmer's wife obtained a capital sum in respect of her contribution to running a farm which was not matrimonial property and therefore not subject to fair division under s 9(1)(a) of the FL(S)A 1985.

As in principle 9(1)(a), in applying principle 9(1)(b) a spouse or civil partner's misconduct is irrelevant unless it has adversely affected the financial resources of the couple.[17]

Principle 9(1)(b) was originally intended to recognise the economic contributions made by women who had followed the traditional child rearing and housekeeping role in marriage. The economic contribution so made and the economic disadvantages sustained in doing so were to be compensated by an award under s 9(1)(b) of the FL(S)A 1985. This has not happened. There are two main reasons. First, an applicant must show that there is an economic imbalance in her favour: unless an attempt is made realistically to assess the economic value of housekeeping and child care services, there is likely to be equilibrium given that she will usually have been alimented by her husband during the marriage.[18] Secondly, since only capital sum payments and/or transfer of property orders are available under s 9(1)(b) of the 1985 Act, the courts are reluctant to make an award if the husband has no capital assets. However, it is submitted that a capital sum payment is nevertheless appropriate in these circumstances – to be paid by instalments out of the husband's future income.[19] The courts are acutely aware of the economic difficulties facing middle aged women who have followed this traditional role. Their solution has been to award periodical allowances under principle 9(1)(e). In the writer's view, this is often a distortion of the function of principle 9(1)(e). Instead, recourse should be made to principle 9(1)(b), which has been designed to compensate women in this situation. The under-utilisation of s 9(1)(b) is perhaps the most disappointing feature of the way in which the FL(S)A 1985 has been applied in practice.

---

1    The economic advantage can be an increase in the value of a spouse or civil partner's non-matrimonial or non-partnership property: *Vance v Vance* 1997 SLT (Sh Ct) 71. Sums of money given by rich W to poor H during the marriage have been held to be economic advantages for the purpose of this principle: *Davidson v Davidson* 1994 SLT 506.

2    In *P v P* [2012] CSIH 15, while the court was satisfied that W had undoubtedly suffered economic disadvantage as a result of giving up her employment in London,

she had not averred that she had done so in order to care for their child: accordingly the s 9(1(b) test was not satisfied]

3     Where a wife had her jewellery forcibly removed from her this was held to constitute an economic disadvantage: *Tahir v Tahir (No 2)* 1995 SLT 451. In *Galloway v Galloway* 2003 Fam LR 10, H transferred 25 per cent of the shares in a private company to W. H administered the fund and took the dividends. W paid tax on the dividends at the higher rate. This was held to be an economic disadvantage.

4     Family Law (Scotland) Act 1985, s 9(2). Construed accordingly, it will read 'economic disadvantage means disadvantage suffered whether before or during the marriage or civil partnership and includes losses in capital, in income and earning power'. It therefore does not include losses which arise *after* the divorce or dissolution, including loss of earning power. Yet we cannot calculate loss of earning power unless we consider how the claimant is likely to fare in the employment market after divorce or dissolution. The view that future losses should not be compensated was upheld by the sheriff in *Dougan v Dougan* 1998 SLT (Sh Ct) 27.

5     FL(S)A 1985, s 9(2).

6     See *Carroll v Carroll* 1988 SCLR 104; *Phillip v Phillip* 1988 SCLR 427; *Muir v Muir* 1989 SCLR 445 (inflationary increase in the value of heritage); *Tyrrell v Tyrrell* 1990 SLT 406 (increase in the value of husband's interest in a pension scheme between the relevant date and the date of divorce); *Christie v Christie* 2004 SLT 95; *Kennedy v Kennedy* 2004 Fam LR 70. Nor is the increase in value a special circumstance for deviation under the FL(S)A 1985, s 10(1): see para **7.11**, note 1.

7     Contributions made after a couple have separated but before the divorce or dissolution are also included.

8     2004 Fam LR 2 at 9. Lady Smith also suggested that before there could be a claim under s 9(1)(b) there has to be an identifiable economic advantage to one spouse which derives from an identifiable contribution by the other: *sed quaere*. In the context of economic disadvantage at least, it is thought that it is enough if the economic disadvantage was sustained in the interests of the other party or the family.

9     *Petrie v Petrie* 1988 SCLR 390; *Welsh v Welsh* 1994 SLT 828; *W v W* [2013] CSOH 136. In *Louden v Louden* 1994 SLT 381, W's economic disadvantages were not set off by the lifestyle she enjoyed during the marriage.

10    See for example, *Wilson v Wilson* 1999 SLT 249; *R v R* 2000 Fam LR 43. Cf *Adams v Adams (No 1)* 1997 SLT 144.

11    *Harris v Harris* 2013 GWD 16-337 (Pursuer's economic disadvantage in using her inheritance to reduce the mortgage over the former matrimonial home was compensated by deviation from equal sharing of the matrimonial property in her favour as a result of s 10(6)(b) special circumstances). An award under FL(S)A 1985, s 9(1)(b) is intended to be *additional* to fair sharing of matrimonial property under s 9(1)(a); therefore it is thought that an imbalance will not have been corrected unless as in *Harris* the payee has obtained more than half the net value of the matrimonial or partnership property under s 9(1)(a). This could arise if, for example, a wife or civil partner had obtained the outright transfer of the family home under s 9(1)(a): see generally *Little v Little* 1990 SLT 230. In *Louden v Louden* 1994 SLT 381, W's share of the matrimonial property was increased to 55 per cent.

12 *Coyle v Coyle* 2004 Fam LR 2.
13 *Symanski v Symanski (No 2)* 2005 Fam LR 2.
14 *Cunniff v Cunniff* 1999 SC 537.
15 1994 SLT (Sh Ct) 25.
16 1999 SLT 249. See also *R v R* 2000 Fam LR 43.
17 FL(S)A 1985, s 11(7)(a). In *Skarpaas v Skarpaas* 1991 SLT (Sh Ct) 15, H's alcoholism was held to amount to such conduct and increased W's claim.
18 See for example, *Welsh v Welsh* 1994 SLT 828; *P v P* [2012] CSHI 15. In *McCormack v McCormack* 1987 GWD 9–287, the wife received a capital sum which was the equivalent of £125 a year for these services!
19 It would appear that this solution was overlooked by Lord Hope in *Miller v Miller; McFarlane v McFarlane* [2006] UKHL 24. This was an appeal to the House of Lords in an English case. Nevertheless Lord Hope took the opportunity to call for reform of the Family Law (Scotland) Act 1985 because a Scottish court could not award a periodical allowance under s 9(1)(b) to compensate a wife who had sustained economic disadvantage in looking after a family. But even if the husband has no capital assets at the date of divorce, a Scottish court can make an order for a capital sum to be paid by instalments over a long period out of the husband's future income. See Clive 'Financial Provision in Divorce' 2006 10 Edin LR 413.

| **Principle 9(1)(c)** | Any economic burden of caring (i) after divorce, for a child of the marriage under the age of 16 years or (ii) after dissolution of a civil partnership, for a child who has been accepted by both partners as a child of the family or in respect of whom they are by virtue of sections 33 and 42 of the Human Fertilisation and Embryology Act 2008, the parents,[1] should be shared fairly between the parties. |
|---|---|

1 On ss 33 and 42 of the 2008 Act see para **9.2**.

**7.18** Where there are dependent children of a marriage or civil partnership[1] which ends in divorce or dissolution, there cannot usually be a clean break as in most cases it will be in the children's best interests to retain contact with both parties.[2] Maintenance calculation and/or aliment for children of the family must be determined before the court will consider claims by the parties for financial provision on divorce or dissolution. But the party who looks after the children may suffer economic disadvantages in doing so: for example, he or she may not be able to take up full-time employment or may have to hire the services of a nanny.

Principle 9(1)(c) was intended to ensure that the economic burden of child care is shared fairly between the parties. In practice this meant that the party who looked after the children received additional financial provision in recognition of the economic burden of child care. But where maintenance calculation is paid, an element of the maintenance is to provide support for the parent who cares for the child. Accordingly, there has been a reduction of claims for financial provision based on principle 9(1)(c).

In determining financial provision under principle 9(1)(c) the court must consider:

(a)     any decree or arrangement for the aliment of the child of the marriage or civil partnership;

(b)     any expenditure or loss of earning capacity caused by the need to care for the child;

(c)     the need to provide suitable accommodation for the child;

(d)     the age and health of the child;

(e)     the education, financial or other circumstances of the child;

(f)     the availability and cost of suitable child care facilities or service;

(g)     the needs and resources of the parties; and

(h)     all the other circumstances of the case.[3]

The court may also take into account the fact that the party from whom financial provision is sought is supporting a person who is maintained as a dependant in his or her household, whether or not he or she owes an obligation of aliment to that dependant; for example, where a husband leaves his wife and is living with and supporting his girlfriend and her children.[4] If the court does so, this will reduce the resources available for financial provision under principle 9(1)(c). A party's misconduct is again irrelevant unless it has adversely affected the financial resources of the couple. This is because principle 9(1)(c) recognises that by contributing to the family by caring for the children, the claimant deserves financial provision.

Unlike orders under principles 9(1)(a) and (b), the court has the power when applying principle 9(1)(c) to make an order for a periodical allowance provided it is satisfied that a capital sum or property transfer is inappropriate or insufficient to satisfy the requirements of s 8(2) of the

Family Law (Scotland) Act 1985.[5] Thus, where a couple have little or no capital assets so that it is not reasonable in the light of their resources to make a capital sum payment or a property transfer order, a periodical allowance may well be justified under principle 9(1)(c)[6]. If a periodical allowance is made, it could – subject to recall or variation – last until the youngest child of the marriage or civil partnership reaches the age of 16.[6] If the couple have extensive capital assets, financial provision under principle 9(1)(c) could take the form of the payment of a capital sum or property transfer order *in addition* to any financial provision under principles 9(1)(a) or (b). Alternatively, if the capital assets were not so extensive, principle 9(1)(c) could be used to justify the transfer of the family home to the party who is looking after the children even though that party would thereby receive more than half the value of the matrimonial or partnership property to which he or she was prima facie entitled under principle 9(1)(a).[7]

---

1   Children of a marriage or civil partnership include children who have been accepted by the spouses or civil partners as a child of the family: Family Law (Scotland) Act 1985, s 27.
2   See **Ch 12**.
3   FL(S)A 1985, s 11(3). See for example, *Miller v Miller* 1990 SCLR 666 (adjusted aliment for children to satisfy claim); *Davidson v Davidson* 1994 SLT 506 (used to *reduce* H's claim against rich W).
4   FL(S)A 1985, s 11(6).
5   FL(S)A 1985, s 13(2). Where there are sufficient assets a capital sum payment will be appropriate; see for example *B v B* [2012] CSOH 21.
6   See for example *Wilson v Wilson* 2013 GWD 54-678 (periodical allowance of £500 until the child reached the age of 16 to begin after expiry of a periodical allowance of £1000 per month for 18 months to be paid to W under s 9(1)(d): see para **7.19** below).
7   A periodical allowance could be competent beyond the child's 16th birthday if the pursuer had incurred a substantial economic burden until the child reached 16 but the defender's means were not sufficient to pay the appropriate periodical allowance which would compensate the pursuer by the time the child reached 16: *Monkman v Monkman* 1988 SLT (Sh Ct) 37.
8   See for example *Cunniff v Cunniff* 1999 SC 537; *Connolly v Connolly* 2005 Fam LR 106. Here a child had a significant disability and W could only work part-time. Her s 9(1)(c) claim was to be satisfied by the increase in value of her share of the family homes when they were finally to be sold.

| | |
|---|---|
| **Principle 9(1)(d)** | A party who has been dependent to a substantial degree on the financial support of the other party should be awarded such financial provision as is reasonable to enable the party to adjust over a period of not more than three years from the date of the decree of divorce or dissolution to the loss of that support. |

**7.19** The purpose of this principle is to provide financial support for a spouse or civil partner who has been financially dependent on the other spouse or civil partner to enable her to readjust to life as a single person after the divorce or dissolution.[1] The financial provision can take the form of a periodical allowance provided the court is satisfied that a capital sum or property transfer is inappropriate or insufficient to satisfy the requirements of s 8(2) of the Family Law (Scotland) Act 1985.[2]

The payment of any periodical allowance is restricted to a maximum period of three years. It might be thought that a three-year maximum period is too short to enable a spouse or civil partner to readjust to life as a single person but the view was taken that it was not the function of the law on financial provision to act as a panacea for the general problem of unemployment. Moreover, it should also be noted that any financial provision awarded under principle 9(1)(d) is *additional* to any capital sum or property transfer order awarded by virtue of principles 9(1)(a) or (b) and any financial provision awarded under principle 9(1)(c), which can last until the youngest child reaches the age of 16.[3]

Before the s 9(1)(d) principle applies, the applicant must have been financially dependent to a substantial degree on the other spouse or civil partner. And so for example, where a wife has been able to find a job during the period between separation and divorce, the principle may not be triggered at all or any support awarded will not be for the maximum period of three years.[4] However, provided she has continued to receive aliment from her husband, a wife can expect some financial provision under this principle even if she has obtained part-time employment.[5]

In making any order the court must have regard to:

    (1)    the age, health and earning capacity of the applicant;

(2)    the duration and extent of the dependence prior to divorce or dissolution (thus for example, a wife who has been a party to a short marriage and has given up her job only shortly before the divorce, is unlikely to receive a periodical allowance for the maximum three years, as opposed to a wife who has been dependent for many years before the divorce);[6]

(3)    the applicant's intention to undertake a course of education or training;

(4)    the needs and resources of the parties; and

(5)    all the other circumstances of the case.[7]

The court may also take into account the fact that the party from whom financial provision is sought is supporting a person who is maintained as a dependant in his or her household whether or not he or she owes an obligation of aliment to that dependant.[8] Unlike s 9(1)(a), (b) and (c) principles, the applicant's misconduct will be taken into account not only when it has affected the couple's financial resources but also if it would be manifestly inequitable to leave the conduct out of account.[9] This is because principle 9(1)(d) is based on equitable considerations and is not a recognition of what a spouse or civil partner has earned or will earn as a result of his or her contributions to the marriage or civil partnership.

Given that financial provision under principle 9(1)(d) is *additional* to any financial provision awarded under principles 9(1)(a), (b) or (c), it is submitted that it will be useful in helping a spouse or civil partner to readjust to being single again. It will be particularly valuable when the applicant intends to embark on a course of further education or retraining. But by restricting the payment of any periodical allowances under this principle to a maximum of three years, any order will not be perceived by the payer as an indefinite financial burden.

---

1    *Morrison v Morrison* 1989 SCLR 574; *Maitland v Maitland* (9 December 1991, unreported) Sh Ct.

2    Family Law (Scotland) Act 1985, s 13(2). See for example *Wilson v Wilson* [2011] CSOH 33 (Periodical allowance of £1000 per month for 18 months) If there are sufficient assets a capital sum payment should be made: *B v B* [2012] CSOH 21, 2012 Fam LR 65.In *McConnell v McConnell* 1995 GWD 3–145 the Inner House ordered W to sell land transferred to her and invest proceeds to provide an income rather than have a periodical allowance under the Family Law (Scotland) Act 1985, s 9(1)(d)).

3   Nevertheless in *Miller v Miller; Mcfarlane v MacFarlane* [2006] UKHL 24 Lord
    Hope argued that the courts should have discretion in exceptional circumstances to
    award periodical allowances under s 9(1)(d) which could extend beyond three years.
    Otherwise it could be unfair to women who have given up their careers to look after
    their families but were facing difficulties in finding employment. But with respect
    this overlooks the power of the court to make a substantial capital sum payment
    under s 9(1)(b) to be payable in instalments out of the husband's future income: these
    instalments could be payable for far longer than three years: see also discussion at para
    **7.17** note 18.
4   *Dever v Dever* 1988 SCLR 352 (six months' support); *Muir v Muir* 1989 SCLR 445
    (one year's support); *Miller v Miller* 1990 SCLR 666 (none at all!).
5   *Tyrrell v Tyrrell* 1990 SLT 406. In *L v L* 2003 Fam LR 101 W received a periodical
    allowance under s 9(1)(d) where a delay was anticipated in the payment by H of a
    substantial capital sum.
6   *Sheret v Sheret* 1990 SCLR 799 (13 weeks only as very short marriage).
7   FL(S)A 1985, s 11(4).
8   FL(S)A 1985, s 11(6).
9   FL(S)A 1985, s 11(7)(b); *Miller v Miller* 1990 SCLR 666 (argued that W had bought
    too large a house).

---

| | |
|---|---|
| **Principle 9(1)(e)** | A party who at the time of divorce or dissolution seems likely to suffer serious financial hardship as a result of the divorce or dissolution should be awarded such financial provision as is reasonable to relieve him of hardship over a reasonable period. |

**7.20** Principle 9(1)(e) is intended to be a 'long stop' measure where adequate financial provision for a spouse or civil partner cannot be achieved by applying the previous four principles. It deals with the situation where, *at the time of the divorce or dissolution*, the applicant is old or is seriously ill[1] and, because he or she is unable to work, will suffer serious financial hardship. The principle does not apply if the applicant is overtaken by illness or other misfortune *after* the date of divorce or dissolution: that is not the concern of a previous spouse or civil partner.

Again financial provision can take the form of a periodical allowance provided the court is satisfied that a capital sum payment or property transfer is inappropriate or insufficient to satisfy the requirements of s 8(2) of the Family Law (Scotland) Act 1985.[2] In making any order, the court must have regard to:

(1)    the age, health and earning capacity of the applicant;

(2)    the duration of the marriage or civil partnership;

(3)    the standard of living of the parties during the marriage or civil partnership;

(4)    the needs and resources of the parties; and

(5)    all the other circumstances of the case.[3]

The court may also take into account the fact that the party from whom financial provision is sought is supporting a person who is maintained as a dependant in his or her household whether or not he or she owes an obligation of aliment to that dependant.[4] Moreover, the applicant's misconduct will be taken into account not only when it has affected the couple's financial resources, but also when it would be manifestly inequitable to leave the conduct out of account.[5] This is because principle 9(1)(e) is clearly based on equitable considerations and accordingly an applicant's responsibility for the break up of the marriage or civil partnership should be a relevant consideration. Nevertheless, it should be stressed that conduct will only be relevant when it would be *manifestly* inequitable to ignore it.

Recourse to the s 9(1)(e) principle should be rare. For example if there has been a long marriage during which a wife has given up employment to look after her family, then even if at the date of the divorce she is too old to enter the labour market, the s 9(1)(e) principle should not be applicable. For in the circumstances of this type of marriage, the wife should have obtained substantial financial provision under principles 9(1)(a) and (b), particularly when it is remembered that matrimonial property includes the husband's interests under any life policies or occupational pension schemes. Nevertheless, the courts have made awards of periodical allowance to middle aged women who have already received generous capital settlements.[6] They had not, however, received an award under principle 9(1)(b) in recognition of their economic contributions in respect of caring for the children and running the household during a long marriage. The courts were concerned about their ability to survive comfortably without an income and therefore made an award of periodical allowance under s 9(1)(e). With respect, this is to distort the scope of s 9(1)(e) as the women were not in *serious* financial hardship since they had received substantial capital settlements. The proper course in these cases was to make an award under s 9(1)(b) of the 1985 Act.

Moreover, since the serious financial hardship must arise *from the divorce or dissolution,* where a couple have very limited resources principle 9(1)(e) should be inapplicable because any periodical allowance awarded simply reduces the amount of income support and other benefits to which the payee would otherwise be entitled as a single person.[7] But the fact that the applicant was not being financially supported by the defender immediately before the divorce or dissolution is not in itself enough to prevent a claim under principle 9(1)(e). In *Haugan v Haugan*[8] the defender had failed to aliment his wife during the marriage. The Inner House of the Court of Session held that she was not precluded from using s 9(1)(e) merely because if she was divorced without any financial provision she would be no worse off financially than she was while married. The absence of support during the marriage was, however, a relevant factor in determining the amount she should be awarded.

Nevertheless, it is thought that on occasions the courts have distorted the scope of s 9(1)(e) by awarding a periodical allowance. In *Stott v Stott,*[9] for example, the husband had a very low income and no capital assets. If there had been no divorce, any award of aliment for the wife would have been no greater than the income support and other benefits she would receive if she did divorce. Yet the court awarded her a periodical allowance. In the present writer's view, the s 9(1)(e) claim should have been rejected because her financial situation was the same whether or not she remained married and therefore no financial hardship arose from *the divorce.* The solution was to have recognised the wife's economic contribution in running the home and looking after the children by making an award of a capital sum under s 9(1)(b) of the 1985 Act, payable by instalments over a long period.[10]

It should only be in very exceptional circumstances that principle 9(1)(e) will be relevant. For example, if there has been a short marriage and the couple have few capital assets but H has a reasonable income, the s 9(1)(e) principle might apply if W was seriously physically disabled at the time of the divorce provided her conduct was not responsible for the break up of the marriage.[11]

If a periodical allowance is ordered under this principle, while subject to recall or variation, it is not limited to any maximum period and can continue until the payee remarries or dies.[12] The fact that it gives rise to a potentially life long financial burden for the payer is another reason why principle 9(1)(e) should be applicable only in the most exceptional circumstances.

1   *Johnstone v Johnstone* 1990 SCLR 358.
2   Family Law (Scotland) Act 1985, s 13(2).
3   FL(S)A 1985, s 11(5).
4   FL(S)A 1985, s 11(6).
5   FL(S)A 1985, s 11(7).
6   *Bell v Bell* 1988 SCLR 457; *Humphrey v Humphrey* (25 May 1988, unreported); *Gribb v Gribb* 1995 SCLR 1007, 1996 SLT 719. Cf the approach of the Inner House in *McConnell v McConnell* 1995 GWD 3–145.
7   *Barclay v Barclay* 1991 SCLR 205: FL(S)A 1985, s 9(1)(e) was not triggered where W was the victim of multiple sclerosis and in hospital. The marriage was short and W was young. H was living with a cohabitant and child. The effect of stopping aliment to W would deprive her of only 5 per cent of her total income. Therefore it was not serious hardship.
8   2002 SC 631.
9   1987 GWD 17–645.
10  On the use of the FL(S)A 1985, s 9(1)(b) in these circumstances, see the discussion at para **7.7**. In *Stott v Stott* 1987 GWD 17–645, the sheriff awarded a periodical allowance under s 9(1)(d) of the 1985 Act to be followed after three years by a periodical allowance under s 9(1)(e) of the 1985 Act. It is submitted that the order under s 9(1)(d) should not have been made. Its purpose is to enable the payee to adjust to the loss of the payer's financial support: by awarding a periodical allowance under s 9(1)(e) to take effect three years later, the payer's financial support continues. In other words, principles s 9(1)(d) and (e) are mutually exclusive. On principle 9(1)(d), see para **7.19**.
11  But even then it is doubtful if H has a low income: *Barclay v Barclay* 1991 SCLR 205. Loss of a wealthy wife has been held to be serious financial hardship for her destitute husband! See *Davidson v Davidson* 1994 SLT 506.
12  FL(S)A 1985, s 13(7)(b); *Johnstone v Johnstone* 1990 SCLR 358.

## Conclusion

**7.21** The Family Law (Scotland) Act 1985, s 9 principles provide sophisticated guidelines which judges must use when exercising their discretion in making orders for financial provision on divorce or dissolution. Principles 9(1)(a) and (b) give recognition through the payment of capital sums and property transfer orders of the economic and other contributions made by the parties to the marriage or civil partnership and provide compensation for any economic disadvantages suffered by them in the interests of the family. As such, they constitute a major step towards a system of deferred community of property and, in effect, perceive marriage and civil partnership as basically an equal relationship between the parties. It is therefore to be regretted that more use has not been made of s 9(1)(b). At the same time, principle 9(1)(c) recognises the need to provide financial provision for the party who sustains an economic burden as a result of continued involvement in caring for any child of the family after the divorce or dissolution;[1] and principle 9(1)(d) is designed to help a spouse or civil partner to readjust to life as a single person – though in this case a periodical allowance is restricted to a maximum period of three years. The final principle is a 'long stop' for very exceptional cases where at the time of the divorce or dissolution serious economic hardship is likely to arise as a result of the divorce or dissolution. Because of the under-utilisation of s 9(1)(b) it is submitted that too great a reliance has been made on s 9(1)(e) thus undermining the economic 'clean break' between the parties which was one of the major aims of the legislation. Finally, unless it has adversely affected the couple's financial resources, misconduct is irrelevant except in relation to principles 9(1)(d) and (e) where it should only be taken into account in so far as it would be manifestly inequitable *not* to do so.[2] This is, of course, consistent with a non-fault system of divorce and dissolution.[3]

Where appropriate, it is important to use all the principles in order to achieve a financial settlement which can best satisfy the claimant's needs: often this will be an attempt to ensure that the party looking after the children can continue to live in the family home.[4]

---

1    But maintenance calculation has overtaken the issue by providing an element of financial support for the parent who cares for the child: see para **7.18**.

2    It is also significant that periodical allowances are most likely to be awarded under these principles.

3    On the operation of the Family Law (Scotland) Act 1985 in practice, see *The Impact of the Family Law (Scotland) Act 1985 on Solicitors' Divorce Practice* (November 1990) Scottish Office Central Research Unit Papers.

4    See, for example, *Cunniff v Cunniff* 1999 SC 537.

## AGREEMENTS FOR FINANCIAL PROVISION

**7.22** It was a cardinal principle of the pre-1985 law that a spouse could validly discharge his or her right to apply for financial provision on divorce.[1] Spouses could agree for themselves the appropriate redistribution of their property and thus achieve an economic 'clean break' on divorce. The problem was that because of the uncertainty on what financial provision a court was likely to order if the case was litigated, lawyers had difficulty in advising their clients on what, in the circumstances of the marriage, constituted a fair settlement. The introduction of the s 9 principles gives greater certainty as to the outcome of litigation and lawyers are in a better position to negotiate financial settlements on behalf of their clients.

Prior to the Family Law (Scotland) Act 1985, an agreement on the financial provision to be made on divorce could not be set aside unless there was evidence of a vitiating factor such as error, fraud, undue influence or misrepresentation. Therefore it was, and is, important for the parties to be separately advised. Section 16 of the FL(S)A 1985, gives the courts limited additional powers to set aside or vary agreements on financial provision to be made on divorce or dissolution.[2]

First, any term in an agreement relating to the payment of a periodical allowance may be varied or set aside provided there is an express term in the agreement to this effect.[3] This can be done at any time after the divorce or dissolution has been granted.[4]

Secondly, any term relating to a periodical allowance can be varied or set aside if the payer has become bankrupt or a child maintenance calculation has been made.[5] This can be done on, or at any time after, granting decree of divorce or dissolution.

Thirdly, on granting decree on divorce or dissolution,[6] the court may set aside or vary any agreement or any term of such an agreement that was not 'fair and reasonable' at the time when the agreement was made.[7] Although the courts now have this power 'to police' such agreements to ensure that they were fair and reasonable *at the time they were made*, because the power can only be exercised when granting decree of divorce or dissolution,[8] the aim of achieving an economic 'clean break' between the parties after the divorce or dissolution will not be frustrated. It is thought that while this power was desirable for the additional protection of parties to such agreements, its limited nature will ensure that it does not operate to discourage parties from self-regulation of their financial arrangements on divorce or dissolution.

1    *Dunbar v Dunbar* 1977 SLT 169; *Thomson v Thomson* 1982 SLT 521; *Elder v Elder* 1985 SLT 471.
2    These include agreements made before as well as during a marriage ie ante nuptial agreements are included: *Kibble v Kibble* 2010 SLT (Sh Ct) 5.
3    Family Law (Scotland) Act 1985, s 16(1)(a); *Mills v Mills* 1989 SCLR 213. It does not matter if the agreement refers – wrongly – to alimentary payments rather than periodical allowances: *Drummond v Drummond* 1995 SCLR 428, 1996 SLT 386.
4    FL(S)A 1985, s 16(2)(a); *Mills v Mills* 1989 SCLR 213; *Drummond v Drummond* 1995 SCLR 428, 1996 SLT 386.
5    FL(S)A 1985, s 16(3).
6    FL(S)A 1985, s 16(2)(b). The court may also exercise its power within such period as the court may specify on granting decree. Although the court cannot set aside the agreement until in a position to grant decree of divorce or dissolution, this does not prevent the court having a preliminary hearing to determine whether or not the agreement is fair: *Gillon v Gillon (No 2)* 1994 SLT 984.
7    FL(S)A 1985, s 16(1)(b). While the onus lies on the pursuer to establish that the agreement is not fair and reasonable, it is not necessary to prove that it was both unfair and unreasonable: *Clarkson v Clarkson* 2008 SLT (Sh Ct) 2. It is an objective test. The agreement is considered from the point of view of both parties. The quality of legal advice is important: *Gillon v Gillon (No 1)* 1994 SLT 978. But the fact that the same solicitor advised both parties is not per se sufficient to render an agreement unfair: *Worth v Worth* 1994 SLT (Sh Ct) 54. The courts are reluctant to overturn agreements validly entered into by the parties: *Inglis v Inglis* 1999 SLT (Sh Ct) 59. It is not enough that a spouse has been overgenerous and then changes his or her mind: *Anderson v Anderson* 1991 SLT (Sh Ct) 11. Nor does the fact that the assets are unevenly distributed per se give rise to an inference of unreasonableness or unfairness: *Gillon v Gillon (No 3)* 1995 SLT 678. In *Clarkson* above, the sheriff accepted the defender's contention that the agreement could not be set aside at common law on the grounds of uninduced error as to the value of the property which was the subject of the agreement.
8    Or within a period specified by the court when granting decree.

## Procedural matters

**7.23** By the Family Law (Scotland) Act 1985, s 18, a spouse or civil partner who has made a claim for an order for financial provision[1] may, not later than a year from the date of disposal of the claim, apply to the court for an order setting aside or varying any transfer of, or transaction involving, property which was effected by the other party not more than five years before the date of making the claim.[2] The court will make such an order if satisfied by the challenger that the transaction had, or was likely to have, the effect of defeating, in whole or in part, the applicant's claim for financial provision. This is an objective criterion: there is no need to establish that the transfer was intended by the transferor to defeat the applicant's claim[3]. Transactions will cover not only dispositions or settlements of property but also gifts of money and other moveables.[4]

An order under s 18 of the 1985 Act does not prejudice the rights of a third party in or to the property where the third party has acquired the property or any rights therein in good faith and for value or has derived title to such property or rights from any person who has done so. Thus, for example, if three years before A's claim for financial provision B, his civil partner, transferred £20K to B's boyfriend, C, the court could set aside the transfer unless C was in good faith and had given value in respect of the money, for example if C had sold to B a painting worth £20K.[5]

Finally, in an action for financial provision,[6] the court can order either party to provide details of his or her resources.[7]

It should also be remembered that before the determination of an action for divorce, dissolution or declarator of nullity, the court has the power to make an award of interim aliment to a party to the action.[8] Only periodical payments can be awarded which are payable until the date of the disposal of the action[9] when the court will make orders for financial provision.

---

1 The section also applies to an action for aliment, or variation or recall of a decree of aliment or order for financial provision.
2 The court has also the power to interdict the party from entering into such a transfer or transaction.
3 *M v M* [2011] CSOH 33.
4 Warrants for inhibition or arrestment on the dependence are also possible, on cause shown, in respect of any property which could be relevant in a claim for financial provision or aliment: Family Law (Scotland) Act 1985, s 19.
5 In *M v M and Wards Estate Trustees Ltd* 2009 SLT 608 prior to the divorce H had transferred assets into a trust for the benefit of children from previous relationships. Because the trustees had not given value, the court granted an interim interdict preventing the trustees from distributing the trust funds to the beneficiaries.

6    Or actions for aliment or interim aliment.
7    FL(S)A 1985, s 20. See, for example, *George v George* 1991 SLT (Sh Ct) 8; *Berry v Berry* 1991 SLT 42. Section 20 of the 1985 Act does not empower the court to order the defender to provide documents to vouch for the value of certain property nor written assurances that there are no further assets: *Nelson v Nelson* 1993 SCLR 149.
8    FL(S)A 1985, s 6. Interim aliment can also be awarded in actions for aliment: *McGeoch v McGeoch* 1998 Fam LR 8.
9    FL(S)A 1985, s 6(3).

Chapter 8

# Cohabitants

## INTRODUCTION

**8.1** One of the features of modern society is the social acceptance of couples who choose to live together without marrying or registering a civil partnership. In some cases the couple will eventually marry, particularly when they decide to have children. But for others their relationship continues simply as cohabitation. How should the law respond to such relationships? At one extreme the law could ignore the fact that the couple lived together and treat them as single persons. At the other end of the spectrum, the law could treat them as though they were married thereby thrusting the obligations of opposite sex or same sex marriage on persons who had chosen not to enter that institution. Over the years Scots law has given rights to and imposed obligations upon cohabitants. It has done so in a haphazard and unprincipled way. The purpose of this chapter is to give an account of the major rights and obligations which arise from cohabitation.

## COHABITATION

**8.2** The fact that a couple are living together does not in itself generate rights and duties. As a general rule it is only when a couple live together as though they were married that their cohabitation will do so[1]. In determining whether a couple are living together as if they were married, the court will consider inter alia the following factors:[2]

(a)   whether the parties have a sexual relationship;

(b)   whether the parties are members of the same household;

(c)   the nature of the parties' financial arrangements;

(d)   the stability of the parties' relationship;

(e)   whether the parties have children together or have accepted children as children of their family;

(f)     whether the parties appear to their family, friends and members of the public as a couple who are married or cohabitants of each other[3]; and

(g)     whether one party has told the other that their relationship was over[4].

It will be clear that before a couple will be treated as living together as though they were married, their relationship must exhibit the characteristics of marriage including sexual relations, emotional commitment, children, shared finances, and some degree of stability and social acceptance as a couple. Whether a couple's relationship exhibits enough of these characteristics for the inference to be drawn that they are or were living together as though they were married is ultimately a question of fact to be determined by the court.

For many years only opposite sex couples were recognised as cohabitants for legal purposes. However, in *Ghaidan v Godin-Mendoza*[5] the House of Lords accepted that statutes which gave rights to opposite sex couples would have to be construed as including same sex couples in order to avoid unlawful discrimination under Article 13 of the European Convention on Human Rights read in conjunction with Article 8 (right to respect for private and family life, home and correspondence). In *Telfer v Kellock*[6] the Lord Ordinary (Lady Smith) accepted that the Damages (Scotland) Act 1976 would have to be interpreted in this way. However, with the introduction of same sex marriage the relevant law applies to same sex as well as opposite sex cohabitants[7].

Because cohabitation has to be inferred from the facts of a particular relationship, unlike marriage or registration of a civil partnership, there will always be a degree of uncertainty on when cohabitation as spouses began or, indeed, ended. This is inevitable. One of the most important and welcome features of Scots law is that there are no minimum periods of cohabitation, for example a year or two years, which must elapse before the couple acquire rights and obligations. The length of their relationship will of course be a relevant factor in determining whether or not their relationship has the element of stability necessary for the inference to be drawn that they were in fact living together as though they were married.

1    Since the introduction of same sex marriage any reference in an enactment to persons living together as if they were in a civil partnership ceases to have effect: Marriage and Civil Partnership (Scotland) Act 2014, s 4(4).
2    Similar criteria have been described as 'admirable signposts' in *Crake v Supplementary Benefits Commission* [1982] 1 All ER 498.
3    In *M v T* 2011 GWD 40-828 the sheriff stressed the importance of how the couple presented themselves to their family and the public] 'given the public nature of the institution of marriage which underpins the issue': ibid at para 30.
4    *Garrad v Inglis* 2014 GWD 1-17.
5    [2004] 3 WLR 113.
6    2004 SLT 1290.
7    Marriage and Civil Partnership (Scotland) Act 2014, s 4.

# SOME LEGAL CONSEQUENCES OF COHABITATION[1]

## Personal effects

**8.3** Unlike spouses, cohabitants are *not* under an obligation to aliment each other. On the other hand, for the purpose of obtaining income support, the needs and resources of a couple who are living together in the same household as if they were married are aggregated.[2] Similarly they are liable relatives.[3] When a person is injured, his or her cohabitant is a relative for the purposes of the Administration of Justice Act 1982.[4] If a person dies as a result of personal injuries, his or her cohabitant is a member of the deceased's immediate family for the purposes of the Damages (Scotland) Act 2011.[5] It is thought that cohabitants would be treated in the same way as a married couple for the purpose of the doctrine of good faith laid down in *Smith v Bank of Scotland*.[6]

1    There are important rights enjoyed by cohabitants under housing legislation: these are beyond the scope of the current text.
2    Social Security Contributions and Benefits Act 1992, s 137(1).
3    Social Security Administration Act 1992, s 78.
4    Sections 8, 9 and 13. The 1982 Act is discussed above at para **3.6**.
5    The 2011 Act is discussed above at para **3.6**.
6    1997 SC (HL) 111, discussed above at para **3.5**.

## Property issues

**8.4** The Family Law (Scotland) Act 2006 contains important property rights for cohabitants. For the purposes of the 2006 Act, s 25(1)(a) states that cohabitant means a member of a couple consisting of a man and a woman who are or were living together as if they were husband and wife[1]. But in determining whether a couple are cohabitants, the court is expressly directed by s 25(2) to have regard to how long the couple have been living together, the nature of their relationship during that period and the nature and extent of any financial arrangements which subsisted between them. Section 25(2) is problematic. To give the definition of cohabitant in s 25(1) and then redefine it in s 25(2) is intellectually incoherent. The provision would have made more sense if it had stated that the factors in s 25(2) were to be considered in determining under s 25(1) whether or not a couple were living together as husband and wife. Alternatively, having determined that a couple were living together as husband and wife, the provision could have stated that in exercising its discretion to make awards of financial provision on separation or death,[2] the court should have regard to the factors in s 25(2).

Section 26 provides that, in any question as to the respective rights of ownership of cohabitants in household goods, there shall be a rebuttable presumption that each cohabitant has an equal share in any household goods acquired during the period of cohabitation. The presumption does not apply to household goods acquired by gift or succession from a third party. Household goods are defined[3] as any goods, including decorative or ornamental goods, kept or used at any time during the cohabitation for their joint domestic purposes in any residence in which the couple were cohabiting. These would include all kinds of domestic furniture and appliances. But because the goods must be used for *joint* domestic purposes, it would not include a wristwatch as opposed to a grandfather clock. The provision only applies to goods, ie moveable property. There is therefore no presumption of common ownership in heritable property, for example the house or flat where the couple live. Money and securities, road vehicles and pets are expressly excluded. Unlike the analogous provision for spouses and civil partners in s 25 of the Family Law (Scotland) Act 1985,[4] there is no equivalent of s 25(2) under which the presumption cannot be rebutted 'by reason only that ... the goods in question were purchased from a third party by either party alone or by both in unequal shares'. It would therefore appear that in relation to cohabitants such evidence could of itself rebut the presumption. It is difficult to see how the factors listed in s 25(2) of the 2006 Act could be used to prevent a couple being treated as cohabitants for the purpose of this section although, of course, the nature and extent of their financial arrangements could be evidence which could be used to rebut the presumption.

Section 27 provides that any savings made from housekeeping allowances by cohabitants or any property bought with such money, should be owned in common between the cohabitants. The rule is subject to any agreement to the contrary between the parties. Unlike the analogous provision for spouses and civil partners under s 26 of the Family law (Scotland) Act 1985,[4] s 27(3) expressly provides that property does not include the house or flat which the cohabitants used as their sole or main residence. Again it is difficult to see how the factors in s 25(2) of the 2006 Act could be used to prevent a couple being treated as cohabitants for the purpose of this section, although their financial arrangements could contain an agreement that any savings from an allowance or any property bought from such savings should not be owned in equal shares.

It is important to emphasise that these provisions are irrelevant in determining the ownership of heritable property which remains governed by the ordinary rules of property law. This is particularly important in relationship to the ownership of the property in which the couple lives. Accordingly, where title is registered in the names of both cohabitants, they are common owners. But if title is registered in the name of only one of the cohabitants, only that cohabitant is the owner of the property. This can give rise to unfairness if the non-owner has directly contributed to the purchase of the property, or has relieved the owner of expenditure by paying household bills, or providing services thus indirectly contributing to the acquisition of the property.

But as Lord Hope explained in the English case of *Stack v Dowden*[6] it may be possible for a remedy to be found in the law of unjustified enrichment. In *Satchwell v McIntosh*[7], for example, title was taken in the name of one of the cohabitants but the other had directly contributed to the purchase price and had paid for some refurbishments. Although the defender was the owner of the property, under principles of unjustified enrichment, the pursuer recovered the monies that she had paid. In *McKenzie v Rutter*[8] the parties agreed to sell their existing properties in order to purchase a house. Only one of the parties sold their property in order to buy the house, title to which was nevertheless taken in joint names. Both were therefore common owners. When the cohabitant who had not sold her property insisted on an action of division and sale of the house, her share of the proceeds was paid to the other cohabitant for otherwise she would have been unjustifiably enriched. However, such cases will now probably proceed under section 28 of the 2006 Act.[9]

---

1   The phrase 'husband and wife' must be construed as including same sex spouses and accordingly same sex cohabitants are included: Marriage and Civil Partnership (Scotland) Act 2014, s 4.
2   On these see below at paras **8.6** and **8.7**.
3   Family Law (Scotland) Act 2006, s 26(4).
4   Discussed above at para **4.5**.
5   Discussed above at para **4.8**.
6   [2007] UKHL 17.
7   2006 SLT (ShCt) 117. See also *Shilliday v Smith* 1998 SC 725.
8   2007 SLT (Sh Ct) 117.
9   See para **8.6**.

---

## The occupation of the family home

**8.5** Cohabitants may experience difficulties in relation to the occupation of their family accommodation when their relationships begin to break down. The Matrimonial Homes (Family Protection) (Scotland) Act 1981 provides some relief. There are generally two situations which occur.

(a) The first situation is where a couple are cohabiting and one partner is entitled to occupy the house and the other partner is not entitled.

The non-entitled partner may apply to a court for the grant of occupancy rights in relation to the house in which they are cohabiting.[1] Occupancy rights can be granted for a period not exceeding six months,[2] although the initial period can be extended for further periods of up to six months with no overall limit. A non-entitled partner's rights of occupation are the same as those of a non-entitled spouse.[3]

A cohabiting couple is defined as a man and a woman who are living with each other as if they were man and wife[4]. In determining whether a couple are cohabiting for the purpose of an application for occupation rights under s 18(1) of the Matrimonial Homes (Family Protection) (Scotland) Act 1981, the court is directed to consider all the circumstances of the case, including the length of their relationship and whether they have any children.[5] The couple must be cohabiting as man and wife at the time of the conduct giving rise to the application for occupancy rights,[6] but the applicant need not be residing in the house at the time of the application. The longer they have been apart, of course, the less likely the court will exercise its discretion under s 18(1) and grant occupancy rights.[7]

When an order granting occupancy rights is in force, certain provisions of the 1981 Act apply to the couple.[8] In particular, regulatory and exclusion orders are available under ss 3 and 4 of the 1981 Act.[9] By s 18A of the 1981 Act the court can grant a domestic interdict: (a) restraining or prohibiting the defender's conduct towards the pursuer or any child in the pursuer's permanent or temporary care; and (b) prohibiting the defender from entering or remaining in: (i) a family home occupied by the pursuer and the defender; (ii) any other residence occupied by the pursuer; (iii) the pursuer's place of work; and (iv) any school attended by a child in the pursuer's care. Where the defender is an entitled partner or has statutory rights of occupation under s 18(1) of the 1981 Act, a domestic interdict cannot be granted prohibiting the defender from entering or remaining in the family home occupied by the pursuer unless it is ancillary to an exclusion order under s 4 of the 1981 Act. Tenancy transfer orders under s 13 of the 1981 Act are also available.[10] However, the non-entitled partner's occupancy rights are not protected from dealings by the entitled partner with third parties.[11]

(b) The second situation is where both partners are entitled to occupy the house.

Here there is no need for an application under s 18(1) of the 1981 Act. But the same provisions of the 1981 Act apply to the couple as though a s 18(1) order was in force.[12] The entitled partners do not have to be residing together at the time of the proceedings; it is enough that they were living together at the time of the conduct which gave rise to the action. Thus for example, where entitled joint tenants were living together as man and wife at the time of the man's misconduct, his partner obtained a tenancy transfer order in an action brought ten months after she had left the house.[13]

It must be stressed that when one partner is non-entitled, the protection afforded by these provisions of the 1981 Act do not apply unless and until there has been a successful application by the non-entitled partner for occupancy rights. Thus in *Clarke v Hatten*[14] an entitled partner was unable to use the 1981 Act to obtain a domestic interdict as the non-entitled partner whose violence she had fled, had not applied for occupancy rights.[15] In contrast, a non-entitled spouse or civil partner has statutory rights of occupation of the matrimonial or family home as a result of simply being married or registering a civil partnership.

Under the Mortgage Rights (Scotland) Act 2001, a person who can apply to have the creditor's rights in respect of the debtor's residential property suspended for a reasonable period includes the debtor's opposite sex or same sex cohabitant if the security subjects are that person's sole or main residence.[16] Where the property is no longer the sole or main residence of the debtor, a person who was the debtor's cohabitant can also apply provided he or she has lived there for at least six months before it ceased to be the debtor's sole or main residence.[17] In addition, the security subjects must be the sole or main residence of a child below the age of 16 who is a child of that person and of the debtor. A child includes a stepchild and any person brought up or treated by the applicant and the debtor as their child.[18]

---

1    Matrimonial Homes (Family Protection) (Scotland) Act 1981, s 18(1).
2    MH(FP)(S)A 1981, s 18(1).
3    MH(FP)(S)A 1981, s 18(6).
4    The phrase 'man and wife' must be construed as including same sex spouses and accordingly same sex cohabitants are included: Marriage and Civil Partnership (Scotland) Act 2014, s 4.
5    MH(FP)(S)A 1981, s 18(2). In *Armour v Armour* 1994 SLT 1127, it was emphasised that s 18(2) applies only to determine whether or not a couple are cohabiting for the purpose of a s 18(1) application.
6    *Armour v Armour* 1994 SLT 1127.
7    *Verity v Fenner* 1993 SCLR 223 (apart for 11 months: applicant had a home in Northern Ireland: occupancy rights not granted).

8     MH(FP)(S)A 1981, s 18(3).
9     For discussion of ss 3 and 4 see above at paras **5.8–5.9**.
10    MH(FP)S)A 1981, s 18(3). See for example, *Souter v McAuley* 2010 GWD 12-218.
11    For discussion see above at para **5.10**.
12    MH(FP)(S)A 1981, s 18(3). Unlike the position of entitled spouses or civil partners, there is no restriction on the grant of a decree in an action of division and sale where the house is owned in common by the entitled partners: for discussion see above at para **5.11**.
13    *Armour v Anderson* 1994 SLT 1127. The same principle would apply if an entitled partner sought an exclusion order under s 4 of the 1981 Act against the other entitled partner.
14    1987 SCLR 527. The entitled partner could now seek an interdict at common law and a power of arrest under the Protection of Abuse (Scotland) Act 2001.
15    It would have been different if both partners had been entitled because MH(FP)(S)A 1981, s 18(3) would operate.
16    MR(S)A 2001, s 1(2)(c).
17    MR(S)A 2001, s 1(2)(d).
18    MR(S)A 2001, s 1(3).

## Financial provision where cohabitation ends otherwise than by death

**8.6** Under s 28 of the Family Law (Scotland) Act 2006, a cohabitant can apply for financial provision when the cohabitation has ended otherwise than by death. The right to apply arises when the couple cease to cohabit.[1] This is ultimately a question of fact. While hard cases can be envisaged, for example where one cohabitant is in jail or hospital, in practice it is unlikely that too many difficulties will arise.[2] The application must be made within a year of the parties' ceasing to live together.[3] Where a couple have cohabited, separated and then resumed cohabitation, the first period of cohabitation can be taken into account provided the action is brought within one year from the date when the second period of cohabitation came to an end.[4]

By s 28(2) of the 2006 Act the court can make the following orders:

(a)    an order for the payment to the applicant of a capital sum of an amount specified in the order;

(b)     an order to pay the applicant such amount as may be specified in the order 'in respect of any economic burden of caring, after the end of the cohabitation, for a child of whom the cohabitants are parents';[5] and

(c)     such interim order as the court thinks fit.

The court can specify the date on which payments must be paid and that a capital sum should be payable in instalments.[6]

In relation to s 28(2)(b), it appears that the court can order periodical payments as well as a capital sum. For the purpose of this provision, a child is a person under the age of 16 of whom the cohabitants are the parents.[7] It does not include a child who has been accepted or treated by the applicant and the defender (or both) as a child of the family. This is surprising as such cohabitants may sustain economic loss after the breakdown from having to care for a child who has been living with them in the same way as cohabitants who are the child's parents.

In considering whether to make any of these orders the court must consider the matters listed in s 28(3) of the 2006 Act. These are:

(a)     whether, and if so to what extent, the defender has derived economic advantage from contributions made by the applicant; and

(b)     whether, and if so to what extent, the applicant has sustained economic disadvantage in the interests of the defender and any relevant child.

While it is readily apparent how fair account of the economic advantages received by the defender and the economic disadvantages sustained by the applicant can form the basis of an order under s 28(2)(a) it is difficult to see why it is applicable to an order under s 28(2)(b) which expressly stipulates that its purpose is to compensate the applicant for the economic burden of caring for a child of the cohabitation after it has come to an end.[8]

The factors in s 28(3) are, of course, important in respect of a claim for a capital sum under s 28(2)(a). These are the economic advantages received by the defender from contributions made by the applicant and economic disadvantages sustained by the applicant in the interests of the defender and a relevant child. In contrast to s 28(2)(b), a relevant child is a person under the age of 16 who is either a child of whom the cohabitants are the parents or who is or was accepted by the cohabitants as a child of their family.[9] The acceptance criterion seems to be the same as creates liability to aliment a child under s 1(1)(d) of the Family Law (Scotland) Act 1985.[10]

Contributions include indirect and non-financial contributions made by looking after any relevant child or any house in which the couple lived.[11] Economic advantage includes gains in capital, income and earning capacity: economic disadvantage includes losses in capital, income and earning capacity.[12] Unlike s 9(1)(b) of the Family (Scotland) Act 1985, the analogous principle which applies in relation to financial provision on divorce or dissolution,[13] s 28(3) does not take account of any economic disadvantage sustained or economic advantages obtained before the couple began to cohabit.

In deciding whether to make an order for a capital sum payment under s 28(2)(a), s 28(4) provides that the court has to consider the matters in s 28(5) and (6). First, the court must consider the extent to which any economic advantage derived by the defender from the applicant's contributions is offset by any economic disadvantage sustained by the defender in the interests of the applicant and any relevant child. Second, the court must consider the extent to which any economic disadvantage sustained by the applicant in the interests of the defender or any relevant child is offset by any economic advantage the applicant has derived from the defender's contributions. It is only if, after this balancing exercise, there is an economic imbalance in favour of the applicant that an award of financial provision can be made under s 28(2)(a). This balancing process is familiar from s 9(1)(b) of the 1985 Act[14]. But unlike spouses and civil partners, cohabitants are not under any obligation to aliment one another. Even so, it is thought that in most relationships it would be unusual if there were not some economic advantages and disadvantages to offset under this provision.

In *Gow v Grant*[15] the Second Division of the Court of Session took an extremely narrow view of the function of s 28. The court stated[16] that the objective of the section was limited in scope: it was intended to enable the court to correct any clear and quantifiable economic imbalance that might have resulted from cohabitation. The section was not designed to confer a general power to deal with any wider financial issues that might have arisen between the parties. It was 'in the nature of compensation for an imbalance of economic advantage or disadvantage'[17].

Given this approach to the purpose of the provision, it is not surprising that the court went on to hold that the only relevant economic disadvantage was that sustained 'in the interests' of the defender ie that the applicant suffered economic disadvantage in a manner intended to benefit the defender. Although the defender had encouraged the applicant to sell her house – her only capital asset – she had not done so in his interest as she had used the proceeds of the sale to pay her debts and make a loan to her son as well as contributing to the couple's extravagant lifestyle.

This decision was overturned by the Supreme Court[18]. The underlying principle of s 28 was one of fairness. The purpose of s 28 was to achieve fairness in the assessment of compensation for contributions made or economic disadvantages suffered in the interests of the relationship[19]. While the economic disadvantage which the applicant sustained had to be in the defender's interests, Lord Hope argued that the provision 'does not say that this must have been his interests only, or that the fact that it was in the applicant's interests also means that it must be left out of account. Still less does it say that "interests" have to be equated with economic advantage or benefit… Provided that disadvantage has been suffered in the interests of the defender to some extent, the door is open to an award of a capital sum even although it may also have been suffered in the interests of the applicant'[20]. The overriding principle was one of fairness rather than precise economic calculation having regard to where the parties were at the beginning of the cohabitation and where they were at the end. The disadvantage that Mrs Gow suffered when she sold her house was her loss of the benefit of the increase in value of her property. She was therefore entitled to compensation for that loss as some of the proceeds of the sale had been used to finance their lifestyle when she cohabited with Grant.

Given that he took the view that s 28 was designed to correct imbalances arising out of a non-commercial relationship where parties are quite likely to make contributions or sacrifices without counting the cost or bargaining for a return, it is not surprising that Lord Hope accepted Lady Hale's contention that in an application under s 28 'it is quite impractible to work out who has paid for what and who has enjoyed what benefits in kind during the cohabitation as people do not keep such running accounts and the cost of working out in detail is quite disproportionate to doing justice between the parties'[21]. In short a broad-brush approach is required. As the principle in 9(1)(b) of the Family Law (Scotland) Act 1985 provides similar compensation for spouses and civil partners[22], Lord Hope considered that 'it may be helpful to refer to cases decided under section 9 (1)(b) when the court is considering what might be taken to be an economic advantage, disadvantage or contribution for this purpose or how the economic burden of caring for a child is to be dealt with under section 28(2)(b). An assessment of what is in the interests of any relevant child cannot sensibly be reduced to purely financial factors'.

The decision of the Supreme Court in *Gow v Grant* has transformed this area of the law[23]. Section 28 is now seen as a way of achieving economic fairness between the parties when their relationship breaks down. While the court must still engage in a balancing exercise, this is to be done in a non-technical and practicable way: common sense rules rather than detailed accounts. In *Whigham v Owen*[24] the couple had lived together for 27 years before they separated. During that time the defender had accumulated substantial assets of approximately £750 K through the success of his business interests. The pursuer had given up her career and acted as the primary carer of their three children. As a result she had assets of less than £10K when they ceased to cohabit. Following the Supreme Court's decision in *Gow*, the Lord Ordinary (Lord Drummond Young)[25] accepted that what was required in a s 28 claim was 'a rough and ready' calculation. In deciding what are economic advantages and disadvantages and contributions, the calculation should take into account the factors that are relevant for that purpose in divorce cases[26]. Nor was there a need to calculate the award on a 'precise mathematical basis'. In the circumstances, Lord Drummond Young awarded the pursuer a capital sum of £250K[27].

As a result of the decision of the Supreme Court in *Gow v Grant* the judges at first instance have a wide discretion in s 28 applications. The view has rightly been expressed that parties must bring evidence of their financial position at the end of their relationship[28]. Evidence of their financial position at the beginning of their cohabitation would also be valuable. Similarly the parties must be able to produce some of the evidence of the facts that they wish the court to consider in any balancing exercise[29]. This is important since, as in all discretionary decisions, there is little scope for interference by appellate courts in s 28 claims[30].

It will be noticed that in a cohabitant's claim for financial provision there is no equivalent of s 9(1)(a) of the 1985 Act, ie fair sharing of the matrimonial or partnership property where fair sharing is prima facie equal sharing.[31] Although there is a presumption of common ownership of household goods,[32] this does not apply in relation to valuable property such as savings and other investments, interests in a pension scheme or the family home. It is because many spouses and civil partners are content with the division of the matrimonial or partnership property under s 9(1)(a), that comparatively little use is made of s 9(1)(b). If there is no matrimonial or partnership property, the courts have taken a rather cavalier approach to the balancing process so that an award of some financial provision can be made under s 9(1)(b).[33] It remains to be seen whether a similar approach will be taken in s 28 applications in the light of *Gow v Grant.*

---

1   Family Law (Scotland) Act 2006, s 28(1).
2   In *Banks v Banks* [2005] CSOH 144 the Lord Ordinary (Carloway) considered how the couple had socialised and managed their finances in order to determine when they had ceased to live together as husband and wife. See  also *M v T* 2011 GWD 40-828 (Couple had not stopped presenting themselves as cohabitants: cohabitation did not cease until they stopped doing so);*Garrad v Inglis* 2014 GWD 1-17  (Couple ceased to cohabit when, after physically separating for two months while the pursuer worked abroad, the defender told him that their relationship was over and began take steps to secure her position by for example changing her will).
3   FL(S)A 2006, s 28(8). In *Simpson v Downie* [2012] CSIH 74 ,2013 SLT 178 an action was raised within the one year time limit. The defender sought to introduce a crave for financial provision on her own account in her defences,which were lodged outwith the one year time period. The court held that the defender's claim was time barred.
4   *Douglas v Bell* 2014 Fam LR 2. To limit the claim to only the most recent period of cohabitation, the sheriff  observed ' would fly in the face of normal human experience': ibid at para 42.
5   FL(S)A 2006, s 28(2). In *F v D* 2009 Fam LR 111, the sheriff awarded the applicant £3000 under s 28(2)(b) in respect of the care of the child and £6000 under s 28(2)(a) in respect of economic advantages given to the defender: as there was no evidence that the defender had suffered any economic disadvantages, the sheriff avoided having to engage in a balancing exercise demanded by s 28(5): s 28(5) is discussed below.
6   FL(S)A 2006, s 28(7). Payment of a capital sum by instalments was made in *M v S* 2008 SLT 871.
7   FL(S)A 2006, s 28(9). It will include a child of whom the cohabitants are the child's parent and second female parent under the Human Fertilisation and Embryology Act 2008, ss 33 and 43, discussed at para **9.2**.
8   In *M v S* 2008 SLT 871 the Lord Ordinary (Matthews) awarded the applicant only half of her prospective economic burden in caring for the child on the assumption that the

cost of the upbringing of the child had to be shared fairly between the applicant and the defender. There is no statutory basis for this assumption.

9   FL(S)A 2006, s 28(9) and (10).
10  For discussion, see para **10.9**.
11  FL(S)A 2006, s 28(9).
12  Losses sustained by one cohabitant as a result of a wrong committed by the other are to be pursued in delict not a claim under s 28(2)(a) because the defender does not receive economic advantages from the wrong: *Cameron v Leal* 2010 GWD 19-379.
13  Discussed at para **7.17**.
14  Discussed at para **7.17** above.
15  [2011] CSIH 25,2011 SC 618.
16  Ibid at para 4.
17  Ibid at para 3.
18  *Gow v Grant* [2012] UKSC 29, 2013 SC(UKSC)1.
19  Ibid per Lord Hope at para 33, In so doing, Lord Hope approved of the approach of Sheriff Miller in *Lindsay v Murphy* 2010 Fam LR 156.
20  Ibid at para 35, approving the approach of Sheriff Dunlop in *Mitchell v Gibson* 2011 Fam LR 53.
21  Ibid at para 33.
22  Discussed at para **17.7** above.
23  For some of the difficulties before *Gow,* see *M v S* 2008 SLT 871 and the discussion in the 6th edition of this book at para **8.6**.
24  [2013] CSOH 29.
25  Who, ironically, gave the judgment of the Second Division in *Gow*.
26  [2013] CSOH 29 at para 10.
27  Lord Drummond Young stated that if they had been married he would have awarded the pursuer £368K. This is because she would have been prima facie entitled to half the value of the matrimonial property under s 9(1)(a) of FL(S)A 1985, discussed at para **7.7** above.
28  *Smith-Milne v Langler* 2013 GWD 13-284.
29  *Cameron v Lukes* 2014 GWD 7-144.
30  It should also be.remembered that, theoretically at least, a court might not treat an applicant as a cohabitant for the purpose of a claim for financial provision because of the length and nature of the relationship and the financial arrangements between the parties during that period FL(S)A 2006, s 25(2).
31  Section 9(1)(a) of the 1985 Act is discussed above at paras **7.7–7.16**.
32  Discussed at para **8.4**.
33  See, for example *Wilson v Wilson* 1999 SLT 249, discussed at para **7.17**.

## Financial provision on intestacy

**8.7**  Unlike a surviving spouse or civil partner,[1] a surviving cohabitant does not have legal rights in the deceased cohabitant's free moveable estate. Nor does a surviving cohabitant have prior rights in respect of the deceased cohabitant's intestate estate, ie when the deceased died without a will. [2] As around 75 per cent of Scots die intestate, a surviving cohabitant can find herself without any capital when her cohabitant dies. Moreover and perhaps more importantly, where the deceased owned the family home in which they lived together, the surviving cohabitant can be evicted by the deceased's heirs on intestacy who will usually be his children or grandchildren.

However by s 29(2) of the Family Law (Scotland) Act 2006, the surviving cohabitant has the right to apply for a share of the deceased cohabitant's property when he has died intestate. At the outset it is important to stress that the right only arises on an intestacy.[3] This means that the cohabitant's right can be defeated if the deceased makes a will before he dies. For example, a man makes a will leaving all his property to a charity. He dies. As he died testate his surviving cohabitant has no right to apply under s 29(2) and as she has no legal rights, she will have no redress against the deceased's estate.

Before an application can be brought the deceased must have been domiciled in Scotland immediately before his death.[4] He must also have been cohabiting with the applicant immediately before his death.[5] It is evident that it is not intended that a former cohabitant should have the right to make a claim under s 29(2). But the use of the word 'immediately' is unfortunate. Surely a surviving cohabitant should still have a claim under s 29(2) even if the deceased had been in hospital or a nursing home for several months before he died? To achieve this result the provision will have to be construed purposively and with sensitivity.

On an application by the surviving cohabitant, the court can make an order: (i) for payment of a capital sum to the applicant out of the deceased's net intestate estate; and (ii) for heritable or moveable property to be transferred from the deceased's net intestate estate to the applicant.[6] The court can specify the date on which the capital sum should be paid, that the capital sum can be paid in instalments and the date when the property should be transferred.[7] The claim must be brought within six months beginning with the day on which the deceased died.[8]

The definition of net intestate estate is significant. It is so much of the intestate estate as remains after provision has been made for the satisfaction of: (a) inheritance tax; (b) other liabilities of the estate having priority over the prior rights and legal rights of a surviving spouse or civil partner; and (c) the prior rights and legal rights of a surviving spouse or civil partner. The last point is important. Where the deceased has died with a surviving spouse or civil partner as well as a surviving cohabitant, then the surviving cohabitant's claim under s 29(2) only applies to what remains of the estate *after* the prior rights and legal rights of the surviving spouse or civil partner have been satisfied. In many cases the prior rights and legal rights of the surviving spouse or civil partner will exhaust the estate[9] and the surviving cohabitant's right under s 29(2) will be valueless.

But of course in the majority of cases the deceased will not be survived by both a spouse or civil partner as well as a cohabitant. A *former* spouse or civil partner does not have legal rights or prior rights in the intestate estates of their ex-spouse or civil partner, having obtained financial provision on divorce or dissolution.

It should also be noticed that in calculating the net intestate estate, no provision has to be made for the satisfaction of the legal rights – legitim – of the deceased's children (and their issue).[10] In other words, a surviving cohabitant's claim under s 29(2) is to be considered before the succession rights of the deceased's children are addressed. In short, it is the deceased's children, as opposed to a surviving spouse or civil partner, who will almost certainly 'lose out' when a claim is successfully brought under s 29(2).

In considering a claim under s 29(2), the court has to consider the following factors in section 29(3):

(i)     the size and nature of the net intestate estate;

(ii)    any benefit received by the cohabitant as a result of the death, for example a pension or life insurance;[11]

(iii)   the nature and extent of any other rights against or claims on the deceased's intestate estate. It is only at this stage that the court can take into account that the deceased's children (and their issue) have legal rights and are the heirs on intestacy; and

(iv)    any other matter the court thinks appropriate.

It should also be remembered that by virtue of section 25(2) the court could consider that, in the light of the length and nature of the relationship and the degree and extent of any financial arrangements which subsisted during the relationship, the applicant should not be treated as a cohabitant for the purpose of a claim under s 29(2). But these factors are surely very important considerations in determining what would be an appropriate award. In order to do so, the sheriff in *Savage v Purches*[12] had to treat them as other matters he considered appropriate under section 29(3). It is thought that he was correct to do so. However the case illustrates the fundamental flaws in the structure of the Act.

There is only one subsection in the 2006 Act that gives a court specific guidance on how to exercise its discretion in a s 29(2) claim. This is s 29(4). It provides that an order under s 29(2) must not have the effect of awarding a surviving cohabitant an amount which is more than that to which she would have been entitled if she had been a surviving spouse or civil partner of the deceased. Put another way, the maximum order a surviving cohabitant can receive is the equivalent of the prior rights and the legal rights that he or she would have received out of the deceased's intestate estate if the survivor had been the deceased's spouse or civil partner.[13] Otherwise little guidance is given on how the court should exercise its discretion. However in *Kerr v Mangan*[14], the Inner House held that the overall fairness approach laid down in *Gow v Grant* for s 28 applications does *not* infuse applications under s 29.

The difficulty is that the purpose of giving a surviving cohabitant a claim under s 29(2) is not clear. Is it to recognise the surviving cohabitant's economic contributions or to compensate for economic disadvantages sustained in the interests of the deceased. Is it to help a surviving cohabitant who has been financially dependent on the deceased by providing her with reasonable financial provision? Or should a surviving cohabitant be treated as a surviving spouse or civil partner unless there are compelling reasons not to do so?[15] What is clear is that judges are unhappy with the unfettered discretion they have been given under the Act[16] and that it is difficult for solicitors to advise clients on the success of a section 29(2) claim. In these circumstances, a cohabitant will be advised to settle. This may account for the paucity of reported decisions.

---

1    For discussion see paras **3.17**.
2    For discussion see para **3.18**.

3  Family Law (Scotland) Act 2006, s 29(1)(a).

4  FL(S)A 2006, s 29(1)(b)(i). This may be difficult to establish: see *Chebotareva v Khandro* 2008 Fam LR 66. Even if the deceased was domiciled in Scotland, the Act does not apply to any heritable property situated outwith Scotland. This is because under the rules of private international law, succession to land is governed by the law of the country where the land is situated: *Kerr v Mangan* 2013 SLT (Sh Ct) 102 approved by the Inner House [2014] CSIH 96.

5  FL(S)A 2006, s 29(1)(b)(ii).

6  FL(S)A 2006, s 29(2). The court has no power to order that the cohabitant should have the same rights as a spouse or civil partner or a percentage thereof. The court's powers are only to make a capital sum payment or property transfer order. However, the SLC has recommended that a cohabitant should be able to obtain a percentage of what she would have inherited if she had been the deceased's spouse or civil partner: Report on Succession (Scot Law Com No 215) Part 4.

7  FL(S)A 2006, s 29(7) and (8).

8  FL(S)A 2006, s 29(6).

9  For discussion, see paras **3.17–3.18**.

10  For discussion of legitim see para **3.17**.

11  In *Savage v Purches* 2009 Fam LR 9, one of the reasons that the cohabitant's claim was unsuccessful was that he had received a substantial lump sum and was in receipt of an income from the deceased's pension trustees.

12  2009 Fam LR 9.

13  This must include the amount that a surviving spouse or civil partner would receive in the unusual circumstances when a surviving spouse or civil partner is the deceased's heir on intestacy.

14  [2014] CSIH 96.

15  An approach which Sheriff Principal Dunlop appears to have supported albeit obiter in *Kerr v Mangan* 2013 SLT (ShCt) 102, para 23.

16  See the stringent criticism of s 29 made by Lady Smith in *Kerr v Mangan* [2014] CSIH 96.

# Chapter 9

# Parents and children

## INTRODUCTION

**9.1** In the law of Scotland, children have passive capacity in the sense that they enjoy a plethora of legal rights. But, as we shall see,[1] they lack active capacity in that they are unable to enforce these rights during their childhood. This must be done on their behalf by an adult who will usually be a parent. In family law, children's most important rights are those which are exigible against their natural parents. The primary purpose of this chapter is to discuss how parentage is established. Before doing so, it is proposed by way of introduction to consider when a child first obtains legal rights[2].

Once a child is conceived, Scottish criminal law provides protection for the foetus by prohibiting the inducement of an abortion.[3] As a result of s 1(1) of the Abortion Act 1967,[4] a person will not be guilty of an offence if a pregnancy is terminated by a registered medical practitioner provided two doctors in good faith are of the opinion:

(1)   that the pregnancy has not exceeded its twenty-fourth week and that its continuance would involve risk, greater than if it were terminated, of injury to the physical or mental health of the pregnant woman or any existing children of her family; or

(2)   that the termination is necessary to prevent grave permanent injury to her physical or mental health; or

(3)   that the continuance of the pregnancy would involve risk to her life, greater than if the pregnancy were terminated; or

(4)   that there is a substantial risk that if the child were born it would suffer from such physical or mental abnormalities as to be seriously disabled.

Where an abortion is sought in the first trimester, ie during the first three months of the pregnancy, the termination will involve a risk to the mother's health which is considerably less than the risks involved in childbirth: accordingly, it is not too difficult to establish ground (1) for a lawful termination in these circumstances.

As in all cases of medical treatment the patient, ie the woman, must consent. Where the grounds for a lawful termination under s 1(1) are established, the consent of the father is not required nor can he obtain an interdict to prevent the pregnancy being terminated.[5] Although ground (1) cannot be used after the twenty-fourth week of the pregnancy, there is no time limit in relation to the other grounds. A later abortion may be necessary, for example if there has been a delay in establishing that the foetus is abnormal for the purposes of ground (4). Although not illegal per se, late termination, ie beyond 24 weeks, is not common in Scotland.

Article 2 of the European Convention on Human Rights[6] provides: 'Everyone's right to life shall be protected by law'. It has been held that 'everyone' usually applies to persons who have been born; consequently lawful termination of a foetus is not a breach of Article 2.[7]

An action in delict will lie when a child is born physically or mentally disabled as a result of injuries sustained in the womb. No action in delict will lie unless the child is born alive. It is only when the child is born alive that the child sustains harm and the delict is completed,[8] albeit that the injuries occurred while the child was a foetus. While there is no authority directly in point it is submitted that, in theory at least, an action would lie even where the injuries were caused as a result of the mother's negligence.[9] A child's right to the physical integrity of the person therefore extends to injuries suffered before the child was born. This conclusion is consistent with the *nasciturus* principle, viz that in matters of private law a child who is *in utero* should be deemed to be already born whenever this would operate for the benefit of the child.

Where a baby is conceived because of a failed sterilisation procedure, the parents cannot recover damages for the economic cost of raising a healthy – if unplanned – child.[10] Where a child is born with a congenital disability, the increased costs incurred by the parents as a consequence of the child's special needs are recoverable, at least where the medical authorities failed to diagnose that the foetus was abnormal.[11] In both situations, the parents may be entitled to solatium.[12]

216

1   See **Ch 10**.
2   On the law of Parent and Child see generally A B Wilkinson and K Norrie *The Law Relating to Parent and Child in Scotland* (3rd edn, 2013) afterwards referred to as *Wilkinson and Norrie*.
3   See generally Michael G A Christie and Sir Gerald H Gordon *The Criminal Law of Scotland* (3rd edn, 2001, SULI/W Greens/Sweet & Maxwell), Vol II, Ch 28; Norrie [1985] Crim LR 475.
4   Abortion Act 1967, s 1(1) .
5   *Kelly v Kelly* 1997 SC 285.
6   Convention for the Protection of Human Rights and Fundamental Freedoms (Rome, 4 November 1950; 213 UNTS 221; TS 71 (1953); Cmd 8969). Most, but not all, of the 1950 Convention has been incorporated into United Kingdom law as Schedule 1 to the Human Rights Act 1998.
7   *Paton v United Kingdom* (1980) 3 EHRR 408.
8   *Hamilton v Fife Health Board* 1993 SC 369. For discussion see Joe Thomson *Delictual Liability* (5th edn, 2014, Bloomsbury Professional), Ch 13.
9   It has long been accepted that actions in delict are competent between parent and child for injuries sustained after the child's birth: *Young v Rankin* 1934 SC 499; *Wood v Wood* 1935 SLT 431.
10  *McFarlane v Tayside Health Board* 2000 SC (HL) 1. It does not matter if the parent of the healthy child is handicapped, for example if the mother was blind: *Rees v Darlington Memorial NHS Trust* [2004] AC 309. The parents will receive a conventional non-compensatory award of around £20K to acknowledge that their right to plan their family has been infringed.
11  *McLelland v Greater Glasgow Health Board* 2001 SLT 446.
12  *McLelland v Greater Glasgow Health Board* 2001 SLT 446.

## ESTABLISHING PARENTAGE

**9.2** In the context of family law, the rights which a child enjoys are those which are prima facie exigible against the child's natural or birth parents. It is therefore important to have rules which establish parentage.

At one time there was little difficulty in determining who was a child's mother: she was the woman who was the biological mother and who gave birth to the child. Advances in reproductive techniques raise difficulties. If an ovum is donated and then fertilised and the resulting embryo transferred to the donee's womb, is the donee to be regarded as the child's mother although genetically unrelated to the child? Section 33(1) of the Human Fertilisation and Embryology Act 2008[1] provides that:

'The woman who is carrying or has carried a child as a result of the placing in her of an embryo or of sperm and eggs, and no other woman, is to be treated as the mother of the child'.

A child's father is determined solely by biological criteria. He is the man whose semen fertilised the ovum leading to the birth of the child. In other words, he must be genetically related to the child. The difficulty is that more than one man may have had intercourse with the mother at the probable date of conception. The law therefore proceeds on the basis of a series of presumptions which can be rebutted by evidence to the contrary.

By s 5(1)(a) of the Law Reform (Parent and Child) (Scotland) Act 1986 a man is presumed to be the father of a child if he was married to the mother of the child at any time during the period beginning with the conception and ending with the birth of the child. Thus the presumption applies when:

(1)    H and W were married both at the date of conception and birth;

(2)    H and W were married at the date of conception but not at the date of the birth: for example, if H had died before the child's birth – a posthumous child – or the couple had divorced before the child's birth;

(3)    H and W were not married at the date of conception but were married at the date of the birth;[2]

(4)    H and W were not married at the date of conception, were married during the pregnancy but were not married at the date of birth.[3]

The presumption does not apply where a child was conceived and born before H and W married.[4] The s 5(1)(a) presumption applies in the case of a void, voidable or irregular marriage in the same way as it applies in the case of a valid and regular marriage.[5]

By s 5 (1)(b) of the Law Reform (Parent and Child) (Scotland) Act 1986, a man will be presumed to be the father of a child, if *both* he and the mother of the child have acknowledged that he is the father and the child has been registered as such.[6]

The presumptions in s 5 (1)(a) and (b) of the 1986 Act may be rebutted by proof on a balance of probabilities[7] that the man was not the father of the child.

Where the presumptions apply, the presumptive father – or the mother if she alleges her husband is not the father – can seek a declarator of non-parentage in the Court of Session or the sheriff court. Where the presumptions do not apply, a declarator of parentage may be sought in the Court of Session or the sheriff court.[8] Thus if a woman has a child, she can seek declarator that a particular man is the father of her child.[9] Conversely, a man can seek declarator that he is the father of a woman's child. If declarator of non-parentage is granted, the presumptions in s 5 of the Law Reform (Parent and Child) (Scotland) Act 1986 are displaced; if declarator of parentage is granted, it will give rise to a presumption to the same effect as the decree.[10] The court shall not grant decree of declarator unless it is satisfied that the grounds of action have been established by sufficient evidence.[11] Thus in an action of declarator of parentage, the pursuer – who will usually be the mother of the child – must establish, by evidence, that on the balance of probabilities the alleged man is the father of the child. Corroborated evidence is no longer required.[12] Similarly, if a man seeks a declarator of parentage, he must establish, by evidence, that on the balance of probabilities he is the father of the child.[13] Finally, in an action of declarator of non-parentage it must be established, by evidence, that on the balance of probabilities the Law Reform (Parent and Child) (Scotland) Act 1986 s 5 presumptions of paternity have been rebutted by, for example, evidence of non-access by the husband to his wife at the probable date of conception. In this context it should be noted that courts have recognised the possibility of abnormal gestation periods.[14]

Where a man has obtained a declarator of paternity that he is the father of a child, he does not thereby automatically obtain parental responsibilities and rights in relation to the child. He can only acquire them with the agreement of the mother or by court proceedings under s 11 of the Children (Scotland) Act 1995.[15]

In cases involving assisted reproduction important statutory rules apply to determine the child's parentage. As we have seen, the woman who is carrying or has carried a child as a result of the placing in her of an embryo or of sperm and eggs, and no other woman, is to be treated as the mother of the child for all legal purposes.[16]

Where a woman is married at the time when she is artificially impregnated and the sperm used is not her husband's, her husband is to be treated as the father of the child for all legal purposes unless it is shown that he did not consent to the treatment.[17] This provision must now be construed as applying to same sex marriages[18]. And so if A and B are same sex female spouses and B has a child by artificial insemination, A shall be treated as the parent of the child unless she did not consent to the treatment. Similarly, where a woman is a party to a civil partnership at the time when she is artificially impregnated, the other civil partner is to be treated as the child's parent for all legal purposes unless it is shown that she did not consent to the treatment.[19] For these purposes, a marriage and civil partnership includes a void marriage or civil partnership if either or both spouses or partners believed that their marriage or civil partnership was valid.[20]

Where the treatment is provided by a person to whom a licence applies, when a woman and a man are not married at the time of the artificial impregnation,[21] the man will be the father of the child for all legal purposes if the agreed fatherhood conditions apply. These are that: (a) he gives notice to the person responsible that he consents to being the child's father; (b) the woman gives notice to the person responsible that she consents to him being so treated; (c) that she does not give a further notice that another man or woman should be the parent of the child; and (d) the mother and the man are not within the prohibited degrees of relationship.[22] There are similar provisions where the mother and another woman are not parties to a same sex marriage or a civil partnership. If the agreed female parenthood conditions apply[23] the other woman will be the parent of the child for all legal purposes (except in relation to succession to a title etc).[24] She is called the second female parent.

Where a person is to be treated as a father or parent by virtue of sections 35 and 36 of the HFEA 2008 or as a parent by virtue of sections 42 and 43, no other person is to be treated as the father or parent of the child.[25] It is also provided that the donor of sperm used for treatment under the 2008 Act is not to be treated as the father of the child[26] and that a woman is not to be treated as the parent of the child merely because she has donated eggs to be used in treatment.

These provisions are of particular relevance to lesbian couples who are not married or in a civil partnership. They enable the mother's partner to be treated as her child's second female parent and, as we shall see, give her the opportunity to have parental responsibilities and rights in relation to the child.

It is important to stress that these provisions only apply where the child has been conceived as a result of assisted reproduction. If a woman has conceived a child as the result of sexual intercourse, her spouse or civil partner or female cohabitant will not be the child's parent though the child may be accepted by them as a child of the family.[27]

---

1 For the previous position, see the fifth edition of this book at para **9.2**.
2 Cf the position at common law in *Gardner v Gardner* (1876) 3 R 695, (1877) 4 R (HL) 56.
3 For example, if H was a soldier who married W when she was pregnant but was killed before the baby was born.
4 This was also the position at common law: *Imre v Mitchell* 1958 SC 439; *James v McLennan* 1971 SLT 162.
5 Law Reform (Parent and Child) (Scotland) Act 1986, s 5(2). A difficulty arises if W marries $H_1$ and later goes through a ceremony of marriage with $H_2$. If W has a child, both $H_1$ and $H_2$ have the benefit of the s 5(1)(a) presumption as the presumption applies both to her valid marriage with $H_1$ and her void 'marriage' with $H_2$. In these circumstances it is submitted that the statutory presumptions cancel each other and $H_1$ and $H_2$ must attempt to establish paternity by evidence. It is irrelevant that the parties to the void marriage were not in good faith: ie knew it was void. Cf the Children (Scotland) Act 1995, s 3(2)(a) and (b), discussed at para **11.3**.
6 LR(PC)(S)A 1986, s 5(1)(b) and Schedule 1, para 8. Cf the position at common law where no presumption arises from cohabitation: *A v G* 1984 SLT (Sh Ct) 65.
7 LR(PC)(S)A 1986, s 5(4). At common law, the presumption *pater est quem nuptiae demonstrant*, ie the father is the man to whom the marriage points, applied when H was married to W at the date of conception. It was a presumption which could only be rebutted by evidence which established beyond reasonable doubt that H did not have access to W at the probable date of conception: see *S v S* 1977 SLT (Notes) 65.
8 LR(PC)(S)A 1986, s 7(2) and (3).
9 The action of affiliation is probably no longer competent: *Canlon v O'Dowd* 1987 SCLR 771.
10 LR(PC)(S)A 1986, s 5(3).
11 Civil Evidence (Scotland) Act 1988, s 8(1).

12 CE(S)A 1988, s 1(1). The doctrine of corroboration by false denial has also been abolished: CE(S)A 1988, s 1(2).
13 See for example, *Docherty v McGlynn* 1985 SLT 237, OH; *Campbell v Grossart* 1988 GWD 24-1004.
14 See for example, *Currie v Currie* 1950 SC 10 (W gave birth 336 days after the couple last cohabited: held not to be an impossible period of pregnancy).
15 For full discussion of parental responsibilities and rights, see **Ch 11.**
16 HFEA, ss 33 and 48(1). In relation to all these rules, legal purposes do not include the right to succeed to any title, coat of arms, honour or dignity: HFEA 2008, s 48(8).
17 HFEA 2008, ss 35(1) and 48(1).
18 Marriage and Civil Partnership (Scotland) Act 2014, s 4.
19 HFEA 2008, ss 42 and 48(1).
20 HFEA 2008, ss 49(1) and 50(1). The provisions do not apply if at the time a judicial separation was in force: ibid.
21 The sperm used must not be that of the man: in addition there must be no other man who is the father of the child by virtue of s 35 and no other woman who is the parent of the child by virtue of s 35 or s 42.
22 HFEA 2008, ss 36, 37 and 48(1).
23 In substance they are the same as the agreed fatherhood conditions.
24 HFEA 2008, ss 43, 44 and 48(1).
25 HFEA 2008, ss 38(1) and 45(1). Note however ss 38(3) and 45(3) which appear to ensure that the presumption of paternity in s 5(1)(a) of the LR(PC)A 1986 is not automatically displaced by the provisions in the HFEA 2008: but since the 2008 Act only applies when the father is not genetically related to the child, the presumption will be easily rebutted and fatherhood will then be determined by the provisions of the 2008 Act.
26 HFEA 2008, s 41.
27 There are also provisions in the Act dealing with the situation where (a) the sperm is used or the embryo is transferred after the death of the donor who had consented to be the child's father (s 39); (b) the embryo is transferred after the death of a spouse or intended father (s 40); and (c) the embryo is transferred after the death of a civil partner or intended second female parent (s 46). Where these apply the particulars of the deceased as the child's father or parent can be entered into a relevant register of births; HFEA 2008, ss 39, 40 and 46.

## DNA PROFILING

**9.3** In actions of declarator of parentage or non-parentage, for many years blood test evidence was of immense importance. By taking blood samples from a child, the mother and the alleged or presumptive father, it was possible to establish that because of his blood group the man could not be the father of the child: ie blood tests could lead to an exclusionary result. If a non-exclusionary result was obtained, the blood tests merely established that any man within that blood group *could* be the child's father. In other words, blood tests could not establish that a man genetically was the child's father.

The utility of blood test evidence has now been overtaken by DNA profiling. By taking samples of bodily fluid or tissue from the child, the mother and the alleged or presumptive father, it is possible by DNA profiling to establish positively whether or not the man is the child's father, ie an inclusionary result can be obtained. The value of DNA profiling evidence in determining issues of paternity is obvious. Nevertheless the law has been uncertain in its application[1] and several problems remain.

The first is to consider who has the power to consent to samples of blood, bodily fluid or tissue being taken from a child. In civil proceedings relating to the determination of parentage, where such a sample is sought from a child below the age of 16 by a party to the proceedings or a *curator ad litem*,[2] any person having parental responsibilities may consent.[3] If a medical practitioner takes the view that a child under 16 understands the nature and purpose of the tests, the child has capacity to consent.[4] Where such a sample is sought from a person, for example a baby, who is incapable of giving consent, by s 6 of the Law Reform (Parent and Child) (Scotland) Act 1986 the court has power to consent to the taking of a sample where:

(1)    there is no person who is entitled to give such consent, for example if the child is an orphan; or

(2)    there is such a person but it is not reasonably practicable to obtain his or her consent, for example if the child's parents are abroad, or a parent is unwilling to accept the responsibility of giving or withholding consent.[5]

A particular difficulty arises if the person with parental responsibilities is the child's presumptive father. Consider the following example. H and W are married at the date of the child's conception and birth. Section 5(1) of the 1986 Act will operate so that H will be presumed to be the child's father and consequently will have parental responsibilities.[6] If H subsequently brings an action of declarator of non-parentage, can he consent to samples being taken from the child when the purpose of so doing is to rebut the s 5 presumption by establishing on the balance of probabilities that he is not the father? *Docherty v McGlynn*[7] is authority that a presumptive father may consent to samples being taken from a child but it is important to note that in this case he wished to do so to establish that he was in fact the child's genetic father. Could therefore a presumptive father rely on the presumption if his purpose was to deny that he was in fact the child's genetic father? In spite of dicta in *Docherty v McGlynn*[8] that he cannot do so, it is submitted that he can. Until the s 5 presumption is rebutted, H is the child's presumptive father and can act as the child's legal representative:[9] *it is in that capacity* that he has the power to consent to the blood or DNA test on the child. Even if his purpose is to establish that he is not the child's genetic father, this does not undermine the legality of his consent to samples being taken from the child which was given in his capacity as the child's legal representative. As we shall see,[10] the court may refuse to admit the evidence so obtained if it would be against the child's interests to do so.

The second problem is that it is a cardinal principle of Scots law that in civil proceedings the courts will not make an order to compel a person to submit to a DNA test against his or her will.[11] Similarly, the court will not make an order to compel a person with parental responsibilities to consent to samples of blood, bodily fluid or tissue being taken from the child.[12] Moreover, it would appear that at common law the court could not make a direction that a sample should be given and then draw adverse inferences if a sample was refused.[13]

Section 70(1) of the Law Reform (Miscellaneous Provisions) (Scotland) Act 1990 now provides that in civil proceedings the court[14] may request a party to the proceedings[15] to provide a sample of blood, bodily fluid or tissue or consent to such a sample being taken from a child in relation to whom the party has power to give consent. This provision still does not give the court the power to *compel* a person to give such a sample or consent to such a sample being taken from a child.

However, if the person refuses or fails to provide such a sample being taken from a child, the court may draw such adverse inference as seems appropriate.[16] In *Smith v Greenhill*,[17] it was held that the court has discretion: (1) whether or not to draw an adverse inference at all; and

(2) if it decides to do so, as to the nature of the inference. In this case, the pursuer sought a declarator of parentage claiming to be the father of W's child. H had also had sexual intercourse with W at the probable date of conception. H refused to consent to samples being taken from the child. It was held that any adverse inference to be drawn from H's refusal was not per se enough to rebut the presumption that H was the father of the child.

Where a person had died, the Scottish courts were prepared to admit hospital records containing the blood group of the deceased where the deceased's blood group was necessary to determine a child's paternity by the use of blood tests.[18]

Finally, in *Docherty v McGlynn*[19] the Inner House of the Court of Session held that in the exercise of its inherent protective jurisdiction in relation to children the court could intervene and refuse to admit such evidence if it was not in the child's interests to do so. Moreover, while it is expressly enacted that a court cannot exercise its powers under s 6(3) of the 1986 Act to consent to a blood sample being taken from a child unless satisfied that it would not be detrimental to the child's health to do so,[20] it is submitted that a court would not consent if the results of the blood tests would be contrary to the child's interests. In reaching its decision in *Docherty v McGlynn*,[21] the Inner House relied upon the English case of *S v S*,[22] where Lord Reid concluded that 'the court ought to permit a blood test of a young child to be taken unless satisfied that it would be against the child's interest'.[23]

In what circumstances will the courts either refuse to make a request under s 70(1) of the 1990 Act that a party to the proceedings should consent to a sample of blood, bodily fluid or tissue being taken from a child or refuse to admit the results of blood or DNA tests which have been carried out on a child with the appropriate consents? In *Docherty v McGlynn*[24] the Inner House considered that there was a 'delicate balance' between the desire for truth in litigation and the advantages for a child in continuing to be regarded as legitimate; Lord Cameron in particular, thought that 'the stigma of illegitimacy is one which in many cases and ranks of society is a cause of pain and distress'.[25] Thus there is authority that the court should not exercise its power to make such a request or admit such evidence if it was likely thereby to establish that a child who was presumptively legitimate was in fact illegitimate. But as we shall see, the status of illegitimacy has now been abolished[26] and consequently it is submitted that the court's observations in *Docherty v McGlynn*[27] no longer carry any weight.

It is therefore submitted that merely because the s 5 presumption of paternity is likely to be rebutted is not in itself sufficient for a court to conclude that it would be contrary to a child's interests to make a request under s 70(1) of the 1990 Act or to admit the results of DNA tests as evidence. Only in very exceptional circumstances[28] will it now be contrary to a child's interests that the truth of the child's paternity should be known: 'The ascertainment of truth must always be in the interests of parties and will usually be in the interests of the child'.[29]

---

1    See for example, *Torrie v Turner* 1990 SLT 718, where the Inner House held that a court has no power to make a direction that a person should give a sample for the purposes of DNA screening though this could lead to a positive result of paternity.

2    A *curator ad litem* is a person appointed by the court to protect the interests of the child in the proceedings.

3    Law Reform (Parent and Child) (Scotland) Act 1986, s 6(1) and (2). On parental responsibilities, see **Ch 11**.

4    Age of Legal Capacity (Scotland) Act 1991, s 2(4), discussed at para **10.2**.

5    LR(PC)(S)A 1986, s 6(3). It should be noted that s 6(3) of the 1986 Act applies to any person – not necessarily a child – who is incapable of consent, for example, a person suffering from mental illness.

6    Children (Scotland) Act 1995, s 3(1)(b). See para **11.3**.

7    1983 SLT 645.

8    1983 SLT 645 at 746, per the Lord President (Emslie) approving *Whitehall v Whitehall* 1958 SC 252 and dicta in *Imre v Mitchell* 1958 SC 439.

9    C(S)A 1995, ss 3(1)(b) and 2(1)(d). See **Ch 11**.

10   See below.

11   *Whitehall v Whitehall* 1958 SC 252; *Torrie v Turner* 1990 SLT 718.

12   *Docherty v McGlynn* 1983 SLT 645; *Torrie v Turner* 1990 SLT 718.

13   *Torrie v Turner* 1990 SLT 718. Cf the approach of Lord Cameron in *Docherty v McGlynn* 1983 SLT 645 at 650.

14   That is, the Court of Session or the sheriff court: Law Reform (Miscellaneous Provisions) (Scotland) Act 1990, s 70(4). The court may make the request *ex proprio motu*: LR(MP)(S)A 1990, s 70(1). Cf the position in the LR(PC)(S)A 1986, s 6(1).

15   A child's grandmother who defended an action of declarator of parentage in the capacity of executrix to her deceased son, the alleged father, has been held to be a party to the proceedings for this purpose: *MacKay v MacKay* 1995 SLT (Sh Ct) 30.

16  LR(MP)(S)A 1990, s 70(2).
17  1994 SLT (Sh Ct) 22.
18  *Docherty v McGlynn* 1985 SLT 237, OH.
19  1983 SLT 645.
20  LR(PC)(S)A 1986, s 6(4).
21  1983 SLT 645.
22  *S v S* [1972] AC 24, HL.
23  [1972] AC 24 at 45.
24  1983 SLT 645.
25  1983 SLT 645 at 650.
26  Law Reform (Parent and Child) (Scotland) Act 1986, s 1. For discussion see para **9.5**.
27  1983 SLT 645.
28  For example, where the child is the product of an incestuous relationship.
29  *Petrie v Petrie* 1993 SCLR 391 at 393, per temporary Sheriff Principal (Coutts) (direction for sample granted to H to remove his suspicions that W's child was *not* his child).

# LEGITIMACY AND ILLEGITIMACY

## Introduction

**9.4** For centuries a child's rights in Scots law were dependent upon whether or not the child was legitimate. A child was legitimate if the parents were validly married at the date of the child's conception or birth or any time in between.[1] When the child was conceived during a valid marriage, the husband was presumed to be the child's father: *pater est quem nuptiae demonstrant.* Thus for example, where a couple were validly married at the date of the child's conception the child was presumed to be the legitimate child of the husband even if the husband died before the child's birth. If a child was conceived and born out of wedlock, the child was illegitimate.[2]

Where the parents' marriage was void, a child conceived or born during the void marriage could be regarded as legitimate as a result of the doctrine of putative marriage. Before this doctrine was applicable, at least one of the parties must have entered into the 'marriage' in the bona fide belief that the marriage was valid, ie in ignorance of any impediment to the marriage. The error had to be one of fact not of law: for example, if a man and a woman married without realising they were uncle and niece, the doctrine was applicable (error of fact) but it did not apply if they had married in the belief that uncle and niece had capacity to marry each other under the law of Scotland (error of law).[3] A child who was conceived or born during a voidable marriage retained the status of legitimacy even if a declarator of nullity of marriage was subsequently obtained.[4]

When a child was born illegitimate, at common law the child could be legitimated by the subsequent valid marriage of the parents: legitimation *per subsequens matrimonium.* Although the effect of the doctrine was retrospectively to treat the child as legitimate from the date of birth, it did not apply if the child's parents lacked the capacity to marry each other at the date of the child's conception.[5] The law was changed by the Legitimation (Scotland) Act 1968. This provided that a child would become legitimated as a result of the parents' subsequent marriage provided that the child was living at the date of the marriage and the father was domiciled in Scotland at that date.[6] It was irrelevant that the parents lacked capacity to marry at the date of the child's conception[7] but, unlike the common law position, the child was only treated as legitimate from the date of the marriage.[8] A marriage for the purposes of the Legitimation (Scotland) Act 1968 included a putative and voidable marriage.[9]

The law took pains to preserve a child's status of legitimacy. Thus for example the presumption *pater est* was only rebuttable by proof beyond reasonable doubt that the husband was not the father of the child.[10] Moreover, because of the scope of the doctrine of putative marriage and the possibility of legitimation by the subsequent marriage of a child's parents, the range of persons treated as legitimate was wide.

Nevertheless, it came to be considered reprehensible that the rights of children should continue to depend on the marital status of their parents. Legal discrimination against illegitimate children was held to a be a breach of Article 8 (right to family life) of the European Convention on Human Rights.[11] The matter was considered by the Scottish Law Commission[12] and its recommendations were enacted in the Law Reform (Parent and Child) (Scotland) Act 1986. That Act has been amended by the Family Law (Scotland) Act 2006[13] so that the status of illegitimacy can finally be erased from Scots law.

1   Bell *Principles of the Law of Scotland* (10th edn, 1899) s 1624. If the child was conceived before marriage and the husband knew at the time of the ceremony that his wife was pregnant and he had had intercourse with her at the probable date of conception, there was a strong presumption that the child was the legitimate child of the husband: *Gardner v Gardner* (1876) 3 R 695, (1877) 4 R (HL) 56.

2   James v McLennan 1971 SLT 162.

3   Purves' Trustees v Purves (1896) 22 R 513.

4   Law Reform (Miscellaneous Provisions) Act 1949, s 4. Since the only ground of a voidable marriage is incurable impotency, the number of children involved was very small: see **Ch 2.**

5   Erskine *An Institute of the Law of Scotland* (8th edn, 1870) I, 67, 52; Bell's *Principles* 1627; *Kerr v Martin* (1840) 2 D 752.

6   Legitimation (Scotland) Act 1968, s 1.

7   By L(S)A 1968, s 4, certain children who failed to be legitimated *per subsequens matrimonium* because their parents lacked capacity to marry at the date of their conception were to be treated as legitimate from the date of the commencement of the 1968 Act. Cf *Wright's Trustees v Callander* 1992 SLT 498.

8   L(S)A 1968, s 1(1).

9   L(S)A 1968, s 8(1).

10  See for example, *Ballantyne v Douglas* 1953 SLT (Notes) 10 at 11, per Lord Patrick. Now the presumption of paternity under the Law Reform (Parent and Child) (Scotland) Act 1986, s 5, can be rebutted by proof on a balance of probabilities: LR(PC)(S)A 1986, s 5(4).

11  Convention for the Protection of Human Rights and Fundamental Freedoms (Rome, 4 November 1950; 213 UNTS 221; TS 71 (1953); Cmd 8969). Most, but not all, of the 1950 Convention has been incorporated into United Kingdom Law as Schedule 1 to the Human Rights Act 1998. See *Marckx v Belgium* (1979) 2 EHRR 330.

12  See Illegitimacy (Scot Law Com No 82).

13  FL(S)A 2006, ss 21 and 45 (2) and Schedule 3.

## The current law

**9.5** Section 1(1) of the Law Reform (Parent and Child) (Scotland) Act 1986 declares:

> 'No person whose status is governed by Scots law shall be illegitimate; and accordingly the fact that a person's parents are not or have not been married to each other shall be left out of account in (a) determining the person's legal status; or (b) establishing the legal relationship between the person and any other person'.

The effect of this provision is that illegitimacy is abolished and all children have legal equality regardless of their parents' marital status at the time of their birth.

To ensure its purpose, s 1(2) of the 1986 Act provides:

> 'Any reference (however expressed) in any enactment or deed to any relative shall, unless the contrary intention appears in the enactment or deed, be construed in accordance with subsection (1) above'.

The 1986 Act amended previous legislation[1] to remove legal inequalities between legitimate and illegitimate children[2] and, so far as possible, references to illegitimate children.[3]

Nevertheless there remained two areas where the distinction between legitimate and illegitimate children could still be important. First, s 1(1) did not apply to any deed executed *before* the commencement of the Law Reform (Parent and Child) (Scotland) Act 1986.[4] But if the deed was executed after the commencement of the Law Reform (Miscellaneous Provisions) (Scotland) Act 1968, any reference in the deed to a relative includes, unless the contrary intention appears, an illegitimate as well as legitimate relationship.[5] Moreover, by s 1(4)(c) of the 1986 Act, s 1(1) did not apply to any deed executed *after* the commencement of the 1986 Act if the deed (however expressed) referred to a legitimate or illegitimate relationship.[6] Thus, for example, if a testator made a bequest in his will expressly to his daughter's legitimate children, the daughter's illegitimate children could not benefit even if the testamentary deed was executed after the commencement of the 1986 Act.

Section 1(4)(c) of the 1986 Act has been repealed by the Family Law (Scotland) Act 2006. Section 1(1) will therefore apply to deeds executed on or after 4 May 2006, the date when the 2006 Act commenced.[7] And so, since illegitimacy has been abolished, a reference in a deed executed after that date to, for example A's legitimate or lawful child, has to be construed in accordance with s 1(1) and must therefore simply refer to any child of A. It could be argued that the use of the words 'legitimate' or 'lawful' indicate a contrary intention for the purposes of s 1(2) so that the deed is not to be construed in accordance with s 1(1). But if this was so, there would have been no need for s 1(4)(c) in the first place and its subsequent repeal by the 2006 Act which was designed to abolish illegitimacy. It is submitted that the use of these terms cannot in themselves amount to such a contrary intention and a testator who, for example, wished to exclude his daughter's illegitimate children would either have expressly to stipulate that s 1(1) was not applicable or that the daughter had to be validly married at the time the beneficiaries were conceived or born or any time in between!

Secondly, the 1986 Act does not apply to the succession or devolution of any title, coat of arms, honour or dignity transmissible on the death of the holder thereof,[8] or affect the functions of the Lord Lyon King of Arms so far as relating to the granting of arms.[9]

Because illegitimacy has been abolished, there is no need for legitimation and the Legitimation (Scotland) Act 1968 has been repealed.[10] Actions for declarator of legitimacy, legitimation and illegitimacy are no longer to be competent except in relation to the succession or devolution of titles, coats of arms, etc.[11]

The 1986 Act does not affect the law in relation to the parental responsibilities and rights of fathers who have not and do not marry the mothers of their children.[12]

---

1 Law Reform (Parent and Child) (Scotland) Act 1986, s 10(1) and Schedule 1.
2 For example in relation to succession, LR(PC)(S)A 1986, Schedule 1, para 7 removes inequalities by the simple expedient of providing that any reference to relative in the Succession (Scotland) Act 1964 shall be construed in accordance with s 1(1) of the 1986 Act. On succession, see para **3.17**.
3 See for example, LR(PC)(S)A 1986, Schedule 1, para 15 in relation to the Damages (Scotland) Act 1976; and LR(PC)(S)A 1986, Schedule 1, para 17 in relation to the Marriage (Scotland) Act 1977 (discussed in **Ch 2**).
4 LR(PC)A 1986, s 1(4)(b). See, for example, *Allan, Petitioner* 1991 SLT 203.
5 Law Reform (Miscellaneous Provisions) (Scotland) Act 1968, s 5. See for example, *Russell v Woods* 1987 SCLR 207.
6 LR(PC)(S)A 1986, s 1(4)(c).
7 Family Law (Scotland) Act 2006, s 45(2) and Schedule 3.
8 LR(PC)(S)A 1986, s 9(1)(c).
9 LR(PC)(S)A 1986, s 9(1)(ca).
10 FL(S)A 2006, s 45(2) and Schedule 3.
11 FL(S)A 2006, s 21(2)(c) adding s 1(6) to the 1986 Act, s 21(4)(a) amending s 9(1)(c) of the 1986 Act and s 45(1) and para 6(2) of Schedule 2 to the 2006 Act.

12 LR(PC)(S)A 1986, s 1(3). See **Ch 11**. The rule that an illegitimate child took the domicile of his mother rather than the domicile of his father has been abolished and replaced by a status neutral set of rules in FL(S)A 2006, s 22. A child is able to acquire a domicile of choice on reaching the age of 16.

# Chapter 10

# Children's legal capacity and rights

## INTRODUCTION

**10.1** The purpose of this chapter is to examine some of the most important legal rights enjoyed by children and how these rights are enforced. As a child matures, there may be a conflict between the child's 'right' to self-determination and the parents' responsibilities and rights in relation to the child's upbringing. Full discussion of this important and controversial issue will be left to the following chapter where parental responsibilities and rights will be discussed in some detail. At present we are concerned with a child's capacity to enter into juristic acts and to seek redress when the child's rights have been infringed: we shall also consider when children may incur liability in respect of their actions. In this context Scots law makes an important distinction between a child below 16 and a young person over that age. At the age of 18 a young person becomes an adult.[1] At the outset it must be emphasised that the treatment of the substantive law on many of these issues is not intended to be exhaustive.

---

1    Age of Majority (Scotland) Act 1969.

---

## LEGAL TRANSACTIONS

### Children under 16

**10.2** In Scots law a child of any age has passive capacity, ie the child enjoys the full complement of legal rights, for example the right to own heritable and moveable property.[1] As a general rule a child under 16 has no active capacity.[2] This means that the child cannot enter into juristic acts, for example make a contract. The child cannot pursue or defend actions when the child's rights have been infringed. Instead, a person entitled to act as the child's legal representative must enter into juristic acts for the child's benefit and pursue or defend actions on the child's behalf. The right

233

to act as a child's legal representative is one of the parental responsibilities and rights[3] which, prima facie, parents have in respect of their children. Accordingly, it is the parent who will usually enter into a transaction[4] on behalf of the child. If a child purports to enter into a transaction without the capacity to do so, the transaction is null.[5] So for example, if a child of ten purported to buy an Armani suit costing £1000, the contract of sale is null. Where a parent enters into a contract on behalf of a child, the contract is valid even if it is to the child's disadvantage. Any remedy[6] the child may have is against the parent, not the other party to the contract.[7] If for example, P enters into a contract with A on behalf of P's child, C, C has no remedy against A if the contract is disadvantageous to C but may have a remedy against P for failing to act as a reasonable and prudent person.[8]

There are important exceptions to the general rule of absence of legal capacity until the child reaches 16.

(i)     A child under the age of 16 has legal capacity to enter into a transaction of a kind commonly entered into by persons of the child's age and circumstances provided the terms of the contract are not unreasonable.[9] If 'commonly' is interpreted as 'not unusually or surprisingly' as opposed to 'often', the scope of this section is potentially very wide. Not only would it cover such transactions as the purchase of sweets or bus and rail tickets but also 'one-off' but not unusual contracts, such as the purchase of a bicycle or computer. It should also be noted that before the child is bound by the transaction, its terms must not be unreasonable.

(ii)    A child aged 12 or over has the legal capacity to make a will;[10] the child can test on both heritable and moveable property.[11]

(iii)   An adoption order or a permanence order (whether or not it contains a provision granting authority for the child to be adopted)[12] cannot be made in respect of a child aged 12 or over unless the child consents.[13]

(iv)    A transaction includes giving any consent having legal effect.[14] Thus giving consent to any surgical, medical or dental procedure on the child is a legal transaction. Where the child is under 16, the parent as the child's legal representative can give consent to such procedures on the child's behalf.[15] However, a child under

16 has capacity to consent if, in the opinion of the qualified medical practitioner attending the child, the child is capable of understanding the nature and possible consequences of the procedure or treatment.[16]

Several points should be noted. First, the child's capacity to consent is determined by the medical practitioner, ie it is the medical practitioner who decides whether or not the child is capable of understanding the nature and possible consequences of the procedure or treatment and consequently whether or not the child has legal capacity to consent.

Secondly, the language of s 2(4) of the Age of Legal Capacity (Scotland) Act 1991 is enabling. It empowers a child under 16 to consent. It is silent on whether a child whom the medical practitioner has decided does understand the nature and possible consequences of the proposed procedure or treatment has capacity to refuse consent.[17] Since an invasion of bodily integrity is an assault in the absence of positive consent, it can be argued that inherent in the capacity to consent is the capacity to refuse consent, viz if a person does not positively consent, an invasion of bodily integrity cannot lawfully take place.[18] Further support for this view is to be found in s 186 of the Children's Hearings (Scotland) Act 2011. This section provides that even if a court or children's hearing specifically directs that a child should undergo medical examination or treatment, this does not override the right of a child who has s 2(4) capacity to refuse consent. Again, s 131A of the Education (Scotland) Act 1980 presupposes that a child with s 2(4) capacity can refuse to consent to medical procedures carried out by school doctors.

However, where the proposed procedure or treatment is in the best interests of the child, the English courts have been prepared to override a young person's refusal to consent.[19] It remains to be seen whether the Scottish courts will find a way to reach a similar conclusion. In practice, if a child is refusing to consent to a proposed procedure or treatment, the medical practitioner is unlikely to take the view that the child is capable of understanding the consequences of the procedure or treatment and consequently the child will not have s 2(4) capacity. In these circumstances, the medical practitioner would then ask the parent as the child's legal representative to consent on behalf of the child.[20]

Finally, there is no express provision in s 2(4) of the ALC(S) A 1991 that the procedure or treatment should be in the best interests of the child. So for example, a child with s 2(4) capacity could consent to being a donor of non-regenerative tissue like a kidney!

(v) A child under 16 has legal capacity to instruct a solicitor in connection with any civil matter provided the child has a general understanding of what it means to do so. A child aged 12 or more is presumed to be of sufficient age and maturity to have such understanding but a child below that age may instruct a solicitor if the child in fact has such understanding.[21]

(vi) If a girl under 16 has a baby, she will automatically have parental responsibilities and rights in respect of her child.[22] Although under 16, the mother may exercise her parental rights and responsibilities.[23] Where a boy under 16 is the father of a child and has parental responsibilities and rights in respect of the child, he is also able to exercise them.[24]

---

1   Age of Legal Capacity (Scotland) Act 1991, s 1(3)(e).

2   ALC(S)A 1991, s 1(1)(a).

3   Children (Scotland) Act 1995, ss 1(1)(d) and 2(1)(d).

4   'Transaction' is defined as a transaction having legal effect: it includes unilateral transactions, the exercise of testamentary capacity, the exercise of a power of appointment, bringing or defending actions, acting as arbiter or trustee, acting as an instrumentary witness and giving consent having legal effect: ALC(S)A 1991, s 9.

5   ALC(S)A 1991, s 2(5).

6   See para **11.2**.

7   This is because the old remedy of reducing the contract as against the other party on the grounds of minority and lesion has been abolished: ALC(S)A 1991, s 1(5). On reduction on the grounds of minority and lesion, see *Wilkinson and Norrie* paras 1.18ff.

8   C(S)A 1995, s 10(1), discussed at para **11.2**.

9   ALC(S)A 1991, s 2(1)(a) and (b).

10  ALC(S)A 1991, s 2(2). A parent as the child's legal representative cannot make the child's will.

11  On children's rights to legitim out of their parents' moveable estate, see para **3.17**.

12  On adoption and permanence orders see Ch 13.

13  Adoption and Children (Scotland) Act 2007, ss 32 and 84(1) and (2).

14  ALC(S)A 1991, s 9.

15  For full discussion, see para **11.9**.

16  ALC(S)A 1991, s 2(4). For the purposes of s 2(4), the storage of gametes in accordance with the Human Fertilisation and Embryology Act 1990 is to be treated as a medical procedure and a person under the age of 16 can consent to the use of his cells for the purpose of research where the child is capable of understanding the nature of the research: ALC(S)A 1991, s 2(4ZA) and (4ZB).

17  In *Houston, Applicant* 1996 SCLR 943 there was a concession that a 15-year-old boy with s 2(4) capacity had the right to refuse to consent to medical treatment. The issue was not explored in depth in this case.

18  The patient does not have to say 'I refuse to consent': if the patient is silent, the proposed procedure or treatment cannot lawfully go ahead without the patient's positive consent. This is subject to the necessity principle where, for example, treatment can be carried out without consent if the patient is unconscious after an accident.

19  *Re W (a minor)* [1992] 4 All ER 627.

20  For full discussion, see para **11.9**.

21  ALC(S)A 1991, s 2(4A). If the child has s 2(4A) capacity he or she will also have capacity to sue or defend in civil proceedings: ALC(S)A 1991, s 2(4B).

22  C(S)A 1995, s 3(1)(a).

23  ALC(S)A 1991, s 1(3)(g).

24  Ibid. He will have parental responsibilities and rights if he was registered as the child's father on or after 4 May 2006 or if the mother agreed he should have them. For discussion see para **11.3**.

## YOUNG PERSONS OVER 16 BUT UNDER 18

**10.3** A young person over 16 has active legal capacity to enter into transactions.[1] When a young person has entered into a transaction between the ages of 16 and 18, the court has power to set the transaction aside if it is a prejudicial transaction.[2] The court can set aside such a transaction until the young person reaches 21.[3] A prejudicial transaction is defined as a transaction which an adult, exercising reasonable prudence, would not have entered into in the circumstances of the young person at the time of entering into the transaction and has caused or is likely to cause substantial prejudice to the young person.[4]

Certain transactions cannot be set aside. These include consent to adoption orders, consent to medical or dental procedures or treatment, transactions in the course of the young person's trade, business or profession, transactions induced by the young person's fraudulent misrepresentation as to age or transactions ratified by the young person after the age of 18 when he or she knew that it could be set aside.[5]

When a young person is between 16 and 18, all the parties to a proposed transaction may make an application to the court to have the transaction ratified.[6] The court cannot ratify the transaction if it is satisfied that an adult exercising reasonable prudence in the circumstances of the young person would not have entered into the transaction. If the transaction is ratified, it cannot be set aside as a prejudicial transaction.[7] Thus for example, if A intends to purchase a house owned by B who is aged 17, A and B should apply to the court to have the proposed sale ratified. The court will ratify the proposed sale if satisfied that an adult exercising reasonable prudence would have sold the house if in B's position. Once ratified, B cannot set the sale aside on the ground that it is a prejudicial transaction.

1    Age of Legal Capacity (Scotland) Act 1991, s 1(1)(b).
2    ALC(S)A 1991, s 3(1).
3    ALC(S)A 1991, s 3(1).
4    ALC(S)A 1991, s 3(2). A typical example of a prejudicial transaction would be if the young person undertook a cautionary obligation.
5    ALC(S)A 1991, s 3(3).
6    ALC(S)A 1991, s 4.
7    ALC(S)A 1991, s 3(3)(j).

## DELICTUAL LIABILITY

**10.4** The Age of Legal Capacity (Scotland) Act 1991 does not affect delictual liability.[1] Where a child under 16 is injured by the wrongous or negligent act of another, the child's legal representative can sue for damages in delict on the child's behalf.[2] Where the young person is over 16, he or she has capacity to bring the action. If a child is injured by his or her parent an action for damages in delict is competent:[3] in these circumstances a *curator ad litem* will be appointed.

Conversely, children can be liable in delict for their wrongful acts if the requisite intention or negligence can be established. Since children are rarely wealthy or insured, there are few, if any, cases where they have been sued for damages in delict. This will not apply if a young person aged 17 causes injury through negligent driving because there is compulsory third party insurance. More importantly, it has been held that a child can be guilty of contributory negligence leading to a reduction of the child's damages when he or she has been injured. In *McKinnell v White*[4] for example, Lord Fraser reduced the damages of a five-year-old child by 50 per cent on the basis that the child had been contributorily negligent when he ran in front of a speeding motorist. Lord Fraser justified his decision on the basis that any child living in an urban area would be bound to be aware by the age of five of the danger of traffic.[5] It should be noted that parents are not automatically vicariously liable for the delicts of their children[6] but a parent will incur personal liability if, as a result of the parent's negligence, this caused or contributed to the child's delict, for example failure to supervise a child properly.[7]

Where a child's parent has died as a consequence of personal injury arising from a wrongful or negligent act of another, a child may claim damages in respect of the parent's death under the Damages (Scotland) Act 2011.[8] Damages are available for loss of support suffered or likely to be suffered as a result of the parent's death[9]. As a general rule, if the child is a dependent child[10] 75% of the deceased's net income is assumed to have been spent in support of the family[11]. There is also compensation for the loss of non-patrimonial benefits, such as the parent's affection and guidance.[12]

---

1   Age of Legal Capacity (Scotland) Act 1991, s 1(3)(c).
2   A child under the age of 16 may have capacity to sue if the child has a general understanding of what it means to do so: ALC(S)A 1991, s 2(4A) and (4B), discussed at para **10.2**.
3   *Young v Rankin* 1934 SC 499; *Wood v Wood* 1935 SLT 431.
4   1971 SLT (Notes) 61.
5   1971 SLT (Notes) 61 at 62. See also *McCluskey v Wallace* 1998 SC 711 (four-year-old child held to be contributorily negligent).
6   But the parents would be liable if they had authorised the child's action or the child was acting as an employee of the parents.
7   *Hastie v Magistrates of Edinburgh* 1907 SC 1102; *Hardie v Sneddon* 1917 SC 1.
8   A child has title to sue even though born after the parent has died: *Cohen v Shaw* 1992 SLT 1022.
9   D(S)A 2011, s 4(3)(a).

10   A child who is under 18 and to whom the deceased owed an obligation of aliment, D(S)A 2011, s 7(3).
11   D(S)A 2011, s 7(1).
12   D(S)A 2011, s 4 (3)(b)  For full discussion, see Joe Thomson *Delictual Liability* (5th edn, 2014, Bloomsbury Professional), Ch 13.

# MARRIAGE AND DOMICILE

**10.5**  A person has capacity to marry or register a civil partnership when aged 16 or over.[1] A young person has the capacity to acquire a domicile of choice on reaching 16.[2]

1   Marriage (Scotland) Act 1977, s 1; Civil Partnership Act 2004, s 86(1)(c).
2   Family Law (Scotland) Act 2006, s 22. Before then, the child will either have a domicile of dependence which follows that of the parents or else will be domiciled in the country with which the child has for the time being the closest connection: see FL(S)A 2006, s 22.

# CRIMINAL LIABILITY

**10.6**  The age of criminal responsibility was not changed by the Age of Legal Capacity (Scotland) Act 1991[1] and remains eight.[2] However a child under the age of 12 cannot be prosecuted in a criminal court.[3] In most situations where a child under 16 has committed a criminal offence,[4] this will be a ground for the referral of the child's case by a Reporter to a children's hearing to determine whether or not the child is in need of a compulsory supervision order.[5] But a child aged 12 or over will be prosecuted in the criminal courts on the instructions of the Lord Advocate if the child has committed a very serious crime, for example murder or culpable homicide.

1   Age of Legal Capacity (Scotland) Act 1991, s 1(3)(c).
2   Children and Young Persons (Scotland) Act 1937, s 55.
3   Criminal Justice and Licensing (Scotland) Act 2010, s 52 adding s 41A to the Criminal Procedure (Scotland) Act 1995.
4   But not when the child is below the age of eight: *Merrin v S* 1987 SLT 193, discussed at para **15.7**.
5   See generally Ch 15 above..

## SPECIFIC AGE LIMITS

**10.7** The Age of Legal Capacity (Scotland) Act 1991 does not affect any age limits laid down for specific purposes by other statutes. In a work of this compass, it is not possible to explore these limits in detail.[1] Sometimes a statute gives a child capacity before the child reaches 16; for example, in Scotland a child aged 12 or more can apply for a maintenance calculation under s 7 of the Child Support Act 1991.[2]

Statutory age limits usually prevent a young person from engaging in a course of conduct until he or she reaches an age beyond 16. Thus for example, a young person has to be 17 or over before he or she can hold a licence to drive a motor car,[3] or obtain a licence to fly a plane.[4] Often Parliament makes it a criminal offence to sell or supply particular goods or services to a child or young person below a particular age, for example to sell tobacco to a child under 16[5] or alcohol to a young person below 18.[6] It is also a criminal offence for a person under 18 to buy or attempt to buy alcohol.[7] Similarly, there are offences relating to betting transactions[8] with young persons below 18.

In relation to sexual activities, it is a criminal offence to have sexual intercourse or engage in sexual activity with a child below the age of 13.[9] It is irrelevant that the child has consented and it is no defence that the accused believed the child was 13 or over.[10] It is also a criminal offence to have sexual intercourse, or engage in sexual activity, with a child who is over 13 but under 16.[11] The offence is committed even though the child consented. It is a defence if the accused reasonably believed that the child was 16 unless the accused has previously been charged with a sexual offence or there is a sexual harm order against him.[12] If both parties are between the ages of 13 and 16, both commit an offence where the sexual acts were consensual.[13] Again there is the defence of reasonable belief that the other party was 16. However, in both situations, there is a further defence that at the time when the sexual conduct took place, the difference in age between the parties did not exceed two years.[14] So, for example, if a boy aged 15 has sex with another boy aged 14, both have a defence as the age difference between them is only a year. Where both parties are over 16 they are free to engage in consensual sexual activity with each other.

---

1   For fuller discussion, see 3 *Stair Memorial Encyclopaedia*, paras 1213 ff.
2   On the Child Support Act 1991, see para **10.11**.
3   Road Traffic Act 1988, s 101.
4   Air Navigation Order 1989, SI 1989/2004, art 20(1)(b)(i).
5   Children and Young Persons (Scotland) Act 1937, s 18(1).
6   Licensing (Scotland) Act 1976, s 68(1).
7   L(S)A 1976, s 68(2).
8   See generally, the Betting, Gaming and Lotteries Act 1963, s 22.
9   Sexual Offences (Scotland) Act 2009, ss 18–26.
10  SO(S)A 2009, s 27.
11  SO(S)A 2009, ss 28–36.
12  SO(S)A 2009, s 39(1) and (2).
13  SO(S)A 2009, s 37.
14  SO(S)A 2009, s 39(3).

---

## LITIGATION

**10.8** Prima facie the general rule of legal capacity applies. Where the child is below 16, any civil action must be pursued or defended on behalf of the child by the child's legal representative. If the child has no legal representative or the legal representative refuses to act, the action can proceed in the child's name in spite of the fact the child is under 16.[1] In any civil proceedings, the court can appoint a *curator ad litem* to protect the child's interests.[2]

If a child under 16 has legal capacity to consult a solicitor, the child also has capacity to pursue or defend in civil proceedings.[3] While a young person over 16 has legal capacity, the young person cannot assent to the variation of a trust until 18;[4] in these circumstances, a *curator ad litem* will be appointed for a young person between the ages of 16 and 18.[5]

It should be noted that prescriptive or limitation periods do not begin to run against a child until he or she reaches 16.[6]

There are special rules which apply to witnesses who are children. Discussion of these are beyond the compass of the present work.

---

1   Age of Legal Capacity (Scotland) Act 1991, s 1(3)(f)(i).
2   ALC(S)A 1991, s 1(3)(f)(ii). This would arise if, for example, there was a potential conflict of interest between the child and the parents and the child's parents were acting as the child's legal representatives.

3    ALC(S)A 1991, s 2(4A) and (4B). On s 2(4A), see para **10.2**.
4    Trusts (Scotland) Act 1961, s 1(2).
5    ALC(S)A 1991, s 1(3)(f)(iii).
6    Prescription and Limitation (Scotland) Act 1973, ss 17(3), 18(3), 18A(2), 22B(4), 22C(3) (limitation); 6(4)(b) (five years' prescription); *McCabe v McLellan* 1994 SLT 346. There is no need for the young person's nonage (ie, being below 16) to be causally related to the failure to pursue the action. In other words, there is a blanket protection due to nonage.

## ALIMENT

**10.9** A child has the right to be alimented by his or her parents. The law of aliment of children is to be found in the Family Law (Scotland) Act 1985. By s 1(1)(c) of the 1985 Act, an obligation of aliment is owed by a father or mother to his or her child. Both parents are under an obligation to aliment their children. Thus liability must be divided between the father and the mother: aliment is not the primary responsibility of the father of a child. The fact that the parents have never married each other is irrelevant. Although the statute speaks of 'father' and 'mother', it is thought that these words must be interpreted as including a mother's same sex spouse or civil partner or a child's second female parent who are parents of the child by virtue of sections 35, 42 and 43 of the Human Fertilisation and Embryology Act 2008.[1]

Section 1(1)(d) of the 1985 Act places an obligation on a person to aliment a child who has been accepted by that person as a child of the family.[2] The absence of a blood tie is irrelevant. The obligation to aliment is therefore extended beyond parents and natural children to include, for example a step-parent or the cohabitant of the child's parent.[3] But s 1(1)(d) would equally apply where a grandparent brings up a grandchild or an uncle or aunt brings up a niece.[4] It is doubtful whether the acceptor must have a family before the child can be accepted since it is expressly provided by s 27 of the 1985 Act that family includes a one-parent family.[5]

Before the obligation arises under s 1(1)(d) the child must have been 'accepted' as a child of the family. This could give rise to difficulties. Consider the following example.

### Example

H and W are married. W has a child. The presumption of paternity in s 5 of the Law Reform (Parent and Child) (Scotland) Act 1986 will apply. If H later rebuts the presumption and establishes that he is not the child's father, does he owe the child an obligation of aliment? Section 1(1)(c) is inapplicable as H is not the child's father. Section 1(1)(d) does not apply if the view is taken that H did not accept the child as a child of his family because he did not know that the child was not his and had therefore not agreed with W to accept another man's child as a child of the family.[6]

The difficulty can be avoided if the criterion was whether a person had 'treated' as opposed to 'accepted' the child as a child of the family.[7]

A child for the purposes of aliment means a person under 18 or a person between 18 and 25 who is reasonably and appropriately undergoing instruction at an educational establishment, or training for employment or for a trade, profession or vocation.[8] Thus, a parent's obligation to aliment a child continues while the child attends university.[9] The obligation to aliment a disabled child with learning difficulties prima facie ceases when the child reaches 18[10] but will continue until 25 if the child attends any course of instruction designed to maximise the child's potential for life.

The obligation of aliment is to provide such support as is reasonable in the circumstances[11] having regard to the factors which the courts use to determine the amount of aliment, ie the needs[12] and resources of the parties, their earning capacities and generally all the circumstances of the case.[13] Where two or more parties owe an obligation of aliment to a child, while there is no order of liability, the court in deciding how much, if any, aliment to award against any of those persons must have regard to the obligation of aliment owed to the child by the other person(s).[14] The following examples illustrate how this provision operates in practice.

### Example 1

H and W are married. They have a child, C. Both H and W therefore have an obligation to aliment C: s 1(1)(c). In quantifying the amount of aliment H should pay, the court must have regard to the fact that W also owes an obligation of aliment to C. Thus if H was unemployed and W was in well-paid employment, the court could take the view that H should only be ordered to pay a fraction of the required aliment or, indeed, no aliment at all, leaving C to pursue a claim against W.

**Example 2**

A, mother, and B, father, have a child, C. Both A and B therefore have an obligation to aliment C: s 1(1)(c). A later marries H who accepts C as a child of his family. H therefore has an obligation to aliment C: s 1(1)(d). In quantifying the amount of aliment H should pay, the court must have regard to the fact that both A and B owe an obligation of aliment to C. Thus even if H was in employment, the court could take the view that H should only be ordered to pay a fraction of the required aliment, leaving C to pursue claims against A and the father, B.

Where a court makes an award of aliment in respect of a child under 16, it may include an amount for the reasonable expenses of the person having care of the child where these are incurred in looking after the child.[15]

An action for aliment can be brought by the child.[16] Thus for example, an 18-year-old child who is attending university can bring a claim for aliment against his or her parents if they have refused to make an appropriate contribution towards the child's maintenance.[17] Where a child is below 18, an action can be brought on his or her behalf by the parent or guardian of the child or any person with whom the child lives or is seeking a residence order in respect of the child.[18] So if for example a grandmother is caring for her daughter's child, she can bring an action of aliment on the child's behalf against the child's mother and father. A woman, whether married or not, may bring an action for aliment on behalf of her unborn child as if the child had been born but no such action will be heard or disposed of prior to the birth of the child;[19] on granting decree after the birth, the court has power to backdate the aliment to the date of the child's birth.[20]

An action for aliment of a child can be brought even if the child is living with the defender; so for example, a child can seek aliment from his or her parents while still living at home with them.[21] In these circumstances, the parents will have a defence if they can show that they are fulfilling their obligation of aliment and are continuing to do so.[22]

Where a couple have separated and the mother, for example, has taken a child under 16 with her, then if the mother brings an action for aliment on behalf of the child against the father, it is no defence to the action that the father has offered to receive the child into his household and thereby fulfil the obligation of aliment.[23] This is because the question of where a child should live is prima facie an issue in proceedings for a residence order where the child's welfare will be the paramount consideration.[24] But where the child is over 16, the father will have a defence to a claim for aliment if he had offered a home to the child which it was reasonable to expect the child to accept.[25] In determining whether it was reasonable for the child to accept such an offer, the defender's conduct will be taken into account.[26] For example, it might not be reasonable for a daughter to accept her father's offer of accommodation if the father's unreasonable behaviour towards her mother had led to the breakdown of the marriage and had been a cause of distress to both the mother and the child.[27]

While an action for aliment simpliciter is competent in both the Court of Session and the sheriff court,[28] in practice a claim is more likely to be made in the course of other proceedings, such as declarator of parentage, actions in relation to parental responsibilities and rights, separation, dissolution of a civil partnership, divorce and claims for financial provision on divorce or dissolution.[29] For example when a woman has a child, if she seeks declarator of parentage,[30] she can bring a claim for aliment on behalf of her child against the alleged father in the same proceedings: if parentage is established, aliment can be ordered from the father of the child. Similarly, in an action for divorce or dissolution, the pursuer can bring claims for aliment on behalf of the children of the marriage or family: these will include not only the spouses' or a civil partner's children, but any children accepted by either spouse or civil partner as children of the family.[31] Any claims for aliment for the children must be satisfied before the court will order financial provision for the spouses or civil partners. Where, at any stage in the proceedings, an action for divorce, dissolution or separation is dismissed, the court is not prevented from making inter alia an order for aliment for any children of the family.[32]

Aliment takes the form of periodical payments, whether for a definite or indefinite period or until the happening of a specified event.[33] The court cannot substitute a lump sum for a periodical payment.[34] But the court can order alimentary payments of an occasional or special nature to meet special needs which it would be unreasonable to expect the claimant to meet out of a periodical allowance.[35] This could, for example, be an order to pay school fees.[36] An award of aliment can be backdated to the date of the bringing of the action and, on special cause shown, to a date prior to the bringing of the action.[37]

On a material change of circumstances since the date of the original decree, an award of aliment can be varied or recalled.[38] An application to vary an award has to be made while the obligation to aliment subsists: it cannot be varied retrospectively when the child has become an adult.[39] The variation can be backdated but not beyond the date of the decree which is being varied.[40] When a variation is backdated, any sums paid under the order before variation can be ordered to be repaid.[41] While an interim award of aliment can be varied or recalled, there is no power to backdate the variation.[42] Where there has been an agreement relating to aliment it can also be varied on a material change of circumstances.[43]

There is no obligation on a child to aliment his or her parent, however wealthy the child or indigent the parent. Where a child is wealthy in his or her own right, a parent can use the child's income for the child's maintenance or education; resort will rarely be made to the child's capital for these purposes unless the parent's circumstances are so reduced that he or she cannot aliment the child.[44]

Finally, the discretionary nature of awards of aliment must be emphasised. What a child will actually receive as an award of aliment depends not only on the child's needs but also on the resources of his or her parents.[45] For children of low income families, awards of aliment will be small. Increasingly resort will have to be made to income support for the basic maintenance of children whose parents are unemployed. But where the parents have separated, in the vast majority of cases their child's right to aliment cannot be enforced in the courts. Instead, an application must be made to the Child Maintenance Service for a maintenance calculation. It is to this statutory system of child support that we now turn.

---

1    Discussed at para **9.2**. Otherwise a child of a lesbian couple would be disadvantaged
     with a resulting breach of the child's human rights.

2  Foster parents are not obliged to aliment children who have been boarded out by a local or other public authority or a voluntary organisation: Family Law (Scotland) Act 1985, s 1(1)(d).

3  See for example, *Telfer v Kellock* 2004 SLT 1290 (child's mother's lesbian lover).

4  See for example, *Inglis v Inglis and Mathew* 1987 SCLR 608.

5  Where a child has been accepted as a child of the family, the acceptor's obligation to aliment continues even if the acceptor no longer wishes a relationship with the child.

6  *Watson v Watson* 1994 SCLR 1097; *Gallacher v Gallacher* 1997 Fam LR 29.

7  'Treated' is now the criterion for the definition of a child of the family in other areas of Scots law, for example ancillary orders for parental responsibilities and rights on divorce or dissolution: Children (Scotland) Act 1995, s 12(4)(b).

8  FL(S)A 1985, s 1(5)(a) and (b). See for example, *Jowett v Jowett* 1990 SCLR 348; *Park v Park* 2000 SLT (Sh Ct) 65; *Watson v Mc Kay* 2002 Fam LR 2.

9  Provided he or she is under 25.

10  *McBride v McBride* 1995 SCLR 1138.

11  FL(S)A 1985, s 1(2). The test for what is reasonable is objective and does not turn on the view of the parent: *Winter v Thornton* 1993 SCLR 389 (whether aliment should be paid for the child's *private* education).

12  In *McGeachie v McGeachie* 1989 SCLR 99 the child was an infant and the mother was in receipt of child benefit; the court reduced an award of aliment on the ground that it was too generous in the light of the baby's existing needs! To be fair, this was an application for interim aliment.

13  FL(S)A 1985, s 4(1). The court may take into account any support given by the defender to any person whom he maintains as a dependent in his household, whether or not the defender owes the dependent an obligation of aliment, for example, a cohabitants' children: FL(S)A 1985, s 4(3)(a). A cohabitant's income could be relevant: *Pryde v Pryde* 1991 SLT (Sh Ct) 26. Conduct is irrelevant unless it would be manifestly inequitable to leave it out of account: s 4(3)(b). In *Walker v Walker* 1991 SLT 649, the court took the father's conduct in lying about his income into account. The fact that a woman agreed to sexual intercourse without contraception – and, indeed, may have indicated to her lover that she was using contraceptives – will not be taken into account to reduce the amount of reasonable aliment to be paid by the father: *Bell v McCurdie* 1981 SC 64. Section 4(3) of the FL(S)A 1985 is discussed in detail in the context of aliment between husband and wife: see para **3.9–3.10**.

14  FL(S)A 1985, s 4(2). See, for example, *Inglis v Inglis and Mathew* 1987 SCLR 608 (action of aliment by uncle and aunt, who had accepted the child, against the child's parents; court took into account the fact that the aunt and uncle also owed an obligation to aliment the child). In *Ahmed v Ahmed* 2004 Fam LR 14, the obligation to aliment the child was proportioned 20:80 between mother and father respectively.

15  FL(S)A 1985, s 4(4); *H v H* 2004 Fam LR 30.

16  FL(S)A 1985, s 2(4)(a). If the child is between 16 and 18, the child has legal capacity to pursue the action; if below 16, the child will have legal capacity to pursue the action if the child has capacity to instruct a solicitor: see para **10.2**. If the child is 18 or over, the child must pursue the action; it is no longer competent for the parent to bring the action on behalf of the child: *Hay v Hay* 2000 SLT (Sh Ct) 95.

17 See *Jowett v Jowett* 1990 SCLR 348. In assessing the amount of aliment to award a student, the court takes into account the availability of student loans and part-time jobs: *Park v Park* 2000 SLT (Sh Ct) 65. There must be evidence of the student's outlays.

18 FL(S)A 1985, s 2(4)(c)(i) and (iii). On residence orders, see **Ch 12**.

19 FL(S)A 1985, s 2(5). This provision might be useful if the father was about to remove himself from the jurisdiction.

20 FL(S)A 1985, s 3(1)(c).

21 FL(S)A 1985, s 2(6).

22 FL(S)A 1985, s 2(7).

23 FL(S)A 1985, s 2(8).

24 The welfare principle is discussed in **Ch 12**.

25 FL(S)A 1985, s 2(8).

26 FL(S)A 1985, s 2(9).

27 See for example, *McKay v McKay* 1980 SLT (Sh Ct) 111. In *Bell v Bell* (unreported) the father's offer was held to be unreasonable as his daughter lived with her mother after the divorce and was currently engaged in higher education in a different town.

28 FL(S)A 1985, s 2(1).

29 FL(S)A 1985, s 2(2).

30 Law Reform (Parent and Child) (Scotland) Act 1986, s 7.

31 FL(S)A 1985, s 1(1)(c) and (d). The court will not be able to make an order in relation to parental responsibilities and rights unless the child has also been treated as a child of the family (and vice versa): Children (Scotland) Act 1995, s 12. Cases where a child has been accepted but not treated as a child of the family will be rare – but a child *in utero* can be accepted as a child of the family even although the child cannot be treated as such until born.

32 FL(S)A 1985, s 21.

33 FL(S)A 1985, s 3(1)(a): for example, aliment could be ordered until the child reaches 18.

34 FL(S)A 1985, s 3(2).

35 FL(S)A 1985, s 3(1)(b).

36 *McDonald v McDonald* 1995 SLT 72; *G v G* 2002 Fam LR 120; *H v H* 2004 Fam LR 30.

37 FL(S)A 1985, s 3(1)(c). The judge should give reasons why the award should be back dated; *Ahmed v Ahmed* 2004 SCLR 247.

38 FL(S)A 1985, s 5(1). The fact that the cost of maintaining a child increases as the child grows older has been held to be a material change of circumstances: *Skinner v Skinner* 1996 SCLR 334. The making of a maintenance calculation in respect of the child for whom the decree of aliment was granted is a material change of circumstances: FL(S)A 1985, s 5(1A).

39 *Paterson v Paterson* 2002 SLT (Sh Ct) 65.

40 FL(S)A 1985, s 5(2) incorporating s 3(1)(c); *Walker v Walker* 1991 SLT 649; cf *Hannah v Hannah* 1988 SLT 82. This is because the material change of circumstances must have arisen after the original decree was awarded. However, the variation will not be backdated unless it is established that the defender can afford to pay the backdated aliment: *Adamson v Adamson* 1996 SLT 427.

41   FL(S)A 1985, s 5(4).

42   *McColl v McColl* 1993 SLT 617; *Adamson v Adamson* 1996 SLT 427.

43   FL(S)A 1985, s 7. See for example *H v H* 2004 Fam LR 30. The court has now the power to backdate any variation: Family Law (Scotland) Act 2006, s 20.

44   The parent on ceasing to act as the child's legal representative is liable to account for intromissions with the child's property but there is no liability if the child's money was used in the proper discharge by the parent of the parent's responsibility to safeguard and promote the child's welfare: C(S)A 1995, s 10, discussed at para **11.2**.

45   It appears that a child of a wealthy parent should be awarded aliment that is to some extent commensurate to the parent's and his family's lifestyle: *H v H* 2004 Fam LR 30; *Ahmed v Ahmed* 2004 Fam LR 14.

## THE CHILD SUPPORT ACT 1991

### Who is covered by the Child Support Act 1991?

**10.10**  The central legal concept of the Child Support Act 1991[1] is that of the 'qualifying child'.[2] This concept is described in more detail below, but in general, a child is only a qualifying child when one or both of the child's parents are not living with the child. Each parent of a qualifying child is responsible for maintaining the child but is taken to have met that responsibility by making periodical payments of child support maintenance in accordance with the Act.[3]

Where a maintenance calculation requiring payments is made under the Act, it is the duty of the non-resident parent to whom the calculation is addressed to make those payments.[4] The person with day-to-day care of the child in effect meets his or her responsibility to maintain by looking after the child and need make no payments to, or for the benefit of, the child. In most cases covered by the Act, the child is being cared for by one of his or her natural parents ('the person with care'), who is separated from the other ('the non-resident parent'). However, the person with care need not be a parent and it is therefore possible for two persons to be non-resident parents for the purposes of the Act.

A child is a qualifying child if one or both of the child's parents are 'non-resident parents'.[5] A parent is a non-resident parent if he or she is not living in the same household with the child and the child has his or her home with another person who is 'a person with care'.[6] A person with care is the person with whom the child has his or her home and who usually provides day-to-day care for the child. The person need not be an individual but may be, for example, a children's home. The prescribed categories for those who may not be persons with care are local authorities and foster parents looking after children who have been boarded out with them by local authorities.[7]

A person only counts as a 'child'[8] for the purposes of the Act if:

(1)   under 16;

(2)   under 20 and satisfies such conditions as may be prescribed.

Category (2) could cover, for example, children attending school or a further education college. A person between 16 and 20 is not a qualified child if the child is engaged in advanced education, or entitled to income support or income-based jobseeker's allowance or engaged in work-based training. In addition, a person who is or has been married or a party to a civil partnership is not a child and this includes cases where the person has celebrated a marriage or civil partnership which is void or a decree of nullity has been granted.

Where a person does not fall within the definition of 'child', that person is not a qualifying child for the purposes of the 1991 Act and therefore no maintenance calculation relating to him or her may be made.[9]

The definition of 'parent' is also important as a person cannot be either a parent with care or a non-resident parent unless he or she falls within the definition of parent. The Act defines 'parent' as 'any person who is in law the mother or father of the child'.[10] This means that the expression covers both natural and adoptive parents but not step-parents. Therefore a person is not liable to maintain a step-child under the Act.[11] The Act makes special provision for determining disputes about parentage for its purposes.[12]

Thus the Act is concerned with defining and enforcing the obligations of parents to maintain their natural and adopted children in those cases where at least one of the parents is neither living with nor looking after the child and the child is living with and being looked after by the other parent or a third party. In most cases to which the Act applies, the courts have no power to award aliment.

---

1    References are to the Child Support Act 1991 as amended. For discussion of child support, see *Wilkinson and Norrie* Ch 14. This chapter was written by John M Fotheringham.

2    CSA 1991, s 3.

3    CSA 1991, s 1.

4    CSA 1991, s 1.

5    Child Support Act 1991, s 3. The term 'non-resident' parent replaces the original 'absent' parent.

6    CSA 1991, s 3.

7    Child Support (Maintenance Assessment Procedure) Regulations 1992, SI 1992/1813, reg 51.

8    CSA 1991, s 55.

9    However, since the person is not a qualifying child, he or she may be able to pursue an action for aliment in the courts: see para **10.9**.

10   CSA 1991, s 54. On the legal concept of parent see **Ch 9**.

11   This means that the child can pursue an action for aliment in the courts against a step-parent who has accepted the child as a child of the family: discussed at para **10.9**.

12   CSA 1991, ss 26–28.

---

## Maintenance calculations[1]

**10.11**   Under s 4 of the 1991 Act either the person with care, or the non-resident parent of a qualifying child may apply to the Child Maintenance Service (CMS) for a maintenance calculation to be made. By virtue of s 7 of the Act, a qualifying child who is habitually resident in Scotland and is 12 or over may apply for a maintenance calculation in his or her own right, provided no application has already been made by either a person with care or a non-resident parent under s 4.

Once a maintenance calculation has been made under any of ss 4 or 7, the non-resident parent comes under a duty to make payments of the amounts specified in the calculation. CMS has powers to arrange for the collection and enforcement of child support maintenance.

Where payments are required under a maintenance calculation they may be made in a variety of ways. The CMS has several important powers with regard to payments. The first is to make a deduction from earnings order, which is in effect an instruction to an employer to deduct maintenance from earnings at source. Such orders may be used both to collect arrears and to collect current maintenance even where there are no arrears. There is no requirement for the CMS to show that there has been any default in payment before imposing an order, although an order should not be used 'in any case where there is good reason not to use it'! The second is the regular deduction order which can be used where: (i) the non resident parent has failed to pay an amount of child support maintenance; and (ii) that person has capital in some form of account. Payments can be ordered from that account to secure payments of arrears and current maintenance on a regular basis. Third is the lump sum deduction order which can be used if the non resident parent has failed to pay an amount of child support maintenance and has a deposit or other savings account from which the arrears can be paid. Finally, there is a liability order which can be made when the non-resident parent has failed to pay an amount of child support maintenance and can be enforced by the usual forms of diligence. A liability order can be appealed to the First Tier Tribunal on the grounds that the non-resident parent has paid the amount or that the amount said to be due is wrong. It must be emphasised that all these are administrative orders ie they are imposed by the CMS without any intervention of a court. In addition once a liability order has been granted, or if other forms of enforcement have failed, the CMS can apply to the sheriff court for one or more of the following orders: committal to prison, disqualification from driving, removal of a passport or imposition of a curfew order.[2]

This is an appropriate point at which to mention the obligation imposed on the CMS by s 2 of the Child Support Act 1991: ie when considering the exercise of any discretionary power conferred by the 1991 Act the CMS is to 'have regard to the welfare of any child likely to be affected by its decision'. This may be contrasted with the obligation of the court in s 11(7) of the Children (Scotland) Act 1995 to regard the welfare of the child as the paramount consideration in any proceedings relating to parental responsibilities and rights.

---

1   The term maintenance 'calculation' replaces the original maintenance 'assessment'.
2   CSA 1991, s 39. Before these sanctions apply the court must be satisfied of the liable relative's wilful refusal or culpable neglect to pay: *Secretary of State for Work and Pensions v McNamara* 2005 SLT (Sh Ct) 125. In relation to the potential removal of

a driving licence or passport, the court must determine in the presence of the non-resident parent what his means are and whether he requires a passport or licence to earn his living.

## The maintenance calculation

**10.12** The basic rate of child support maintenance[1] is calculated as a percentage of the non-resident parent's gross weekly income:

12 per cent, where there is one qualifying child;

16 per cent, where there are two qualifying children; and

19 per cent, where there are three or more qualifying children.

The basic rate applies provided the non-resident parent's gross income is less than £800 a week. If it is more than £800 the non-resident parent will pay 9 per cent, 12 per cent and 15 per cent of that part of his income which exceeds £800 for one, two or more children respectively. The maximum gross weekly income is £3000. The income of the person with care of the qualifying child is ignored as is the income of any new partner of the non-resident parent[2]. On the other hand, if the non-resident parent has one child[3] in his new family, the gross income is reduced by 12 per cent before the formula is applied. If he has two children, the reduction is 16 per cent. If there are three or more children, the reduction is 19 per cent.

For example, a non-resident parent has two children and gross earnings of £600 a week. The maintenance calculation is £96, ie 16 per cent of £600. If he has two children in his new family, his gross earnings are reduced by 16 per cent, ie £504. The maintenance calculation is therefore reduced to £80.64 ie 16 per cent of £504.

There can be a further reduction in the maintenance calculation if the non-residential parent has residential contact with a child from an earlier family. The reduction is as follows:

52–103 nights' residential contact: 1/7th reduction

103–156 nights' residential contact: 2/7th reduction

156–174 nights' residential contact: 3/7th reduction

174 + nights' residential contact: maintenance calculation is halved.

Here it is the maintenance calculation, not the gross income used for the calculation, that is reduced. Thus if, in our example, the non-resident parent has residential contact of 60 days with the children of his first family, the maintenance calculation is reduced by 1/7th, ie 1/7th of £96 = £13.70 a week. Only residential contact with the non-residential parent counts: staying with the non-residential parent's mother or father ie the child's grandparents, for example, will not lead to any reduction.

The non-resident parent may apply to have the normal maintenance calculation *reduced* because he is incurring special expenses.[4] These are[5]:

(1)    high costs of exercising contact with his children;

(2)    long term illness or disability of a child living with him;

(3)    debts incurred for the benefit of his earlier family while they were living together;

(4)    boarding school fees paid for qualifying children: this is limited to the boarding part of the cost; and

(5)    mortgage payments which he pays in respect of a home which he shared with the person with care and in which she continues to live. He must have no real right of property in the house. This provision is intended to encourage the non-resident parent to agree that the parent with care and the children should continue to live in the former family home without having to pay the mortgage, knowing that this will lead to a reduction of the maintenance calculation.

---

1    See Child Support Act 1991, Schedule 1 (as amended).

2    For many years the rules in respect of cohabitants discriminated against a non-resident parent who cohabited with a same sex partner. In *M v Secretary of State for Work and Persons* [2006] UKHL 11 the House of Lords held that this did not amount to a breach of the non-resident parent's human rights under Article 8 (right to respect for private and family life) or Article 1 of the First Protocol (right to possessions). The discrimination has been removed by amendments made by the Civil Partnership Act 2004.

3    The child can be his biological child or step-child.

4    CSA 1991, ss 28A–28F.

5    CSA 1991, Schedule 4B.

## Respective roles of the courts and the CMS

**10.13** The jurisdiction of the courts to award aliment for qualifying children has been largely, but not entirely, replaced by the powers of the CMS to make maintenance calculations.[1] Section 8 of the Child Support Act 1991 provides that no court shall exercise any power which it would otherwise have to make, vary, or revive an award of aliment in any case where the CMS would have jurisdiction to make a maintenance calculation. In other words, it is not competent for the court to make any order which has the effect of awarding aliment in cases where a child support calculation may be made under s 4 or 7 of the CSA 1991[2]. This has the effect of excluding the court's jurisdiction to award aliment under the Family Law (Scotland) Act 1985 in cases where at least one of the parents of the relevant child or children is a non-resident parent for the purposes of the 1991 Act. However, s 8 of the 1991 Act does not prevent an order for aliment being made against a person with care of the child. Accordingly a child can sue the person caring for him or her for aliment even where a maintenance calculation could be made against the non-resident parent.

There are three exceptions to the general principle that no award of aliment may be made where a maintenance calculation could be made. First, under s 8(6) of the 1991 Act an order for aliment may be made where the non-resident parent has more than enough assessable income to meet fully the maximum child maintenance allowable under the formula and the court is satisfied that the circumstances of the case make it appropriate for an award to be made. This is colloquially referred to as a 'top-up' award.[3] The great majority of non-resident parents will not be sufficiently well off to reach the threshold for top-up awards.

Secondly, under s 8(7) of the 1991 Act, an award for aliment may be made solely for the purpose of meeting some or all of the expenses incurred by a child in receiving instruction at an educational establishment or undergoing teaching for a trade, profession or vocation.[4]

Thirdly, under s 8(8) of the 1991 Act, an award of aliment may still be made where the child is disabled and the order is made solely for the purpose of meeting some or all of the expenses due to the disability. This exception applies where a disability living allowance is being paid in respect of the child, or the child is blind, deaf or dumb or substantially and permanently disabled.

These three exceptions apply where a person is a qualifying child for the purposes of the 1991 Act. Their effect is to allow the court to make an award of aliment – or vary an award or an alimentary agreement – even though a child maintenance calculation has been or could be made. But since the court's jurisdiction is only excluded in the first place where there is jurisdiction to make a maintenance calculation, it follows that the general law of aliment is still relevant in all cases where a child who is not a qualifying child is owed an obligation of aliment. Thus for example, a university student may sue a parent for aliment and a step-child may sue a step-parent who has accepted the child as a child of his family.

In terms of s 9 of the 1991 Act, there is nothing to prevent persons entering into a maintenance agreement even though a child maintenance calculation has been or might be made.[5] The existence of such an agreement does not prevent any party to it from applying for a maintenance calculation provided the agreement has been in force for a year or more[6]: this applies to post 2003 agreements. Agreements made before that date prevent an application for a maintenance calculation.[7] Any provision of the agreement which purports to restrict the right to apply for a maintenance calculation is void. In any case where the jurisdiction of the court to make an award of aliment would be excluded by s 8 of the 1991 Act, the court has no power to vary any maintenance agreement by inserting a provision requiring a non-resident parent to pay aliment or by increasing the amount payable under such an existing provision.

---

1    Child Support Act 1991, ss 11 and 13.
2    It should be emphasised that the court's jurisdiction is excluded if a maintenance calculation *could* be made: there is no need for the calculation to have taken place before the court's jurisdiction is excluded.
3    See for example, *H v H* 2004 Fam LR 30.
4    *H v H* 2004 Fam LR 30.
5    The court also retains the power to make a maintenance order to enforce the terms of the agreement; s 8(5) of the 1991 Act. See *Otto v Otto* 2002 Fam LR 95.
6    CSA 1991, ss 4 (10)(ab), 7(10) and 9(3).
7    CSA 1991, ss 4(10)(a), 7(10) and 9(3).

# Chapter 11

# Parental responsibilities and rights

## INTRODUCTION

**11.1** It is a hallmark of a democratic society that while parents have the primary responsibility to look after their children, they are free to bring them up in the manner which they deem best for the children's welfare. In order to fulfil their responsibilities, parents enjoy important rights in respect of the upbringing of their children. Parental autonomy is not absolute. The criminal law protects children from serious physical, emotional or sexual abuse by their parents. Moreover, if a parent neglects or physically ill-treats a child, the child can be made subject to a compulsory supervision order under the Children's Hearings (Scotland) Act 2011 and can, if necessary, be removed from the parents.[1] In addition, children and young people will have a named person who is not their parent to promote, support and safeguard their welfare.[2].

However within these parameters Scots law gives parents the rights, inter alia to choose a child's religion, to decide how a child should be educated, to discipline the child, to consent to medical treatment on the child's behalf and to determine, generally, the place and manner in which the child's time is spent. As maturity is gained, increasingly children will wish to make important decisions in relation to such matters as medical treatment for themselves. Accordingly, it is submitted that the nature of a parental right alters as the child matures: beginning with the right to take decisions on the child's behalf, it becomes, in time, a right merely to give guidance to the child.

The purpose of this chapter is to examine the nature and extent of parental responsibilities and parental rights. We shall consider:

(1)    what, in general, these responsibilities and rights are;

(2)    who has parental responsibilities and rights; and

(3)    some specific parental responsibilities and rights.

---

1    On the Children's Hearings (Scotland) Act 2011, see **Chs 14** and **15** below.
2    Children and Young People (Scotland) Act 2014, Part 4 discussed in **Ch 14** below.

## WHAT ARE PARENTAL RESPONSIBILITIES AND RIGHTS?

**11.2** A parent[1] has the following responsibilities to a child:[2]

(1) to safeguard and promote the child's health, development and welfare;

(2) to provide direction and guidance to the child in a manner appropriate to the stage of the child's development;

(3) if the child is not living with the parent, to maintain personal relations and direct contact with the child on a regular basis; and

(4) to act as the child's legal representative.[3]

These responsibilities supersede any analogous duties imposed on a parent at common law;[4] but they do not replace specific statutory duties, for example to aliment the child[5] or to ensure the child's education.[6] The parental responsibilities have to be carried out to the extent that it is practicable and in the interests of the child to do so.[7]

In order to fulfil these responsibilities, a parent has the following rights:

(1) to have the child living with the parent or otherwise to regulate the child's residence;

(2) to control, direct or guide the child's upbringing in a manner appropriate to the child's stage of development;

(3) if the child does not live with the parent, to maintain personal relations and direct contact with the child on a regular basis; and

(4) to act as the child's legal representative.[8]

These parental rights supersede any analogous right enjoyed by a parent at common law[9] but they do not replace specific statutory rights.[10] Because these rights are given in order that parents can fulfil their parental responsibilities, they can only be exercised in so far as it is practicable and in the interests of the child to do so.[11]

Parental rights end when the child reaches 16.[12] Parental responsibilities end at that age, except the responsibility to give a child guidance which lasts until a young person reaches 18.[13] When reaching any major decision in fulfilling parental responsibilities or exercising parental rights, the parent must have regard so far as practicable to the views of the child, if the child wishes to express them.[14] Account should be taken of the child's age and maturity. It is presumed that a child of 12 or over is of sufficient age and maturity to form a view but the views of younger children are relevant if they have *in fact* sufficient maturity. This obligation to consult the child may be difficult to enforce,[15] but it is indicative of the child-centred decision-making process which the Children (Scotland) Act 1995 is intended to promote. The obligation arises only in respect of *major* decisions: it is thought that the importance of a decision will be determined objectively rather than from the child or parent's perspective.

If two or more persons have parental rights, each can exercise a right without the consent of the other.[16] But a child cannot be removed from the United Kingdom without the consent of a person who has the parental rights relating to the child's residence or contact with the child.[17]

The parental responsibility in s 1(1)(a) of the C(S)A 1995 is sufficiently amorphous to cover a wide range of matters: the child's education, health, religion, discipline etc. Similarly, the s 1(1)(b) responsibility is of wide import, ie the provision of counsel for the child in every aspect of the child's life. The s 1(1)(c) responsibility is of the utmost significance. The 1995 Act proceeds on the basis that it is in a child's best interests to have the benefit of two parents: thus the responsibility – and corresponding right in s 2(1)(c) – of a parent to maintain personal relations and direct contact with the child when that parent no longer lives with the child. The parental rights in s 2(1)(a) and (b) are to help a parent fulfil the parental responsibilities in s 1(1)(a) and (b). We shall consider these responsibilities and rights in greater detail later in this chapter.

The parental responsibility[18] and right[19] to act as a child's legal representative enables a parent to enter into transactions on behalf of a child when the child lacks active legal capacity. When the child has capacity to enter into a legal transaction the parent cannot act as the child's legal representative.[20] The parent should consult the child before entering any major transaction[21] on the child's behalf; but if the other party to the transaction entered into it in good faith the transaction cannot be challenged on the ground of the legal representative's failure to consult the child.[22]

Where a parent, acting as the child's legal representative, administers the child's property[23] the parent must act as a reasonable and prudent person would act on his or her own behalf.[24] While enabled to do anything in relation to the property which the child could do if of full age and capacity,[25] the parent is liable to account to the child for the intromissions with the child's property.[26] This will usually occur when the child reaches 16. No liability is incurred by the parent in respect of funds which have been used in proper discharge of the parent's responsibility under s 1(1)(a), ie to safeguard and promote the child's health, development and welfare.[27] If a parent enters into a transaction on behalf of a child below 16, the transaction cannot be set aside on the ground that it is prejudicial to the interests of the child. If the transaction involved the use of the child's own funds, redress may be sought by the child against the parent under s 10.[28]

'Transaction' is widely defined.[29] Consequently, the parent acting as the child's legal representative can enter into a wide range of juristic acts on behalf of the child as well as administer the child's own property.[30] Moreover, as legal representative a parent can give consent on behalf of the child.[31] Thus for example, while the responsibility to obtain medical care for a child falls within s 1(1)(a) of the C(S)A 1995, the duty and right to consent to medical treatment on the child's behalf derives from the parent being the child's legal representative.[32] It is also for this reason that a parent cannot consent to medical treatment on the child if the child has gained the capacity to consent on his own behalf under s 2(4) of the Age of Legal Capacity (Scotland) Act 1991.[33]

Parents cannot abdicate parental responsibilities and rights but can arrange for them to be carried out by other people, for example the headmaster of a boarding school.[34] Liability for failure to fulfil the responsibilities remains with the parents.[35]

---

1　A parent is the child's genetic mother or father: Children (Scotland) Act 1995, s 15(1). In spite of the absence of a genetic relationship, a person is a parent if that person has adopted the child or parentage is established by the Human Fertilisation and Embryology Act 1990, ss 27–30 or Part 2 of the Human Fertilisation and Embryology Act 2008: C(S)A 1995, s 15(1).

2　A child is a person below 18 years old: C(S)A 1995, s 15(1).

3　C(S)A 1995, s 1(1)(a), (b), (c) and (d).

4　C(S)A 1995, s 1(3).

5    Family Law (Scotland) Act 1985, s 1(1)(c) and (d), discussed at para **10.10**.
6    Under the Education (Scotland) Act 1980.
7    C(S)A 1995, s 1(1); if it is not practicable and in the interests of the child for a parent to carry out a parental responsibility, it would appear that the responsibility no longer exists: *White v White* 1999 Fam LR 28; *sed quaere*?
8    C(S)A 1995, s 2(1)(a)–(d).
9    C(S)A 1995, s 2(5).
10   For example under the Education (Scotland) Act 1980.
11   C(S)A 1995, s 1(1).
12   C(S)A 1995, s 2(7).
13   C(S)A 1995, s 1(2)(a) and (b).
14   C(S)A 1995, s 6(1). The views of other persons having parental responsibilities and rights should also be considered.
15   What would Leopold Mozart have thought if told he had to consult the five-year-old Wolfgang as to the wisdom of going on a concert tour – albeit that Wolfgang Amadeus Mozart was an infant prodigy?
16   C(S)A 1995, s 2(2).
17   C(S)A 1995, s 2(3) and (6). If the child's parents have such rights the consent of both is required.
18   C(S)A 1995, s 1(1)(d).
19   C(S)A 1995, s 2(1)(d).
20   C(S)A 1995, s 15(5).
21   On the duty to consult, see above.
22   C(S)A 1995, s 6(2).
23   Where the child is the beneficiary under a trust or executory, the property may be administered by a judicial factor or the Accountant of Court: C(S)A 1995, s 9. Where a child is awarded damages, the court can order that the fund is to be administered by persons other than the parents, for example the Accountant of Court: C(S)A 1995, s 13. In the absence of any criticism or suspicion of the parents' ability to look after the child's funds, a defender is not obliged to raise s 13 proceedings. The court's discretion under s 13 is unfettered by the need to be satisfied that the administration of the damages could not be reasonably secured except by the appointment of a factor: *I v Argyll and Clyde Health Board* 2003 SLT 231.
24   C(S)A 1995, s 10(1)(a).
25   C(S)A 1995, s 10(1)(b); for example, *sell* the child's property, including heritage.
26   C(S)A 1995, s 10(1).
27   C(S)A 1995, s 10(2).
28   A parent is no longer a trustee for the purposes of the Trusts (Scotland) Act 1921: C(S)A 1995, Schedule 4, para 6.
29   It has the same meaning as in s 9 of the Age of Legal Capacity (Scotland) Act 1991, discussed at para **10.2**: C(S)A 1995, s 15(1).
30   C(S)A 1995, s 15(5)(a).
31   C(S)A 1995, s 15(5)(b). However, a parent has no right to consent on behalf of the child to the storage of gametes under the Human Fertilisation and Embryology Act 1990: C(S)A 1995, s 15(7).

32   Discussed in detail at para **11.9**.
33   C(S)A 1995, ss 1(1)(d) and 2(1)(d).
34   C(S)A 1995, s 3(5).
35   C(S)A 1995, s 3(6).

## WHO HAS PARENTAL RESPONSIBILITIES AND RIGHTS?

**11.3** A child's mother automatically has parental responsibilities and rights in relation to her child.[1] It does not matter that she has never been married to the child's father: her age is also irrelevant.[2] A child's father automatically obtains parental responsibilities and rights in two situations. First if he is or was married to the child's mother at the date of the child's conception or at any time thereafter.[3]

### Examples

(1)   H and W are married at the date of conception and birth. H is presumed to be the father of the child[4] and will automatically have parental responsibilities and rights.

(2)   H and W are married after the date of conception but before the birth. H is presumed to be the father of the child and will automatically have parental responsibilities and rights.

(3)   H and W marry after the date of conception and birth. H will *not* be presumed to be the father of the child[5] but if H's paternity is established, H will automatically acquire parental responsibilities and rights when H marries W.

For this purpose, marriage includes a voidable marriage and a 'marriage' which is void provided *both* parties believed in good faith that the marriage was valid (whether or not the error was one of fact or law).[6]

Secondly, where a father has not married the child's mother he will automatically obtain parental responsibilities and rights if he is presumed to be the father of the child because he was registered as the child's father.[7] This rule only applies when the man was registered as the child's father on or after 4 May 2006, the date when the Family Law (Scotland) Act 2006 came into force.[8]

Where a woman is a parent by virtue of sections 35 or 42 of the Human Fertilisation and Embryology Act 2008 ie when she is married to or in a civil partnership with the child's mother,[9] she will automatically have parental responsibilities and rights in respect of the child.[10] Similarly if a woman is the child's second female parent by virtue of s 43 of HFEA 2008, ie when the mother has agreed that she should be the child's second female parent,[11] she will automatically have parental responsibilities and rights if she was registered as the child's parent.[12]

Where none of these principles applies, there are two ways that a father[13] or the child's second female parent[14] can obtain parental responsibilities and rights. First, if the mother has not previously been deprived of some or all of her parental responsibilities and rights,[15] she may enter an agreement: (i) with the father under which he is to obtain the responsibilities and rights which he would have got if he had married the mother;[16] or (ii) with the child's second female parent under which she is to obtain the responsibilities and rights she would have obtained if she had been a spouse of, or a party to a civil partnership with, the mother.[17] Thus a father and second female parent can obtain *all*[18] the parental responsibilities and rights by agreement with the mother. The agreement will stipulate the appropriate date upon which the father or second female parent is to acquire the responsibilities and rights. It is expressly enacted that the mother and father have capacity to make such an agreement 'whatever age they may be'.[19] This means that if either or both are below 16, the age of legal capacity,[20] they can still enter into such an agreement and both will be able to exercise their parental responsibilities and rights in respect of their child.[21] However there is no such provision in respect of an agreement between the mother and the second female parent. Such an agreement does not have effect unless it is in the prescribed form and registered in the Books of Council and Session at a time when the mother still has the parental responsibilities and rights that she had when she made the agreement.[22] It is important to note that the father or second female parent acquires their responsibilities and rights solely by the mother's agreement. No court is involved and it is irrelevant that a court would take the view that it was not in the child's interests that the father or second female parent should have parental responsibilities and rights. Once registered, the agreement is irrevocable[23] except by court order.[24] Section 4 and 4A agreements only enable a mother to give parental responsibilities and rights to the man who is the biological father of her child or the woman who is the second female parent: they cannot be used to give parental responsibilities and rights to other relatives of the child, for example the child's grandmother.

Secondly, the father or the second female parent could apply to the sheriff court or Court of Session under s 11 of the Children (Scotland) Act 1995 for an order giving him or her parental responsibilities and rights.[25] He or she has title to sue as a person who 'not having, and never having had, parental responsibilities and rights in relation to the child, *claims an interest*'.[26] The genetic and/or emotional ties towards the child are per se sufficient to constitute an interest.[27] The welfare of the child is the paramount consideration,[28] and the court will give the father or second female parent parental responsibilities and rights only if it is in the child's best interests to do so. There is no onus of proof and the only question is to determine what is in the child's best interests. In *T v M*[29] the court held that the following factors should be considered: the degree of commitment that the applicant has towards the child; the degree of attachment between the applicant and the child; the importance of that commitment and attachment to the child's welfare; the reasons or motives behind the application; whether the applicant will take account of the child's views; any need to protect the child from the applicant's conduct; whether the applicant and any other person having parental responsibilities and rights will have to cooperate with each other in matters affecting the child and whether they will be able to do so; and whether it is better for the child that the order be made than no order being made at all.

Any person, for example the child's grandparents or a step-parent, can apply under s 11(3)(a)(i) of the C(S)A 1995 to obtain parental responsibilities and rights. Again their genetic and/or emotional ties would constitute sufficient interest.[30] Moreover, it is open to any person with an interest in the welfare of a child to apply under s 11(3)(a)(ii) for a specific parental responsibility or right; for example a doctor seeking the right to consent to medical treatment on behalf of a child whose parents are refusing to consent. It has been held that these provisions should not be interpreted restrictively and that Parliament should be presumed to have legislated in accordance with the UN Convention on the Rights of the Child and the European Convention on Human Rights. Thus a 14 year old girl had title to sue for a contact order in respect of her half–brother and half-sister: the welfare of the children is the paramount consideration.[31]

Where a person aged 16 or over has *de facto* care or control of a child below that age then, if the carer does not have parental responsibilities or rights in relation to the child, the carer has a statutory responsibility to do what is reasonable in all the circumstances to safeguard the child's health.[32] Even though the carer does not have the right to act as the child's legal representative[33] in fulfilling the responsibility to safeguard the child's health the carer can consent to any surgical, medical or dental treatment, or procedure on behalf of the child. However, this right to consent only applies if:

(1)     the child does not have legal capacity to consent on his or her own behalf;[34] *and*

(2)     the carer has no reason to believe that the child's parent would refuse to consent.[35]

Thus for example, a person who has care of a child and knows that the child's parents are Jehovah's Witnesses cannot consent to a blood transfusion on behalf of the child. If in fulfilling this responsibility the carer must make a major decision, the child has to be consulted.[36] The responsibility does not arise when a person has care or control of a child at school.[37]

A child's parent can appoint a person to be the child's guardian in the event of the parent's death.[38] To be effective the appointment must be in writing and signed by the parent.[39] In addition, the parent must have been entitled to act as the child's legal representative at the date of the parent's *death*.[40] When a parent appoints a guardian, this is regarded as a major decision and there is a duty to consult the child.[41] An appointment as guardian does not take effect unless the person named in the deed accepts the appointment, either expressly or by acts which are not consistent with any other intention.[42] Once the appointment is accepted, the guardian automatically acquires the full complement of parental responsibilities and rights.[43] Where the child has a surviving parent, the parent's responsibilities and rights continue and are fulfilled and exercised along with the parental responsibilities and rights of the guardian.[44] Guardianship ends when the child reaches 18, or the child or guardian dies, or is terminated by an order under s 11 of the C(S)A 1995.[45]

1    Children (Scotland) Act 1995, s 3(1)(a).
2    Age of Legal Capacity (Scotland) Act 1991, s 1(3)(g).
3    C(S)A 1995, s 3(1)(b)(i). This would also be the case where the husband was the child's father by virtue of the Human Fertilisation and Embryology Act, s 35: on s 35 see para **9.2**.
4    Law Reform (Parent and Child) (Scotland) Act 1986, s 5(1)(a), discussed at para **9.2**.
5    Unless both H and W have acknowledged that H is the father of the child and the child has been registered as such: LR(PC)(S)A 1986, s 5(1)(b), discussed at para **9.2**. If the registration took place on or after 4 May 2006, the father would automatically obtain parental responsibilities and rights: see below.
6    C(S)A 1995, s 3(2)(a) and (b). Accordingly, if W is in bad faith, H does not obtain parental responsibilities and rights under this provision: W will of course have parental responsibilities and rights by virtue of being the child's mother. Cf s 5(1) and (2) of the LR(PC)(S)A 1986, discussed at para **9.2**.
7    C(S)A 1995, s 3(1)(b)(ii). This presumption of paternity arises under the LR(PC)(S)A 1986, s 5(1)(b) and Schedule 1, para 8, discussed above at para **9.2**. This would also be the case when the man was the child's father by virtue of the HFEA 2008, s 35 ie mother agreed that man should be the child's father: on s 35 see para 9.2.
8    FL(S)A 2006, s 23(4).
9    On HFEA 2008, s 42 see para **9.2**.
10   C(S)A1995, s 3(1)(c).
11   On HFEA 2008, s 43 see para **9.2**.
12   C(S)A 1995, s 3(1)(d).
13   Ie who has not been registered as such.
14   Ie who has not been registered as such.
15   For example, as a result of the child having been adopted or a s 11(2)(a) order or a permanence order. On adoption see **Ch 12**; on s 11 orders see para **12.4**; and on permanence orders, see paras **13.13** and **14.7**. If the mother has been deprived of any parental responsibilities and rights, she cannot make such an agreement.
16   C(S)A 1995, s 4(1).
17   C(S)A 1995, s 4A(1).
18   Unless there is a s 11 order in force affecting some of the mother's responsibilities and rights, for example, if there was a residence order in favour of a third party. Such an order does not normally deprive the parent of his or her responsibilities and rights: C(S)A 1995, s 11(11), discussed at para **12.4**. Accordingly, for example, the mother could still enter into a s 4 agreement with the father, even if a residence order had been made in favour of the child's grandparents.
19   C(S)A 1995, s 4(1).
20   Discussed in Ch 9.
21   ALC(S)A 1991, s 1(3)(g): for discussion see para **10.2**.
22   C(S)A 1995, s 4(2)(a) and (b). The date of registration is the appropriate date, ie it is the date when the father or second female parent obtains parental responsibilities and rights.
23   C(S)A 1995, s 4(4).

24 C(S)A 1995, s 11(11).
25 C(S)A 1995, s 11(1), (2)(b)(i) and (ii). The court can do so, even if the applicant is under 16: s 11(11).
26 C(S)A 1995, s 11(3)(a)(i). Italics added.
27 *D v Grampian Regional Council* 1994 SLT 1038 (Inner House); upheld 1995 SLT 519 (House of Lords). In *X v Y* 2002 Fam LR 58 the homosexual father of a child conceived by artificial insemination obtained parental responsibilities and rights although the case was defended by the mother and her same sex cohabitant.
28 C(S)A 1995, s 11(7)(a). See for example, *T v A* 2001 SCLR 647.
29 2007 SCLR 447 (Sh Ct).
30 A mother's same sex cohabitant was denied title to sue in *X v Y* 2002 Fam LR 58. However, same sex cohabitants were granted parental responsibilities and rights in relation to each other's child in *W v M, M v W* (2002 Sh Ct). It is thought that *X v Y* is unsound in principle.
31 *E v E* 2004 Fam LR 115.
32 C(S)A 1995, s 5(1).
33 C(S)A 1995, s 2(1)(d).
34 On the capacity of a child below 16 to consent to medical treatment etc, see the ALC(S)A 1991, s 2(4), discussed at para **10.2**.
35 C(S)A 1995, s 5(1).
36 C(S)A 1995, s 6(1)(a). On the duty to consult the child see para **11.2**.
37 C(S)A 1995, s 5(2).
38 C(S)A 1995, s 7(1). A guardian of a child may appoint a person to be the child's guardian in the event of the guardian's death: s 7(2). The same rules apply as in the appointment of a guardian by the child's parent.
39 C(S)A 1995, s 7(1)(a)(i). The appointment will usually be in the parent's will or a codicil to the will. If the will or codicil is revoked, the appointment is also revoked: C(S)A 1995, s 8(4). Where the appointment is made in a deed other than a will or codicil, it is revoked if the deed is destroyed by the granter or the granter has another person destroy the deed in the granter's presence: s 8(3). If A appoints B to be the guardian, then B's appointment is revoked if A later appoints C to be the guardian unless it is clear that the appointment of C is an additional appointment: s 8(1). However, the appointment of B is not revoked unless the appointment of C is in writing and signed by A: s 8(2). It does not matter if the appointment of B is in an unrevoked will or codicil.
40 C(S)A 1995, s 7(1)(a)(ii).
41 C(S)A 1995, s 7(6).
42 C(S)A 1995, s 7(3). If two or more persons are appointed, any one can accept the appointment even if the other(s) refuse to do so unless the appointment otherwise provides.
43 Children (Scotland) Act 1995, s 7(5). This is subject to any s 11 orders and any parental responsibilities order in force at the time the appointment was accepted.
44 C(S)A 1995, s 7(1)(b). Each can exercise a parental right without the consent of the other: s 2(3), discussed at para 11.1.
45 C(S)A 1995, s 11(2)(h).

## SPECIFIC PARENTAL RESPONSIBILITIES AND RIGHTS

**11.4** In this section, we shall consider some of the most important parental responsibilities and rights.[1] The statutory responsibilities and rights are expressed in very general terms and it is valuable to consider specific aspects. The responsibility to safeguard and promote the child's health, development and welfare and to give the child direction and guidance will be considered along with the right to have the child living with the parent and the parent's right to control, direct or guide the child. The responsibility and right to act as the child's legal representative have already been discussed.[2] It must always be remembered that a parent is expected to fulfil the statutory responsibilities only in so far as it is practicable for the parent to do so.[3] However, in exercising parental rights there is a duty to consult the child when making a major decision and the parent must always act in the child's interests.[4] Accordingly, parental rights can be regarded as prima facie rights in the sense that any purported exercise of the right must further the child's welfare or, at least, must not be against the interests of the child: this is known as 'the welfare principle'.

If a purported exercise of a parental right is against the child's interests, there is no obligation on the child or a third party to act in accordance with the parent's decision. The ultimate arbiter of whether or not a purported exercise of parental rights is *in fact* contrary to a child's welfare is the Court of Session or the sheriff court which have the power to make any order in relation to parental responsibilities and rights.[5] Thus for example, a child or a third party can petition the court for a declarator that a purported exercise of a parental right by a parent is not in the interests of the child or that a parent's acts or omissions are in breach of the parent's statutory responsibilities.

---

1   For full discussion see *Wilkinson and Norrie* Ch 7.
2   At para **11.2**. They will arise incidentally in the present discussion.
3   Children (Scotland) Act 1995, s 1(1). There would, for example, be no failure to comply with s 1(1)(a) if a parent had to refuse a child's request to be educated at boarding school or holiday in Florida because the parent could not afford to do so.
4   C(S)A 1995, ss 1(1), 2(1) and 6. On the duty to consult, see para **11.2**.
5   C(S)A 1995, s 11(1) and (2). The orders listed in s 11(2) are 'without prejudice to the generality' of s 11(1).

## Residence

**11.5** Parents have the right to have their child live with them or otherwise to regulate their child's residence,[1] for example to allow the child to holiday with friends. It is generally accepted that children thrive in a stable home environment and consequently this right can be seen as enabling parents to fulfil their responsibility to promote the child's development.[2] It is only a prima facie right and must be exercised in the child's interests. Accordingly, parents may lose the right to have their child live at home if it would be against the child's interests to remain with or be returned to the parent.

This is illustrated by the leading case of *J v C*,[3] a decision of the House of Lords in an English appeal, but accepted as authoritative in Scotland.[4] A couple had a child. They were advised that because of the child's health he should remain with foster parents in England and not return with his parents to Spain where the family lived. The parents left their child in England but retained contact with him through visits etc. When, several years later, the child's health had improved, the parents decided that the child should come to Spain and live there with the rest of the family. The child was made a ward of court. The court had then to determine whether or not the parents should be permitted to take their child to Spain. The proceedings were protracted and the case was eventually heard by the House of Lords. The House of Lords decided that in spite of the fact that the parents' conduct was unimpeachable, the child should nevertheless remain with his foster parents in England. After eight-and-a-half years, the boy had become integrated into his foster parents' family and to remove him to Spain would be likely to cause him distress and possible long-term psychological harm: and so the parents could not exercise their prima facie right to have their child live with them because it would be contrary to the child's interests to do so.

*J v C*[5] is authority for the proposition that the parental right of residence is governed by the welfare principle.[6] A parent cannot validly exercise the right if it is not in the best interests of the child to do so. A striking example is provided by *M v Dumfries and Galloway Regional Council*.[7] A child was being looked after by a local authority. The mother who had not been deprived of her parental rights,[8] asked the local authority to return her child. The local authority refused. The sheriff held that since there was suspected abuse, the return of the child was not in the child's interests and consequently the authority was not under any obligation to accede to the mother's request.[9]

---

1   Children (Scotland) Act 1995, s 2(1)(a).
2   C(S)A 1995, s 1(1)(a).
3   [1970] AC 668, HL, [1969] 1 All ER 788.
4   See *Cheetham v Glasgow Corporation* 1972 SLT (Notes) 50.
5   [1970] AC 668.
6   See in particular, the speech of Lord McDermott, [1970] AC 668 at 701. This is now enacted in s 1(1) of the C(S)A 1995.
7   *M v Dumfries and Galloway Regional Council* 1991 SCLR 481.
8   For example, as a result of a permanence order, see paras **13.13** and **14.7**. The child was not subject to the then equivalent of a compulsory supervision order: discussed in **Ch 15**.
9   The case of the child should, of course, have been referred to a Reporter to consider whether the child was in need of the then equivalent of a compulsory supervision order.

---

## Discipline

**11.6** A parent has the right to control a child.[1] This can include physical chastisement. In theory, the exercise of this right must be in accordance with the welfare principle: in practice, physical chastisement must be reasonable. Unless the law has sufficiently clear standards of what amounts to reasonable punishment there will be a violation of Article 3 of the European Convention on Human Rights which provides: 'No one shall be subjected to torture or to inhuman or degrading treatment or punishment'.[2]

Excessive physical ill-treatment of a child will lead to criminal proceedings for cruelty[3] and will constitute grounds for a compulsory supervision order under the Children's Hearings (Scotland) Act 2011.[4] But any physical ill-treatment will constitute an assault for which the parent is criminally responsible unless the parent can show that the assault was justifiable. In determining whether the assault is justifiable, the court must have regard to: (a) the nature of what was done, the reason for it and the circumstances in which it took place; (b) its duration and frequency; (c) any effects – physical or mental – which it has been shown to have had on the child; (d) the child's age; and (e) the child's personal characteristics (including sex and state of health) at the time of the parent's conduct.[5] If the assault on the child included or consisted of a blow to the head, shaking or the use of an implement, the court must hold that the assault was unjustifiable.[6] The 'right' lasts until the child reaches 16.[7]

1    Children (Scotland) Act 1995, s 2(1)(b).
2    *A v United Kingdom* (1999) 27 EHRR 611.
3    Children and Young Persons (Scotland) Act 1937, s 12(1).
4    On compulsory supervision orders, see Ch 15.
5    Criminal Justice (Scotland) Act 2003, s 51(1).
6    CJ(S)A 2003, s 51(3)
7    C(S)A 1995, s 2(7). At common law, school teachers had an independent right physically to chastise school children: *McShane v Paton* 1922 JC 26. However, corporal punishment has been abolished in Scottish schools: Standards in Scotland's Schools etc Act 2000, s 16.

## Education

**11.7**  Parents are under a duty to ensure that their children receive a suitable education until they reach 16.[1] In particular, they must ensure that the child attends school.[2] In order to fulfil these specific obligations and fulfil the general statutory responsibility to promote the child's development,[3] a parent has the right to choose a child's education.[4] This right must be exercised in accordance with the welfare principle.[5] Unless the parent has sufficient means to afford private education, the exercise of this right will be limited. Parents' rights to choose a local authority school which is suitable for the needs of their children have been strengthened as a result of legislation.[6]

It should be noted that the rights and obligations in respect of a child's education vest not only in the parent but also the child's guardian, any person obliged to aliment the child and any person having day-to-day care of the child.[7]

1    Education (Scotland) Act 1980, ss 30–31.
2    E(S)A 1980, s 35. The parent is relieved of this obligation if the parent provides the child with effective education by other means. A parent's failure, without reasonable excuse, to ensure that a child attends school is an offence: see for example, *Wyatt v*

*Wilson* 1994 SLT 1135. In *Hagan v Rae* 2001 SLT (Sh Ct) 30, it was held that reasonable excuse had to be interpreted in a way to allow a parent to defend herself on the ground that it was not fair in the circumstances that she should face criminal sanctions in respect of her child's truancy. Otherwise there could be a violation of Article 6(2) of the European Convention on Human Rights which provides that: 'Everyone charged with a criminal offence shall be presumed innocent until proved guilty by law'.

3    E(S)A 1980, s 30(1).
4    Where both parents have parental rights any dispute over choice of school etc can be resolved by a specific issue order under the Children (Scotland) Act 1995, s 11(2)(e): see for example, *G v G* 2002 Fam LR 120. While the child's welfare is the paramount consideration, the court will give weight to maintaining the status quo. In *CAM v HM* [2012] CSOH 127 the court made a specific issue order that the children should remain at their current primary school and refused their mother's request that she could remove them to another school in the town where she had gone to live after she had separated from their father.
5    *J v C* [1969] 1 All ER 788, [1970] AC 668 at 702, HL, per Lord McDermott.
6    E(S)A 1980, ss 28 and 28A–28H (as amended). See Alison L Seager 'Parental Choice of School' 1982 SLT (News) 29. The right is not absolute: *Keeney v Strathclyde Regional Council* 1986 SLT 490. In *Regan v Dundee City Council* 1997 SLT 139 it was held that parents should have been consulted before a school was closed. Note also the parental involvement in school boards: see the School Boards (Scotland) Act 1988.
7    E(S)A 1980, s 135(1).

## Religion

**11.8**  In an increasingly pluralistic society, religious toleration is of the first importance. Scots law recognises that in fulfilment of their responsibility for the child's development, parents have a prima facie right to choose a child's religion. This right must be exercised in accordance with the child's welfare. Where a parent's or, indeed a child's, religious convictions will result in physical harm to the child, the parents' and the child's wishes will be overridden. For example, while parents are free to decide that a child should be brought up as a Jehovah's Witness, if the child should require a blood transfusion the law will not countenance the parent's refusal to consent to such treatment.[1]

Scottish courts have accepted that where parents are of different religions, it matters little to the child whether he or she is brought up in one faith rather than another: the matter will be decided in the light of all the circumstances of the case in accordance with the welfare principle. In *McNaught v McNaught*,[2] a mother who was a Protestant had the children of the marriage living with her. In spite of the fact that she had agreed to bring up the children in her husband's Roman Catholic faith, the husband failed to obtain an order that at least his youngest child, a son, should continue to be brought up as a Roman Catholic. As it was otherwise in the child's best interests to be with his mother, she was free to bring up the child as a Protestant since either faith was for the benefit of the child. In *S v S*[3] the husband was Egyptian and a Muslim: the wife was Scottish and a Protestant. They had three children. After they had separated, the mother who was the primary carer, began to send the children to the Church of Scotland. The husband objected and sought a specific issue order that the children should be brought up in the Islamic faith to which the mother had agreed at the time of the marriage. In refusing the order on the grounds that it was not in the children's best interests that such an order be made, the sheriff stated[4] that 'Regardless of the religious obligation, if there is any conflict between that obligation and the interests of the children, then the interests of the children must prevail.'

At one time the courts were adamant that it was in a child's interests to be brought up in a religious faith. In *M'Clements v M'Clements*,[5] the Lord Justice-Clerk (Thomson) said that in his opinion a child 'ought not to be denied the opportunity of being brought up in the generally accepted religious beliefs of the society in which he lives'.[6] Nevertheless, it is thought that today parents would not be in breach of any parental responsibility if they chose to bring up their child as an atheist or agnostic.[7] It is interesting to note in this context that religious instruction is a 'compulsory' element in the curricula of public, ie education authority, schools.[8]

On reaching 16, a young person can choose his or her own religion.[9] While parents retain the responsibility to guide their child on such matters,[10] they have no power to veto the child's choice. A child below 16 may wish to choose a religion different from that of the child's parents. Given their duty to consult the child, the parents may fulfil their statutory responsibilities by agreeing with the child's choice. In these circumstances it is thought that the parents would only be in breach of their parental responsibilities if it would be against the child's interests to change religion. This could arise if the child proposed to join an extreme sect.

---

1 In practice an application would be made for a permanence order and the local authority could consent to the child having medical treatment: Adoption and Children (Scotland) Act 2007 Part 2 discussed at paras **13.13** and **14.7**. Alternatively, a person could apply for the parental right to consent to medical treatment by bringing proceedings for a specific issue order under s 11(2)(e) of the C(S)A 1995: see para **12.4**.
2 1955 SLT (Sh Ct) 9.
3 2012 GWD 37-739.
4 Ibid at para 147.
5 1958 SC 286.
6 1958 SC 286 at 289.
7 Cf *MacKay v MacKay* 1957 SLT (Notes) 17, per the Lord President (Clyde).
8 Education (Scotland) Act 1980, ss 8–10. Religious observance can only be discontinued after a poll of local government electors: E(S)A 1980, s 8(2). Parents can elect that their child should not take part in religious observance or education.
9 The parental responsibility and right ceases when the child is 16: C(S)A 1995, ss 1(2)(a) and 2(7).
10 The parental responsibility to give guidance lasts until the child is 18: C(S)A 1995, s 1(2)(b).

---

## Medical procedures

**11.9** In fulfilment of their responsibility to safeguard and promote their children's health,[1] parents have the prima facie right to consent to medical treatment on the child's behalf.[2] The exercise of this right is subject to the welfare principle. There is little Scottish authority on the point but English decisions are instructive.

In *Re D (a minor)*[3] for example, a mother consented to the sterilisation of her mentally disabled daughter who had reached the age of puberty. Before the operation took place the child was made a ward of court. The court overrode the mother's decision on the ground that the operation was not in accordance with the welfare of the child. Heilbron J based her decision on the grounds that although mentally disabled the child probably had sufficient capacity to enter into marriage; there was no evidence that she was promiscuous; and any unwanted pregnancy could be terminated. In those circumstances, the proposed operation was not in the child's interests. On the other hand, in *Re B (a minor)*[4] the House of Lords held that a sterilisation operation could be carried out on a mentally disabled girl of 17 who had a mental age of 5. Pregnancy and childbirth would have been physically and mentally disastrous for the young woman and therefore it was in her best interests that the operation go ahead.[5]

The right to consent implies the right to refuse consent to medical treatment. This right must again be exercised in accordance with the welfare principle. In *Re B (a minor)*[6] the Court of Appeal overrode the parents' refusal to consent to an operation to remove an intestinal blockage from their new born infant who had Down's Syndrome. The parents had taken the view that since the child was mentally disabled, it was better for the child to die as a result of the blockage rather than live. The court held that this purported exercise by the parents of their prima facie right to withhold consent was not in accordance with the child's welfare. The child had the prospect of a reasonably happy life, albeit with the syndrome. In the circumstances, the court overrode the parents' decision and consented to the operation on behalf of the child.[7] On the other hand, *Re B (a minor)*[8] was distinguished in *Re C (a minor)*[9] where a new born baby, suffering from congenital hydrocephalus, was dying. It was in the infant's best interests to receive care which merely relieved her suffering and there was no need to give treatment which might achieve a short prolongation of life.

Where the proposed treatment is generally accepted as therapeutic, it is thought that a parent's consent to such treatment on a child will be upheld as a valid exercise of the parent's prima facie right since it would be in the child's best interests to consent. Conversely, where a parent refuses to consent to therapeutic medical treatment on a child, the purported exercise of the prima facie right will be overridden as it would be against the child's interests not to have the benefit of the treatment.[10] In *Re A*,[11] the Court of Appeal took the view that prima facie a court cannot sanction an operation that is clearly against the interests of a child. This case concerned Siamese twins both of whom would die unless separated; but it was also clear that one would undoubtedly die a short time after the operation. In these unique circumstances, the court held that in applying the welfare principle, it had to choose the lesser of two evils and the least detrimental choice was to allow the operation to go ahead since it allowed one of the twins the chance to live.

*Re A* was a case where the procedure was clearly against the interests of the twin who was going to die when separated from her sister. But what of procedures which if not clearly in the child's best interests are not clearly against the child's interests? If an analogy be taken from the law on blood tests and DNA profiling,[12] *Docherty v McGlynn*[13] suggests that a medical procedure can be carried out on a child provided it is not positively *against* the child's interests to do so. It is submitted that in Scots law parents can lawfully consent to medical procedures on their children which, while not in the child's best interests, are not positively against the child's interests. These would include, for example, non-therapeutic circumcision of male infants;[14] the taking of blood samples from healthy children for the purpose of medical research and the donation of regenerative tissue, for example bone marrow.[15] However, it is expressly provided that a parent cannot consent on behalf of a child to the storage of the child's gametes under the Human Fertilisation and Embryology Act 1990.[16]

When a child reaches 16, the child can consent on his or her own behalf.[17] Given the importance of patient autonomy, this must include the right to refuse medical treatment. As we have seen,[18] a child below 16 may have capacity to consent by virtue of s 2(4) of the Age of Legal Capacity (Scotland) Act 1991. The 1991 Act does not expressly stipulate that parents lose their right to consent on behalf of a child who has s 2(4) capacity. Where the proposed medical treatment is unarguably therapeutic, there is no difficulty if the parents and the child both consent. If the child has s 2(4) capacity, the child's consent is sufficient – even if the parents would not consent. The difficulty arises if the child has s 2(4) capacity and refuses to consent. Can the parents override their child's refusal and consent on the child's behalf? Conversely, if a child with s 2(4) capacity consents to medical treatment which is not unarguably therapeutic, can the parents veto the child's decision: for example, if the child consents to a termination of pregnancy or to donate non-regenerative tissue?

There are two possible views. The first is that when the child has s 2(4) capacity then the parents lose their right to consent as the right is no longer needed. The parent consents as the child's legal representative. Section 15(5) of the C(S)A 1995, provides that a parent can only consent as a legal representative when the child has no capacity to consent to a legal transaction; once a child has s 2(4) capacity under the ALC(S)A 1991, the parent must cease to act as the child's legal representative in relation to medical procedures.[19]

The second is that as the parents retain the responsibility to give direction to the child until the child is 16[20] – and guidance until the child is 18[21] – the parents cannot simply be ignored. The difficulty is that if the parents are to give direction or guidance, they must be told of the proposed medical treatment. In the case of *Gillick v West Norfolk and Wisbech Area Health Authority*,[22] in an English appeal the House of Lords held that, in exceptional circumstances, a parent need not be informed when a girl under 16 seeks contraceptives or contraceptive advice from a doctor.

There are two threads of reasoning in the speeches of the majority. Lord Scarman took the view that parental rights exist only in so far as a child lacks the capacity to take decisions for him or herself; thus, when a girl has sufficient understanding, intelligence and maturity to make decisions in relation to inter alia sexual matters, the parent's rights cease.[23] This supports the first view discussed above. But whether or not the child has gained this degree of maturity is a question of fact and it is difficult to see how this will be determined, particularly in relation to sexual matters. Parents will argue that a child has not reached that degree of maturity when the child's proposed course of conduct appears to be contrary to the parents' concept of what is in the best interests of the child.

Lord Fraser, on the other hand, did not deny that the parents had a prima facie right to be informed. But he maintained that there could be exceptional circumstances where this was not necessary, ie when the child:

(1)  understood the nature and effect of contraceptives;

(2)  had been strongly advised to consult her parents but had refused;

(3)  was likely to have or continue to have sexual intercourse without contraceptives;

(4)  her physical or mental health would suffer without contraceptive advice; and

(5)  that it was in the child's best interests to be prescribed contraceptives without the parents' knowledge or consent.

Whether an exceptional case had arisen could in his Lordship's opinion safely be left to the clinical judgment of the doctor concerned.[24]

It should be noted that before Lord Fraser's exception applies, the proposed course of treatment must be in the child's best interests. This could provide a solution to the problem where a child with s 2(4) capacity under the Age of Legal Capacity (Scotland) Act 1991 refuses to have medical treatment which would be in the child's best interests, for example a blood transfusion. Since the child is acting *against* his or her interests, Lord Fraser's exception would *not* apply and the parental consent would be valid. In other words, if Lord Fraser is correct, a child with s 2(4) capacity can in exceptional circumstances consent without the parent's knowledge to medical procedures which are in the child's interests but cannot refuse to consent to such procedures if this would be clearly against the child's interests.[25]

*Gillick*[26] was, of course, an English decision and is not binding on Scottish courts where the matter is ultimately one of construction of s 2(4) of the ALC(S)A 1991. To the extent that the House of Lords rejected the contention that parents have a right to veto such treatment, it is important. On the other hand, it is precisely where medical treatment is not unarguably in the child's best interests that parents should have the right to be informed and be able to advise their children before they embark on a course of action which they might later regret. In the context of the prescription of contraceptives to a girl under 16, her parents have a statutory obligation to proffer advice, to discuss, for example, whether or not it is in her long-term interests to enter sexual relationships at such an early age. If they persuade her that this is not in her interests, then no further difficulties arise; but if they do not, they cannot prevent her obtaining contraceptives if she has s 2(4) capacity. In the case of a sexually active girl who is determined to continue to have sexual intercourse, it is the present writer's view that the Scottish courts would accept that it was not against her interests to be prescribed contraceptives without her parents' consent. But this would be a decision that the parents had purported to exercise their right improperly – ie in a way which was contrary to the welfare principle – not that the right to be informed does not exist.[27]

It is thought that a similar approach would be taken in respect of other medical procedures. If for example a 14-year-old girl sought termination of a pregnancy then – even if she had s 2(4) capacity – it can be argued that her parents have the right to be informed in order to discuss with her the alternatives to termination and the possible long-term effect on her of having an abortion. If the child was still determined to have the termination it is thought that any purported veto by her parents would be ineffective as it is surely against a child's interests to compel her to continue with an unwanted pregnancy.[28] On the other hand if, for example, parents purported to veto a 14-year-old boy's decision to donate a kidney for a school friend, the parents' decision would probably be upheld even if the boy had s 2(4) capacity since it is prima facie contrary to his interests to donate non-generative tissue.[29] However this remains an uncertain area of the law until s 2(4) of the ALC(S)A 1991 has been the subject of authoritative judicial scrutiny.[30]

---

1   Children (Scotland) Act 1995, s 1(1)(a).
2   This is by virtue of their responsibility and right to act as the child's legal representative: C(S)A 1995, ss 1(1)(d) and 2(1)(d).
3   [1976] 1 All ER 326, [1976] Fam 185.
4   [1988] AC 199, [1987] 2 WLR 1213.
5   The court indicated that before such an operation was to be performed, the consent of the court should always be obtained: [1987] 2 WLR 1213 at 1218, per Lord Templeman. In Scots law this could be done by an application under C(S)A 1995, s 11(1). Given that consent can only be given where it is in the child's best interests to do so, it could be argued that the consent of the court is otiose: however, it is thought that it would nevertheless be prudent to obtain the court's approval in such a sensitive area.
6   [1981] 1 WLR 1421, CA.
7   See also *Re C* [2000] Fam 48 where the court overrode the parents' refusal to allow their child to be tested for HIV.
8   [1981] 1 WLR 1421.
9   [1990] Fam 26. See also *Finlayson, Applicant* 1989 SCLR 601 where a ground for the then equivalent of a compulsory supervision order was established when parents refused medical treatment for their haemophiliac son even though they were genuinely concerned that the child might be infected with AIDS as a result of the treatment: the child's physical condition had deteriorated as a result of non-treatment.
10  *Re C* [2000] Fam 48.
11  [2000] 4 All ER 961.
12  Discussed at para **9.3.**
13  1983 SLT 645.
14  Non-therapeutic male circumcision has been authorised in England: *Re J (Specific Orders)* [2000] 1 FLR 571. Non-therapeutic female circumcision cannot lawfully be carried out in the United Kingdom: Prohibition of Female Circumcision Act 1985.
15  The donation of non-regenerative tissue, for example a kidney, would be against the child's ie the donor's interests: consequently a parent cannot consent to this procedure

on behalf of a child. However, if the child had capacity under s 2(4) of the Age of Legal Capacity (Scotland) Act 1991, it would appear that the child could consent.

16   C(S)A1995, s 15(7).

17   ALC(S)A 1991, s 1(1)(b).

18   For discussion, see para **10.2.**

19   For full discussion see *Wilkinson and Norrie*, paras 8.50 ff.

20   C(S)A 1995, s 1(1)(b)(i) and (2)(a).

21   C(S)A 1995, s 1(1)(b)(ii) and (2)(b).

22   [1985] 3 All ER 402, HL.

23   [1985] 3 All ER 402 at 422.

24   [1985] 3 All ER 402 at 413.

25   Lord Fraser's approach was followed by the Court of Appeal in *Re W* [1992] 4 All ER 627. (If a child refuses to consent to life-saving treatment, the parents can give a valid consent.)

26   *Gillick v West Norfolk and Wisbech Area Health Authority* [1985] 3 All ER 402.

27   Cf the approach of Lord Scarman in *Gillick v West Norfolk and Wisbech Area Health Authority* [1985] 3 All ER 402 at 402 and the first view of the effect of s 2(4) capacity discussed above.

28   See for example, *Re P (a minor)* (1982) 80 LGR 301.

29   But the parents would not be able to do so if the first view of the effect of s 2(4) of the ALC(S)A 1991 was correct.

30   In *Houston, Applicant* 1996 SCLR 943, a concession was made in relation to the first view of the ALC(S)A 1991, s 2(4) being correct. The sheriff (McGowan) thought it 'illogical that on the one hand a person under the age of 16 should be granted the power to decide upon medical treatment for himself but his parents have the right to override his decision. I am inclined to the view that the minor's decision is paramount and cannot be overridden': 1996 SCLR 943 at 945.

## Looking after children

**11.10** Ensuring that a child receives medical care is only one aspect of a parent's responsibility to safeguard and promote the child's health, development and welfare.[1] Apart from alimenting the child,[2] parents should give their children love and affection and provide them with opportunities to play and socialise with other families.[3] Parents must ensure the safety of their children and that their children are looked after in the parents' absence.

In the event of abandonment or neglect, not only could the child be in need of a compulsory supervision order,[4] but the parents could be liable to criminal sanctions under s 12(1) of the Children and Young Persons

(Scotland) Act 1937. Wilful abandonment is a question of fact and degree depending on the period during which the children have been left and the steps, if any, which were taken for their care.[5] Merely to leave a child unattended is not wilful neglect: it will depend on all the circumstances of the case including the age of the child, the age of any babysitter, the time the child was left alone and the reason why the child was left unattended. But it is neglect if a very young child is left alone for a substantial period and through the absence of care is likely to experience unnecessary suffering.[6]

Parents must also be prepared to give their children direction and guidance whenever it is in the child's interest to do so.[7] This clearly covers a wide range of issues, for example recreational pursuits, educational opportunities, career opportunities etc. In practice this will merge with the parent's obligation to consult the child on any major decision which will affect the child, for example moving house, changing school etc.[8]

1   Children (Scotland) Act 1995, s 1(1)(a).
2   On aliment, see **Ch 10.**
3   For full discussion, see *Wilkinson and Norrie*, paras 8.22 ff.
4   Discussed in **Ch 15.**
5   *M v Orr* 1995 SLT 26.
6   *H v Lees* 1994 SLT 908 (not neglect when mother was intoxicated and unable to look after baby for several hours when no evidence that child required food or changing during that period); *D v Orr* 1994 SLT 908; (not neglect when father left 13-year-old son alone for several hours); *M v Normand* 1995 SLT 128 (not neglect merely to leave a child of 20 months sleeping unattended in a car for 45 minutes: there must be circumstances which suggest that the child would be likely to experience unnecessary suffering).
7   C(S)A 1995, s 1(1)(b).
8   On the duty to consult, see para **11.2.**

## Names

**11.11** A name is one of the most fundamental elements of a person's sense of self and it has been argued that parents therefore have the responsibility to name their child.[1] It is customary for a 'legitimate' child to take the surname of the father. Difficulties arise when parents divorce and the children live with their mother. If she remarries can she unilaterally change the children's surname to that of their step-father? It could be argued that it would be in their best interests to alter their surnames if, as a result of the retention of their surname, the children experience difficulties at school or settling into their new family. However, the retention of their original surname is a valuable link in maintaining the children's relationship with their father. This would be particularly important if the children knew their father before the divorce and he had been having successful contact with them. Unless there was evidence of genuine distress to the children in being known by their original surname, as opposed to inconvenience for the mother and step-father, in such circumstances it is submitted that it would be contrary to the children's interests to alter the surname. Conversely, if the children had had little contact with their father there would be a strong case that a change of surname to that of their step-father would be in the children's interests as this would strengthen their relationship with their step-father who is in the circumstances the only father figure that they have known.[2]

It is thought that the change of name is a matter relating to parental responsibility under s 1(1)(a) of the Children (Scotland) Act 1995 as it concerns the welfare of the child. However, in exercising such responsibility, one parent does not have to consult the other: so a child's surname can be changed unilaterally by one of the parents. If the other parent maintains that the change of name is against the child's interests the court has jurisdiction to consider the issues under s 11(1) of the 1995 Act.[3]

1    *Wilkinson and Norrie*, paras 8.61 ff.
2    *W v A* [1981] 1 All ER 100, [1981] Fam 14, CA; cf *Cosh v Cosh* 1979 SLT (Notes) 72.
3    *M v C* 2002 SLT (Sh Ct) 82.

## Contact

**11.12** We have been considering specific examples of the nature of parental responsibilities and rights where the child is living with the parents. A parent who is not living with a child has the responsibility to maintain personal relations and direct contact with the child on a regular basis;[1] and the parent enjoys the corresponding right to maintain the relationship and have direct contact with the child.[2] As with the other parental rights, the right to contact is a prima facie right in the sense that it must be exercised in accordance with the welfare principle. This is not inconsistent with Article 8 of the European Convention on Human Rights which provides that 'Everyone has the right to respect for his private life and family life, his home and his correspondence'. Although the European Court of Human Rights has held[3] that 'the mutual enjoyment by parent and child of each other's company constitutes a fundamental element of family life', it is recognised that the right of a parent to see his child cannot be absolute. In particular, it must be balanced against the rights of others, including the child. If a court deprived a parent from exercising his right of contact because it was against the child's interests to do so that would not violate Article 8 provided the parent's interests had been taken into account.[4]

Before the enactment of the Children (Scotland) Act 1995, Scottish courts insisted that a father was not entitled to have contact with his child unless he could show that it was positively in the child's best interests to do so.[5] The onus lay on the father to provide such evidence: there was no presumption that contact would be in the interests of the child.[6] The position can be summarised as follows:

'The father's application for access [contact] was made by him on his own admission, because he is the father. He gave no other reason for his application. A father does not have an absolute right to access to his child. He is only entitled to access if the court is satisfied that it is in the best interests of the child'.[7]

Before an application for contact was successful, the parent had to prove that contact was positively in the child's best interests: the fact that contact was not against the child's interests was not enough. In these circumstances, the right to contact was a right without substance.[8]

The C(S)A 1995 not only gives parents the right to have contact with their children but also imposes an *obligation* upon them to do so. The rationale for such an obligation is that prima facie it is in the interests of children to have a continuing relationship with the parent who does not live with the child. The opportunity was therefore open for the courts to assert that there is now a presumption that contact is in a child's best interests and that a parent should only be denied contact if it is established that contact would be contrary to the interests of the child. Nevertheless, in *White v White*[9] the Inner House of the Court of Session held that there was no presumption that contact with a parent was in the best interests of the child. On the other hand, the court rejected the idea that disputed contact cases should be resolved by considerations of onus of proof. Instead, the Lord President (Rodger) favoured 'a third way'. The welfare of the child was always the paramount consideration but in determining what was in the child's best interests:

> 'the court should have regard to the general principle that it is conducive to a child's welfare to maintain personal relations and direct contact with his absent parent. But the decision will depend on the facts of the particular case and, if there is nothing in the relevant material on which the court, applying that general principle, could properly take the view that it would be in the interests of the child for the order to be granted, then the application must fail'.[10]

---

1      Children (Scotland) Act 1995, s 1(1)(c).

2      C(S)A 1995, s 2(1)(c).

3      *B v United Kingdom* (1988) 10 EHRR 87. The right includes families where the parents are unmarried: *Marckx v Belgium* (1979) 2 EHRR 330.

4      *White v White* 2001 SLT 485.

5      *Crowley v Armstrong* 1990 SCLR 361; *Sanderson v McManus* 1997 SC (HL) 55.

6      *O v O* 1995 SLT 238. But see the dissenting judgment of Lord McCluskey in an Extra Division in *Sanderson v McManus* 1995 SLT 750.

7      *Porchetta v Porchetta* 1986 SLT 105 at 105, per Lord Dunpark. The word '[contact]' has been added.

8      For full discussion, see Joe Thomson 'Whither the "Right" of Access'? 1989 SLT (News) 109.

9      2001 SLT 485.

10    2001 SLT 485 at 491. Lord Rodger had argued at 489 that courts should have regard to 'the common conception of what will, generally speaking, be in the interests of the children so far as contact is concerned', ie that it is usually in the child's welfare to retain contact. See also *Sanderson v McManus* 1997 SC (HL) 55 where the natural link between a father and his child was described as being of 'intrinsic value' and *NJDB v JEG* [2010] CSIH 83, 2011 SC 191.

---

Chapter 12

# Actions in relation to parental responsibilities and rights

## INTRODUCTION

**12.1** A mother automatically has parental responsibilities and rights in relation to her child.[1] The child's father will also automatically have the full complement of parental responsibilities and rights if: (i) he was married to the child's mother at the date of conception or subsequently; or (ii) has been registered as the father of the child.[2] Where the child was born as a result of assisted reproduction, the mother's partner will automatically have parental responsibilities and rights if: (i) she was the mother's spouse or civil partner; or (ii) has been registered as the child's second female parent.[3] But it is possible for other persons to acquire parental responsibilities and rights as a result of an application to the court under s 11 of the Children (Scotland) Act 1995. For example, unless he has obtained parental responsibilities and rights under an agreement with the child's mother,[4] the father of a child who does not automatically have parental responsibilities and rights can only obtain parental responsibilities and rights by virtue of a s 11 order. On divorce or dissolution, the court has power to regulate the parental responsibilities and rights of the parties in relation to any children of the marriage or civil partnership. The purpose of this chapter is to discuss the procedures which are applicable and the principles which are applied in litigation relating to parental responsibilities and rights.

---

1 Children (Scotland) Act 1995, s 3(1)(a), discussed at para **11.3**.
2 C(S)A 1995, s 3(1)(b), discussed at para **11.3**. The registration must be on or after 4 May 2006.
3 C(S)A 1995, s 3(1)(c) and (d).
4 C(S)A 1995, s 4, discussed at para **11.3**.

## TITLE TO SUE

### (1) Independent applications in relation to parental responsibilities and rights

**12.2** The Court of Session and the sheriff court have the power to make any order in relation to parental responsibilities and rights as it thinks fit.[1] An application can be brought by the following persons:

(a)   A person who does not have and never has had parental responsibilities and rights in relation to the child, but claims an interest.[2] In other words, any person claiming an interest can bring an application. An interest can be a genetic or emotional tie between the applicant and the child. Applicants include the father of a child or the child's second female parent who does not automatically have parental responsibilities and rights, a step-parent[3] or the child's grandparents.[4] In addition, a person with an interest in the outcome of the specific application as it relates to the welfare of the child also has title to sue. For example, a doctor could apply under this provision for the right to consent to medical treatment on behalf of a child whose parents were refusing to consent.

It is expressly enacted that a child has title to sue in respect of the fulfilment of parental responsibilities and rights vis-à-vis him or herself.[5] If a child wished to live elsewhere than at home, or the child was unhappy with parental decisions relating to the child's education etc, or was concerned about how his or her property was being administered, the *child* could apply under s 11(1) of the Children (Scotland) Act 1995 for a ruling by the court. A local authority has no title to sue under s 11 for an order in relation to parental responsibilities and rights.[6] If the local authority wishes to have parental responsibilities and/or rights, it must apply for a permanence order under Part 2 of the Adoption and Children (Scotland) Act 2007.[7] If a social worker considered the child to be in need of a compulsory supervision order, the case should be referred to a Reporter.[8]

(b)   Any person who has parental responsibilities or rights in relation to a child.[9] If for example, both parents have parental rights and responsibilities but cannot agree on the child's religion or education etc, either could apply under s 11 of the 1995 Act for a ruling by the court on the matter.

(c)     Any person who has had parental responsibilities or rights in relation to the child.[10] If for example, a mother has been deprived of her parental responsibilities and rights by a s 11(1)(a) order because she was a drug addict, she could apply for parental responsibilities and rights when she was successfully cured of her addiction and wished to resume her responsibilities towards her children. But persons deprived of parental responsibilities and rights by the following orders have no title to sue:[11]

(i)     when the parental responsibilities and rights have been extinguished as a result of an adoption order. This means that if a child has been adopted the natural mother or father cannot seek parental responsibilities and rights under s 11 of the 1995 Act. There is one exception. With leave of the court, the parent can apply for a contact order;[12]

(ii)    when the parental responsibilities have been extinguished by virtue of a parental order under s 54 of the Human Fertilisation and Embryology Act 2008 (fast-track adoption procedure for child born as a result of surrogacy);[13] or

(iii)   where the parental responsibilities and rights have vested in a local authority as a result of a permanence order. In this situation, the parent can apply to have the permanence order varied or revoked.[14]

In these three situations, decisions have been made for the long-term future of the child and the parents' interests will have been taken into account on making the relevant order. It would defeat the certainty inherent in adoption and permanence orders if the whole procedure could be undermined by applications under s 11 of the Children (Scotland) Act 1995 for parental responsibilities and rights by parents who had recently been denuded of these rights and responsibilities as a consequence of such orders.

---

1     Children (Scotland) Act 1995, s 11(1)(a), (b) and (2). The court can also make any order relating to the guardianship of the child and the administration of the child's property: C(S)A 1995, s 11(1)(c) and (d).

2  C(S)A 1995, s 11(3)(a)(i).
3  This would include the parent's cohabitant. The fact that it is a same sex cohabitation is irrelevant to the preliminary issue of title to sue as opposed to the merits of the case. In *X v Y* 2002 GWD 12-344 the sheriff took the view that a parent's same sex cohabitant was not a member of the child's family and could not apply. This decision is wrong. Cf the decision in *W v M, M v W* (2002) Sh Ct, where same sex cohabitants obtained parental responsibilities and rights in relation to each other's children. In *Telfer v Kellock* 2004 SLT 1290, the Lord Ordinary (Lady Smith) held that a child was a member of the family of the child's mother's lesbian partner who had accepted the child as a child of the family. Siblings have also applied for parental responsibilities and rights in respect of other siblings, for example contact: it is thought that such actions are competent: *E v E* 2004 Fam LR 115: cf *D v H* 2004 Fam LR 41.
4  *D v Grampian Regional Council* 1994 SLT 1038 (IH); approved 1995 SLT 519, HL.
5  C(S)A 1995, s 11(5): we are assuming the child has legal capacity to sue: see **Ch 10**.
6  C(S)A 1995, s 11(5). It can make representations to the court that it would be against a child's interests to award parental responsibilities and rights to the applicant: *McLean v Dorman* 2001 SLT 97.
7  On permanence orders, see paras **13.13** and **14.7**.
8  On compulsory supervision orders, see **Ch 15**.
9  C(S)A 1995, s 11(3)(a)(ii).
10  C(S)A 1995, s 11(3)(ab).The application must be for an order other than a contact order.
11  C(S)A 1995, ss 11(4)(a), (c) and 11A.
12  C(S)A 1995, s 11 (3)(aa).
13  Discussed at para **13.15**.
14  C(S)A 1995, s 11A.

## (2) Ancillary actions in relation to parental responsibilities and rights

**12.3** We have been considering the question of title to sue when a person brings an application relating to parental responsibilities and rights independently of other proceedings. In addition, the courts have the power under the Children (Scotland) Act 1995 to make s 11 orders in any action of divorce or dissolution, judicial separation or declarator of nullity of marriage or civil partnership.[1] Even if no application has been made, the court must consider whether or not to make a s 11 order in the light of such information as is before the court, relating to the arrangements or proposed arrangements for the upbringing of any child of the family.[2] A child of the family is *either* a child of both parties to the action *or* any other child (other than a child placed with them as foster parents by a local authority) who has been treated by both of them as a child of the family.[3] A child is a person below the age of 16.[4]

The court can postpone granting decree in the principal action if it feels unable to make a s 11 order without further consideration and there are exceptional circumstances which make it desirable in the interests of the child to delay granting decree until the court is able to exercise its s 11 powers.[5] In these circumstances, the court can call on a local authority to provide a report as to the arrangements for the upbringing of the child.[6] The report will often contain recommendations with regard to the residence of the child and while the decision is that of the court alone,[7] in practice the recommendations will often be followed. The use of this power is not extensive and even if social background reports were made mandatory in all divorce or dissolution actions, it is considered that in the vast majority of cases they would merely confirm the arrangements agreed by the parties. Moreover, with the gradual acceptance of the value of family mediation, parties are increasingly making voluntary agreements as to the upbringing of their children after they have separated.[8] Family mediation is not compulsory but the court has power to recommend mediation in relation to disputes over parental responsibilities and rights.[9]

Where the court considers that a s 11 order should be made, it can make the order even if there was no application for such an order: moreover, the court can make a s 11 order even if it declines to make an order in respect of the principal action.[10] Thus for example, if H brings an action of divorce against W the court could order that their children should reside with W, even though the court refuses H's action for divorce.

---

1  Children (Scotland) Act 1995, s 12(1). Ancillary orders are also possible in actions for declarator of parentage: *Robb v Gillan* 2004 Fam LR 121; *Y v M* 2013 GWD 27-550.
2  C(S)A 1995, s 12(1).
3  C(S)A 1995, s 12(4)(a) and (b). But the court cannot order aliment for such a child unless the child was also accepted as a child of the family: FL(S)A 1985, ss 1(1)(d) and 2(2)(a).
4  C(S)A 1995, s 12(3).
5  C(S)A 1995, s 12(2).
6  Matrimonial Proceedings (Children) Act 1958, s 1.
7  *MacIntyre v MacIntyre* 1962 SLT (Notes) 70.
8  Solicitors are enjoined to encourage clients to use mediation in appropriate cases: Practice Notes of 11 March 1977.

9   For the Court of Session Rules, see the Act of Sederunt (Rules of the Court of Session 1994) 1994, SI 1994/1443, RCS 49.23 (as amended). For the sheriff court rules, see the Sheriff Courts (Scotland) Act 1907, Schedule 1 (Ordinary Cause Rules 1993), rule 33.22. See also E M Clive *The Law of Husband and Wife in Scotland* (4th edn, 1997) W. Greens/Sweet & Maxwell, p 55.
10   C(S)A 1995, s 11(3)(b).

## THE NATURE OF S 11 ORDERS

**12.4** Whether a s 11 order is sought in an independent action or as an ancillary action, the court has the power to make any order in relation to parental responsibilities and rights as it thinks fit.[1] Without prejudice to the generality of this power, the Children (Scotland) Act 1995, s 11(2) specifies the following orders.

(a)   An order depriving a person of some or all of that person's parental responsibilities and rights. For example, if H is convicted of sexual abuse of his children, W could apply under s 11(2) (a) for an order depriving H of his parental responsibilities and rights.

(b)   An order: (i) imposing upon a person parental responsibilities; or (ii) giving a person parental rights. The person must be 16 or over unless that person is a parent of the child.[2] This is the provision under which a person who does not have parental responsibilities and rights can obtain them: for example a father who does not automatically have parental responsibilities and rights,[3] a step-parent or the child's grandparent.

(c)   An order Regulating the arrangements as to: (i) with whom a child under 16 is to live; or (ii) if with different persons alternately or periodically, with whom and during what periods a child under 16 is to live. This is known as 'a residence order'. This order can be used where H and W divorce and the court wishes to regulate the residence of their children, for example that they are to live with W for six days a week and with H for the other day. Because the court can make any order 'it thinks fit', residence need not be awarded to H or W but to a third party, for example the child's grandparent. It should be noted that a child can apply for a residence order.[4]

(d) An order regulating the maintenance of personal relations and direct contact between a child under 16 and a person with whom the child is not living. This is known as 'a contact order'. This order can be used where for example H and W divorce and W obtains a residence order: H can apply for a contact order in order to maintain his personal relationship with his children who are living with W. It is also the way in which a father who does not automatically have parental responsibilities and rights or grandparents who have successfully applied for the parental right of contact can exercise that right. A child can also apply for a contact order.[5] A contact order can be varied on a change of circumstances. An appeal court will only intervene if the order was one which no reasonable judge could reach: its function is not to determine what is in the best interests of the child.[6]

(e) An order regulating any specific question which has arisen in respect of parental responsibilities and rights, guardianship or the administration of a child's property. This is known as a specific issue order. The scope of such orders is potentially very wide. Consider the following examples:

(i) H and W cannot agree on the education[7] or religion of their child. An application could be made for a specific issue order to resolve the impasse.

(ii) A child is unhappy with the parents' decision to send the child to boarding school or to move house or not to holiday in Florida. The child could apply for a specific issue order to resolve the matter.

(iii) The mother of a mentally disabled girl with learning difficulties wishes to have her daughter sterilised: the doctors are concerned. The mother or the doctors can apply for a specific issue order to determine whether the operation is in the girl's interests and consequently whether or not the sterilisation can go ahead.

(iv) A mother wishes to take her child to Australia for an extended period although this will frustrate the father's right of contact with the child. She can apply for a specific issue order to resolve the matter.[8]

(f)   An interdict to stop any conduct which purports to be done in fulfilment of parental responsibilities or to be an exercise of parental rights relating to a child or the administration of the child's property. Again the scope of this provision is potentially very wide. Consider the following examples:

   (i)   The parents of a 12-year-old girl with s 2(4) capacity[9] consent on her behalf to the termination of their daughter's pregnancy even though the girl refuses to consent. The girl or a nurse or a doctor could apply for an interdict prohibiting the operation going ahead until the court has made a specific issue order as to the legality of the operation.

   (ii)  The parents enter into the sale of a house owned by their 12-year-old child. The child could apply for an interdict preventing the sale going ahead until the court had determined whether or not the sale was in the child's interests.

(g)   An order appointing a judicial factor to manage a child's property or remitting the matter to the Accountant of Court.

(h)   An order appointing or removing a person as guardian of the child.[10]

In practice, the most common orders are residence orders and contact orders and orders giving or depriving persons of parental responsibilities and rights. A s 11 order includes an interim order,[11] the variation of an order or the discharge of an order.[12] For the purpose of s 11 of the 1995 Act, a child is a person below 18, except in the case of residence and contact orders when the child must be below 16.[13] If in the course of s 11 proceedings[14] the court considers that a ground of referral exists,[15] it may refer the case to a Reporter who can arrange a children's hearing to consider whether or not the child requires a compulsory supervision order.[16]

It will be clear that often more than one person will have parental responsibilities and rights in respect of a child.[17] Where this is the case, each can exercise a parental right without the consent of the other(s).[18]

What then is the effect of a s 11 order on a person's parental responsibilities and rights? Consider the following example:

H and W are married. Both have parental responsibilities and rights in respect of C. H and W divorce. W obtains a residence order in respect of C. H is awarded a contact order in respect of C. How do these orders affect H and W's parental responsibilities and rights?

By s 11(11) of the 1995 Act, an order has the effect of depriving a person of parental responsibilities and rights[19] only in so far as the order expressly so provides and only to the extent that it is necessary to do so to give effect to the order. Thus in the example, the residence order will not deprive H of *any* of his parental responsibilities and rights unless this is expressly stipulated in the order. While not being deprived of his responsibilities and rights, H cannot act in any way which would be incompatible with the residence order.[20] So even though he has still the prima facie right to have his child living with him, H cannot insist that the child live with him rather than W during the periods stipulated in the residence order that W is to have C living with her. Similarly, W retains the full complement of parental responsibilities and rights but cannot prevent H from seeing C at the times stipulated in the contact order. If the court took the view that H and W would not act sensibly, it could in the residence order expressly deprive H of his s 2(1)(a) right to have C living with him, and in the contact order expressly deprive W of her right to have contact with C during the period C is to have contact with H. The court is enjoined *not* to do so unless satisfied that it would be better for the child to make such orders than that no order to that effect be made at all.[21]

The importance of s 11(11) cannot be over-emphasised. The C(S)A 1995 takes the view that a child should have the benefit of the support and guidance of *both* parents. A s 11 order should have the minimal effect on the parents' existing parental responsibilities and rights. Indeed, if a child's parents agree on the steps to be taken in respect of the child's upbringing after they divorce,[22] there should be no need for a s 11 order as the court *cannot* make a s 11 order unless satisfied that it is better for the child to make the order than that none should be made at all.

Even if a s 11 order is made and a person is expressly deprived of a parental responsibility or right, this must be the *minimum* necessary to give effect to the order. If in the example, H was deprived of his right to have C live with him,[23] H still retains the right to determine C's education[24] or act as

C's legal representative:[25] these rights are exercised *along with* W, who also retains parental responsibilities and rights.

Where a residence order is made which requires a child to live with a person who does not have pre-existing parental responsibilities and rights in relation to the child, the effect of the order is to give that person the parental responsibilities in s 1(1)(a), (b) and (d) and the parental rights in s 2(1)(b) and (d) of the 1995 Act for as long as the order is in force.[26] So in the example, if residence was awarded to C's grandmother, she would have the relevant responsibilities and rights as a result of the residence order.[27] Unless H or W was expressly deprived of parental responsibilities and rights in the residence order, they would continue to fulfil their responsibilities and exercise their rights *along with* C's grandmother, provided they did not act in any way that was incompatible with the order.[28]

The C(S)A 1995 adopts a minimalist approach to orders relating to parental responsibilities and rights. No s 11 order can be made unless the court is satisfied that it is better for the child to make an order than that none should be made at all.[29] This is particularly pertinent where a residence order or a contact order is sought when a marriage breaks down. In these circumstances, the parties are to be encouraged to reach agreement, if necessary through mediation services, on how their children are to be brought up after the divorce. If this can be done, each parent will retain the full complement of parental responsibilities and rights after divorce. There will be no need for a residence or contact order: indeed, the court *cannot* make the orders.[30] But to achieve this objective the parents must put the interests of their children first and recognise the importance of the children's need to retain personal relationships with both parents after the breakdown of a marriage. This has led to the introduction of a parenting agreement to guide and help parents whose relationship has broken down to make arrangements which best promote the interests of their children.[31]

---

1   Children (Scotland) Act 1995, s 11(1) and (2).
2   'Parent' means the genetic mother or father subject to Chapter 3 of the Adoption and Children (Scotland) Act 2007, the Human Fertilisation and Embryology Act 1990, ss 27–30 and Part 2 of the Human Fertilisation and Embryology Act 2008.
3   There is no reason in principle why the court cannot make such an order even if the applicant could not immediately discharge his parental responsibilities and rights: *T v A* 2001 SCLR 647.

4   C(S)A 1995, s 11(5).
5   C(S)A 1995, s 11(5).
6   *M v M* 2002 SC 103; *NJDB v JEG* [2010] CSIH 83;*S v S* [2012] CSIH 17 (Appeal rejected on the basis that 'the high threshold for appellate intervention has not been met and that the appeal must fail').
7   *G v G* 2002 Fam L R 120.
8   *Shields v Shields* 2002 SLT 579; *McShane v Duryen* 2006 Fam LR 15.
9   That is, capacity to consent to medical treatment by virtue of the Age of Legal Capacity (Scotland) Act 1991, s 2(4), discussed at para **10.2**.
10  On guardianship, see para **11.3**. In *L v H* 1996 SC 86 the father of an illegitimate child applied for guardianship so that he would become a relevant person who would then have the right to attend a children's hearing in respect of the child. The application was refused on the basis that guardianship was for the benefit of the child – not for the benefit of the guardian.
11  *G v G* 2002 Fam LR 120.
12  C(S)A 1995, s 11(13).
13  C(S)A 1995, ss 15(1), 11(2)(c) and (d).
14  C(S)A 1995, s 54(2)(b). This power also exists in an action of divorce, dissolution, judicial separation, declarator of marriage, nullity of marriage, nullity of a civil partnership, and parentage or non parentage: C(S)A 1995, s 54(2)(a) and (aa). The child must normally be below 16.
15  On grounds of referral, see para **15.7**. The provision does not apply where the ground of referral is that the child has committed an offence: s 54(1).
16  C(S)A 1995, s 54(3). For full discussion, see **Ch 15**.
17  For full discussion, see para **11.3**.
18  C(S)A 1995, s 2(2). But a parent cannot take a child out of the country without the consent of the other parent: C(S)A 1995, s 2(3) and (6).
19  But the court can revoke a s 4 or s 4A agreement if necessary to do so: C(S)A 1995, s 11(11). On s 4 and s 4A agreements, see para **11.3**.
20  C(S)A 1995, s 3(4).
21  C(S)A 1995, s 11(7)(a).
22  Discussed at para **12.5**.
23  C(S)A 1995, s 2(1)(a).
24  C(S)A 1995, s 2(1)(b).
25  C(S)A 1995, s 2(1)(d).
26  C(S)A 1995, s 11(12). These are known as relevant responsibilities and rights.
27  Subject to any provision in the order that she was *not* to have any relevant responsibility or right.
28  C(S)A 1995, s 3(4).
29  C(S)A 1995, s 11(7)(a). There must be evidence that it would be better for the child that an order should be made: *G v G* 1999 Fam LR 30; *CR or D v D* [2005] CSOH 88.
30  C(S)A 1995, s 11(7)(a).
31  For the parenting agreement, see Appendix I.

## THE WELFARE PRINCIPLE

**12.5**  In considering whether or not to make a s 11(1) order and, if so, the nature of the order, the court has to exercise discretion. In so doing s 11(7)(a) of the 1995 Act provides that the court:

> 'shall regard the welfare of the child concerned as its paramount consideration and shall not make any such order unless it considers that it would be better for the child that the order be made than that none should be made at all'.

We have discussed the non-interventionist aspect of this provision in the preceding section; in this section we shall explore the welfare principle in some detail.

It is a fundamental tenet of the 1995 Act that decisions relating to parental responsibilities and rights should be child centred. Not only is the child's welfare the paramount consideration in s 11 proceedings but by s 11(7)(b) the court is also enjoined so far as practicable, taking account of the child's age and maturity, to do the following:[1]

(1)     give the child an opportunity to indicate whether the child wishes to express any views;

(2)     if the child so wishes, give the child an opportunity to express his or her views; and

(3)     have regard to such views as the child may express.

We shall call this the duty to consult the child.[2] A child aged 12 or over is presumed to be of sufficient age and maturity to form a view, but the views of a child below that age can be taken into account if the child *in fact* is of sufficient age and maturity.[3] In giving his or her views, the child does not have to be legally represented if he or she does not wish to be.[4] Thus the views of the child at the centre of the proceedings must be fed into the court's decision-making process.[5] Difficulties can arise if the child requests that his views be kept confidential. The parties are entitled to a fair hearing under Article 6 of the European Convention on Human Rights and this usually involves disclosure of the evidence that the court has taken into account in reaching its decision. Accordingly, the court should disclose the child's views unless there is a real possibility of significant harm to the child. The interests of the child have to be balanced against the interests of the other parties. Non-disclosure should be the exception rather than the rule.[6] However, it is the *court's* view of what is in the child's best interests which will ultimately prevail, not the views of the child.

Although under s 11(7)(a) the welfare principle is the paramount consideration, s 11(7A) provides that in carrying out this duty the court must have regard to the matters listed in s 11(7B). These are:

(a)    the need to protect the child from abuse or the threat of abuse which might affect the child;

(b)    the effect such abuse or the risk of such abuse may have on the child;

(c)    the ability of the abuser to care for or otherwise meet the needs of the child; and

(d)    the effect of such abuse or the risk of such abuse on a person with parental responsibilities (or who would have such parental responsibilities by virtue of an order under s 11(1)) from carrying out these responsibilities.

Abuse is very broadly defined. It includes violence, harassment, threatening conduct giving rise to physical or mental injury, fear, alarm or distress.[7] Conduct includes speech and being present at a particular place or area.[8] Importantly, abuse includes abuse directed at a person other than the child.[9] So in determining under s 11(7)(a) what is in the child's best interests, a court must take into account the fact that the child's mother has been abused even if the abuser has not abused the child. Also included in abuse is 'domestic abuse'.[10] It has been held that the abuse, or risk of abuse, does not have to be directed towards the child (or a third party), nor does it have to be intentional.[11] In other words, the test for the existence of abuse is objective. A person who behaves aggressively when drunk, or under the influence of drugs, engages in abuse even although his aggression is unintentional and not directed towards his family.

These provisions focus on abuse or risk of abuse to the person who has care of the child, usually the child's mother, as well as the direct abuse or possibility of abuse of the child. Because abuse of the carer may affect the quality of her care, it is a matter which indirectly affects the child's welfare which must always remain the paramount consideration in s 11 applications. An abuser's ability to care for the child is a relevant factor when he has directly abused the child in the past. But the fact that he has abused the carer when she was his partner in the past may not be relevant to his ability to care for the child in the future. This is particularly important given the width of the definition of abuse which includes any language which could give rise to distress, or the mere presence of a person in a particular place. In *R v R*[12] the court emphasised that evidence of abuse or the risk of abuse did not in itself give rise to a presumption against granting parental responsibilities and rights. Once again it is important to remember that in the end of the day it is the child's welfare, not whether a parent was an abusive partner, that is the paramount consideration and that the child's views are always to be taken into acount.[13]

Nevertheless, it is the welfare principle that has to be used to determine the difficult questions that can be raised in s 11 proceedings. It would apply in deciding, in what would be exceptional circumstances, that a parent should be deprived of parental responsibilities. The interests of a child will also be the paramount consideration in determining whether or not to give parental responsibilities and rights to a father or a second female parent who does not automatically have them, or a step-parent or a grandparent of the child. Acute problems can be envisaged in specific issue orders, but again the welfare principle must provide the solutions. An exception is made to this in proceedings relating to a child's property to the extent that the court must endeavour not to affect adversely a person who has 'in good faith and for value, acquired any property of the child concerned, or any right or interest in such property'.[14] This could arise if the child's parents had leased heritable property owned by the child to a bona fide tenant when it was not in the child's best interests to do so.

Where the welfare principle was most commonly applied before the enactment of the 1995 legislation was in actions for custody and access. These cases are also illustrative of how it is used in applications for residence and contact orders. The decisions must be used with caution given that under the 1995 Act: (1) the court should not make any order unless it is better for the child to do so than that no order should be made at all;[15] and (2) the court *always* has a duty to consult the child.[16]

---

1   Children (Scotland) Act 1995, s 11(7)(b)(i), (ii) and (iii).
2   The obligation to consult continues throughout all the proceedings until a final order is made: *Shields v Shields* 2002 SLT 579. There the court stressed that the only proper and relevant test was whether, in all the circumstances, it was practicable to consult the child.
3   C(S)A 1995, s 11(10).
4   C(S)A 1995, s 11(9): the presumption in s 11(10) applies to a child's decision under s 11(9).
5   *Shields v Shields* 2002 SLT 579.
6   *Re D (minors)* [1995] 4 All ER 385; followed in *McGrath v McGrath* 1999 SLT (Sh Ct) 90; *Dosoo v Dosoo* 1999 SLT 86.
7   C(S)A 1995, s 11(7C)(a).
8   C(S)A 1995, s 11(7C)(a) and (b).
9   C(S)A 1995, s 11(7C)(b).
10  C(S)A 1995, s 11(7C)(c).
11  *R v R* 2010 GWD 23-442.
12  2010 GWD 23-442; *W v G* 2012 GWD 34-692 (Father awarded a residence order even though there had been bouts of violence towards the mother during their volatile relationship and evidence of alcohol and drug abuse. In the course of his judgment the sheriff stated that 'At the end of the day it comes down to a question of risk. Whilst no one can ever predict with certainty what the future holds for anyone, I am satisfied on the evidence that the pursuer will always put the welfare of [the child] at the top of his list of priorities. I am not satisfied that the defender will always do so': ibid at para 19).
13  C(S)A 1995, ss 11(7D) and (7E) obliges the court to consider whether it should make an order where the result of doing so is that two persons – usually the child's parents – will have to co-operate with each other. The inference is that if they can't co-operate the court should not make the order. But if such an order were otherwise in the best interests of the child why should the court not make an order even though the parents may find it difficult to co-operate with each other?
14  C(S)A 1995, s 11(8).
15  Discussed at para **12.4**.
16  See above.

---

## The relevant factors in applying the welfare principle in residence orders

**12.6**  While the welfare of the child is the paramount consideration, all the factors of the case are considered to the extent that they point to the course of action which is best for the child. As Lord MacDermott explained in *J v C*,[1] the welfare principle connotes:

> 'a process whereby, when all the relevant facts, relationships, claims
> and wishes of parents, risks, choices and other circumstances are taken
> into account and weighed, the course to be followed will be that which
> is most in the interests of the child's welfare ...'.[2]

Specific factors are relevant in so far as they pertain to the child's welfare.
In determining what is best for the child, a judge will be influenced not
only by medical and psychological knowledge of the development of
children but, almost inevitably, by his or her own conception of how a
child should be brought up. This is recognised in the rule that in such
cases[3] an appellate court will not interfere with the decision of the judge at
first instance unless the court is satisfied either that the judge exercised his
or her discretion upon a wrong principle, or that the decision is so plainly
unreasonable that the judge must have exercised his or her discretion
wrongly.[4]

At the beginning of the twentieth century, it was the practice of the Court
of Session in divorce actions to apply a presumption that the 'innocent'
spouse whose conduct was not responsible for the break up of the marriage
should be granted custody; this presumption was rebuttable on evidence
that it would be against the child's welfare to award custody to the innocent
spouse.[5] Such a presumption has no place in modern Scots law where the
welfare of the child is the paramount consideration in s 11 proceedings and
the law of divorce and dissolution is, theoretically at least, based on the
non-fault concept of irretrievable breakdown of the relationship.[6] Instead,
a person's 'conduct' should only be relevant in so far as it suggests that it
would not be in the child's best interests to live with that person. So for
example, if all other factors suggest that it would be in a girl's interests that
she should live with her mother, the fact that the mother was an adulterous
wife is irrelevant. Similarly, it should also be irrelevant that a woman
is a prostitute provided she is a competent mother and has satisfactory
accommodation for the child. But if the accommodation was such that the
child was in danger of physical or sexual assault by the woman's clients
then the prostitution would be relevant because of its probable effects on
the welfare of the child.

It is submitted that a similar approach should be taken when the person
seeking residence or contact is gay or lesbian. In the past it is clear that

a parent's sexual orientation has been considered to be an important factor. In *Early v Early*[7] a lesbian mother lost custody of her child who had lived happily with her for several years. The court held, inter alia, that the boy, who was approaching adolescence, required a suitable male role model and could better adjust to his mother's sexuality if he lived with his father and siblings.[8] However, in *Salgviero da Silva Mouta v Portugal*,[9] the European Court of Human Rights held that the decision of a Portuguese court to award custody of a child to his mother simply because she was heterosexual, while the father was gay, constituted a violation of the father's rights under Article 8 and unlawful discrimination under Article 14 of the European Convention of Human Rights. The approach evidenced in *Early*[10] can therefore no longer be justified.

In weighing up the factors which determine what is best for the child, in the past the Scottish courts also gave considerable importance to ensuring that a child obtained a religious upbringing. The 'solace and guidance' of a religious faith was regarded as so important for the welfare of a child that on divorce it was difficult for an atheist spouse to obtain custody if the other spouse was prepared to provide a religious environment. In *M'Clements v M'Clements*[11] for example, an adulterous mother was awarded custody rather than an atheist father because she would give the children a religious upbringing.[12] Where both parties were prepared to offer the child a religious upbringing, there was no bias in favour of any particular Christian denomination and custody was determined by weighing up other factors in accordance with the welfare principle.[13] These cases were decided 60 or so years ago. It is submitted that given our increasingly secular society, a religious upbringing is no longer an important factor in applying the welfare principle. On the other hand, a child's ethnicity and cultural background are becoming increasingly relevant.[14]

The Scottish courts have rejected any presumption that a young child should prima facie live with his or her mother. In *Hannah v Hannah*,[15] the Lord Ordinary had proceeded on the basis that it was 'more in accordance with nature' that a child should be removed from the custody of her father and his cohabitant where she had been living for several years after the marriage had broken down and be returned to the mother. In reversing the judge's decision, in the Inner House of the Court of Session Lord Walker observed:

> 'What exactly the Lord Ordinary meant by nature, or what precisely nature has to do with it, I must confess I find difficulty in appreciating as a proper test in matters of this kind. It is not nature but the welfare of the child which is the material matter.'[16]

The evidence established that the child – who had lived with her father for six years – was happy and well adjusted: in these circumstances, the court held that it was in her best interests that custody be awarded to her father.

In *Brixey v Lynas*[17] the sheriff awarded custody to the father of an illegitimate child. The decision was upheld by the Sheriff Principal. Since her birth and throughout the proceedings, the child had been in the care of her mother and was well looked after. In reversing the decisions of the sheriff and Sheriff Principal, the Inner House of the Court of Session held that the child should remain with her mother. In the course of his judgment, Lord Morison took the view that the sheriff had given insufficient weight to:

> 'the practice of the courts in Scotland to recognise as an important factor which has to be fully taken into account in a dispute concerning custody between the mother and father of a very young child, that during his or her infancy the child's need for the mother is stronger than the need for a father'.[18]

At the same time Lord Morison recognised that 'This principle should not be regarded as creating any presumption in favour of the mother, nor, certainly, as a rule of law'.[19] On appeal, the House of Lords held that the contention that a young child should be in the care of his or her mother was neither a presumption nor a principle but rather the recognition of a widely held belief of ordinary people based on nature![20]

It is thought that although the judges overstated the importance of a *mother's* – as opposed to a *parent's* – role in the upbringing of a child, the result in *Brixey* is justified on the basis that the child was thriving in the *de facto* care of her mother. In *Re B (a child)*[21] the Supreme Court approved the dictum of Lady Hale delivered in the earlier case of *Re G*[22]:

> 'All consideration of the importance of parenthood in private law disputes about residence must be firmly rooted in an examination of what is in the child's best interests. This is the paramount consideration.

It is only as a contributor to the child's welfare that parenthood assumes any significance. In common with all other factors bearing on what is in the best interests of the child, it must be examined for its potential to fulfil that aim.'

Acute difficulties arise in relation to relocation cases. This is where a parent who has a residence order wishes to relocate with the child. This may make it difficult if not impossible for the other parent to retain contact with the child. To permit relocation therefore goes against the shared parenting philosophy of the Children (Scotland) Act 1995. In England, however, the Court of Appeal in *Payne v Payne*[23] considered that the reasonable proposals of the resident parent seeking to relocate were factors of great weight giving rise in effect to a presumption in favour of a resident parent's wishes. This approach was rejected by the Inner House in *M v M*[24]. The reasoning was affirmed in *S v S*[25]. In Scots law there is no presumption in favour of *either* parent. Instead, the welfare and best interests of the child or children concerned are paramount and fall to be judged without any preconceived leaning in favour of the rights and interests of others. The onus therefore rests on the party seeking relocation to establish that it would be in the best interests of the child to do so[26].

It is submitted that cases such as *Hannah v Hannah*[27] and *Brixey v Lynas*[28] illustrate the most important factor which the court will take into account in determining where a child should live, viz the preservation of the status quo. Provided a child is secure in the environment where he or she has lived since the breakdown of the marriage or relationship, prima facie it is in the child's best interests to remain in the care of that parent. For example in *Whitecross v Whitecross*[29] a mother failed to obtain the custody of a young child who had lived with his father since the break up of the marriage. The court took the view that it was in the child's best interests not to disturb the continuity of the child's relationship with his father with whom he had been living:

'To disturb the situation which admittedly is satisfactory in all respects and would involve removing the child from the custody of a parent with whom he has lived in family since his birth inevitably involves a certain degree of disturbance of his life, the effects of which it is impossible to assess or estimate with any accuracy.'[30]

Consequently, other things being equal, it is considered to be in a child's best interests to preserve the status quo and allow the child to live with the parent who has looked after the child since the break up of the marriage or the relationship.[31]

It must be stressed that this is only a prima facie presumption. If it is established that it is in the best interests of the child to be moved, the courts should not hesitate to do so. In *Hastie v Hastie*,[32] a child aged nine had been in the care of his father's mother, ie the child's grandmother, for four years. The grandmother, who was 63, attempted to indoctrinate the child against his mother. In these circumstances, Lord Davidson ordered that the child should live with his mother because this would restore a 'normal' parent child relationship which was in the child's best interests.[33] Similar concern for a 'normal' family relationship has resulted in a child being removed from the care of his lesbian mother to that of his father.[34] Other factors, for example if a child would be removed from a school where he or she was settled, may result in the child residing with a parent who has not hitherto had care and control of the child.[35]

If it is generally accepted that the preservation of the status quo operates for the benefit of the child, then an important consequence follows. When a marriage, civil partnership or other relationship breaks down, the children will generally remain in the care of their mother. In practice there are few disputed cases.[36] Instead, the couple agree that the child should continue to reside with the parent who has cared for the child since the break up: in the vast majority of the cases, this will be the mother. A residence order simply reflects this arrangement.[37] Even in the few contested cases, the courts were reluctant to disturb the status quo.[38] This practice has been reflected in the principle of non-intervention in s 11(7)(a) of the Children (Scotland) Act 1995 so even fewer residence orders are awarded since it is not in the child's interests to make an order which simply reflects what the parties have already agreed.[39]

A final point. While a child has the right to be heard in residence disputes, a child does not have the right to decide where he or she should live. To talk in terms of the child's rights as opposed to the child's best interests diverts from the focus which the child's welfare should occupy in the minds of judges called upon to make decisions as to the child's residence.[40]

1   [1970] AC 668 at 710–711, HL.
2   In *Campins v Campins* 1979 SLT (Notes) 41 at 42, Lord Cameron emphasised that nothing can override or be superior to the child's welfare.
3   It is thought that this is true for all applications under s 11(1) of the Children (Scotland) Act 1995, not merely residence and contact orders.
4   *Britton v Central Regional Council* 1986 SLT 207; *Early v Early* 1990 SLT 221; *J v J* 2004 Fam LR 20; *Y v M* 2013 GWD 27-550; *M v M* [2011] CSIH 65; *S v S*[2012] CSIH 17; *A v S* [2014] GWD 14-257.
5   *Hume v Hume* 1926 SC 1008.
6   See **Ch 6**.
7   1989 SLT 114, approved 1990 SLT 221.
8   In *Hill v Hill* 1990 SCLR 238, a child was returned to his gay father in Canada on the ground that the father was not a danger to the child with whom he had had a good relationship. In *X v Y* 2002 Fam LR 58, a gay father was given contact to his son who had been born as a consequence of AID.
9   2001 Fam LR 2.
10  1989 SLT 114.
11  1958 SC 286.
12  Cf *MacKay v MacKay* 1957 SLT (Notes) 17, where the atheist father was awarded custody on condition that the child's grandmother gave the child religious instruction.
13  *McNaught v McNaught* 1955 SLT (Sh Ct) 9.
14  *Osbourne v Mathan (No 2)* 1998 SC 682; *Perendes v Sim* 1998 SLT 1382.
15  1971 SLT (Notes) 42.
16  1971 SLT (Notes) 42 at 43.
17  1994 SLT 847.
18  1994 SLT 847 at 849.
19  1994 SLT 847 at 849.
20  *Brixey v Lynas* 1996 SLT 856. This view was endorsed by the House of Lords in *Re G (children)* [2006] UKHL 43 (order in favour of natural mother of children conceived by AID during a lesbian relationship). In the course of his speech, Lord Scott profoundly observed, 'Mothers are special'.
21  [2009] UKSC 5.
22  [2006] UKHL 43 at para 37.
23  [2001] Fam 473.
24  [2011] CSOH 65, 2009 SLT 608.
25  [2012] CSIH 17, 2012 Fam LR 32.
26  Factors to be taken into account include: the reasonableness of the proposed move; the motive of the parent wishing to move; the importance of contact with the other parent; the importance of the child's relationship with other members of the family; the extent of the contact that is able to be maintained; the extent to which the child may gain from a relationship with family members should the move go ahead; the child's views; the effect of the move on the child; the effect of refusal on the applicant; the effect of refusal on the child; whether it is better for the child to make the order rather than

refuse it. See Sheriff Morrison in *M v M* 2008 Fam LR 90, cited with approval by the Inner House in *M v M* [2011] CSIH 65, 2012 SLT 428.

27   1971 SLT (Notes) 42.

28   1996 SLT 856.

29   1977 SLT 225.

30   *Whitecross v Whitecross* 1977 SLT 225 at 228, per Lord Cameron. See also, for example, *L v L* 2013 GWD 25-496.L. In *Senna-Cheribbo v Wood* 1999 SC 328, a two-year-old girl who was being looked after by her paternal grandparents was allowed to remain there in spite of her grandmother's age and diminution in energy; her mother who sought a residence order was simply incapable of coping with a child on a permanent basis

31   The preservation of the status quo is consonant with the 'least detrimental' criteria for custody disputes advocated by Goldstein, Freud and Solnit in their influential book, *Beyond the Best Interests of the Child* (1973, New York). In *Breingan v Jamieson* 1993 SLT 186, a child who had been living with her mother was allowed to remain with her mother's family after the mother's death. In refusing the father's application for custody Lord Maclean observed at 190: 'Her [the child's] life has been disturbed enough so far. To remove her now to a totally different environment would be disruptive of her settled, happy life and detrimental to her best interests ...'. The status quo is also preserved in other aspects of parental responsibilities and rights, for example education: *G v G* 2002 Fam LR 120; *CAM v HM* [2012] CSOH 127.

32   1985 SLT 146.

33   See also *Clark v Clark* 1987 GWD 35-1240 (child removed from grandparents to mother).

34   *Early v Early* 1989 SLT 114, approved 1990 SLT 221. On the continued legality of this approach to homosexual parents see above.

35   *Clark v Clark* 1987 GWD 13-441. See also *Jesner v Jesner* 1992 SLT 999.

36   Eekelaar and Clive *Custody after Divorce* (1977), p 52. In the Scottish sample, custody was disputed at the time of the divorce proof in only 1 per cent of the cases.

37   Thus Eekelaar and Clive found that the wife was awarded custody in 76 per cent and the husband awarded custody in 9 per cent of the cases: *Custody after Divorce* p 56 and Table 34.

38   It was irrelevant whether or not the preservation of the status quo favoured the child's father or mother. For full discussion, see Maidment *Child Custody and Divorce* (1984), pp 61–66.

39   See para **12.4**; *G v G* 1999 Fam LR 30.

40   In *Re B* [2009] UK SC 5.

## Relevant factors in applying the welfare principle in contact orders

**12.7**  Before the Children (Scotland) Act 1995, in actions for access the Scottish courts insisted that the onus lay on the pursuer to prove that access was positively in the child's best interests.[1] As a result of the 1995 Act,[2] where a person already has parental responsibilities and rights, prima facie that person has both the duty and the right to maintain a personal relationship with a child who is no longer living with him or her. This responsibility and right to contact remain even if the child is subject to a residence order unless the person has been expressly deprived of the responsibility and right.[3] In other words, the whole thrust of the 1995 legislation is that it is prima facie in a child's best interests to have contact with an absent parent as this reinforces the child's sense of identity.[4]

In *White v White*,[5] the Inner House of the Court of Session held that a father did not have to establish that contact was positively in the child's best interests. On the other hand, his right to contact will not be automatically enforced in the absence of evidence that contact would be *against* his child's interests. Instead the welfare principle should prevail and the common conception that contact between a father and his child is good for the child should be an important factor in that calculus[6]. The father in *White*[6] already had parental responsibilities and rights. However, the *exercise* of his rights is governed by the welfare principle. In those circumstances, he is in a similar position to a father who does not have parental responsibilities and rights. It is now recognised that the natural link between father and child in this situation may also have intrinsic value[7], and this factor will be important in determining whether it is in his child's interests that a father should be granted a right of contact and allowed to exercise it. The fact that during their relationship a father has been abusive towards the child's mother does not conclusively prevent direct contact being in the best interests of the child[9].

In contact cases, the views of the children are of particular importance; but where a child says he or she does not wish to see the pursuer, the court should take pains to see that the refusal is genuine.[10]

---

1     *Porchetta v Porchetta* 1986 SLT 105; *Crowley v Armstrong* 1990 SCLR 361; *O v O* 1995 SLT 238; *Sanderson v McManus* 1997 SC (HL) 55.
2     Children (Scotland) Act 1995, ss 1(1)(c) and 2(1)(c).
3     C(S)A 1995, s 11(11); see para **12.4**.
4     *Cooper v Cooper* 1987 GWD 17-628; *McCabe v Goodall* 1989 GWD 30-114.
5     2001 SLT 485.

6   However in *A v S* 2014 GWD 14-257, the court emphasised that there was no presumption in favour of contact once the biological father and child relationship had been established.

7   *White v White* 2001 SLT 485.

8   *Sanderson v McManus* 1997 SC (HL) 55.

9   *S v J* [2012] CSOH 49.

10  *Cosh v Cosh* 1979 SLT (Notes) 72; *Clement v Clement* 1987 GWD 18-660; *Brooks v Brooks* 1990 GWD 2-62 *B v B* [2010] CSOH 127. (Contact stopped between a mother and her child. There was little emotional attachment between them, the mother was suffering from mental illness and the child did not want contact to continue.)

## Conclusion

**12.8** In theory, any proceedings in relation to parental responsibilities and rights are determined by the welfare principle. But in relation to the residence of children whose parents' marriage ended in divorce, Maidment[1] has concluded that British socio-legal studies have produced three findings:

> 'Firstly, about 94 per cent of divorcing parents agree between themselves the arrangements for the care of their children after the divorce. Secondly, about 90 per cent of these arrangements provide for the mother being the main caretaker in that the children live with her. Thirdly, the court, which need not but usually is asked to confirm the private consensual arrangements, rarely disturbs parents' agreements and almost invariably preserves the residential status quo of the child ...'.

Whatever the theoretical powers of the court, even if a residence order was thought necessary the judge will invariably 'rubber stamp' the arrangements which have been negotiated by the parties. In so far as these arrangements will normally confirm that the child should live with the mother where she has had the care of the child since the break up of the relationship, this preserves the status quo. This is thought to be conducive to the child's welfare as it does not disturb the continuity of the child's relationship with the *de facto* caring parent.

Moreover, unless he has been expressly deprived of his parental responsibilities and rights, a residence order does not deprive the father of exercising his rights and fulfilling his responsibilities in relation to the upbringing of the child. It will often have been agreed that the non-residential parent should have contact with the child. Before the Children (Scotland) Act 1995, such contact often became irregular, particularly if the parents subsequently entered into new family relationships. Even though parents have a statutory responsibility under the 1995 Act to maintain personal relations with children who are not living with them,[2] there is little evidence that matters have improved. It should be noted that the normal arrangements under which a child lives with the mother operates to reinforce the traditional view that women should bear the major burden of the child-rearing function.

There is growing evidence that children will make a better recovery from the traumatic effects of the breakdown of their parents' relationship when they can sustain an emotional tie with both parents. As a consequence of the principle that no s 11 order should be made unless it is better for the child to make the order than that none be made at all, and that when such orders are made they should have the minimum effect on a parent's existing responsibilities and rights, the C(S)A 1995 has given Scots law the framework to achieve this end. There is some evidence that many family law practitioners and parents have taken the opportunity to make this aspiration everyday actuality. It is thought that the parenting agreement will also help.

Nevertheless, there are still cases where residence and contact are bitterly disputed between parents resulting in protracted proceedings: these long proofs are not in the interests of the children involved. They are also extremely expensive and the expenses will often be met from the public purse. In *NJDB v JEG*[3] the Lord President (Hamilton) described such proceedings as a 'highly unsatisfactory' state of affairs and reminded professional advisers of their duty to their clients and the court to attempt to obtain an expeditious disposal by taking steps to identify and concentrate on, and only on, what is in the best interest of the children at the centre of the case. When the case proceeded to the Supreme Court[4] Lord Reed was highly critical of the length of time the dispute had lasted and the costs involved. He focused on the lack of judicial control over the process due to the extensive pleadings of both parties which then resulted in an extensive proof. In his view 'The glacial pace of the proceedings was itself inimical to the best interests of the child... the proceedings have overshadowed the life of this young child, perpetuating and deepening the conflict between his parents which has caused him such distress'[5].

Moreover even if a parent obtains an order for residence or contact, difficulties will arise if the other parent refuses to obtemper [obey] the decree. The ultimate sanction is to imprison the parent for contempt of court. While the Scottish Courts have been robust in upholding this sanction in extreme cases,[6] the absence of a parent in prison is hardly conducive to the child's welfare. Thus the necessity to achieve agreement on child related issues and at all costs avoid litigation.

---

1    Maidment *Child Custody and Divorce* (1984), p 68.
2    Children (Scotland) Act 1995, s 1(1)(c).
3    2010 CSIH 83.
4    [2012] UKSC 21, 2012 SC (UKSC) 293.
5    Ibid at para 21.
6    See for example *M v S* [2009] CSIH 44; *G v B* [2011] CSIH 56, 2011 SLT 1253.

---

# Chapter 13

# Adoption

## INTRODUCTION

**13.1** Adoption is the legal process by which the relationship of parent and child is created by the order of a court. The law has been subject to important reforms and is now to be found in the Adoption and Children (Scotland) Act 2007.[1] The effect of an adoption order is to vest parental responsibilities and rights in relation to the child in the adoptive parents.[2] An adopted child is treated in law as the child of the adopter, as if he or she had never been the child of any person other than the adoptive parents.[3] Thus the parental responsibilities and rights of the parents towards their child are extinguished when the child is adopted and the child's rights are enforceable against the adopters and not the parents. Adoption is therefore a radical interference with the rights of children and their parents to respect for family life under Article 8 of the European Convention on Human Rights. Accordingly the procedure must carefully balance the interests of those persons if a violation of Article 8 is to be avoided.[4]

There are exceptions to the general principle that on adoption the child is no longer regarded as the child of his or her parents. In determining prohibited degrees of relationship for the purpose of the law of marriage, civil partnership and incest, the child remains the child of his or her parents;[5] in addition, an adopted child cannot marry an adoptive parent.[6] Adoption does not affect the law on nationality or citizenship.[7] Similarly, adoption does not affect a child's entitlement to a pension which was in payment at the time of the adoption.[8] Finally, while as a general rule an adopted child is treated for the purposes of the law of succession as the child of the adopters and no other person,[9] the child retains rights in relation to a parent's estate if the adoptive parent died before the commencement of the Succession (Scotland) Act 1964 and the parent dies after the commencement of the Law Reform (Miscellaneous Provisions) (Scotland) Act 1966.[10]

In spite of these exceptions it must be emphasised that the effect of an adoption order on the child's relationship with his or her parents is drastic. Put simply, the parents lose all parental responsibilities and rights when their child is adopted. In particular it should be noted that under ss 11(4)(a) and 11A of the Children (Scotland) Act 1995, the parent loses the right to apply for parental responsibilities and rights, including contact, after a child has been adopted or is subject to a permanence order.[11] These provisions have been held to be proportionate and necessary in a democratic society and do not amount to a breach of a parent's rights under Article 8.[12] Nevertheless, in order to avoid a violation of Article 8, the law of adoption must have regard to the rights of the child's parents as well as the interests of the child. While traditionally considered as a way of providing a home for a new born infant, usually with a childless couple, adoption is increasingly perceived as a long-term solution for children in need.[13] In these circumstances, adoption orders should not be made without the agreement of the parents unless they have clearly forfeited their prima facie rights and responsibilities to bring up their child.

Scottish Ministers are to make arrangements for the establishment of a register to be known as Scotland's Adoption Register for the purposes of facilitating adoption[14].

---

1   See generally *Wilkinson and Norrie* , Ch 21.
2   Adoption and Children (Scotland) Act 2007, s 28(1).
3   AC(S)A 2007, s 40 (1) and (4). Where the person adopting a child is a member of a relevant couple with the child's birth parent the effect of the adoption order is to treat the child as the child of the couple and not the child of any other person except the adopter and the other member of the couple: AC(S)A 2007, s 40(2) and (3). On relevant couples see para **13.4**.
4   *City of Edinburgh Council v D* 2001 SLT (Sh Ct) 135; *City of Edinburgh Council v W* 2002 Fam LR 67; *G v City of Edinburgh Council* 2002 SLT 828; *Aberdeen City Council v R* 2004 SLT (Sh Ct) 53; *Midlothian Council v W* 2005 SLT (Sh Ct) 146; *Dundee City Council v K* 2006 SLT 63, 2006 Fam LR 2.
5   AC(S)A 2007, s 41(1).
6   Adoptive siblings can marry: A C (S)A 2007, s 41(2). For full discussion, see para **2.6**.
7   AC(S)A 2007, s 41(3).
8   AC(S)A 2007, s 42.
9   Succession (Scotland) Act 1964, s 23(1). See *Cameron v MacIntyre's Executor* 2006 SLT 176. The adopted child inherits by virtue of the provisions in the 1964 Act and not by virtue of s 40 of the AC(S)A 2007: AC(S)A 2007, s 44.

10  Law Reform (Miscellaneous Provisions) (Scotland) Act 1966, s 5.
11  See para **12.2** above.
12  *Dundee City Council v K* 2006 SLT 63, 2006 Fam LR 2.
13  See Chs 14 and 15.
14  AC(S)A 2007, ss 13A–G.

## ADOPTION AGENCIES

**13.2** It is the duty of every local authority to establish and maintain a comprehensive adoption service to meet the needs of all those who are or would be affected by the adoption – in particular the children, their parents, the rest of the child's family and the adoptive parents.[1] The facilities to be provided include arrangements for assessing children and prospective adopters, placing children for adoption and giving information.[2] The adoption service must also provide adoption support services which include counselling, guidance and any other assistance in relation to the adoption process that the local authority considers appropriate in the circumstances of a particular case.[3] In doing so the local authority must have regard to the other social services that it provides so that help can be given in a co-ordinated manner.[4] Where a local authority does not have an adoption service it may use the services of registered adoption services.[5] For the purpose of the Adoption and Children (Scotland) Act 2007, the local authority adoption service and a registered adoption service is known as an adoption agency.[6]

It is a fundamental tenet of the AC(S)A 2007 that all the preliminary arrangements for an adoption should be made by an adoption agency. It is a criminal offence for a person other than an adoption agency to make arrangements for the adoption of a child or place a child for adoption.[7] The person who makes the placement and the person who receives the child, knowing the placement is with a view to adoption, can be prosecuted.[8]

There is one exception where arrangements made by persons other than an adoption agency are lawful. A private person can place a child for adoption where the proposed *adopter* is the child's parent or, where the parent is a member of a relevant couple, the other member of the couple, or any other relative of the child.[9] Thus for example, a mother can place her child for adoption by her sister, ie the child's aunt.

---

1   Adoption and Children (Scotland) Act 2007, s 1(1) and (2).
2   AC(S)A 2007, s 1(3).
3   AC(S)A 2007, s 1(4) and (5). Except when the services have to be provided as a matter of urgency, on a request for such services the local authority will make an assessment of the needs of the person for such services: AC(S)A, ss 9, 10 and 11. The local authority has the power to provide the person entitled to the services with a payment instead of the service: AC(S)A 2007, s 12.
4   AC(S)A 2007, s 2(1)(a). It must also have regard to any registered adoption service provided in the local authority area: AC(S)A, s 2(1)(b).
5   AC(S)A 2007, s 2(2).
6   AC(S)A 2007, s 119.
7   AC(S)A 2007, s 75(1).
8   AC(S)A 2007, s 75(3).
9   AC(S)A 2007, s 75(2). On relevant couples, see para **13.4**.

---

## WELFARE OF CHILDREN

**13.3** Where a court or adoption agency is coming to a decision relating to the adoption of a child it must have regard to all the circumstances of the case and is to regard the need to safeguard and promote the welfare of the child throughout the child's life as the paramount consideration.[1] So far as is reasonably practicable to do so, they must have regard in particular to:

(a)   the value of a stable family unit in the child's development;

(b)   the child's ascertainable views regarding the decision taking into account the child's age and maturity;

(c)   the child's religious persuasion, racial origin and cultural and linguistic background;

(d)   the likely effect on the child, throughout the child's life, of making the adoption order.[2]

A child of 12 or more is presumed to be of sufficient age and maturity to form a view;[3] but the views of a child below 12 should be taken into account if the child has *in fact* sufficient age and capacity to form a view.

Thus at *every* stage of the adoption procedure when a court or adoption agency makes a decision which involves a degree of discretion – as opposed to a finding of fact – the welfare of the child *throughout his life* is the paramount consideration and the views of the child must be fed into that decision-making process[4]. Again, problems can arise where the child requests that his or her views should be treated as confidential. This should only be granted by the court in exceptional circumstances where there is a risk of significant harm to the child.[5]

Before placing a child for adoption, an adoption agency *must* consider whether or not adoption is the best way to meet the needs of the child or whether there is some better, practical alternative: if there is a practical alternative, the adoption agency must not make arrangements for the adoption of the child.[6] For example, if H1 and W divorce and W marries H2, it may be better for the children of H1 that he retains his parental rights and responsibilities than that his children are adopted by H2. H2 could, of course, obtain parental responsibilities and rights in respect of the children;[7] these would be exercised jointly with H1. Similarly, if the prospective adopters are relatives of the child, for example the child's grandparents, uncle or aunt, it may be better for the child that they apply for parental responsibilities and rights rather than distort the natural relationships through the adoption process.

In placing a child for adoption, an adoption agency must have regard so far as is reasonably practicable to the views of the child's parents, guardians and other relatives.[8] Nevertheless, the child's welfare is the paramount consideration[9] and the adoption agency should give effect to the family's views only when it is consistent with the child's welfare to do so. Only children who are under 18[10] and who have not been married or registered a civil partnership[11] can be adopted in Scots law. An adopted child can be adopted again.[12] Where the child is aged 12 or over, an adoption order cannot be made without the child's consent.[13] However, in reaching any decision, the views of a child of any age must be given due consideration by a court or adoption agency.[14]

A failure to consult the child's parents in deciding to place the child for adoption or to *apply* for an adoption order, has been held not to amount to a breach of the birth parents' rights under Articles 6 and 8.[15]

---

1    Adoption and Children (Scotland) Act 2007, s 14(2) and (3).
2    AC(S)A 2007, s 14(4).
3    AC(S)A 2007, s 14(8). This is without prejudice to the need for the consent of a child aged 12 or over to the adoption order: AC(S)A 2007, s 32.

4    For example, in *H v M* 1995 SCLR 401 when the child's mother died, the father, who had never married the child's mother, obtained parental rights including residence. The sheriff refused the father's application to adopt his daughter on the basis that adoption was no better for the child's welfare than the existing situation which allowed the child to have contact with her maternal grandmother. The child was too young to express an informed opinion It is, of course, impossible for anyone to know what will be best for a child for the rest of her life: in the author's opinion the statutory criterion is ludicrous!

5    *Re D (Minors)* [1995] 4 All ER 385; for discussion see para **12.5**.

6    AC(S)A 2007, s 14(6) and (7).

7    H2 would apply under the Children (Scotland) Act 1995, s 11; for discussion, see Ch 12.

8    AC(S)A 2007, s 14(5).

9    AC(S)A 2007, s 14(3). The *child's* religious persuasion, racial origin and cultural and linguistic background are factors to be fed into the welfare principle: AC(S)A 2007, s 14(4)(c).

10   AC(S)A 2007, s 119. An adoption order can be made in respect of a person aged 18 or over, if the application was made before the child was 18: AC(S)A 2007, s 28(4). If an adoption order was made in respect of a person aged 18 or over, the decree could be reduced: *Cameron v MacIntyre's Executor* 2006 SLT 176.

11   AC(S)A 2007, s 28(7).

12   AC(S)A 2007, s 28(6).

13   AC(S)A 2007, s 32(1). The court may dispense with the child's consent if satisfied that the child is incapable of giving consent: AC(S)A 2007, s 32(2).

14   AC(S)A 2007, s 14(4)(b). In *C, Petitioners* 1993 SLT (Sh Ct) 8, it was held to be impracticable to ascertain the views of a six-year-old child when the prospective adopters refused to allow her to be interviewed since they did not wish her to know that she was adopted: the prospective adopters were the child's birth mother and stepfather. The adoptive order was nevertheless made.

15   *Dundee City Council v M* 2004 SLT 640.

## PROSPECTIVE ADOPTERS

**13.4** A relevant couple can apply to adopt a child jointly. A couple is 'relevant' if its members:

(a)    are married to each other;

(b)    are civil partners of each other;

(c)    are living together as if husband and wife in an enduring family relationship.[1]

Each member of the relevant couple must be 21 or over and neither of them must be the parent of the child.[2]

A spouse or civil partner who is not the child's parent and is 21 or over can adopt a child alone if the court is satisfied that the other spouse or civil partner cannot be found, or that the spouses or civil partners have separated and are living apart and the separation is likely to be permanent, or the other spouse or civil partner is by reason of ill health (whether physical or mental) incapable of making an application for an adoption order.[3] A member of a relevant couple (by virtue of living together as spouses) who is not the child's parent and is 21 or over can adopt a child alone if the court is satisfied that the other member of the couple is by reason of ill health (whether physical or mental) incapable of making an application for an adoption order.[4]

Where a person is a member of a relevant couple and the other member of the couple is a parent of the child, then that person can adopt the child alone provided that person is 21 or over and the parent is 18 or over.[5] Here the effect of the adoption order is that the child is to be treated as the child of the couple concerned and as not being the child of any person other than the adopter and the other member of the couple ie the child's parent.[6] The adoption order does not affect the parental responsibilities and parental rights which immediately before the order were vested in the member of the couple who is the child's parent: similarly that parent's duty to aliment the child is not extinguished.[7] However the parental responsibilities and parental rights of the child's other parent are extinguished by the adoption order as is his duty to aliment the child.[8]

Where a person is not a member of a relevant couple and is 21 or over she or he can adopt the child alone.[9] However, if that person is the natural parent of the child, before the application can go ahead the court must be satisfied that:

(a)   the other natural parent is dead; or

(b)   the other natural parent cannot be found; or

(c)   by virtue of provisions in the Human Fertilisation and Embryology Acts 1990 and 2008 there is no other parent[10]; or

(d)   the exclusion of the other natural parent from the application for adoption is justified on some other ground.

The situations when a natural parent will wish to adopt his or her child alone will be rare. It could arise for example when a father has no parental responsibilities or parental rights and decides to adopt his child after the mother has died.

1    Adoption and Children (Scotland) Act 2007, s 29(3). Since the introduction of same sex marriage any reference in the enactment to persons living together as if they were in a civil partnership ceases to have effect. Marriage and Civil Partnership (Scotland) Act 2014, s 4(4). By s 4(1) of CP(S)A 2014, 'husband and wife' refers to same sex spouses and therefore same sex couples can be a relevant couple. It is difficult to see how a couple will establish that they live in 'an enduring family relationship'. The statutory implication seems to be that the relationship of spouses need not be enduring!

2    AC(S)A 2007, s 29(1). Parent means a parent who has any parental responsibilities or parental rights in relation to the child: AC(S)A 2007, s 29(4). A member of the couple must be domiciled in part of the British Isles or each member of the couple has been habitually resident in part of the British Isles for at least one year ending with the date of the application: AC(S)A 2007, s 29(2).

3    AC(S)A 2007, s 30(4). Parent means a parent who has any parental responsibilities or parental rights in relation to the child: AC(S)A 2007, s 30(8).

4    AC(S)A 2007, s 30(5). If, of course, the couple had separated they would not qualify as a relevant couple. Parent means a parent who has any parental responsibilities and rights in relation to the child: AC(S)A 2007, s 30(8).

5    AC(S)A 2007, s 30(3). Parent means a parent who has any parental responsibilities or parental rights in relation to the child: AC(S)A 2007, s 30(8).

6    AC(S)A 2007, s 40(2)(b) and (3).

7    AC(S)A 2007, s 35(1).

8    AC(S)A 2007, s 35(2). Where the duty arises under a deed or arrangement which constitutes a trust or expressly provides that the duty is not to be extinguished by the making of an adoption order, then the duty will not be extinguished: AC(S)A 2007, s 35(3).

9    AC(S)A 2007, s 30(1) and (2)

10   1990 Act, s 28 (disregarding s 28(5A) to (5I)) or 2008 Act, ss 34 to 47 (disregarding ss 39, 40 and 46).

## PROCEDURE

**13.5** Where the child was placed with the applicants by an adoption agency or where the applicant is a parent, step-parent or relative of the child, the child must be at least 19 weeks old before an adoption order can be made and have lived with the applicant at all times during the preceding 13 weeks.[1] If a child was not placed with the applicants by an adoption agency and they are not related to the child, the child must be at least 12 months old before an adoption order can be made and have lived with the applicants at all times during the preceding 12 months.[2] This would apply where for example foster parents want to adopt a child who has been looked after by them.

Where a child has not been placed with the applicants by an adoption agency, the applicants must give notice to the local authority within whose area the child has his or her home of their intention to adopt the child. The notice must be given at least three months before the date of the order. During that period the local authority investigates the suitability of the adoptive parents etc and makes a report to the court.[3] Where a child has been placed by an adoption agency, the adoption agency submits a report to the court on the suitability of the adoptive parents etc.[4] An adoption order will not be made unless the court is satisfied that the applicants have afforded the adoption agency or the local authority sufficient opportunities to see the child in the home environment.[5]

Where the child has been placed by an adoption agency and the child's parents have consented to the placement, the parents cannot remove the child without the leave of the adoption agency or the appropriate court.[6] Where an application for an adoption order is made by a person with whom the child has had his or her home for the preceding five years, no person can remove the child from the applicant's home while the application is pending unless the prospective adopters consent, or the appropriate court grants leave for the removal of the child, or the child is arrested, or the removal is authorised by virtue of an enactment.[7] This protection extends to foster parents who decide to adopt a child who is being looked after by a local authority but who has lived with the applicants for the preceding five years.[8]

An application for an adoption order can be made to the Court of Session or the sheriff court of the sheriffdom where the child is.[9] The proceedings are heard in private.[10] A *curator ad litem* must be appointed with the duty of safeguarding the child's interests; in particular it is the *curator's* duty to provide the court with a comprehensive report dealing with all the circumstances of the adoption application.[11] Thus the court will have an independent assessment of whether the adoption will be in the interests of the child.

Difficulties can be experienced when an application is made for an adoption order in respect of a child who, at the same time, is also the subject of an action for parental responsibilities and rights in another court. These conflicts of jurisdiction should be avoided in the best interests of the child.[12]

1   Adoption and Children (Scotland) Act 2007, s 15(1), (2) and (3).
2   AC(S)A 2007, s 15(1) and (4).
3   AC(S)A 2007, ss 18 and 19.
4   AC(S)A 2007, s 17.
5   AC(S)A 2007, s 16.
6   AC(S)A 2007, s 20.
7   AC(S)A 2007, s 22. Similar protection exists for the period during which a prospective adopter has given notice of intention to adopt a child to a local authority but before the application is made: the child must have lived with the prospective adopters for the preceding five years: AC(S)A 2007, s 21.
8   AC(S)A 2007, s 23.
9   AC(S)A 2007, s 119.
10  AC(S)A 2007, s 109.
11  AC(S)A 2007, s 108(a). A reporting officer must also be appointed for witnessing agreements etc: AC(S)A 2007, s 108(b). The same person can be both *curator ad litem* and reporting officer.
12  See for example, *F v F* 1991 SLT 357.

## PARENTAL CONSENT

**13.6** It is a fundamental principle of the law of adoption that an adoption order cannot be made unless the court is satisfied that each parent or guardian of the child 'understands what the effect of making an adoption order would be and consents to the making of the order (whether or not the parent or guardian knows the identity of the persons applying for the order)'.[1] For this purpose, parent means a parent who has *any* parental responsibilities or parental rights in relation to the child.[2] Consider the following examples:

(1)   M and F are married at the child's conception or subsequently: both have parental responsibilities and rights and are parents;[3]

(2)   M is an unmarried mother: she has parental responsibilities and rights and is a parent;[4]

(3)   F has not married M and has not been registered as the father of the child: he has no parental responsibilities and rights and is not a parent;[5]

(4)     F has not married M but has obtained a contact order under
        s 11(2)(d) of the Children (Scotland) Act 1995: he has the
        parental responsibility and right to contact and is a parent;[6] or

(5)     M and F are married at the child's conception but both have been
        deprived of parental responsibilities and rights under s 11(2)
        (a) of the C(S)A 1995: neither has parental responsibilities and
        rights and therefore neither is a parent.[7]

A guardian is a person appointed to be the child's guardian by deed or
will or court order.[8] The agreement of a person, other than the child's
mother or father, who has parental responsibilities and rights is *not*
required unless that person has been appointed to be the child's guardian.
A mother's agreement is ineffective if given less than six weeks after the
child's birth.[9]

---

1   Adoption and Children (Scotland) Act 2007, s 31(2)(a).
2   AC(S)A 2007, s 31(15)(a). Parent also means a parent who, by virtue of a permanence
    order which does not include provision granting authority for the child to be adopted,
    has no parental responsibilities and rights: AC(S)A 2007, s 31(15)(b). On permanence
    orders, see paras **13.13** and **14.7**.
3   Children (Scotland) Act 1995, s 3(1)(a) and (b).
4   C(S)A 1995, s 3(1)(a).
5   C(S)A 1995, s 3(1)(b).
6   On C(S)A 1995, s 11(2)(d), see para **12.4**. F would also be a parent if he obtained the
    responsibilities and rights by agreement with M: C(S)A 1995, s 4, discussed at para
    **11.3**. See for example *West Lothian Council v M* 2002 SLT 1155. The existence of a
    s 4 agreement in favour of F has been held to rebut the presumption that the mother's
    husband was father of the child: *Aberdeen City Council v J* 1999 SLT 953. *Sed quaere*
7   On C(S)A 1995, s 11(2)(a), see para **12.4**.
8   AC(S)A 2007, s 119. On guardianship, see para **11.3**.
9   AC(S)A 2007, s 31(11).

---

## Dispensation with Consent

**13.7** As we have seen, the consent the child's parent or guardian is
necessary before an adoption order can be made. However, under section
31 (2) (b) of the Adoption and Children (Scotland) Act 2007 the court has
power to dispense with their consent in certain circumstances; these will
be discussed in this section.

It has been a feature of the law of adoption in Scotland that dispensation with consent involves the court in a two-stage process.[1] First, the court must be satisfied that a ground for dispensation exists. This is primarily a question of fact. If a ground is established, the court must then consider whether the consent of the parent or guardian *should* be dispensed with on that ground. In reaching this decision, the court must apply the welfare principle in s 14(2) of the AC(S)A 2007, ie the welfare of the child is the paramount consideration. But it must be emphasised that s 14(2) is only relevant at this second stage, ie *after* the ground has been established. But as we shall see,[2] the 2007 Act has introduced a new 'welfare' ground which appears to conflate the two stages: unsurprisingly, this ground has caused considerable controversy. We shall consider the grounds in turn:

1    *L v Central Regional Council* 1990 SLT 818.
2    See para **13.12**.

*(1)  Parent or guardian is dead[1]*

**13.8** When the parent or guardian is dead, he or she cannot give consent. Therefore there is no need to dispense with their consent. Moreover, when a parent is dead he or she cannot have parental responsibilities and parental rights and accordingly is not a parent within the definition of 'parent' in section 31(15) of the AC(S)A 2007. For these reasons, the death of a parent or guardian cannot technically be a ground for dispensing with their consent. In these circumstances, we must conclude that this provision has been included for the avoidance of any doubt.

1    AC(S)A 2007, s 31(3)(a).

*(2)  Parent or guardian cannot be found or is incapable of giving consent[1]*

**13.9** Whether a parent or guardian cannot be found is usually decided on the information contained in the report of the *curator ad litem* and the productions. The court must be told what steps were taken to find the parent or guardian and in particular it is important to 'follow up' evidence that relatives or friends may still be in contact with the missing person.[2] Evidence of incapacity to give agreement will usually be a medical report on the parent's or guardian's physical or mental condition.

Once the ground is established, the court must apply s 14(3) of the Adoption and Children (Scotland) Act 2007 to determine whether consent *should* be dispensed with on that ground. Consider the following examples:

### Example 1

A mother is unconscious in hospital after a road accident. Clearly the s 31(3)(b) ground is established as she is incapable of giving consent. The medical prognosis is that she is likely to regain consciousness within a month. This evidence is relevant to the second stage, ie whether the court should dispense with her agreement on the ground that she is incapable of giving it. The issue is determined by s 14(3) of the 2007 Act. Since it is prima facie in a child's best interests to be brought up by his or her mother, giving paramount consideration to the welfare of the child, it is thought that the court should not dispense with the mother's agreement and the adoption order should therefore not be made.

### Example 2

A mother is unconscious in hospital after a road accident. Clearly the s 31(3)(b) ground is established as she is incapable of giving consent. The medical prognosis is that she is severely brain damaged and unlikely to regain consciousness. This evidence is relevant to the second stage, ie whether the court should dispense with her agreement on the ground that she is incapable of giving it. The issue is determined by s 14(3) of the 2007 Act. Giving paramount consideration to the welfare of the child, it is thought that the court should dispense with the mother's agreement on this ground and make the adoption order.

---

1    AC(S)A 2007, s 31(3)(b).
2    In *S v M* 1999 SC 388 no steps were taken to contact the mother's father in an attempt to find her: since not all reasonable steps had been taken to find her, the inference could not be drawn that she could not be found.

---

*(3) Inability to discharge parental responsibilities and parental rights*[1]

**13.10** This ground is concerned with parents who have parental responsibilities and parental rights. However, it does not apply to those parents whose only parental responsibilities and rights are the responsibility of maintaining personal relations and direct contact with the child and the right to do so. Accordingly, when a parent has merely contact responsibilities and rights, the failure to have contact cannot trigger s 31(4) and another ground must be used to dispense with the parent's consent.

Where a parent has parental responsibilities and parental rights beyond contact responsibilities and rights, then s 31(4) applies if in the opinion of the court: (i) the parent is unable satisfactorily to discharge those responsibilities and exercise those rights; and (ii) the parent is likely to continue to be unable to do so. It will be noticed that the crucial issue is the parent's *inability* to discharge the rights and duties satisfactorily: there is no implication of blame. That said, where a parent has abused a child or neglected a child, it is thought that the court is entitled to infer from these facts not only that the parent was unable satisfactorily to discharge parental responsibilities and parental rights but the abuse or neglect are also relevant to the question whether the parent will be able satisfactorily to discharge them in the future[2]. In considering whether or not the incapacity ground applies it has been said that the court is engaged essentially in a fact finding exercise.[3]

The ground applies even although the parent's responsibilities and rights have been curtailed or suspended by the terms of a compulsory supervision order[4]. The ground is concerned with whether the parent is unable satisfactorily to discharge her parental responsibilities and rights and is not restricted as to how she has in fact treated the child in the past.

The court must also be satisfied that the parent is likely to continue to be unable satisfactorily to discharge parental responsibilities and rights in the future. It may be difficult to assess the 'parenting abilities' of a person whose children have not resided with them. However in *M v R*[5]. Lord Glennie, while accepting that it involved some suspension of belief, thought that 'the proper approach is for the court to assess the parents' parenting abilities by assuming that the child will return to live with the birth parents; and asking whether, in such circumstances, the parents can satisfactorily discharge their parental responsibilities and exercise their parental rights'. It must be an inability of enduring significance. Thus if a parent's inability was due to drug addiction, the ground of dispensation would not be satisfied if she had recovered after successfully undergoing treatment and was now able to look after her child.

Even if the ground is established, the court must apply s 14(3) of the 2007 Act to determine whether the agreement *should* be dispensed with. However, as the court must be satisfied that the parent is likely to continue to be unable satisfactorily to discharge parental responsibilities and parental rights in order for the ground to be established, circumstances will be rare when it will not be in the child's best interests to dispense with the parent's consent on this ground.

1    AC(S)A 2007, s 31(4).
2    *D Petitioner* 2012  SLT (Sh Ct) 73.
3    *S for the Authority to Adopt the Child FY* [2014] CSIH 42.
4    Ibid. It is thought that the Lord Ordinary (Glennie) was wrong when he opined in *M v R* [2012] CSOH 186 that the ground was not available in these circumstances.
5    [2012] CSOH 186 at para 74.

*(4)  Absence of parental responsibilities and rights as a result of a permanence order[1]*

**13.11**  As we shall see[2] a local authority has the power to apply for a permanence order when the child's residence with the parent is or is likely to be seriously detrimental to the welfare of the child.[3] The effect of a permanence order is to transfer the parent's parental responsibilities and parental rights to the local authority. This ground arises when the parent has no parental responsibilities and parental rights by virtue of a permanence order which does not contain authority to adopt and the court is satisfied that it is unlikely that such responsibilities will be imposed on, or such rights given to, the parent. Given that before a permanence order can be made, the parental environment must be seriously detrimental to the child's welfare and that for the ground to be established the court must be satisfied that it is unlikely that the parent will regain parental responsibilities and rights, it is thought that it will almost always be in the child's best interests to dispense with the parent's consent on this ground.

---

1 AC(S)A 2007, s 31(4) and (5).
2 Paras **13.13** and **14.7**.
3 AC(S)A 2007, ss 80 and 84(5)(c)(ii).

---

*(5) The child's welfare*

**13.12** Section 31(3)(d) of the Adoption and Children (Scotland) Act 2007 provides that where neither section 31(4) (inability to discharge parental responsibilities and parental rights) nor section 31(5) (absence of parental responsibilities and rights as a result of a permanence order) applies the consent of a parent or guardian can be dispensed with if 'the welfare of the child otherwise requires the consent to be dispensed with'.

Accordingly, section 31(3)(d) is triggered when: (a) consent cannot be dispensed with under section 31(4) because the court takes the view that the parent might become able to discharge parental responsibilities and exercise parental rights; or (b) consent cannot be dispensed with under section 31(5) because the court takes the view that it is likely that parental responsibilities will be imposed on or parental rights given to the parent. If this is so, then having failed to establish a section 31(4) or (5) ground, the court can dispense with parental consent if the child's welfare requires it.

This would mean that if section 31(3)(d) could be used to dispense with parental consent whenever adoption was in the child's best interests in accordance with the welfare principle in section 14(3), a competent and reasonably capable parent could have her consent dispensed with if adoption were a better option for the future of the child. This it was argued could amount to an infringement of the parent's Article 8 right to family life.[1]

In *ANS v ML (AP)*[2] the Supreme Court held that when properly construed, s 31 (d) was not an infringement of Article 8. Lord Reed explains[3]:

'It follows that legislation authorizing the severing of family ties between parents and their children will not readily be construed as setting anything less than a test of necessity. Section 31(3)(d),in stipulating that the welfare of the child must "require" that parental consent be dispensed with, is consistent with such a test. There must, in other words, be an overriding requirement that the adoption proceed for the sake of the child's welfare, which remains the paramount consideration. The court must be satisfied that the interference with the rights of parents is proportionate: in other words, that nothing less than adoption will suffice. If the child's welfare can be equally well secured by a less drastic intervention, then it cannot be said that the child's welfare "requires" that consent to adoption be dispensed with. That requirement is consistent with section 28(2),which prohibits the court from making an adoption order unless it considers that it would be better for the child that the order be made than not.'

Put another way, the scope of section 31(3)(d) is restricted to the situation where the child's welfare *requires* the court to dispense with the parent's consent because adoption is the best way to protect the child from a positively harmful situation and not merely a better outcome than continuing to remain a member of the child's existing family.[4]

---

1   See for example *Olsson v Sweden* (1988) 11 EHRR 259; *Kav Finland* [2003] 1FLR 696; *Buchberger v Austria* (2003) 37 EHRR 13; *Haase v Germany* (2004) 40 EHRR 19.
2   [2012] UKSC 30, 2013 SC (UKSC) 20.
3   Ibid at para 34.
4   The welfare ground was used in *M v R* [2012] CSOH 186.

---

## PERMANENCE ORDERS

**13.13** By section 80 of the Adoption and Children (Scotland) Act 2007, a local authority can apply for a permanence order. A permanence order consists of a mandatory provision under which the parental right to provide guidance appropriate to a child's stage of development[1] and the parental right to regulate the child's residence[2] vest in the local authority.[3] The order may contain a wide range of ancillary orders vesting other parental responsibilities and rights in the local authority or a third party.[4] Most importantly an ancillary order can be made extinguishing the parent's parental responsibilities and rights[5]. In so doing the court must ensure that that each parental responsibility and right vests in a person[6] However, even if all the parent's parental responsibilities and rights have been extinguished by the permanence order, the parent retains the right to refuse to consent to the adoption of the child unless the court can dispense with parental consent under s 31(5) (or arguably s 31(3)(d)).[7]

Before the court can make a permanence order, it must be satisfied either (a) that no one has the right to have the child living with them or (b) where there is such a person, the child's residence with that person is or is likely to be seriously detrimental to the welfare of the child.[8] It cannot be sufficiently emphasised that before a permanence order can be made on the latter ground it must be established that the child's continuing residence with the parent is likely to be *seriously* detrimental to the child's welfare: it is not sufficient that it would be better for the child to be removed from the care of the parents. Moreover, once such a ground has been established, in determining whether to make the order, the need to safeguard and promote the welfare of the child throughout childhood is the paramount consideration and the court cannot make an order unless it is better for the child that the order be made than if it was not made.[9]

A permanence order cannot be made in respect of a child aged 12 or over without the child's consent.[10] The child should be given the opportunity to express his or her views[11] and if the child is aged 12 or over it is presumed that the child is of sufficient age and capacity to form a view[12] In addition the court must have regard to the child's views, the child's religious persuasion, racial origin and cultural and linguistic background, and the likely effect on the child if the order is made.[13] A permanence order can be made in respect of a child who has been adopted but not if the child is or has been married or is or was a party to a civil partnership.[14]

When applying for a permanence order, the local authority can request the court for a provision granting authority for the child to be adopted.[15] Before such authority can be granted, the court must be satisfied that the child has been or is likely to be placed for adoption.[16] The parents of the child must understand the effect of making an adoption order and consent to such an order being made in respect of the child.[17] But the court can dispense with parent's consent on exactly the same grounds as the court can use to dispense with parental consent to an adoption order itself.[18] The court can rely on the same body of evidence in deciding whether to grant authority to adopt as it relied on in deciding to make the permanence order[19].

Even although a ground exists, the court should only dispense with the consent if the welfare test in section 14(3) is satisfied as an order granting authority for adoption is a decision relating to the adoption of the child.[19] Since a permanence order can only be made when the child's residence with the parent is or would be likely to be seriously detrimental to the child's welfare, in most cases grounds will exist to dispense with the parent's consent. If the authority to adopt is granted in the permanence order, then there is no need to obtain or dispense with the parent's consent to the adoption order itself.[20] Where a permanence order is in force without a provision granting authority for the child to be adopted, the local authority can apply to have the order amended to include such authority.[21] The permanence order comes to an end once the adoption order has been made.[22]

Permanence orders are an important innovation. They will help local authorities who are looking after children in need to place these children for adoption when adoption is considered by the authority to be in the long term interests of a child.[23]

---

1    Children (Scotland) Act 1995, s 1(1)(b)(ii).
2    C(S)A 1995, s 2(1)(a).
3    AC(S)A 2007, s 81.
4    AC(S)A 2007, s 82.
5    AC(S)A 2007, s 82(1)(c).
6    AC(S)A 2007, s 80(3).
7    AC(S)A 2007, s 31(15)(b).
8    AC(S)A 2007, s 84(5)(c)(i) and (ii).
9    AC(S)A 2007, s 84(2) and (3). See *Midlothian Council v M* [2013] CSIH 71;2014 SC 1684. *Dumfries and Galloway Council Petitioner* 2013 GWD 31-62.
10   AC(S)A 2007, s 84(1). The child's consent is not required if the child does not have the capacity to consent: s 84(2).
11   AC(S)A 2007, s 84(5)(a)(i) and (ii).
12   AC(S)A 2007, s 84(6).
13   AC(S)A 2007, s 84(5)(b)(i), (ii) and (iii).
14   AC(S)A 2007, s 85.
15   AC(S)A 2007, s 80(2)(c).
16   AC(S)A 2007, s 83(1)(b).
17   AC(S)A 2007, s 83(1)(c)(i).
18   Discussed above paras **13.ff**. The necessity criterion must be satisfied before the court can dispense with consent on the welfare ground in s 83(2)(d): see para **13 12.**

19  *S v City of Edinburgh Council* [2012] CSIH 95, 2013 SCLR 534.

20  *City of Edinburgh Council Ptrs* 2010 GWD 25-472.

21  AC(S)A 2007, s 31(7).

22  AC(S)A 2007, s 93. The consent of the parent is necessary or have been dispensed with on the same grounds as in the case of the adoption order itself.

23  AC(S)A 2007, s 102.

24  On children in need, see **Ch 13**. See further on permanence orders, para **14.7**.

## THE ADOPTION ORDER

**13.14**  If the child is the subject of a permanence order with authority for adoption or the relevant parental consents have been obtained or dispensed with, the court can then proceed to make the adoption order. It will do so having regard to section 14(3) of the Adoption and Children (Scotland) Act 2007 viz the need to safeguard and promote the welfare of the child throughout the child's life is the paramount consideration. However, the court must not make an adoption order unless it considers that it would be better for the child that the order be made than if it was not.[1] In *T, Petitioner*[2], for example, the Inner House of the Court of Session made an adoption order in favour of a male nurse who was living with his same sex cohabitant. The child had been rejected by his mother. It was in his best interests to be cared for by the applicant and his partner: their sexual orientation was not important in the circumstances. On the other hand, a court has refused to make an order when, for example, the purpose of the adoption was to avoid immigration requirements and not to integrate the child into the proposed adopters' family.[3] But the most common situation where an adoption order would not be made would be if the court was not satisfied with the verification of the statements in the petition.

By s 28(3) of the AC(S)A 2007 the court has power to attach any terms or conditions to the order as it thinks fit. This discretion is governed by the welfare principle in s 14(3) of the 2007 Act. This power can be used to allow the child to have contact with his or her birth family after the adoption and thereby support open adoptions.[4]

Adoption orders are registered in the Adopted Children Register. On reaching 16 an adopted person is entitled to obtain information in respect of his birth; counselling services are available for adopted persons who have received such information.[5]

1    AC(S)A 2007, s 28(2).
2    1997 SLT 724.
3    In *Re W (a minor)* [1985] WLR 945, CA; cf *Re H (a minor)* [1982] 3 All ER 84, [1982] Fam 121.
4    *B v C* 1996 SLT 1370; *City of Edinburgh Council v D* 2001 SLT (Sh Ct) 135. In *West Lothian Council v M* 2002 SLT 1155 the court called for greater flexibility in the adoption procedure better to balance the interests of the birth parents, the adoptive parents and the child.
5    See generally AC(S)A 2007, Chapter 5 and Schedule 1.

## Surrogacy

**13.15** Where a couple have commissioned a surrogate mother, and either party (or both) is the genetic parent,[1] after the child is born they can apply within six months of the birth for a parental order.[2] For this purpose, the applicants must be: (a) husband and wife; (b) civil partners; or two persons who are living as spouses in an enduring family relationship and are not within the prohibited degrees of relationship in relation to each other.[3] Both applicants must be 18 or over.[4] The agreement is required of the surrogate mother, ie the woman who gave birth to the child, and any other person who is a parent of the child.[5] Their agreement is not necessary if the mother or any other parent cannot be found or is incapable of giving agreement.[6] The agreement of the mother is ineffective if given within six weeks of the birth.[7] The effect of the order is that the commissioning couple in effect adopt the child, ie the child is to be treated in law as the child of the applicants.[8] The court must be satisfied that no money or other benefit (other than for expenses reasonably incurred) has been given or received by the applicants for or in consideration of the making of the order, the parental agreement, handing the child over to the applicants or the making of arrangements in respect of the order.[9]

1    M by supplying sperm or W by supplying the ovum.
2    Human Fertilisation and Embryology Act 2008, s 54(1) and (3). Where the child was born before the 2008 Act came into force and the couple were ineligible to obtain a parental order under the Human Fertilisation and Embryology Act 1990 because they

were not married, an application can be made within a period of six months after the 2008 Act came into force: HFEA 2008, s 54(11).

3   HFEA 2008, s 54(2).
4   HFEA 2008, s 54(5).
5   HFEA 2008, s 54(6).
6   HFEA 2008, s 54(7).
7   HFEA 2008, s 54(7).
8   HFEA 2008, s 54(1). If the surrogate mother or another parent of the child refuses to agree, the couple can apply to adopt the child: the parent's consent can then be dispensed with if grounds exist. See *C v S* 1996 SLT 1387. The adoption went ahead in this case even though the couple had given the mother a payment in breach of A(S) A 1978, s 51(1)(c), and of HFEA 1990, s 30(7).
9   HFEA 2008, s 54(8).

# Chapter 14

# Children: responsibilities and powers of local authorities

## INTRODUCTION

**14.1** Although family autonomy may be regarded as a hallmark of a democratic society, it is accepted that a modern state should provide general services in relation to health, education, housing and leisure which indirectly benefit all children. But it has also been recognised that a local authority should make provision through its social work agencies for the assistance, support and protection of children who are vulnerable when the family of which they are part becomes dysfunctional. At one extreme, this provision may simply take the form of advice and guidance to the family; at the other, it might involve the compulsory removal of a child from the family.

In the latter situation, two points must be stressed. First, not only are parental responsibilities and rights being overridden, but also the child is being deprived of liberty. Clearly, serious human rights issues arise under Article 5 (right to liberty and security of person) and Article 8 (right to respect for private and family life) of the European Convention on Human Rights.[1] Article 5(d) of the European Convention recognises that the detention of a child can be justified if it is made by lawful order for the purpose of educational supervision or to bring him before a competent legal authority. To avoid violations of these Articles, it is therefore important that the law should provide procedural safeguards to ensure that these interests are adequately represented before a decision is made which would deprive parents of their child and the child of his or her family – even if, ultimately, this step must be taken to secure the welfare of the child. This in turn can raise human rights issues, in particular Article 6 of the European Convention (right to a fair and public hearing). In short, the procedures must satisfy the minimum standards of a fair hearing set down in Article 6, which provides as follows:

'(1)  In the determination of his civil rights and obligations or of any criminal charge against him, everyone is entitled to a fair and public hearing within a reasonable time by an independent and impartial tribunal established by law. Judgment shall be pronounced publicly but the press and public may be excluded from all or part of the trial in the interests of morals, public order or national security in a democratic society, where the interests of juveniles or the protection of the private life of the parties so require, or to the extent strictly necessary in the opinion of the court in special circumstances where publicity would prejudice the interests of justice.

(2)  Everyone charged with a criminal offence shall be presumed innocent until proved guilty according to law.

(3)  Everyone charged with a criminal offence has the following minimum rights:

(a)  to be informed promptly, in a language which he understands and in detail, of the nature and cause of the accusation against him;

(b)  to have adequate time and facilities for the preparation of his defence;

(c)  to defend himself in person or through legal assistance of his own choosing or, if he has not sufficient means to pay for legal assistance, to be given it free when the interests of justice so require;

(d)  to examine or have examined witnesses against him and to obtain the attendance and examination of witnesses on his behalf under the same conditions as witnesses against him; and

(e)  to have the free assistance of an interpreter if he cannot understand or speak the language used in court.'

The second point which must be stressed is that although a large degree of discretion must be given to social work agencies, their decisions in relation to a child may have serious consequences for the child and the child's family. It is therefore crucial that the parameters in which this discretion can lawfully be exercised are clearly laid down. The law in this area is governed by provisions in the Children (Scotland) Act 1995, the Children's Hearings (Scotland) Act 2011 and the Children and Young Persons (Scotland) Act 2014.[2]

---

1    Convention for the Protection of Human Rights and Fundamental Freedoms (Rome, 4 November 1950; 213 UNTS 221; TS 71 (1953); Cmd 8969). Most, but not all, of the 1950 Convention has been incorporated into United Kingdom law as Schedule 1 to the Human Rights Act 1998.
2    See generally *Wilkinson and Norrie*, Chs 15-20.

---

## THE RESPONSIBILITIES AND DUTIES OF LOCAL AUTHORITIES

**14.2** Under Part 3 of the Children and Young People (Scotland) Act 2014 every three years a local authority and the relevant health board must prepare a children's services plan for the area of the local authority. This plan is to be used so that children's services in the area are provided in the way that: (i) best safeguards, supports and promotes the wellbeing of children in the area; (ii) ensures that any action to meet needs is taken at the earliest appropriate time and that where appropriate, action is taken to prevent needs arising; (iii) is most integrated from the point of view of the recipients and (iv) constitutes the best use of available resources[1]. It is therefore anticipated that such plans will help prevent children becoming children 'in need'[2].

Under Part 4 of the CYP(S)A 2014, a local authority must make available a named person service to children and young persons in their area[3]. Where the child is preschool age, the responsibility for the provision of a named person service rests on the health board[4]. The named person is an individual who is an employee of a service provider who has met such requirements as to training, qualifications, experience or position as may be specified by Scottish Ministers[5]. The named person cannot be the parent of the child[6]. Where the named person considers it to be appropriate in order to promote, support or safeguard the well being of the child or young person, the named person can[7]:

(i)    Advise, inform or support the child or young person or their parent;

337

(ii) Help the child or young person or their parent to access a service or support; or

(iii) Discuss or raise, a matter about the child or young person with a service provider or relevant authority.

The responsibility for the exercise of these functions lies with the service provider rather than the named person[8]. Information must be published about the named person's service[9].

It is clear that the purpose of the named person service is to attempt to ensure that a child or young person is helped at an early stage and prevent the child or young person from becoming a child in need. For some this would appear to be a sensible, indeed enlightened, policy, if sufficient resources are available. But since the service is provided to all children and not only those whose families have become or are likely to become dysfunctional, it may be seen as too great an intrusion into family autonomy and a potential breach of Article 8.

Under Part 5 of the CY(P(S)A 2014, if a responsible authority considers that a child has a wellbeing need and the need is not capable of being met except by a targeted intervention, the child will be provided with a child's plan. A child has a wellbeing need if the child's well being is, or is at risk of, being adversely affected by any matter[10]. Assessment of wellbeing is done by reference to the extent to which the child may or would be safe, healthy, achieving, nurtured, active, respected, responsible and included[11]. A targeted intervention is a service provided by a relevant authority directed at meeting the needs of children whose needs cannot be met by the services which are generally provided to children by the authority[12]. In considering whether a child's plan is required, the responsible authority should consult with the child's named person, the child and the child's parents[13]. The plan will contain a statement of the child's wellbeing need and the targeted intervention which is required and the relevant authority who should provide the intervention[14]. In so far as is reasonably practicable the relevant authority must provide the service and secure that the targeted intervention takes place[15]. The plan will be kept under review[16]. Again this might see a sensible policy but again there is an infringement of traditional family autonomy.

By s 12 of the Social Work (Scotland) Act 1968[17] it is the duty of a local authority to make available general advice, guidance and assistance to persons living in its area. Assistance can be given to a relevant person in kind or, in exceptional circumstances constituting an emergency, in cash. A relevant person is any person aged 18 or over.[18] Assistance is generally given in kind. It may be given in cash if to do so would avoid the local authority incurring greater expense in giving assistance to that person in some other way either then or in the future;[19] for example, giving a mother cash to avoid having to look after her child in local authority accommodation. In this way, by helping adult members of their family, the local authority indirectly helps children in need.

By s 22(1) of the Children (Scotland) Act 1995, a local authority is under an obligation:

(a)     to safeguard and promote the welfare of children[20] in its area who are in need; and

(b)     so far as is consistent with that duty, to promote the upbringing of such children by their families so that the children can be helped within their home environment.

In *Crossan v South Lanarkshire Council*[21] it was held that this provision amounted to a *general* duty to provide services with the detailed nature and extent of those services being left to the authority's discretion; it does not oblige local authorities to provide services to individual children in respect of their individual needs. However, the authority has a discretion – not an enforceable obligation – to provide services for a particular child and members of the child's family if it will safeguard or promote the child's welfare to do so.[22] The services may include giving assistance in kind or, in exceptional circumstances, cash. In providing child care services, the local authority should, so far as is practicable, have regard to the child's religion, racial origin and linguistic background.[23]

Information about the services available for children is to be publicised.[24] There is emphasis on co-operation between the local authority, the health boards, national health trusts and other local authorities in the provision of appropriate services.[25] Among its services, a local authority should provide help for physically and mentally disabled children[26] and day care for pre-school age children.[27]

A local authority *may* provide accommodation for any child within its area if it considers that it would safeguard or promote the child's welfare to do so.[28] A local authority *must* provide accommodation for any child, residing or found in its area, if it appears to the local authority that the child requires accommodation because:

(1)   no one has parental responsibility[29] for the child;

(2)   the child is lost or abandoned; or

(3)   the person who has been caring for the child is prevented, whether or not permanently and for whatever reason, from providing the child with suitable accommodation or care.[30]

A 'child' for these purposes is a child who has not attained 18.[31] Before providing a child with accommodation, the local authority, so far as practicable, must have regard to the child's views (if the child wishes to express them) taking account of the child's age and maturity; a child aged 12 or over is presumed to be of sufficient age and maturity to form a view, though the views of younger children should be considered if they *in fact* have sufficient maturity.[32]

It is the policy of the C(S)A 1995 to enable children in need to be supported at home rather than in local authority accommodation. Accordingly, a local authority cannot provide accommodation for a child if any person with parental responsibilities and parental rights[33] objects *and* is willing and able to provide or arrange accommodation for the child.[34] Any such person can remove the child from local authority accommodation at any time.[35] But a child cannot be removed from local authority accommodation if the child is 16 or over and agrees to remain in the local authority accommodation.[36] Where the child is subject to a residence order[37] the child cannot be removed by a person with parental responsibilities and parental rights if the person in whose favour the residence order was made agrees that the child should be looked after in accommodation provided by the local authority.[38] Where a child has been provided with accommodation by a local authority for a continuous period of six months or more, any persons with the relevant parental rights and responsibilities cannot remove the child without having given the local authority at least 14 days' notice in writing of their intention to do so.[39]

The accommodation provided by the local authority can be with foster parents, the child's relatives or any other suitable person but the child cannot be accommodated with any persons who have parental responsibilities or with whom the child has been living.[40] In so far as placement with relatives is concerned, under the Looked After Children (Scotland) Regulations 2009 the local authority can approve a child's relative, for example the child's grandmother, or a person known to the child and with whom the child has a pre-existing relationship as kinship carers[41]. A kinship carer is eligible to receive the same allowances as foster parents. If relative or friend of the child obtains an order under s 11 of the Children (Scotland) Act 1995 under which the child is to reside with them, this is a kinship care order and the local authority has to provide them with kinship care assistance[42]. The child can also be maintained in a residential establishment or other appropriate place.[43]

When a local authority is looking after a child for whom it is providing accommodation, the authority must act to promote and safeguard the child's welfare: this is the paramount consideration.[44] Use can be made of the services available for children who are being cared for by their parents.[45] The services of 'corporate parents', for example a health board, can be used[46]. The authority must take steps to promote personal relationships and direct contact between the child and any person with parental responsibilities provided it is practicable and appropriate to do so.[47] In reaching any decision in relation to the child, the local authority, so far as is reasonably practicable, must ascertain the views of the child, the child's parents, any person with parental rights who is not a parent of the child and any other person whose views the authority considers relevant.[48] The child's views, if any, those of the other persons described above and the child's religion, race, and cultural and linguistic background must all be regarded by the local authority in making its decision.[49] In addition the local authority must have regard to the general principle that its functions should be exercised in relation to children and young people in a way which is designed to safeguard, support and promote their wellbeing[50]. In short all these factors must be fed into the welfare principle which is the paramount consideration.[51] The authority can depart from the welfare principle only if it is necessary for the protection of the public from serious harm.[52] When a child is being looked after by a local authority, the child's case must be reviewed periodically.[53]

It is important to emphasise that this duty to look after the child arises not only when the child has been provided with accommodation under s 25 of the C(S)A 1995, but also when the child is in local authority accommodation as a result of a compulsory supervision order[54] or any order, warrant or authorisation made under the CH(S)A 2011 as a result of which the local authority has responsibilities in respect of the child.[55]

When a child who is at least 16 ceases to be looked after by a local authority, the authority must provide the young person with continuing care[56]. In addition when the child is at least 16 but not yet 19, was on his 16th birthday or at any subsequent time looked after by a local authority, the local authority is under a duty to provide the young person with advice, guidance and assistance when the young person leaves local authority accommodation.[57] Between the ages of 19 and 26, the young person can apply to the local authority for such advice, guidance and assistance; and the local authority may grant the application unless satisfied that the young person's welfare does not require it.[58] The assistance may include assistance in kind or cash.[59] The local authority can also make grants to help such a young person meet expenses in relation to education and training,[60] and can contribute towards the costs of the young person's maintenance and accommodation in any place where the young person is, or is seeking, employment or receiving education or training until the young person is 26.[61] These 'after-care' provisions are important as they help the young person make the difficult transition from the local authority environment to independence in the general community.

The C(S)A 1995 also provides for short-term refuges for children at risk of harm.[62] When a *child* requests refuge and it appears to the local authority (or the manager of a registered residential establishment) that the child is at risk of harm, the local authority may provide the child with accommodation for a period of up to 7 days or, in exceptional circumstances, 14 days. During that period the local authority can determine what further steps should be taken to safeguard and promote the welfare of the child.[63]

---

1   CYP(S)A 2014, s 9(1).
2   On children in need see beyond.
3   CYP(S)A 2014, s 19.
4   CYP(S)A 2014, s 20.
5   CYP(S)A 2014, s 19(2) and (3).
6   CYP(S)A 2014, s 19 (4).
7   CYP(S)A 2014, s 19(5).
8   CYP(S)A 2014, s 19(8).

9    CYP(S)A 2014, s 24.
10   CYP(S)A 2014, s 33(2).
11   CYP(S)A 2014, s 96.
12   CYP(S)A 2014, s 33(4).
13   CYP(S)A 2014, s 33(6).
14   CYP(S)A 2014, s 34.
15   CYP(S)A 2014, s 38.
16   CYP(S) A 2014, s 39.
17   The Social Work (Scotland) Act 1968, s 12.
18   SW(S)A 1968, s 12(2).
19   SW(S)A 1968, s 12(1). Giving assistance in kind or cash is also subject to the provisions in s 12(3), (4) and (5) of the 1968 Act.
20   A child is a person under 18: C(S)A 1995, s 93(2)(a).
21   2006 SLT 441.
22   C(S)A 1995, s 22(3)(a).
23   C(S)A 1995, s 22(2).
24   C(S)A 1995, s 20.
25   C(S)A 1995, s 21.
26   C(S)A 1995, s 23. See *Crossan v South Lanarkshire Council* 2006 SLT 441 where it was held that the provision of such services for an individual child was not an enforceable obligation but a matter for the local authority's discretion. In this case the authority's decision not to provide out of and after school care free of charge to the pursuer's son was not unreasonable.
27   C(S)A 1995, s 27.
28   C(S)A 1995, s 25(2).
29   On parental responsibilities, see **Ch 10.**
30   C(S)A 1995, s 25(1).
31   C(S)A 1995, s 93(2)(a). A local authority *may* provide accommodation for a young person in their area aged between 18 and 21 if it would safeguard or promote that young person's welfare to do so: C(S)A 1995, s 25(3).
32   C(S)A 1995, s 25(5).
33   On parental rights, see **Ch 10**.
34   C(S)A 1995, s 25(6)(a).
35   C(S)A 1995, s 25(6)(b).
36   C(S)A 1995, s 25(7)(a).
37   On residence orders, see para **12.4**.
38   C(S)A 1995, s 25(7)(b).
39   C(S)A 1995, s 25(7).
40   C(S)A 1995, s 26(1)(a).
41   For details see 2009 Regulations, reg 11(2).
42   CYP(S)A 2014, Part 13.
43   C(S)A 1995, s 26(1)(b) and (c).
44   C(S)A 1995, s 17(1)(a). This includes the duty to provide the child with advice and assistance to prepare the child for when he or she is no longer looked after by the local authority: s 17(2). See below.

45   C(S)A 1995, s 17(1)(b).
46   CYP(S)A 2014. For a full list of corporate parents, see Sch 4 to the 2014 Act.
47   C(S)A 1995, s 17(1)(c).
48   C(S)A 1995, s 17(3).
49   C(S)A 1995, s 17(4).
50   C(S)A 1995, s 23A.
51   C(S)A 1995, s 17(1)(a).
52   C(S)A 1995, s 17(5).
53   C(S)A 1995, s 31(1). Where a child is being looked after by a local authority, any natural person who has parental responsibilities must inform the local authority of any change of address: C(S)A 1995, s 18(1).
54   See **Ch 15**.
55   See **Ch 15**.
56   C(S)A 1995, s 26A.
57   C(S)A 1995, s 29(1).
58   C(S)A 1995, s 29(2).
59   C(S)A 1995, s 29(3). The local authority must carry out an assessment of the young person's needs: C(S)A 1995, s 29(5).
60   C(S)A 1995, s 30(1)(a).
61   C(S)A 1995, s 30(1)(b).
62   C(S)A 1995, s 38.
63   A local authority is also under an obligation to safeguard and promote the welfare of a child if the authority receives notice from the managers of a hospital in its area that the parents of a child in the hospital have not been in contact with their child for a continuous period of three months or more (or it is likely that there will be no contact with the child for three months or more taking into account any preceding period of absence of parental contact). On receipt of such notice the local authority must consider what further steps, if any, it should institute under the C(S)A 1995 to safeguard and promote the child's welfare: see C(S)A 1995, s 36.

## THE POWERS OF LOCAL AUTHORITIES

**14.3** We have seen that when children are in need a major objective of the Children (Scotland) Act 1995 is that local authorities should provide services to support children in their family environment.[1] The 1995 Act also gives a local authority the right to apply to the sheriff for a range of court orders to help the local authority fulfil its obligations in respect of children. These orders are discussed in this section.

1   Children (Scotland) Act 1995, s 22(1)(a) and (b).

## The court's duty to consult the child

**14.4** At the outset, it is important to appreciate that in determining any matter relating to the child, the welfare of the child throughout his or her childhood is the paramount consideration of the court.[1] Where a local authority applies to a sheriff for an assessment order,[2] exclusion order,[3] or a permanence order,[4] the sheriff must, so far as is practicable and taking into account of the age and maturity of the child concerned, give the child an opportunity to indicate whether or not he or she wishes to express a view. If the child wishes to express a view, the sheriff must give him or her the opportunity to express that view; and have regard to the view expressed.[5] A child of 12 or more is presumed to be of sufficient age and maturity to form a view, but younger children's views must also be heard if they *in fact* have sufficient age and maturity.[6] This will be referred to as 'the duty to consult'. The importance of the obligation to consult the views of the child cannot be over-emphasised. It is a central policy of the Children (Scotland) Act 1995 that the child at the centre of the judicial proceedings should have the opportunity to state his or her views and that these are fed into the sheriff's decision-making process which is ultimately governed by the welfare principle, the paramount consideration. A sheriff can only depart from the welfare principle if this is necessary for the protection of the public from serious harm.[7] Consonant with the underlying philosophy of the 1995 Act – that help for a child in need should take place within the child's own family environment – the sheriff should not make any order unless satisfied that it would be better for the child that the order be made than that none should be made at all.[8]

---

1 Children (Scotland) Act 1995, s 16(1).
2 See para **14.5**.
3 See para **14.6**.
4 See para **14.7**.
5 C(S)A 1995, s 16(2) and (4)(b)(i).
6 C(S)A 1995, s 16(2) and (4)(b)(i). The court should not grant a child's request that his or her views should be kept confidential unless there is a risk of serious harm to the child should they become known. For discussion, see para **12.5**.
7 C(S)A 1995, s 16(5).
8 C(S)A 1995, s 16(3).

## Child assessment orders

**14.5** In order to safeguard and promote the welfare of children, local authority social workers may require access to the child in order to make an assessment of the child's needs. After the assessment is made, the local authority can determine what steps should be taken to help the child by way of provision of services or taking further proceedings under the Children's Hearings (Scotland) Act 2011.

If the local authority social workers experience difficulties in seeing the child, for example if the child's family denies access, the local authority can apply to a sheriff for a child assessment order.[1] The purpose of this order is to assess the state of the child's health or development or the way in which the child has been treated or neglected. For the purpose of a child assessment order, a child is a person below 16.[2] Before an order can be made the sheriff must be satisfied that:

(1)   the local authority has reasonable cause to suspect that the child is suffering or is likely to suffer *significant* harm as a result of the way the child is being treated or neglected;

(2)   that an assessment is necessary in order to establish whether or not there is reasonable cause to believe that the child is being badly treated or neglected; and

(3)   the local authority is unlikely to be able to make such an assessment unless the order is made.[3]

Nevertheless, the welfare of the child throughout the child's childhood is the paramount consideration.[4] The duty to consult the child applies in proceedings for an assessment order[5] and the sheriff must also be satisfied that it is better to make the order than that none should be made at all.[6]

The sheriff must specify the date on which the assessment is to begin and the period during which the child is to be assessed.[7] This period must begin no later than 24 hours after the order is granted and not exceed three days.[8] An assessment order cannot be renewed. The person who has the child must produce the child, allow the assessment to be carried out and comply with any directions in the order relating to contact.[9] The assessment is carried out by an authorised person, ie the local authority or any person authorised by the local authority, for example a doctor or social worker.[10]

The sheriff has the power to order the child to be taken to any place for the purpose of making the assessment, for example a hospital, and can authorise the child to be kept there for a specified period. During that time, the court can make directions for the child to have contact with any person, for example the child's parents. The assessment will usually involve the medical examination of the child. If the child is under 16 but has capacity to consent under s 2(4) of the Age of Legal Capacity (Scotland) Act 1991,[11] the child's rights are preserved by s 186 of the CH(S)A 2011. Thus the child could refuse to consent to the medical examination.

The order lasts for a maximum period of three days. It may be for this reason that the CH(S)A 2011 does not expressly provide an appeals procedure for such orders. This may appear odd given that the child can be removed from home for the purposes of the assessment. However, it is thought that the normal appeals procedure from an order of a sheriff is available but given the constraints of time an appeal would only be possible where the assessment was not to take place until several weeks after the proceedings in court.

By s 36(3) of the CH(S)A 2011, where an application is made for an assessment order, if the sheriff considers that the conditions exist for making a child protection order, the sheriff may grant a child protection order instead.[12]

After the assessment has taken place, the local authority will be in a position to determine what steps should be taken to help the child. These could include further orders under the C(S)A 1995 or the CH(S)A 2011, referral of the case to a Reporter to arrange a children's hearing[13] or, if practicable, support for the child at home through the provision of services.[14]

---

1   Children's Hearings (Scotland) Act 2011, s 35(1).
2   CH(S)A 2011, s 199(1). Also included is a child between 16 and 18 who is subject to a compulsory supervision order: on compulsory supervision orders, see **Ch 15**.
3   CH(S)A 2011, s 36(2).
4   CH(S)A 2011, s 25.
5   CH(S)A 2011, s 27.
6   CH(S)A 2011, s 29(1)(a) and (2).
7   CH(S)A 2011, s 35(4).
8   CH(S)A 2011, s 35(5).
9   CH(S)A 2011, s 35(3).
10  CH(S)A 2011, s 35(2).
11  Discussed at para **10.2**.

12  On child protection orders, see para **15.2**.
13  On children's hearings, see **Ch 15**.
14  Children (Scotland) Act 1995, s 22(1)(a) and (b).

### Exclusion orders

**14.6** The philosophy underlying an exclusion order is simple viz that where a child is being abused it is better for the alleged abuser to leave the home environment than that the child be removed from home. This is consonant with the aim of the Children (Scotland) Act 1995 that, so far as it is consistent with the local authority's duty to safeguard and promote the child's welfare, a child should be brought up by his or her own family.

A local authority can apply to a sheriff for an order excluding any person named in the order (a named person) from the child's family home.[1] A child for the purpose of an exclusion order is a person below 16.[2] Family home means any house, caravan, houseboat or other structure used as a family residence in which the child ordinarily resides with a person who has parental responsibilities[3] in relation to the child, or who ordinarily has charge of or control over the child: it includes any garden or other ground or building attached to, or usually occupied with, the home.[4]

The sheriff *may* grant an exclusion order if the following conditions are satisfied:

(a)   that the child has suffered, is suffering, or is likely to suffer, *significant* harm as a result of any conduct, or any threatened or reasonably apprehended conduct,[5] of the named person;

(b)   that the making of an exclusion order against the named person—

(i)   is *necessary* for the protection of the child, irrespective of whether the child is for the time being residing in the family home; and

(ii)   would better safeguard the child's welfare than the removal of the child from the family home; and

(c)   that, if an order is made, there will be a person specified in the application who is capable of taking responsibility for the provision of appropriate care for the child and any member of the family who requires care and who is, or will be, residing in the family home (an appropriate person).[6]

Although condition (b) prescribes that the test is 'necessity', unlike the position under s 4 of the Matrimonial Homes (Family Protection) (Scotland) Act 1981,[7] in an application for an exclusion order under the C(S)A 1995, the welfare of the child *is* the paramount consideration.[8] Moreover, in determining whether an exclusion order should be made, the sheriff has a duty to consult the child.[9] In addition, the sheriff cannot make an order unless satisfied that making the order is better than that none should be made at all.[10]

It is difficult to give the appropriate weight to the statutory conditions for an exclusion order within the context of the paramount consideration being the welfare of the child. For if the welfare of the child is indeed paramount, some, at least, of the statutory conditions would be redundant. This issue has not been litigated.[11] What is clear is that an exclusion order can be made even where the child is not residing in the family home at the time of the application thus avoiding the problems initially experienced in relation to exclusion orders under s 4 of the 1981 Act.[12]

An exclusion order cannot be finally determined unless the named person has been afforded an opportunity of being heard or represented before the sheriff, and the sheriff has considered the views of any person on whom notice of the application has been served.[13] If the sheriff is satisfied that the conditions in s 76(2) of the C(S)A 1995 are met but the conditions in s 76(3) are not fulfilled, ie the named person etc has not been heard, the sheriff may grant an interim order which will have the effect of an exclusion order pending a hearing before the sheriff within a period to be specified in rules.[14] At that hearing, the sheriff can confirm or vary the interim order until the case is finally determined.[15] An interim order can be made – even if the conditions in s 76(3) of the 1995 Act are met – at any time before the final determination of the case. Since an exclusion order is defined as including an interim exclusion order,[16] the obligation to consult the child applies in proceedings for such an order.

As a consequence of provisions similar to those in s 4 of the Matrimonial Homes (Family Protection) (Scotland) Act 1981,[17] the sheriff is enjoined *not* to make an exclusion order if it appears to the sheriff that it would be unjustifiable or unreasonable to grant the order having regard to all the circumstances of the case[18] including:

(1)   the conduct of the members of the child's family (whether in relation to each other or otherwise);

(2)   the respective needs and financial resources of the members of the family; and

(3)   the extent, if any, to which the family home and any relevant item in that home is used in connection with a trade, business or profession by any member of the family.[19]

Other relevant factors in this context are whether the named person must reside in the family home because it is or is part of an agricultural holding, or is let to the named person by an employer as an incident of employment. As with s 4 of the 1981 Act, it is difficult to envisage situations where it would be unjustifiable or unreasonable to grant an exclusion order when *ex hypothesi* the sheriff is satisfied that the condition in s 76(2)(b)(i) of the C(S)A 1995 is met, ie the order is *necessary* for the protection of the child.[20] *A fortiori* this would appear to be the case, when we remember that the welfare of the child is the paramount consideration in determining whether or not to make an exclusion order under the 1995 Act.[21]

If in an application for an exclusion order, the sheriff considers that the conditions for a child protection order under Part 5 of the Children's Hearings (Scotland) Act 2011 are satisfied, the sheriff *may* make a child protection order rather than an exclusion order if it is in the child's best interests to do so.[22]

The effect of an exclusion order is to suspend the named person's rights of occupancy[23] (if any) in the family home and to prevent the named person from entering the home except with the express permission of the *local authority* which applied for the order. A wide range of ancillary orders is available;[24] these include:

(1)   a warrant for the summary ejection of the named person from the home;

(2)   an interdict prohibiting the named person from entering the home without the express permission of the local authority;

(3)     an interdict preventing the named person removing any item from the home (ie an item reasonably necessary to enable the home to be used as a family residence);

(4)     an interdict prohibiting the named person from entering or remaining in a specified area in the vicinity of the home;

(5)     an interdict prohibiting the named person from taking any step specified in the interdict in respect of the child, for example meeting the child at school or telephoning the child; and

(6)     an order regulating contact between the child and the named person.[25]

With the exception of an interdict prohibiting the named person from entering the home, the sheriff cannot make any of these ancillary orders if the named person satisfies the sheriff that it is unnecessary to do so.[26] A contact order can be made by the sheriff *ex proprio motu* if it is in the best interests of the child to do so.[27] But it must be remembered that, unless the named person is interdicted from seeing the child, if the named person has parental responsibilities and rights he or she will retain the responsibility and right to have contact with the child on a regular basis and a contact order is strictly not necessary.[28] The local authority may, at any time an exclusion order is in force, apply to the sheriff to have a power of arrest attached to any interdict granted by the sheriff. This power applies to an interim exclusion order as well as a final order. The detailed provisions in respect of powers of arrest are to be found in s 78 of the C(S)A 1995.

A final exclusion order ceases to have effect six months after being made[29] unless the sheriff directed that it should end earlier or any permission given by a third party to the spouse or partner of the named person to occupy the home is withdrawn.[30] 'Partners' are persons who live together as if they were husband and wife.[31]

On the application of the local authority or the named person or an appropriate person (ie a person who has responsibility for the care of the child) or the spouse or partner of the named person (if not excluded from the home or if not an appropriate person), the sheriff may vary or recall an exclusion order or any ancillary order:[32] the welfare of the child is, of course, the paramount consideration. If the exclusion order is recalled, it ceases to have effect.[33]

An exclusion order cannot be renewed. It only allows a breathing space of six months to enable appropriate steps to be taken by the local authority for the long-term support of the child. But because the time limits are so tight it was held in *Glasgow City Council v H*[34] that after an interim exclusion order had lapsed, a fresh application for an exclusion order was not an abuse of process. The crucial role given to local authorities in relation to exclusion orders can be seen as an aspect of their general obligations under the C(S)A 1995 to safeguard and promote the welfare of children in need.

1   Children (Scotland) Act 1995, s 76(1).
2   C(S)A 1995, s 93(2)(b).
3   On parental responsibilities, see **Ch 12**.
4   C(S)A 1995, s 76(12).
5   It can be reasonably apprehended that a Schedule 1 offender will repeat similar offences if he has repeated them in the past and has refused to acknowledge his guilt: *Russell v W* 1998 Fam LR 25. It does not matter that the child is subject to a compulsory supervision order which contains a condition that the named person should not have contact with the child if there is reason to believe that the named person will not comply with it. On Schedule 1 offences, see the Criminal Procedure (Scotland) Act 1995, Schedule 1, and para **15.7**.
6   C(S)A 1995, s 76(2).
7   Discussed at para **5.9**.
8   C(S)A 1995, s 16(1).
9   C(S)A 1995, s 16(2) and (4)(b)(i).
10  C(S)A 1995, s 16(3). This provision appears to make little sense in the context of exclusion orders: *sed quaere*.
11  There is a paucity of reported decisions on C(S)A 1995, s 76. It would appear to be little used. See, however, *Russell v W* 1998 Fam LR 25.
12  For discussion, see para **5.9**.
13  C(S)A 1995, s 76(3).
14  C(S)A 1995, s 76(4).
15  C(S)A 1995, s 76(5).
16  C(S)A 1995, s 76(12).
17  Discussed at para **5.9**.
18  C(S)A 1995, s 76(9).
19  C(S)A 1995, s 76(10).
20  A possible scenario is when other orders are available under the C(S)A 1995 or CH(S)A 2011 that would equally protect the child.
21  Cf the Matrimonial Homes (Family Protection) (Scotland) Act 1981, s 4.
22  C(S)A 1995, s 76(8). On child protection orders, see para **15.2**.
23  On occupancy rights, see **Ch 5**.
24  C(S)A 1995, s 77(3).

25  C(S)A 1995, s 77(3).
26  C(S)A 1995, s 77(4).
27  C(S)A 1995, s 77(6).
28  See generally **Ch 11**.
29  C(S)A 1995, s 79(1). Interim orders also cease after six months: *Glasgow City Council v H* 2004 SC 189.
30  C(S)A 1995, s 79(2)(a) and (c).This provision does not appear to have been amended to include civil partners.
31  C(S)A 1995, s 79(4). Husband and wife include same sex spouses as a result of Marriage and Civil Partnership (Scotland) Act 2014, s 4(1). Therefore same sex couples are included.
32  C(S)A 1995, s 79(3).
33  C(S)A 1995, s 79(2)(b).
34  2004 SC 189.

## Permanence Orders

**14.7**  Although a local authority must endeavour to support a child who is in need within the child's own family environment, situations arise when it is neither practicable nor conducive to the child's welfare to do so. The child's case may be passed to a Reporter to refer the matter to a children's hearing to determine whether the child is in need of a compulsory supervision order.[1] However, the local authority could apply to the court for a permanence order vesting parental responsibilities and rights in respect of the child in the local authority. A permanence order consists of: (a) the mandatory provision; (b) such of the ancillary provisions as the court thinks fit; and (c) if the appropriate conditions are satisfied, a provision granting authority for the child to be adopted.[2]

The mandatory provision vests in the local authority the parental responsibility to provide guidance appropriate to the child's stage of development and the parental right to regulate the child's residence.[3] These are the parental responsibility in s 1(1)(b)(ii) and the parental right under s 2(1)(a) of the C(S)A 1995 respectively. The responsibility lasts until the child reaches the age of 18 and the right until the child reaches the age of 16.[4] When the order is made the parent's s 2(1)(a) right in relation to the child is extinguished.[5]

The ancillary provisions are provisions:

(i)   vesting in the local authority such of the responsibilities to safeguard and promote the child's health, development and welfare, to provide guidance to the child and to act as the child's legal representative; and such of the parental rights to control, direct or guide the child's upbringing, and to act as the child's representative as the court considers appropriate;[6]

(ii)  vesting such of the C(S)A 1995 s 1 parental responsibilities and such of the parental rights mentioned above in a person other than the local authority as the court thinks appropriate.[7] Where parental responsibilities and rights vest in the local authority under (i), or another person under (ii), and the parent still retains parental responsibilities and rights, they can each exercise their parental rights without the consent of the other;[8]

(iii) extinguishing any parental responsibilities and parental rights which immediately before the order was made vested in the child's parent or guardian but which by virtue of s 82(1)(a) or (b) now vest in the local authority or another person.[9] It will be clear that making an ancillary order to extinguish a parent's parental responsibilities and rights is a serious inroad into the parent's right under Article 8 to respect for family life and must be necessary to protect the child from serious harm;

(iv)  specifying arrangements for contact between the child and his or her family where it is in the child's best interests to do so;[10] and

(v)   determining any question in relation to any parental responsibilities and rights and any other aspect of the welfare of the child.[11]

The conditions for an order granting authority for adoption and the effect of granting such authority have already been discussed.[12]

It will be clear that the effect of such an order is that the child will often be removed from home and the local authority will have the right to make the major decisions in relation to the upbringing of the child. In doing so, the local authority must act in accordance with the principles already discussed in the context of the provision of accommodation for children being looked after by the authority.[3] In addition the court can also make an ancillary order extinguishing the child's parents' responsibilities and rights in respect of the child. If a permanence order is made it revokes any existing order relating to parental responsibilities and rights.[13]

Given the potentially drastic effects of such an order on both the child and the parents, it can only be made if one of the following grounds can be established:-

(i)     that there are no persons who have the parental right to have the child living with them.[14] In practice this will arise when the child is an orphan.

(ii)    where there is such a person, the child's residence with that person is, or is likely to be, seriously detrimental to the welfare of the child.[15] It cannot be emphasised too much that this ground will only be satisfied if it would be *seriously* detrimental to the welfare of the child to remain at home with his or her parent. It is not enough that it would be in the child's best interests to be removed from home.

Even when one of the grounds exists, there are further conditions which must be satisfied before an order can be made. The need to safeguard and promote the child's welfare throughout childhood is the paramount consideration in considering whether or not to make an order and what provision the order should contain[16]. Moreover the court cannot make a permanence order unless it considers that it would be better for the child that the order be made than that it should not be made.[17] The views of the child must be taken into consideration[18] and the court should have regard to the child's religious persuasion, racial origin and cultural and linguistic background as well as the likely effect on the child of making the order.[19] There is no hierarchy among these conditions: all of them have a bearing on whether a permanence order should be made[20].

Where the child is aged 12 or over, a permanence order cannot be made unless the child consents.[21] While a permanence order can be made in respect of a child who is adopted, it cannot be made in respect of a child who is or has been married or is or has been a civil partner.[22]

In proceedings for a permanence order, the court must allow representations from the local authority, the child, the child's parents and any person who claims an interest.[23] These persons can also apply for the variation of ancillary provisions in a permanence order[24] but apart from a local authority, they must obtain the leave of court to do so.[25] Leave must be granted if there has been a material change of circumstances or that for any other reason it is proper to allow the application to be made.[26]

A local authority and any of these persons with leave of court can apply to have a permanence order revoked. The court will revoke the order if satisfied it is appropriate to do so in all the circumstances of the case including in particular any material change of circumstances directly relating to any of the order's provisions and any wish by the parents to have their parental responsibilities and rights reinstated.[27] If the court revokes a permanence order, it must consider whether or not to make an order under section 11 of C(S)A 1995 imposing parental responsibilities on and giving parental rights to any person, for example a step-parent of the child.[28]

---

1    On compulsory supervision orders, see **Ch 15**.
2    Adoption and Children (Scotland) Act 2007, s 80(1).
3    AC(S)A 2007, s 81(1).
4    AC(S)A 2007, s 81 (2).
5    AC(S)A 2007, s 87.
6    AC(S)A 2007, s 82(1)(a).
7    AC(S)A 2007, s 82(1)(b).
8    AC(S)A 2007, s 91.
9    AC(S)A 2007, s 82(1)(c) and (d).
10   AC(S)A 2007, s 82(1)(e).
11   AC(S)A 2007, s 82(1)(f).
12   See para **13.13**.
13   AC(S)A 2007, s 88.
14   AC(S)A 2007, s 84(5)(c)(i).
15   AC(S)A 2007, s 84(5)(c)(ii). See *W v Aberdeen Council* [2012] CSIH 37, 2013 SC 108.
16   AC(S)A 2007, s 84(4). See *West Lothian Council Petitioner* [2014] CSOH 73 In *Dumfries and Galloway Council Petitioner* 2013 GWD 31-62, the sheriff said at para 20 'if the order sought would best promote and safeguard the child's welfare it is difficult to see how it would not be necessary to make the order unless, of course, what the order sought to achieve would happen without it. Not to do so would be to disregard the paramountcy of the child's welfare. So in that sense, the section 84(4) welfare test is one of necessity'.
17   AC(S)A 2007, s 84(3) See *Midlothian Council v M* [2013] CSIH 71, 2014 SC 168.
18   AC(S)A 2007, s 84(5)(a) and (b)(i).
19   AC(S)A 2007, s 84(5)(b)(ii) and (iii).
20   *W v Aberdeenshire Council* {2012] CSIH 37, 2013 SC 108.

21  AC(S)A 2007, s 84(1). The child's consent is not necessary if the child is incapable of consenting: s 84(2).
22  AC(S)A 2007, s 85(1) and (2).
23  AC(S)A 2007, s 86(1) and (2).
24  AC(S)A 2007, s 92.
25  AC(S)A 2007, s 94(4).
26  AC(S)A 2007, s 94(5).
27  AC(S)A 2007, s 98.
28  AC(S)A 2007, s 100.

## Parenting Orders

**14.8** As we shall see[1] when a child commits a criminal offence, this will usually result in the child being referred to a children's hearing. However, under the Antisocial Behaviour Etc (Scotland) Act 2004,[2] a local authority or the Principal Reporter can apply for a parenting order in respect of the parent of the child.[3]

When a local authority applies, the court must be satisfied that either the behaviour or the conduct condition is satisfied.[4] The behaviour condition is that the child has engaged in antisocial behaviour and that the making of the order is desirable in the interests of preventing the child from engaging further in such conduct.[5] The conduct condition is that the child has engaged in criminal conduct and that the making of the order is desirable in the interests of preventing the child from engaging further in such conduct.[6] For this purpose a child engages in criminal conduct if the conduct constitutes a criminal offence or would do so if the child had attained the age of eight.[7]

When the application is brought by the Principal Reporter in addition to the behaviour or conduct conditions, the Principal Reporter can also rely on the welfare condition, viz that the making of the order is desirable in the interests of improving the welfare of the child.[8] Before an application is brought by a local authority, it must consult the Principal Reporter and vice versa when the application is brought by the Principal Reporter.[9]

Before a parenting order can be made the court must give the child an opportunity to express his or her views.[10] The parents must also be given the opportunity to be heard.[11] The court must also obtain information about the family circumstances of the parent and the likely effect of the order on those circumstances.[12] It must also explain in ordinary language the effect of the order and any requirements proposed to be included, the consequences of failing to comply with the order and the right of the parent to appeal against the making of the order.[13]

When determining whether to make the order, the paramount consideration is the welfare of the child.[14] The court must also have regard to: (i) the child's views; (ii) the information about the family circumstances; (iii) whether the parent has taken 'relevant voluntary steps' viz steps to prevent the child engaging in antisocial behaviour or criminal conduct or which were intended to improve the child's welfare; and any other behaviour of the parent that appears to be relevant.[15] In so far as practicable the court must ensure that the requirements of the parenting order avoid any conflict with the religious beliefs of the parent or any interference with the times at which the parent normally works or attends an educational establishement.[16]

When the order is made, the parent must comply with its requirements during a specified period beginning with the making of the order and not exceeding 12 months: this includes a requirement to attend such counselling or guidance sessions as may be directed by an officer appointed by the local authority within the first three months of the specified period.[17] If the parent fails without reasonable excuse to comply with any requirements or directions, the parent is guilty of a criminal offence.[18]

A parenting order can be varied or revoked on an application by the parent, the child or local authority.[19] Similar principles apply to the variation or revocation of a parenting order as to the making of such an order.[20]

It will be seen that a parenting order is directed at the child's parents not the child. Yet the welfare of the child remains the paramount consideration when making, varying or revoking such an order. It is an attempt to help a child whose behaviour has been antisocial or criminal by supporting the parents to fulfil their parental responsibilities rather than removing the child from the family environment.

---

1   **Ch 15**.

2   ABE(S)A 2004, s 102(1).
3   Parent is defined as any parent having parental responsibilities and rights in respect
    of the child, any person in whom parental responsibilities and rights have vested, any
    person in whom parental responsibilities and rights have vested under a permanence
    order, any person who appears to be a person who ordinarily (and other than by reason
    only of his employment) has charge of or control over the child: ABE(S)A 2004, s 117
    and C(S)A 1995, s 93(2)(b).
4   ABE(S)A 2004, s 102(20).
5   ABE(S)A 2004, s 102(4).
6   ABE(S)A 2004, s 102(5).
7   ABE(S)A 2004, s 102(7).
8   ABE(S)A 2004, s 102(30) and (6).
9   ABE(S)A 2004, s 102(9).
10  ABE(S)A 2004, s 108(1)(a): a child aged 12 or more is presumed to be of sufficient
    age and maturity to form a view: ABE(S)A 2004, s 108(6).
11  ABE(S)A 2004, s 108(1)(b).
12  ABE(S)A 2004, s 108(1)(c).
13  ABE(S)A 2004, s 108(2).
14  ABE(S)A 2004, s 109(1).
15  ABE(S)A 2004, s 109(2)–(6).
16  ABE(S)A 2004, s 110.
17  ABE(S)A 2004, s 103.
18  ABE(S)A 2004, s 107.
19  ABE(S)A 2004, s 105.
20  ABE(S)A 2004, s 109(3).

# Chapter 15

# Children in need: emergency procedures and compulsory supervision orders

## INTRODUCTION

**15.1** We have been discussing the obligations and powers of a local authority to provide support for children. As we have seen, the local authority should endeavour to safeguard and promote the child's welfare by providing support within the child's home environment. As such, the child and the child's family voluntarily accept the local authority's help through its social work department.[1] However, circumstances can arise where it is not possible to provide support for a child on a voluntary basis and the only way to safeguard and promote the child's welfare is through *compulsory* supervision of the child.

In Scots law, compulsory supervision orders are made by a children's hearing.[2] A child's case is referred to a children's hearing by a Reporter[3] to the children's panel who acts independently of any local authority. In this chapter we shall examine the operation of this system.[4] At the outset, it is important to emphasise that in deciding any matter in relation to a child, the welfare of the child throughout his or her childhood is the paramount consideration of the children's hearing.[5] A children's hearing can only depart from the welfare principle if this is necessary to protect the public from serious harm and even here the welfare of the child is the primary, as opposed to the paramount, consideration.[6] Moreover, as a general rule when reaching its decision, the children's hearing is under the same obligation to consult the child as a sheriff when making a court order.[7] The children's hearing is also enjoined not to make a compulsory supervision order unless the hearing considers that it would be better for the child to make the order than that none should be made at all.[8]

---

1    An exception is, of course, a permanence order.
2    On the constitution of children's hearings, see para **15.6**.

361

3    The Children's Hearing (Scotland) Act 2011 refers to 'the Principal Reporter', but this includes other officers of the Scottish Children's Reporter Administration to whom the Principal Reporter's functions are delegated, ie Reporters: CH(S)A 2011, Sch 3, para 10.
4    On the role of the Reporter in the system, see para **15.4** below.
5    CH(S)A 2011, s 25(2).
6    CH(S)A 2011, s 26.
7    CH(S)A 20110, s 27(3). A child aged 12 or over is presumed to be of sufficient age and maturity to form a view: CH(S)A 2011, s 27(4). On the obligation to consult, see para **14.4**.
8    CH(S)A 2011, s 28(1) and (2).

## EMERGENCY PROCEDURES: CHILD PROTECTION ORDERS

**15.2** Situations can arise where it is necessary to act quickly to protect a child from serious ill-treatment by removing the child to a place of safety. A Reporter can then consider whether the child is in need of a compulsory supervision order and, if so, arrange a children's hearing. A child for these purposes is a person below 16.[1]

On an application by a local authority or any other person (for example, a police constable or a local authority) a sheriff *may* make a child protection order if satisfied that:

(a)    there are reasonable grounds to believe that:

(i)     the child has been or is being treated in such a way that the child is suffering or is likely to suffer significant harm,

(ii)    the child has been or is being neglected and as a result of the neglect the child is suffering or is likely to suffer significant harm,

(iii)   the child is likely to suffer significant harm if the child is not removed to and kept in a place of safety,

(iv)   the child is likely to suffer significant harm if the child does not remain in the place at which the child is staying (whether or not the child is resident there) and

(b)    the order is *necessary* to protect the child from that harm or from further harm.[2]

When the applicant is a local authority, a sheriff *may* also make a child protection order if satisfied that:

(a)   the local authority has reasonable grounds to suspect that

(i)   the child has been or is being treated in such a way that the child is suffering or is likely to suffer significant harm,

(ii)   the child has been or is being neglected and as a result of the neglect the child is suffering or is likely to suffer significant harm, or

(iii)   the child will be treated or neglected in such a way that is likely to cause significant harm to the child.

(b)   the local authority is making enquiries to allow it to decide whether to take action to safeguard the welfare of the child, or is causing those enquiries to be made,

(c)   those enquiries are being frustrated by access being unreasonably denied, and

(d)   the local authority has reasonable cause to believe that access is required as a matter of urgency.[3]

It should be noted that, theoretically at least, the sheriff has a discretion whether or not to make the order. The application must identify the applicant and, where it is practicable, the child concerned; state the grounds for the application; and be accompanied by supporting evidence.[4] As soon as practicable after the child protection order has been made, the applicant must give notice to the person required to produce the child, each relevant person in relation to the child,[5] the relevant local authority if the local authority is not the applicant, the Reporter and any other person to whom the applicant is required to give notice under rules of court. When the Reporter receives such notice, the Reporter must give notice of the order to any person other than a relevant person whom the Reporter considers to have or recently have had a significant involvement in the upbringing of the child.[6]

The effect of the order is to require any person in a position to do so to produce the child and to authorise the removal of the child to a place of safety[7] (or prevent the child being removed from the place the child is currently being accommodated): it also authorises an assessment of the child's health or development and the way in which the child has been or is being treated or neglected.[8] The order can include an information non-disclosure direction under which the location of the place of safety or any other information is not be disclosed to any person specified in the order.[9] An applicant's actions in respect of the child are restricted to those acts the applicant believes are necessary to safeguard or promote the welfare of the child.[10]

The sheriff must consider whether to include a contact direction in the order. A contact direction can prohibit contact between the child and the child's parent, or any person with parental responsibilities and any specified person or class of persons; it may also direct contact between the child and such persons subject to any conditions which the sheriff considers appropriate to safeguard and promote the welfare of the child.[11] The applicant may apply for a direction in relation to the fulfilment of parental responsibilities and the exercise of parental rights in relation to the treatment of the child arising out of any assessment authorised by the order or any other matter the sheriff considers appropriate.[12] Such a direction can authorise a medical examination of, and related treatment for, the child but if the child has capacity under s 2(4) of the Age of Legal Capacity (Scotland) Act 1991,[13] no examination or treatment can take place if the child refuses to consent.[14]

Unless the Reporter has received notice of an application to set aside or vary the protection order,[15] the Reporter must arrange a children's hearing to determine whether or not the protection order should continue.[16] This initial children's hearing must take place on the second working day after the order has been made.[17] If satisfied the conditions for making a child protection order are established, the children's hearing can continue the order and any directions (with or without variations) until a second children's hearing can be arranged to consider whether or not the child is in need of a compulsory supervision order.[18] This second hearing must take place on the eighth working day after the order was made. The duty to consult the child does *not* arise where the sheriff is deciding whether or not to make a child protection order.[19]

When a child is removed to a place of safety provided by a local authority, the local authority has the same duties towards the child as if the authority was looking after the child by virtue of s 17 of the Children (Scotland) Act 1995.[20]

An application can also be made by any person to a justice of the peace for an order requiring any person who can do so to produce the child and for authorisation to remove a child to, or prevent the child's removal from, a place of safety.[21] The justice of the peace must be satisfied that the conditions for a child protection order are met and that it is not practicable in the circumstances for an application for a child protection order to be made to a sheriff.[22] This is an emergency procedure; the duty to consult the child does not arise. The authorisation ceases after 12 hours if arrangements have not been made to remove the child to, or prevent the child's removal from, a place of safety.[23] Where these steps have been taken, the authorisation ceases after 24 hours or when an application to a sheriff for a child protection order has been disposed of, if earlier.[24] In other words, it is essential to apply to a sheriff for a child protection order as soon as possible within the 24 hours that the authorisation lasts and that steps are taken to protect the child within 12 hours of the authorisation being granted.

A police constable has the power to remove a child to a place of safety if the grounds for a child protection order are met and the removal of the child is necessary to protect the child from harm and it is not practicable in the circumstances for an application to be made to a sheriff for such an order.[25] As soon as practicable the constable must inform the Reporter that the child has been removed.[26] A child may not be kept in a place of safety under this provision for more than 24 hours,[27] during that period the Reporter can apply for a child protection order.

There is no appeal from the sheriff's decision to grant a child protection order or the decision of the initial children's hearing to continue the order. However, an application can be made to a sheriff to terminate or vary the protection order and directions (if any): this must be done *before* the initial children's hearing has commenced to consider whether or not the order should be continued.[28] An application can also be made to a sheriff to set aside (or vary) a decision of the initial children's hearing that the order and directions (if any) should continue: this must be done within two working days of the hearing's decision.[29] The application can be brought by the child; a relevant person; any person not being a relevant person who has, or recently has had, a significant involvement in the upbringing of the child; the person who had applied for the child protection order; the person specified in the order to produce the child; the Reporter and any other person prescribed by rules of court.[30] Notice of the application must also be given to these persons.[31] The Reporter can then arrange a children's hearing to provide advice for the sheriff hearing the application.[32]

Before determining the application the sheriff must give the following persons the opportunity to make representations: the applicant; the child; each relevant person; any person who is not a relevant person ie who the sheriff considers to have or recently has had a significant involvement in the child's upbringing; the applicant for the child protection order; the relevant local authority if not the applicant for the child protection order and the Reporter. The sheriff must make the determination within three working days after the day on which it was made otherwise the order ceases to have effect. The sheriff will terminate the order if the sheriff is not satisfied that the conditions for a child protection order are not met.[33] If they are met, the order and any directions can be varied or the child protection order can simply be confirmed.[34]

A child protection order ceases to have effect in the following circumstances:

(1)     if no attempt has been made to implement the order by the end of 24 hours of a child protection order being made;

(2)     where the initial children's hearing does not continue the order;

(3)     where an application to have the order terminated or varied is not determined timeously, ie within three days of the application;

(4)     where a sheriff terminates the order;

(5)     where the Reporter considers that the conditions for a child protection order are no longer satisfied and the person who implemented the order or the applicant has received notice of the Reporter's decision;

(6)     where the Reporter decides not to arrange a second children's hearing to determine whether the child is in need of a compulsory supervision order and the person who implemented the order or the applicant has received notice of the Reporter's decision;

(7) where a child protection order has been continued, on the commencement of a second children's hearing to consider whether the child is in need of a compulsory supervision order;

(8) where a child protection order contains the authorisation to remove the child to a place of safety, the end of 8 working days beginning on the day after the day on which the child was removed to the place of safety;[35]

(9) where the order does not contain such authorisation, the end of eight working days beginning on the day after the day on which the order was made.[36]

Child protection orders have been discussed in considerable detail. The reason for doing so is that these orders deprive the child of his or her family and parents of their child. They are paradigmatic of the tension inherent in any system of child protection law between the autonomy of the family and the obligation of the state to intervene in order to protect a child. Unless the procedures are fair and recognise the interests of the child and the family, there could be a violation of Article 5 (right to liberty), Article 8 (right to respect for private and family life) or Article 6 (right to a fair trial) of the European Convention on Human Rights. In the Children's Hearings (Scotland) Act 2011, the Scottish Parliament has enacted a complex system of strict time limits, hearings and reviews in order to balance these two potentially competing interests. In particular, they ensure that the parents of the child involved are given an opportunity to be heard within a reasonable time of the child being removed.[37].

---

1    Children Hearings (Scotland) Act 2011, s 199(1). Also included is a child between 16 and 18 who is already subject to a compulsory supervision order: CH(S)A 2011, s 199(6) and (7).

2    CH(S)A 2011, s 39(2).

3    CH(S)A 2011, s 38(2).

4    CH(S)A 2011, s 37(5).

5    On relevant persons see para **15.5**.

6    CH(S)A 2011, s 43(1) and (2).

7    A place of safety is a residential or other establishment provided by a local authority, a community home, a police station, a hospital or surgery whose management is willing temporarily to receive the child, the dwelling house of a suitable person or any other suitable place the occupier of which is willing to receive the child: CH(S)A 2011 s 202. A child may be kept or detained in a police station only if it is not reasonably practicable to keep or detain the child in a place of safety which is not a police station: steps must

be taken to identify a place of safety which is not a police station and transfer the child to that place as soon as is reasonably practicable: CH(S)A 2011, s 189C.

8   CH(S)A 2011, s 37(2).
9   CH(S)A 2011, s 40.
10  C(S)A 2011, s 58(1) and (2).
11  CH(S)A 2011, s 41.
12  CH(S)A 2011, s 42.
13  Discussed at para **10.2**.
14  CH(S)A 2011, s 186.
15  CH(S)A 2011, ss 45(1)(c) and 46(1)(c).
16  CH(S)A 2011, ss 45(2) and 46(2). This is known as 'an initial hearing'.
17  CH(S)A 2011, ss 45(3) and 46(3).
18  CH(S)A 2011, s 47. If not satisfied that the conditions are met, the hearing terminates the order.
19  CH(S)A 2011, s 27(2).
20  CH(S)A 2011, s 44. On s 17 of C(S)A 1995, see para **14.2**.
21  CH(S)A 2011, s 55(1).
22  CH(S)A 2011, s 55(2).
23  CH(S)A 2011, s 55(4).
24  CH(S)A 2011, s 55(5).
25  CH(S)A 2011, s 56(1).
26  CH(S)A 2011, s 56(2).
27  CH(S)A 2011, s 56(3).
28  CH(S)A 2011, s 48(3)(a).
29  CH(S)A 2011, s 48(3)(b).
30  CH(S)A 2011, s 48(1) and (2). The Reporter cannot bring an application to have the order terminated as opposed to varied: CH(S)A 2011, s 48(2).
31  CH(S)A 2011, s 49.
32  CH(S)A 2011, s 50.
33  CH(S)A 2011, s 51(5)(a).
34  CH(S)A 2011, s 51(5)(b) and (c).
35  CH(S)A 2011, s 54(c).
36  CH(S)A 2011, s 54(d).
37  A child protection order was made in *City of Edinburgh Council v C* 2012 GWD 38-758 on the basis of the parents' unstable and volatile relationship and their abuse of alcohol and drugs.

## COMPULSORY SUPERVISION ORDERS

### Information that a child may be in need of a compulsory supervision order

**15.3** We have been considering the situation where a child enters the children's hearing system as a result of a child protection order. This is an emergency procedure which should only be used in exceptional circumstances. The more usual route is that the Reporter receives information that a child may be in need of a compulsory supervision order. Any person who considers that a child is in need of protection, guidance, treatment or control and that it might be necessary for a compulsory supervision order to be made in relation to the child may inform a Reporter[1]. A police constable is obliged to inform the Reporter if the constable considers that a child needs a compulsory supervision order.[2] If a local authority acquires information, for example from social workers, that a child may be in need of a compulsory supervision order, the local authority must make all necessary inquiries into the child's circumstances and give the information to the Reporter.[3]

A court also has the power to refer a case to the Principal Reporter, if during relevant proceedings[4] it is satisfied that one (or more) of the grounds of referral for a compulsory supervision order[5] – other than the commission by the child of an offence – exists.[6] Where criminal proceedings are not to be proceeded with against a child who has been detained in a place of safety, a police constable must inform the Reporter who can direct that the child be released from the place of safety or that the child remain there until the Reporter determines whether or not the child requires a compulsory supervision order.[7]

Under s 12(1A) of the Antisocial Behaviour etc (Scotland) Act 2004, if the sheriff makes an antisocial behaviour order and considers that a ground of referral – other than the offence ground – has been established, the sheriff can require the Principal to arrange a children's hearing.[8] Where a child or another person has pled guilty or been found guilty of a criminal offence, the court can remit the case to the Principal Reporter to arrange for the disposal of the case by a children's hearing.[9]

---

1   Children's Hearings (Scotland) Act 2011, s 64.
2   CH(S)A 2011, s 61.
3   CH(S)A 2011, s 60. This could involve the application for a child assessment order: for discussion, see para **14.5**.
4   That is actions for divorce, separation, declarators of marriage, nullity of marriage, dissolution or declarator of nullity of a civil partnership or separation of civil partners, declarators of parentage or non-parentage, proceedings in relation to parental responsibilities and rights, applications for adoption orders or permanence orders, proceedings in relation to offences under the Education (Scotland) Act 1980 and

an application for a forced marriage protection order under the Forced Marriage etc (Protection and Jurisdiction) (Scotland) Act 2011: CH(S)A 2011, s 62(5).
5     On these grounds, see para **15.7**.
6     CH(S)A 2011, s 62(1).
7     CH(S)A 2011, s 65. The Lord Advocate may direct that in any specified case or class of case that evidence lawfully obtained in the investigation of a crime or suspected crime be given to the Principal Reporter: CH(S)A 2011, s 63.
8     CH(S)A 2011, s 70. For the purposes of the children's hearing the ground is to be taken as established.
9     Criminal Procedure (Scotland) Act, s 49. For the purposes of the children's hearing this is to be taken as conclusive evidence that the offence committed by the child or the other person: CH(S)A 2011, s 71.

## The role of the Reporter

**15.4** When a child has entered the system by the routes described above, the decision whether or not to refer the case to a children's hearing is that of the Reporter. The Reporter (an officer of the Scottish Children's Reporter Administration) acts independently.[1] The Reporter who need not have a legal background has the right of audience before a sheriff or sheriff principal.[2]

After having received the information, if it appears to the Reporter that a child might be in need of protection, guidance, treatment or control, the Reporter must determine whether or not grounds of referral exist and if so whether it is necessary for a compulsory supervision order to be made.[3] If the Reporter takes the view that no ground of referral exists or it is not necessary for a compulsory order to be made, the Reporter must inform the child, each relevant person, the relevant local authority, any person specified in a child protection order and the persons who provided the information, of the decision not to proceed.[4] If the Reporter considers that the family may be able to benefit from social work support, the Reporter can refer the case to the relevant local authority to provide advice, guidance and assistance to the child and the family.[5] If the child is being kept in a place of safety, the Reporter must arrange for the child's release.[6]

However, if the Reporter feels that the child is in need of a compulsory supervision order, it is the Reporter's duty to arrange a children's hearing to consider the case[7] and to call upon the local authority for a report on the child and the child's social background. As we shall see, the Reporter has important powers and duties in relation to the conduct of the children's hearing and subsequent proceedings. The Reporter is, in effect, the lynchpin of the whole system and the importance of the Reporter's role cannot be over-emphasised.

---

1 Children's Hearings (Scotland) Act 2011, s 22.
2 CH(S)A 2011, s 19.
3 CH(S)A 2011, s 66.
4 CH(S)A 2011, s 68(3) and(4).
5 CH(S)A 2011, s 68(5).
6 CH(S)A 2011, s 68(2).
7 CH(S)A 2011, s 69(2). If the child is being kept in a place of safety under s 43 of the Criminal Procedure (Scotland) Act 1995 the hearing must take place no later than the third day after the reporter has received the information from the constable: CH(S)A 2011, s 69(3).

---

## The child and relevant persons

**15.5** A child is a person who is under the age of 16 (or between the ages of 16 and 18 if already subject to a supervision requirement).[1] The child must be present in Scotland at the date of the referral.[2]

A 'relevant person' includes:[3]

(a) a parent or guardian having parental responsibilities or parental rights in relation to the child. However it is expressly provided that a parent does not have parental responsibilities and rights for this purpose merely by virtue of having a contact order or a specific issue order under sections 11(2)(d) or (e) of the Children (Scotland) Act 1995.[4] Read literally this means that a father of a child is not a relevant person under this provision unless he has parental responsibilities and rights. Nor does he qualify as a relevant person under this provision even if he has a contact order in his favour. However in *Principal Reporter v K*[5] the Supreme Court held that where an unmarried father had established family life with the child, to deny him the status of a relevant person amounted to a breach of his Article 8 right to family life. Therefore to avoid any incompatibility with the ECHR, the Court used section 3 of the Human Rights Act 1998 to construe the definition of a relevant person in s 93(2)(b) of the Children

(Scotland) Act 1995 – which was then the relevant legislation – in such a way as to include a father who had established family life with his child as a relevant person.

In order to avoid a breach of Article 8 the Scottish Ministers have provided in regulations[6] that all parents are within the definition of relevant persons (except those whose parental responsibilities and parental rights have been removed by court order).

(b)      a person in whom parental responsibilities or parental rights are vested under s 11(2)(b) of the Children (Scotland) Act 1995 viz an order imposing on a person parental responsibilities and giving parental rights. This is the way that a child's relative, for example the child's grandmother, should proceed.

(c)      a person having parental responsibilities or parental rights under section 11(12) of the Children (Scotland) Act 1995 viz a person who has relevant responsibilities and rights by virtue of a residence order under s 11(2)(c).

(d)      A person in whom parental responsibilities or parental rights are vested by virtue of a permanence order.

(e)      Any other person specified by order made by Scottish Ministers.

A specific issue order cannot be made for the purpose of enabling a person to qualify as a relevant person.

However, a person *must be deemed* to be a relevant person if a pre-hearing panel[7] considers that that person has or has recently had a significant involvement in the upbringing of the child.[8] In *AG v Principal Reporter*[9] the sheriff observed[10] 'Note the word "must". The pre-hearing has no discretion once it is considered that there is or has recently been a significant involvement in the upbringing of the child or children.' The panel is not concerned with whether or not it is in the best interests of the child to deem the individual to be a relevant person. The test is purely factual rather than judgmental. Nevertheless, it is not sufficient that the person has had some involvement in the child's upbringing. The involvement must have been significant so that the person's views are important when considering the welfare of the child.[11]

The issue must be referred to the pre-hearing panel by the Principal Reporter at the request of the child or a relevant person in relation to the child or by the individual concerned.[12] So for example the child's grandmother may be deemed to be a relevant person by a pre-hearing panel if she is playing a significant part in the upbringing of the child. If a person is deemed to be a relevant person, that person will have the right and duty to participate in subsequent hearings. The case can be referred back to the pre-hearing panel to consider whether a person should no longer be deemed to be a relevant person[13].

There is a right of appeal to the sheriff from the pre-hearing panel's decision whether or not an individual should be deemed to be a relevant person.[14]

---

1   Children's Hearings (Scotland) Act 2011, s 199. In relation to failure to attend school, a child includes a person over 16 who is not over school age. Where the case has been remitted to the Principal reporter under s 49 of the Criminal Procedure (Scotland) Act 1995, a child is any person up to the age of 18.
2   *Mitchell v S* 2000 SC 334.
3   CH(S)A 2011, s 200(1). Also included are parent and persons having parental responsibility under the Children Act 1989 and the Adoption and Children Act 2002.
4   CH(S)A 2011, s 200(2).
5   [2010] UKSC 56, [2011]1 WLR 18.
6   The Children's Hearings (Review of Contact Directions and Definition of Relevant Persons) Order 2013, art 3.
7   The panel consists of three members of the Children's Panel selected by the National Convener.
8   CH(S)A 2011, s 81(3).
9   [2013 SLT (Sh Ct) 125 (Foster parents deemed to be relevant persons).
10  Ibid at para 3.
11  *MP v Elizabeth Templeton* [2014] CSIH 66.
12  CH(S)A 2011, s 79(2).
13  CH(S)A 2011, ss 79(5A) and 81A; *F v Principal Reporter* 2014 GWD 13-235.
14  CH(S)A 2011, s 160(2). See, for example, *MP v Elizabeth Templeton* [2014] CSIH 66.

---

## The children's hearing

**15.6** Whether or not a child is in need of a compulsory supervision order and, if so, what steps should be taken to promote the child's welfare, are prima facie issues for a children's hearing. The National Convener of Children's Hearings Scotland is an independent officer who selects members of the children's hearing from the Children's Panel whose members have in turn been appointed by the National Convener and includes persons from all local authority areas.[1] The children's hearing consists of three members of the Children's Panel and the National Convener must ensure that it includes both male and female members and so far as practicable consists only of members who live and work in the local authority which is relevant for the child concerned in the hearing.[2] The National Convener may select one of the members of the children's hearing to chair the hearing.[3]

While the National Convener may provide advice to the children's hearings about any matter in connection with carrying out their functions, for example, advice on the law, procedural matters, the consequences of their decisions and how they are to be implemented, neither the National Convener nor the Principal Reporter can direct or guide the hearings on how they carry out their functions in a particular case.[4] In other words, the children's hearing is independent.

The members of the Children's Panel are ordinary members of the public who have a knowledge of, and an interest in, children and who are anxious to help children in need of help and support. The National Convener makes arrangements for the training of panel members and potential panel members. The training should involve persons under the age of 25 who have had experience of a children's hearing. In particular, the training must have regard to how panel members can best elicit the views of children. The performance of panel members is monitored by the National Convener.[5]

A children's hearing was not intended to be a court. Its proceedings were relatively informal and conducted in private with the Reporter, the child and any relevant person usually present. Although the child and any relevant person had the right to legal representation, this was not encouraged.[6] The basic rules of evidence applied[7] but in exceptional circumstances the rules of natural justice were suspended in the interests of the child.[8] In *S v Miller*,[9] the system was challenged on the ground that it was incompatible with Article 6 of the European Convention on Human Rights.[10] The Inner House held that where the ground of referral was that the child had committed an offence,[11] the child was *not* being charged with an offence. Consequently, the mandatory protections of Article 6(3) did not apply. But the court held that in every referral a child is entitled to a fair hearing under Article 6(1) of the European Convention. To avoid a violation of Article 6(1), the Lord President (Rodger) considered that the child was entitled to legal representation (and legal aid) at the hearing if:

(1)    the child might be held in secure accommodation;[12]

(2)    the case involved difficult issues of fact and law;

(3)    because of his age or intelligence, it was difficult for the child to understand the issues involved; or

(4)    the child could not present an effective case and therefore was unable to exercise his right of access to justice.

The opportunity was taken in the Children's Hearing (Scotland) Act 2011 to introduce a child's advocacy service to provide a child with support and representation[13] and to amend the Legal Aid (Scotland) Act 1986 so that children may receive legal aid and legal assistance.[14] Detailed procedural rules are to be introduced.[15] These developments introduce a far greater degree of legal formality into the system and are no doubt necessary to ensure conformity with the ECHR: but it is a far cry from the original conception of a welfare based system of justice for juveniles administered by lay persons.

On the other hand, a children's hearing (and a sheriff) must consider whether to appoint a person to safeguard the interests of the child.[16] The safeguarder can be legally qualified. The safeguarder will then prepare a report setting out anything that, in the opinion of the safeguarder, is relevant to the consideration of the matter before the children's hearing.[17]

---

1   Children's Hearings (Scotland) Act 2011, ss 1, 2, 4 and 6(2).
2   CH(S)A 2011, ss 5 and 6(3)(a) and (b). The relevant local authority is the local authority where the child predominantly resides or where the child does not predominantly live in the area of a particular local authority, the local authority with which the child has the closest connection: CH(S)A 2011, s 201.
3   CH(S)A 2011, s 6(4).
4   CH(S)A 2011, ss 8 and 9.
5   CH(S)A 2011, Sch 2 para 3.
6   C(S)A 1995, s 42(2)(i). Legal aid was not available.
7   *Kennedy v B* 1973 SLT 38; *F v Kennedy (No 2)* 1993 SLT 1284.
8   *Kennedy v A* 1986 SLT 358 at 362, per the Lord Justice-Clerk (Ross).
9   2001 SLT 531. See also *S v Miller (No 2)* 2001 SLT 1304.
10  The text of Article 6 is to be found at para **14.1**.
11  See para **15.7**.
12  On secure accommodation, see para **15.10**.
13  CH(S)A 2011, s 122.

14   CH(S)A 2011, Part 19.
15   CH(S)A 2011, s 177.
16   CH(S)A 2011, ss 30 and 31.
17   CH(S)A 2011, Part 4.

## The grounds of referral

**15.7** Before a child will be considered to be in need of a compulsory supervision order, the Reporter must be satisfied that one or more grounds of referral exist. But even if there is a ground of referral, the Reporter is not obliged to refer the case to a children's hearing unless the Reporter takes the view that it is necessary that a compulsory supervision order be made.[1] The grounds of referral are listed in the 2011 Act, s 67(2):

(a)     the child is likely to suffer unnecessarily, or the health or development of the child is likely to be seriously impaired, due to a lack of parental care. Earlier incidents of parental neglect can be used to show the likelihood of the child's suffering or impairment of health or development.[2] In *McGregor v L*[3] the Inner House of the Court of Session held that the ground[4] was established in relation to a newborn infant who had never left hospital but whose parents had a history of neglecting their children. It was not necessary for the child actually to have suffered parental neglect before the ground was made out:

'If it is proved that the habits and mode of life of these parents are such as to yield the reasonable inference that they are unlikely to care for this child in a manner likely to prevent unnecessary suffering or serious impairment of her health or development, the ground of referral would be established.'[5]

The test whether lack of parental care is likely to cause a child unnecessary suffering or seriously to impair a child's health or development is objective, ie whether a reasonable person could draw that inference from the nature and extent of the parental lack of care;[6]

(b)   a Schedule 1 offence has been committed in respect of the child.[7] The ground is established if, on the balance of probabilities, an offence was committed against the child.[8] It is not necessary to be able to identify the perpetrator of the offence. Even if the alleged perpetrator is identified, the balance of probabilities is still the correct standard of proof: it is irrelevant that the alleged perpetrator is ultimately acquitted of the offence in criminal proceedings;[9]

(c)   the child has, or is likely to have, a close connection with a person who has committed a Schedule 1 offence. For these purposes[10] a child is to be taken to have a close connection with a person: (a) if the child is a member of the same household as the person; or (b) the child is not a member of the same household as the person but the child has significant contact with the person. Household has a wide meaning which is discussed in the cases concerned with the next ground;

(d)   the child is, or is likely to become, a member of the same household as a child in respect of whom a Schedule 1 offence has been committed.[11] The extent of the concept of household is illustrated by *McGregor v H.*[12] Child A's brother, B, had been a victim of a schedule 1 offence. At the date of the hearing, B was being looked after by foster parents, ie was no longer physically in the same house as A. However, the Inner House of the Court of Session was prepared to give 'household' an extended meaning. In the court's view, 'household' connoted a family unit, ie a group of persons held together by a particular tie, usually a blood relationship: while a family unit normally lived together, it did not cease to be a family unit if individual members were temporarily separated. Although at the time of the hearing B was physically separated from A, they were still part of the same family unit and therefore the same household. Accordingly, the ground of referral was applicable vis-à-vis A, as A was a member of the same household as B who had been the victim of a Schedule 1 offence.[13]

In *A v Kennedy*,[14] the ground was established in respect of a child whose sibling had died of a Schedule 1 offence almost ten years before! Although there had been changes in the membership of the family, it was still the same household as at the time the child had died. Where the perpetrator of a Schedule 1 offence has physically left the family this is *not* decisive of the question whether or not a child is a member of the perpetrator's household. Since the criterion for the existence of a household turns on relationship rather than locality, the household could continue if the person who looked after the child still felt affection for the perpetrator and there was regular contact between them.[15] In particular, the court will be reluctant to accept that a household has changed if the separation only took place as a consequence of intervention by a local authority when investigating whether or not a child was in need of a compulsory supervision order.[16] The making of a contact order does not of itself mean that the parent and child are members of the same household.[17]; or

(e)   the child is being, or is likely to be, exposed to persons whose conduct is (or has been) such that it is likely that:

   (i)    the child will be abused or harmed, or

   (ii)   the child's health, safety, or development will be seriously adversely affected;

(f)   the child has, or is likely to have, a close connection with a person who has carried out domestic abuse;

(g)   the child has, or is likely to have, a close connection with a person who has committed an offence under Parts 1, 4 or 5 of the Sexual Offences (Scotland) Act 2009;

(h)   the child is being provided with accommodation by a local authority under section 25 of the Children (Scotland) Act 1995[18] and special measures are needed to support the child;

(i)    a permanence order[19] is in force in respect of the child and special measures are needed to support the child ;

(j)    the child has committed an offence. The Children's Hearings (Scotland) 2011 proceeds on the basis that when a child commits a criminal offence this is merely symptomatic of the child's failure to develop social skills. This failure will often be the result of dysfunctionalism in the child's family. The child who commits an offence is therefore in need of help, not punishment.[20]

As we have seen[21], although the age of criminal responsibility is only 8, no child below the age of 12 can be prosecuted in a criminal court. In exceptional cases, for example very serious crimes such as murder or where the child has committed an offence with an adult, a child between the ages of 12 and 16 may be prosecuted in the High Court or sheriff court. But as a general rule where a child has committed an offence the case will be referred by the Reporter to a children's hearing to determine whether the child is in need of a compulsory supervision order. In *Merrin v S*[22] the Inner House of the Court of Session held that before this ground can be used the child must have reached the age of criminal responsibility, ie be aged eight or over. The case proceeds in exactly the same way as the case where a referral is made on any other of the grounds;

(k)    the child has misused alcohol;

(l)    the child has misused a drug, whether or not a controlled drug within the meaning of the Misuse of Drugs Act 1971;

(m)    the child's conduct has had, or is likely to have, a serious adverse effect on the health, safety or development of the child or another person;

(n)    the child is beyond the control of a relevant person;

(o)    the child has failed to attend school regularly without reasonable excuse. In the absence of an allegation of misconduct on the child's part, it has been held that an order excluding the child from school is a reasonable excuse for non-attendance;[23]

(p)    the child –

    (i)    is being, or is likely to be, subjected to physical, emotional or other pressure to enter into a marriage or civil partnership, or

    (ii)    is, or is likely to become, a member of the same household as such a child.[24]

---

1    Children's Hearings (Scotland) Act 2011, s 66(2).

2    *Kennedy v S* 1986 SLT 679. The fact that the child was put out of the house at night by the father's cohabitant did not prevent the court establishing the ground against the father.

3   1981 SLT 194.
4   Technically the lack of parental care ground under the previous law.
5   *McGregor v L* 1981 SLT 194 at 196.
6   *M v McGregor* 1982 SLT 41; *D v Kelly* 1995 SLT 1220. Thus the ground was established in *Finlayson (Applicant)* 1989 SCLR 601 although the parents' refusal to allow conventional medical treatment on their haemophiliac child was the result of concern that the child might thereby be infected by AIDS.
7   That is an offence listed in Schedule 1 to the Criminal Procedure (Scotland) Act 1995: the offences include physical and sexual abuse of a child. They are not restricted to crimes against children; for example incest with an adult is included. The ground can be established if for example, physical chastisement of a child is not reasonable: see *B v Harris* 1990 SLT 208; *G v Templeton* 1998 SCLR 180. The current relevant offences are in Schedule 1 to the CP(S)A 1995. It does not matter that the offence was committed outside Scotland: *S v Kennedy* 1996 SLT 1087.
8   *S v Kennedy* 1987 SLT 667.
9   *Harris v F* 1991 SLT 242. Evidence can be led to establish the ground even if criminal proceedings are imminent: *P v Kennedy* 1995 SLT 476.
10  And grounds (f) and (g).
11  Evidence of the facts in issue is required where there has been no proof of the original Schedule 1 offence because the accused accepted an earlier ground of referral based on (d): *M v Constanda* 1999 SC 348.
12  1983 SLT 626.
13  See also *Cunningham v M* 2005 SLT (Sh Ct) 73.
14  1993 SLT 118.
15  *Kennedy v R's Curator ad Litem* 1993 SLT 295.
16  *Kennedy v R's Curator ad Litem* 1993 SLT 295.
17  *Templeton v E* 1998 SCLR 672. The length and circumstances of the physical separation are important factors. But the continued existence of family ties is not necessarily the same as continued membership of the same household: this is consistent with *McGregor v H* 1983 SLT 626 if the physical separation is no longer temporary.
18  On s 25 see para **14.2**.
19  On permanence orders, see paras **13.13** and **14.7**.
20  See generally *Report on Children and Young Persons* (the Kilbrandon Report) Cmnd 2306 upon which the Social Work (Scotland) Act 1968 was based and which, in this respect, continues to be followed in the CH(S)A 2011. In *S v Miller* 2001 SLT 531, the Inner House held that where a referral was brought on this ground the child was not being charged with a criminal offence for the purposes of Article 6(3) of the European Convention on Human Rights; for text of Article 6 see para **14.1**.
21  Para **10.6**.
22  1987 SLT 193.
23  *D v Kennedy* 1988 SCLR 31.
24  On marriages or civil partnerships entered into under duress, see para **2.18**.

## Procedure in referrals

**15.8** Where a case is referred by the Reporter to a children's hearing, the child has the right to attend all stages of the hearing[1] and is obliged to do so.[2] However, the child can be excused from attending all or part of the hearing if the children's hearing is satisfied:

(a) in a case concerned with a Schedule 1 offence or a sexual offence, the attendance of the child at the hearing, or that part of the hearing, is not necessary for a fair hearing; or

(b) attendance of the child at the hearing, or that part of the hearing, would place the child's physical, mental or moral welfare at risk; or

(c) taking account of the child's age and maturity, the child would not be capable of understanding what happens at the hearing or that part of the hearing.[3]

The question whether the child's attendance should be excused can be determined by a pre-hearing panel. It is the Reporter's responsibility to secure the attendance of a child whose attendance at the hearing has not been excused. If such a child fails to attend, the Reporter can apply to a children's hearing which on cause shown can grant a warrant to secure the child's attendance at the hearing.[4] The warrant authorises a police officer to apprehend the child, take the child to a place of safety and bring the child to the hearing.[5] Whether or not a warrant to secure attendance is granted, the grounds hearing may, where the child has failed to attend, require the reporter to arrange another grounds hearing[6] Because the child has a statutory right to be present, the child can insist on attending.[7]

Where a children's hearing is considering a child's case, a relevant person has the right to attend all stages of the hearing.[8] and is obliged to do so.[9] Failure to attend is a criminal offence.[10] But if it is appropriate to do so the hearing can proceed in the relevant person's absence. However, a relevant person's attendance may be excused if the children's hearing is satisfied that it would be unreasonable to require that person's attendance or that person's attendance is unnecessary for the proper consideration of the matter before the hearing.[11] The question whether a relevant person's attendance should be excused can be determined by a pre-hearing panel.[12]

The children's hearing can exclude a relevant person (and his or her representative) from any part(s) of the case for so long as it is necessary in the interests of the child where the hearing is satisfied that it must do so in order to obtain the child's views or because the presence of the relevant person is causing, or is likely to cause, significant distress to the child.[13] After the relevant person (or representative) has returned the chairman of the hearing must explain to the relevant person what has taken place during the excluded person's absence.[14]

The Reporter is under a duty to prepare a statement of the grounds of referral which the Reporter believes apply to the case and the facts on which that belief is based.[15] The children's hearing is arranged. This is known as a grounds hearing. When the child and the relevant persons appear, it is the chairing member's duty to explain to them the ground(s) of referral and the supporting facts in relation to the ground(s). The chairing member then asks them whether they accept that each ground applies in relation to the child and that they accept each of the supporting facts.[16] If the relevant persons and the child accept each ground of referral, the hearing will then consider how best to dispose of the case.[17] The hearing can also dispose of the case if at least one of the grounds is accepted and the hearing considers it appropriate to consider making a compulsory supervision order on the basis of the ground(s) that was accepted.[18]

The hearing can defer a decision on whether or not to make a compulsory supervision order until a subsequent children's hearing.[19] If the grounds hearing considers that the nature of the child's circumstances is such that for the protection, guidance, treatment or control of the child it is necessary as a matter of urgency that a compulsory supervision order be made, the hearing can make an interim compulsory supervision order.[20] The interim order comes to an end at the next hearing arranged for the child or the expiry of 22 days beginning with the date the interim order was made whichever is earlier.[21] But before the expiry of the interim order, the Principal Reporter can apply to a sheriff for an extension of the interim compulsory supervision order which in turn can be further extended by the sheriff.[22] The extended order expires 22 days after the order was extended unless it is further extended.[23]

If the grounds hearing considers that it is necessary to do so for the purpose of obtaining any further information or carrying out any further investigation that is needed before the subsequent children's hearing, the grounds hearing can make a medical examination order.[24] This can contain the following measures:[25]

(a)    a requirement that the child attend or reside at a specified clinic, hospital or other establishment;

(b)    a requirement that a specified authority arrange a specified medical examination of the child. But if the child has capacity under section 2(4) of the Age of Legal Capacity (Scotland) Act 1991,[26] the child can refuse to consent;[27]

(c)    a prohibition on the disclosure of the place specified in (a);

(d)    a secure accommodation authorisation;[28]

(e)    a direction regulating contact between the child and a specified person or class of persons;

(f)    any other specified condition appearing to the children's hearing to be appropriate for the purposes of ensuring that the child complies with the order.

If the grounds hearing decides not to defer making a decision, it must make a compulsory supervision order if satisfied that it is necessary to do so for the protection, guidance, treatment or control of the child. If it is not so satisfied, the children's hearing must discharge the referral.[29]

If either the child or a relevant person does not accept the ground(s) of referral,[30] unless they are prepared to discharge the referral, the hearing must direct the Reporter to make an application to the sheriff for a determination on whether each ground not accepted by the child or relevant person is established.[31] The chairing member must explain to the child and the relevant person the purpose of the application and inform the child that the child must attend the hearing before the sheriff unless the sheriff excuses the child's attendance.[32] If it considers that it is necessary to do so, the hearing can make an interim compulsory supervision order.[33] Before the determination of the application before the sheriff, the Reporter may arrange a children's hearing to consider whether a further interim compulsory supervision order should be made. The children's hearing can make the further order if it is necessary to do so unless it would be the third such in consequence of the original interim compulsory supervision order.[34]

A direction for an application by the Reporter to the sheriff is also necessary[35] if the child is not capable of understanding or has not understood the explanation of the ground(s) of referral.[36] Again, if it is necessary to do so, an interim compulsory supervision order can be made.[37]

The application by the Reporter must be heard by the sheriff within 28 days of being lodged.[38] Unless excused, the child has a duty to attend.[39] The sheriff can release the child from the obligation to attend where:

    (a)    in a case concerned with a Schedule 1 offence or a sexual offence, the child's attendance is not necessary for the just hearing of the application;

    (b)    the attendance of the child at the hearing, or a part of the hearing, would place the child's physical, mental or moral welfare at risk; or

    (c)    taking into account of the child's age and maturity, the child would not be capable of understanding what happens at the hearing or part of the hearing.[40]

If the child fails to attend, the sheriff may grant a warrant to secure the child's attendance.[41] The child and the relevant persons have the right to be represented.[42]

The onus lies on the Reporter to establish by evidence that the ground(s) of referral exist. The sheriff can dispense with hearing evidence if:

    (i)    the child and the relevant persons accept the ground(s) before the application is determined;[43] or

    (ii)    the application has been brought because of the child's incapacity to understand the explanation of the grounds and the relevant persons accept the grounds.[44]

In these circumstances the grounds of referral are deemed to have been established.

The standard of proof normally required is that on the balance of probabilities the ground(s) exist.[45] There is no need for corroboration.[46] There is an important exception. When the ground of referral is that the *child* has committed an offence, the standard of proof is the criminal standard, ie it must be proved to the sheriff beyond reasonable doubt that the child committed the offence and corroboration is required.[47] A sheriff can entertain an application as to whether the ground of referral that the child has committed an offence is established, even though the prosecution of the offence, for example rape, would not have been competent in the sheriff court.[48]

If the sheriff decides that none of the grounds of referral is established, the sheriff dismisses the application and discharges the referral.[49] If a ground of referral is established (or deemed to be established), the sheriff remits the case to the Reporter to arrange a children's hearing to consider and determine the case.[50] The sheriff can make an interim compulsory supervision order if it is necessary to do so.[51]

Where there has been a determination that a ground(s) of referral has been established – a grounds determination, the child or a relevant person has the right to apply to a sheriff for a review of the grounds determination.[52]

---

1   Children's Hearings (Scotland) Act 2011, s 78(1)(a).
2   CH(S)A 2011, s 73(2).
3   CH(S)A 2011, s 73(3).Where the children's hearing is a grounds hearing, the child can only be excused from attending the hearing to hear the grounds explained if the child is incapable of understanding the explanation: CH(S)A 2011, s 73(4).
4   CH(S)A 2011, s 123.
5   CH(S)A 2011, s 88(1). A warrant may include a secure accommodation authorisation. The warrant expires 7 days after the child has been first detained or the beginning of the hearing if earlier. In *Martin v N* 2004 SC 358 the Inner House of the Court of Session held that the child's detention under the parallel provisions under the previous law was not in breach of Article 5 of the European Convention (right to liberty) because it fell within the proviso in Article 5(d) *viz* detention of a minor by lawful order for the purpose of educational supervision or his lawful detention for the purpose of bringing him before the competent legal authority.
6   CH(S)A 2011, s 95. The grounds hearing can make an interim compulsory supervision order.
7   CH(S)A 2011, s 78(1)(a).
8   CH(S)A 2011, s 78(1)(c): unlike the child's right to attend, the relevant person's right is expressly subject to the children's hearing's power to exclude a relevant person under s 76(2).
9   CH(S)A 2011, s 74(2).

10  CH(S)A 2011, s 74(4).
11  CH(S)A 2011, s 74(3).
12  CH(S)A 2011, s 79(3).
13  CH(S)A 2011, s 76(1) and (2) and s 77(1) and (2).
14  CH(S)A 2011, s 76(3) and s 77(3). This may satisfy any potential breach of Articles 6 and 8 of the European Convention on Human Rights: *McMichael v United Kingdom* 51/1993/446/525. Regulations must ensure that a relevant person has access to the documents before the children's hearing; but this may lead to a child being reluctant to disclose information which the child knows will be given to a relevant person. It has now been accepted that the *child* should have access to any relevant documentation: *S v Miller* 2001 SLT 531.
15  CH(S)A 2011, s 89.
16  CH(S)A 2011, s 90(1)(1A). The chairing member must ask the child whether the documentation accurately reflects any views the child expressed before the hearing; CH(S)A 2011, s 121.
17  CH(S)A 2011, s 91(1)(a).
18  CH(S)A 2011, s 91(1)(b).
19  CH(S)A 2011, s 91(2).
20  CH(S)A 2011, s 92(2).
21  CH(S)A 2011, s 86(3)(a) and (d).
22  CH(S)A 2011, ss 98 and 99.
23  CH(S)A 2011, s 86(3)(e).
24  CH(S)A2011, s 92(3).
25  CH(S)A 2011, s 87(2).
26  Discussed at para **10.2**.
27  CH(S)A 2011, s 186.
28  Discussed at para **15.10**.
29  CH(S)A 2011, s 91(3).
30  Or where at least one of the grounds has been accepted but the hearing does not consider it appropriate to make a compulsory supervision order on the basis of the ground(s) that has been accepted.
31  CH(S)A 2011, s 93(2).
32  CH(S)A 2011, s 93(4).
33  CH(S)A 2011, s 93(5).
34  CH(S)A 2011, s 96. But before the expiry of the 66 days, the Principal Reporter can apply to a sheriff for an extension of the interim order which in turn can be further extended by the sheriff: CH(S)A 2011, ss 98 and 99.
35  Unless the hearing discharges the case.
36  CH(S)A 2011, s 94(1) and (2).
37  CH(S)A 2011, s 94(5).
38  CH(S)A 2011, s 101(2).
39  CH(S)A 2011, s 103(2).
40  CH(S)A 2011, s 103(3).
41  CH(S)A 2011, s 103(5).

42  CH(S)A 2011, s 104(2) and (3). The person representing the child or relevant person at the hearing need not be a solicitor or advocate: CH(S)A 2011, s 104(4).
43  CH(S)A 2011, s 105.
44  CH(S)A 2011, s 106(1). However, the child, relevant persons, a safeguarder and the Principal Reporter can request that a hearing be held and the sheriff may consider that it is not appropriate to determine the application without a hearing: CH(S)A 2011, s 106(3) and (4).
45  *S v Kennedy* 1987 SLT 667; *Harris v F* 1991 SLT 242.
46  Civil Evidence (Scotland) Act 1988, s 1(1).
47  CH(S)A 2011, s 102(3). If the offence cannot be proved beyond reasonable doubt, the child's alleged criminal act cannot per se establish the existence of another ground on the balance of probabilities test: *Constanda v M* 1997 SC 217.
48  *Walker v SC* 2003 SC 570.
49  CH(S)A 2011, s 108(3).
50  C(S)A 2011, s 108(2).
51  CH(S)A 2011, s 109(3).
52  CH(S)A 2011, ss 110–117.

## Disposal of the case

**15.9**  If the child and the relevant persons accept the ground(s) of referral or if the ground(s) of referral have been established in proceedings before the sheriff, the children's hearing will then consider how it should dispose of the case.[1] The hearing will have the social background report and any other relevant information.[2] If the hearing considers that further investigation is necessary into the child's circumstances, the case can be deferred.[3] If the children's hearing considers that the nature of the child's circumstances is such that for the protection, guidance treatment or control of the child it is necessary to make an interim compulsory supervision order or a medical examination order, it can do so.[4]

1  Children's Hearing's (Scotland) Act 2011, s 119(3). This is also the situation where the case has been referred to the Reporter by a court which is satisfied in relevant proceedings that a ground of referral exists.
2  This can include allegations against a relevant person which were not used in respect of the ground of referral that was accepted or established: *O v Rae* 1993 SLT 570. But the hearing cannot rely on allegations specifically rejected by the sheriff: *M v Kennedy* 1993 SLT 431.
3  C(S)A 2011, s 119(2).
4  CH(S)A 2011, s 120.

### Children in need of compulsory supervision orders

**15.10**  The children's hearing must proceed on the course which, in its view, is in the best interests of the child: the welfare of the child throughout the child's childhood is the paramount consideration[1] The child's views must be taken into account.[2] Where the children's hearing feels that no further action is required, it must discharge the referral.[3] However if the hearing is satisfied that it is necessary for the protection, guidance, treatment or control of the child to make a compulsory supervision order it must do so.[4] In doing so, the hearing is under a duty to consult the child and must be satisfied that it is better for the child to make a compulsory supervision order than that none be made at all.[5]

The compulsory supervision order contains measures which the hearing considers necessary to safeguard and promote the child's welfare.[6] The same measures can be made in interim compulsory supervision orders.[7] It also specifies the local authority which is to be responsible for giving effect to the measures included in the order (the implementation authority).[8] The measures include:

(i)    a direction regulating contact between the child and a specified person, for example the child's parents and family The hearing must consider wheter a contact requirement should be made.[9]

(ii)   a requirement that the implementation authority arrange a medical (or other) examination of or treatment for the child;[10] but if the child has capacity under s 2(4) of the Age of Legal Capacity (Scotland) Act 1991,[11] the child can refuse to consent.[12]

(iii)  a requirement that the child reside in a specified place, for example with foster parents or residential care.[13] A direction can be made authorising the person in charge of the place in which the child is to reside to restrict the child's liberty as that person considers appropriate having regard to the measures included in the order, for example to ensure that the child receives counselling at a particular time and place.[14] Disclosure of the place where the child resides can be prohibited.[15]

(iv)   a movement restriction condition. This restricts the child's movements and may require the child to comply with arrangements specified in the condition for monitoring the child's compliance with the restriction.[16] A movement condition can only be made if (a) the child had previously absconded and is likely to abscond again and, if the child were to abscond it is likely that the child's physical, mental or moral welfare would be at risk, or (b) the child is likely to engage in self-harming conduct, or (c) the child is likely to cause injury to another person and the children's hearing is satisfied that it is necessary to include a movement restriction order.[17] If the hearing considers the restriction condition is necessary to protect members of the public from serious harm, the welfare of the child is not the paramount consideration but remains the primary consideration.[18]

(v)    a secure accommodation authorisation. This requires the child to reside at a residential establishment which contains secure and not secure accommodation.[19] The authorisation allows the child to be placed and kept in secure accommodation within the establishment.[20] An authorisation can only be made if (a) the child has previously absconded and is likely to abscond again and, if the child were to abscond, it is likely that the child's physical, mental or moral welfare would be at risk or (b) the child is likely to engage in self-harming conduct or (c) the child is likely to cause injury to another person and having considered the other options available – including a movement restriction condition – the children's hearing is satisfied that it is necessary to include a secure accommodation authorisation.[21] If the hearing considers that a secure accommodation authorisation is necessary to protect the public from serious harm, the welfare of the child is not the paramount consideration but remains the primary consideration.[22] The chief social worker can only implement the secure authorisation with the consent of the person in charge of the residential establishment containing the secure accommodation.[23] There is an appeal to the sheriff in respect of any decision to implement the authorisation.[24]

(vi)   a requirement that the child comply with any other specified condition, for example to receive counselling or psychiatric support.[25]

(vii)  a requirement that the implementation authority carry out specified duties in relation to the child.[26]

A compulsory supervision order ceases to have effect on the day one year after it was made unless it has been continued: if it has been continued, it ends on the day one year after it was last continued. The order will automatically come to an end on the day the child attains 18.[27]

However, the supervision requirement should not continue any longer than is necessary in the interests of the child. The Reporter must initiate a review of a compulsory supervision order by a children's hearing if the order will expire within three months and it would not otherwise be reviewed before it expires.[28] The implementation authority must by notice to the Reporter require a review if it considers that the order should be terminated or varied or is not being complied with, or that the child should be subject to a permanence order or be placed for adoption.[29] Moreover, and perhaps even more importantly, the child and any relevant person have the right by giving notice to the Reporter to have the order reviewed by a children's hearing.[30] On review, the children's hearing may continue the order, vary the order, or terminate it.

The child or relevant person may appeal to the sheriff against any decision of the children's hearing.[31] An appeal is competent not only in relation to the making of the compulsory supervision order itself but also as to any of the measures it contains. The sheriff may hear evidence from the child and any relevant person.[32] If the sheriff is satisfied that the decision of the children's hearing is not justified the sheriff may:

(1)     require the Reporter to arrange a children's hearing;

(2)     continue, vary or terminate the order;

(3)     discharge the child from any further hearing;

(4)     make an interim compulsory supervision order or interim variation of a compulsory supervision order; or

(5)     grant a warrant to secure attendance.[33]

If satisfied that the hearing's decision is justified, the sheriff must confirm the decision.[34] If satisfied that the appeal was frivolous or vexatious the sheriff can order that for a period of 12 months from the date of the order the person who appealed must obtain leave from the sheriff before making another appeal.[35]

There can be further appeals from the sheriff to the Sheriff Principal and the Court of Session.[36]

The implementation authority must give effect to the compulsory supervision order. This includes securing or facilitating the provision of services for the child.[37] The child is regarded as being looked after by the authority.[38] Consequently the principles in s 17 of the 1995 Act which determine how a local authority is to look after the child apply. Where the child is residing with the child's own family, the implementation authority must from time investigate whether any conditions imposed by the order are being complied with while the child is living there.[39]

If it appears to a children's hearing that the implementation authority is in breach of these duties, the hearing may direct the National Convener to give notice to the authority of an intended application by the Convener to enforce the authority's duty.[40] The Convener's notice must set out the respects in which the authority is in breach and state that if the authority does not perform the duty within 21 days, the National Convener at the direction of the hearing will make an application for the enforcement of the duty.[41] At the same time the National Convener sends a copy of the notice to the child and each relevant person.[42] If the hearing gives such direction, it must require a further review of the order and if on that further review it appears that the authority is still in breach the hearing can direct the National Convener to make the application.[43] In determining whether to direct the National Convener to make an application, the hearing must *not* take into account the adequacy of the means available to the local authority to enable it to comply with the duty.[44] The National Convener makes the application to the Sheriff Principal who can order the implementation authority to carry out its duties in respect of the compulsory supervision order.[45]

---

1    Children's Hearings (Scotland) Act 2011, s 25(2).
2    CH(S)A 2011, s 27.
3    CH(S)A 2011, s 119(3)(b).
4    CH(S)A 2011, s 119(3)(a).
5    CH(S)A 2011, s 28(2).
6    CH(S)A 2011, s 83(1)(a).
7    CH(S)A 2011, s 86(1)(a).
8    CH(S)A 2011, s 83(1)(b).

9   CH(S)A 2011, s 83(2)(g) and (3).
10  CH(S)A 2011, s 83(2)(f).
11  Discussed at para **10.2**.
12  CH(S)A 2011, s 186.
13  CH(S)A 2011, s 83(2)(a).
14  CH(S)A 2011, s 83(2)(b).
15  CH(S)A 2011, s 83(2)(c).
16  CH(S)A 2011, ss 83(2)(d) and s 84.
17  CH(S)A 2011, s 83(4) and (6).
18  CH(S)A 2011, s 26.
19  Or two establishments one of which is not secure accommodation.
20  CH(S)A 2011, s 83(2)(e) and s 85.
21  CH(S)A 2011, s 83(5) and (6).
22  CH(S)A 2011, s 26.
23  CH(S)A 2011, s 151(3). The implementation of secure accommodation authorisations is the subject of detailed regulations.
24  CH(S)A 2011, s 162.
25  CH(S)A 2011, s 83(2)(h).
26  CH(S)A 2011, s 83(2)(i).
27  CH(S)A 2011, s 83(7).
28  CH(S)A 2011, s 133.
29  CH(S)A 2011, s 131.
30  CH(S)A 2011, s 132(2) and (3). They can do so after three months from the making or continuation or variation of the order: CH(S)A 2011, s 132(4).
31  CH(S)A 2011, s 154(1): the appeal must be made within 21 days beginning with the day the decision was made by the children's hearing.
32  CH(S)A 2011, s 155(5)(a) and (b).
33  CH(S)A 2011, s 156(2) and (3).
34  CH(S)A 2011, s 156(1). The sheriff can take any of the steps outlined above if the sheriff is satisfied that the circumstances of the child have changed since the decision was made.
35  CH(S)A 2011, s 159.
36  CH(S)A 2011, ss 163–167. The appeal is restricted to a point of law or procedural irregularity. It is inappropriate in fact sensitive issues. *JM v Eileen Taylor* [2014] CSIH 62.
37  CH(S)A 2011, s 144.
38  Children (Scotland) Act 1995, s 17(6)(b).
39  CH(S)A 2011, s 145.
40  CH(S)A 2011, s 146(1) and (2).
41  CH(S)A 2011, s 146(3).
42  CH(S)A 2011, s 146(4).
43  CH(S)A 2011, s 146(5) and (6).
44  CH(S)A 2011, s 146(7).
45  CH(S)A 2011, ss 147 and 148.

## The effect of a compulsory supervision order

**15.11** Parents do not lose their parental responsibilities and rights in respect of a child who is subject to a compulsory supervision order. Not only does a court have jurisdiction to regulate residence or contact in relation to such children but the parent retains title to sue.[1] In exceptional situations, the court can consider the merits of a s 11 application[2] in relation to parental responsibilities and rights even though the child is subject to a compulsory supervision order.[3] But this is often of little value for, even if the parent is awarded residence or contact, the parent cannot *exercise* the parental responsibilities and rights if it would be incompatible with the supervision order and any measures it contains, for example in relation to the parent's contact with the child. As a relevant person, the parent could seek a review and ask the children's hearing to vary the condition in relation to contact.

The reason why parental responsibilities and rights do not automatically cease when a compulsory supervision order is made is because in many cases it is desirable that the child should continue to live, or at least, retain links, with his or her family. If the local authority social workers take the view that in order to safeguard and promote the welfare of the child it is necessary that the child should no longer be part of his or her family, the local authority could apply for a permanence order.[4] Before doing so, the local authority must refer the case to the Reporter who must arrange a children's hearing to review the case.[5] If the children's hearing agrees that it is in the best interests of the child to do so, it can vary the supervision order to allow the local authority to proceed.

---

1   *P v P* 2000 SLT 781.
2   On the Children (Scotland) Act 1995, s 11, see **Ch 12**.
3   *P v P* 2000 SLT 781 (application by a grandmother when the children's hearing had made it a condition of the requirement that the child live with her grandmother).
4   Discussed at para **14.7**.
5   Children's Hearings (Scotland) Act 2011, s 131(2).

---

# CONCLUSION

**15.12** The system of children's hearings is not only a bold attempt to introduce a welfare-based approach to the problem of juvenile crime but also provides personnel with expertise and experience to make decisions which are in the best interests of children who, because of the dysfunctionalism of their family or otherwise, are in need. The danger of such paternalistic legislation is that insufficient weight is given to the rights of children and their families. By insisting that a hearing cannot proceed unless the child and relevant persons accept the grounds of referral or, where they do not, that the grounds are established to the satisfaction of a judge, the present system recognises the importance of family autonomy. By imposing a duty to consult the child at all the important procedural stages, the Children's Hearings (Scotland) Act 2011 also places emphasis on children's rights. Nevertheless, the procedures will continue to be scrutinised to ensure they do not violate Articles 5, 6 and 8 of the European Convention on Human Rights.

On the other hand, the responsibility for implementing the supervision requirements rests on local authorities. Many local authorities simply do not have the resources – particularly social workers – to discharge this obligation. It will be interesting to see how the procedure to force local authorities to fulfil their duties towards children who are subject to compulsory supervision orders will operate in practice at this time of severe cuts in public spending.

Appendix

# Parenting Agreement for Scotland – Plan

## INTRODUCTION

**This 'Plan' is the second of the two documents which make up the Parenting Agreement for Scotland. The Plan is for you and your children's other parent to complete together.**

There should be two copies, one for each of you. It is intended to be a record of the arrangements you have agreed on with regard to the future care of your children.

The Plan is complemented by a 'Guide'. The Guide aims to help you consider some of the key issues which are important for parents who have separated. You may find it helpful to refer to the Guide as you are completing the Plan but it's up to you how you use the *Parenting Agreement for Scotland.*

At the end of this document there is a space for you and your former partner to sign, indicating your joint commitment to the arrangements you have agreed on. As well as each of you keeping a copy of the Plan, you may wish to give a copy to other people who will be involved in your children's lives, such as grandparents – but again, that's up to you

## PUTTING YOUR CHILDREN FIRST

**It is important to bear in mind how vulnerable and insecure some children can feel when their parents separate.**

It can really help them if you put aside your differences with one another and make arrangements which will bring stability and continuity into their lives at a time of doubt and change.

Some things that all separating parents should take account of:

- Children find change unsettling and thrive on stability and a regular routine.

- When change is unavoidable, children need to have the new arrangements explained to them, so they understand what is happening and why.

- Children should be involved in decisions made about their future – so don't forget to ask them what they feel.

- However, while children's views should be listened to, children should never be asked to take responsibility for decisions which will have a major impact on their, or either of your, lives.

- A particularly difficult and sensitive area for children and former partners arises if a new partner is introduced into either home. This requires great sensitivity by all concerned.

## EFFECTIVE COMMUNICATION

The purpose of the *Parenting Agreement for Scotland* is to encourage parents who have separated to come together and talk about future arrangements for their children. No one would suggest that this is easy. Your feelings towards each other may be far from positive but if you can agree on sensible, workable arrangements for your children now, it could help prevent disagreements arising in future and make things easier for your children.

Always remember that you are making plans for your children and that it's their welfare and happiness which is at stake. Below are some general guidelines about how separated parents should talk to one another and their children.

### Talking to your children

- Explain the fact of your separation so that they understand the changes that are taking place.

- Reassure them that your separation does not alter the fact that you both love them and will continue to be their parents.

- Don't criticise or blame the other parent.

- Keep your promises. Your children need to be able to trust and rely on you. This is very important right now.

- Reassure them that they are not to blame for your separation.

### Talking to each other

- Try to avoid arguing or criticising each other in front of your children. Even when you can't agree, respect one another's views.
- As much as possible, show a united front to your children and assure them that you both want what's best for them.
- Be reasonable. Don't make demands that can't possibly be met.
- Always look to reach a compromise.
- Communicate directly with your former partner – don't send messages through your children.
- Once you have come to an agreement with your former partner, stick to it.
- Recognise that circumstances will change over time and be flexible.

## YOU AND YOUR CHILDREN

The following sections in the Plan focus on some specific areas of your children's lives which, as parents, you will need to consider. Before you move onto this, you can fill in your names and those of your children in the space below.

Parents' Names

_____

_____

## Children

**Name**                                    **Date of Birth**

_____        _____

_____        _____

_____        _____

_____        _____

If you feel that there are any other people with a close involvement in caring for your children whose names you would also like to record in the Plan (e.g. grandparents or step-parents) you can include their details below.

## Others

**Name**                              **Relationship to Children**

_____     _____

_____     _____

_____     _____


## LIVING ARRANGEMENTS

Page 5 of the Guide discusses some of the issues to be considered when agreeing living arrangements for your children. You may wish to read this before completing the following section.

Where will your children live and for what periods? (This may include more than one address)

_____

_____

_____


How much time will they spend with each of you in a way which is realistic, practical and in the children's best interests?

_____

_____

_____


How might you best spend this time with your children?

_____

_____

_____

If a visit needs to be postponed by an adult, how and by whom will this be explained to the children?

_____

_____

_____

If your child needs to postpone or rearrange a planned visit, how will this be managed?

_____

_____

_____

Will the children be able to stay overnight at each of your homes?

_____

_____

_____

How else will the children keep in contact, e.g. e-mail, phone calls, text message, post?

_____

_____

_____

Are there any firm rules that you want to agree on for your children?

(Depending on their ages, these might include bedtimes, staying out late or smoking, for example).

_____

_____

_____

Which other people do you feel are suitable to look after your children? (This might include grandparents, other relatives, neighbours).

_____

_____

_____

If either of you have a new partner, how will you introduce them to your children?

_____

_____

_____

How might you deal with any reluctance by either your former partner, or particularly your children, to be involved with a new partner?

_____

_____

_____

## KEEPING IN TOUCH

Page 9 of the Guide discusses some of the issues to be considered concerning other people your children will keep in touch with. You may wish to read this before completing the following section.

Which family members and friends who are important to your children will they stay in contact with?

_____

_____

_____

(For younger children, you may even want to ask them to fill in the diagram below).

## People who are important to me

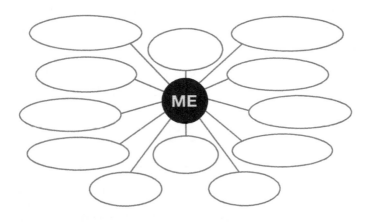

How will you arrange for your children to stay in contact with these people?

_____

_____

_____

How often will contact take place?

_____

_____

_____

Other than visits, can your children be encouraged to stay in touch with these other people by other means, such as by e-mail, letter or phone?

_____

_____

_____

## SCHOOL

Page 11 of the Guide discusses some of the issues to be considered concerning your children's schooling. You may wish to read this before completing the following section.

How will the school be informed about your family's change of circumstances – will you meet with the school's guidance staff, for example?

_____

_____

_____

How will you ensure that each parent receives school reports and other details of yours children's progress?

_____

_____

_____

How will you ensure that each parent receives information about school events?

_____

_____

_____

Will both of you attend school functions such as parents' evenings and sports days? Will you attend these functions together or separately?

_____

_____

_____

How will you and your former partner make decisions about which school the children will attend; how will you help them make decisions about their choice of subjects and future career options?

_____

_____

_____

If one of your children is ill, or if there is any kind of emergency, who should the school contact?

_____

_____

_____

If one of your children has problems at school, who should the school contact?

_____

_____

_____

Have you informed the school about who will be picking up the children on particular days?

_____

_____

_____

Who should be consulted on, and give consent to, school trips? How will these be paid for?

_____

_____

_____

## HOLIDAYS AND OTHER 'SPECIAL' DAYS

Page 13 of the Guide discusses some of the issues to be considered around your children's holidays. You may wish to read this before completing the following section.

When school holidays come along, how will you share responsibility for caring for your children?

_____

_____

_____

During the holidays, will the children be spending time with other people, such as grandparents or other relatives?

_____

_____

_____

Can either of you take the children away on holiday? Abroad?

_____

_____

_____

How will holidays be paid for?

_____

_____

_____

What arrangements will you make for other days when schools are closed, such as inservice days?

_____

_____

_____

What arrangements will you make for birthdays and other 'special' days?

_____

_____

_____

Have you discussed these arrangements with your children to see what their views are?

_____

_____

_____

## HEALTH

Page 15 of the Guide discusses some of the issues to be considered relating to your children's health care. You may wish to read this before completing the following section.

How will your children's GP be informed about the family's change of circumstances, including where the children are now living as well as contact details of both parents?

_____

_____

_____

Who will be responsible for ensuring that your children keep routine medical and dental appointments?

_____

_____

_____

If one of your children has a chronic or long-term illness, what arrangements have you made to ensure they can get the help they need at all times, no matter who they are living with?

_____

_____

_____

If one of you is ill and unable to look after the children, what arrangements will you make to deal with this?

_____

_____

_____

In the event of an emergency, who can you call on to help with childcare?

_____

_____

_____

Who will give parental consent to medical treatment when consent is required by a GP or hospital?

_____

_____

_____

## MONEY MATTERS

Page 17 of the Guide discusses some of the issues to be considered concerning financial support for your children. You may wish to read this before completing the following section.

Have you discussed the cost of financially supporting your children?

_____

_____

_____

Are there regular payments already being made by either of you?

_____

_____

_____

How will things like children's clothes and shoes be paid for?

_____

_____

_____

How will bigger things such as a computer or bicycle be paid for?

_____

_____

_____

Have you considered making long-term provision for your children's future needs, such as the cost of further education?

_____

_____

_____

Will you consider discussing together what might be appropriate 'big' presents at Christmas and on birthdays?

_____

_____

_____

## OTHER ARRANGEMENTS

There are any number of other situations relating to your children's care which you will need to consider. The previous sections have dealt with some of the major ones. If there are any other arrangements which you wish to include in this Plan, you may wish to record these in the space below.

_____

_____

_____

_____

_____

_____

## MAKING CHANGES

Page 19 of the Guide asks you to consider reviewing and updating the arrangements you have made about your children's care. You may wish to read this before completing the following section.

Will you arrange to regularly reassess the arrangements you have agreed on? If so, at what intervals would you think reassessment would be appropriate?

_____

_____

_____

Alternatively, do you prefer to update arrangements as and when new circumstances present themselves?

_____

_____

_____

As your children get older and their needs change, how will you involve them in discussions about arrangements you are making for them?

_____

_____

_____

# JOINT AGREEMENT

Now that you have made these important decisions about the future care and welfare of your children, you may each wish to sign in the space below to confirm your joint commitment to what you have agreed.

"As parents of the children named on page 6 of this Plan, we jointly accept responsibility for the future welfare, stability, development and happiness of our children. We have discussed and agreed the arrangements laid out in this Plan and commit ourselves to these arrangements. We have also discussed these arrangements with our children."

"We will jointly re-visit these arrangements in future, as necessary. In this way we will take account of changing circumstances and ensure that our children's best interests come first."

Name                                    Name

_____        _____

Signature                               Signature

_____        _____

Date                                    Date

_____        _____

If you feel that they are old enough, you may want to give your children the opportunity to sign the Plan as well. This would allow them to show that they understand and are agreeable to the arrangements which have been made on their behalf.

*"I have read the Parenting Agreement reached by my parents. They have discussed these arrangements with me and taken my views into account."*

Name                                    Name

_____        _____

Signature                               Signature

_____        _____

Date                                    Date

_____        _____

Please remember that the *Parenting Agreement for Scotland* is not a legal contract. The completed 'Plan' reflects the arrangements which you have agreed to set in place for the future care and well-being of you children. By signing above, you are simply confirming what you have jointly agreed and there is no legal commitment in doing so. As with all parts of this document, you don't have to complete this section if you don't want to.

## NOTES

_____

_____

_____

# Index

*[references are to paragraph]*